RISK MANAGEMENT

"*Risk Management* is a complete fixed income toolkit. Focused, with powerful, clear examples and straight to the point formalism. I strongly recommend it to everyone involved in studying, analyzing, or managing fixed income and derivatives portfolios."

—Lev Borodovsky
Co-Chairman, Global Association of Risk Professionals (GARP)
Director, Risk Management, Credit Suisse First Boston

"A valuable contribution to the field, providing perspective and industry knowledge to a subject often lost in the details."

—Ronald Kahn
Managing Director, Barclays Global Investors

"An excellent discussion of modern risk management methodologies enriched with valuable lessons learned from their practical application. The emphasis on combining quantitative models with subjective expert judgement and intuition will help portfolio and risk managers make better investment decisions."

—Stewart Morrison
Senior Vice President & Chief Investment Officer,
Keyport Life Insurance Company

WILEY FRONTIERS IN FINANCE

Series Editor: Edward I. Altman, New York University

FORTHCOMING:

RISK MANAGEMENT

Approaches for Fixed Income Markets

Bennett W. Golub
Leo M. Tilman

John Wiley & Sons, Inc.

New York • Chichester • Weinheim • Brisbane • Singapore • Toronto

ISBN: 0-471-33211-9

Printed in the United States of America

10 9 8 7 6 5 4 3 2 1

"And of course, stability isn't nearly so spectacular as instability."
Aldous Huxley, *Brave New World*

Contents

Frequently Used Abbreviations and Notations

Abbreviations

ALM	asset/liability management
ATM	at-the-money
CCD	coupon curve duration
CMBS	commercial mortgage-backed security
CMO	collateralized mortgage obligation
CMS	constant maturity swap
CMT	constant maturity treasury
DER	debt-to-equity ratio
EROR	expected rate of return
ERP	effective risk profile
IntRR	interest rate risk
IO	interest-only stripped mortgage-backed security
IR	information ratio
ITM	in-the-money
KRD	key rate duration
KTRD	key treasury rate duration
LEDUR	long-end duration
LIBOR	London Interbank Offered Rate
MBS	mortgage-backed security
MTB	mortgage/treasury basis
OAC	option-adjusted convexity
OAD	option-adjusted duration
OAS	option-adjusted spread
OAV	option-adjusted value
OCD	option-adjusted spread curve duration
OTM	out-of-the-money
OTR	on-the-run

PCA	principal components analysis
PCD	principal components duration
PDF	probability density function
PO	principal-only stripped mortgage-backed security
ROE	return-on-equity
SEDUR	short-end duration
TBA	to-be-announced
TE	tracking error
TSOV	term structure of volatility
TSY	U.S. Treasury security
USD	U.S. dollar
VaR	Value-at-Risk
WAC	weighted-average coupon
YTM	yield-to-maturity
ZCB	zero-coupon bond
ZVO	zero volatility [option-adjusted] spread

Notations

CF_i	set of cash flows
$det(X)$	determinant of matrix X
$\bar{e}$	vector of one standard deviation dollar exposures
$fx_{A/B}$	foreign exchange rate between currencies A and B
I	identity matrix
$\$krd_i$	dollar key rate duration
krd_i	key rate duration
$ktrd_i$	key treasury rate duration
$\Lambda = \{\lambda_i\}$	diagonal matrix of principal components' variances (eigenvalues)
$mpl(\bar{z})$	magnitude plausibility of spot curve shock $\bar{z}$
$N(\mu, \sigma)$	normal random variable with mean μ and standard deviation σ
P	price
$\bar{p} = \{p_i\}$	vector of principal components (random variables)
ρ	correlation matrix
$SSDir$	coefficient of interest rate directionality of swap spreads
s	swap spread or credit spread in general, depending on context
r	parallel interest rate movement (spot curve shock)
r_i	key spot rates
$spl(\bar{z})$	shape plausibility of spot curve shock $\bar{z}$
σ	volatility or one standard deviation
Σ	covariance matrix of changes in systematic risk factors
$\Omega = \{p_{i,j}\}$	matrix of principal components' factor loadings (eigenvectors)
V	market value
$VOLDir$	coefficient of interest rate directionality of implied volatility
X^T	transposed matrix or vector X
χ_n^2	chi-squared distributed random variable with n degrees of freedom
y	yield-to-maturity
ζ_i	percentages of the total variance explained by principal components

Foreword

Much has been written about the emergence of the Information Age. Nowhere is this more evident than in the evolution of financial markets over the past two decades. Fueled by rapid advances in the availability and sophistication of technology, securities are becoming increasingly complex and capital markets are becoming more global. Whether a business operates in one country or many, on the ground or on-line, it can now be invested in multiple countries and financed through a variety of currencies and markets. Investors are afforded substantially greater opportunities, but face far greater challenges in evaluating investments and monitoring and managing portfolios through changing market cycles. Without sound risk management practices, last year's hero can become next year's victim because what was once perceived as skill may turn out to have been fleeting luck of the draw. Now more than ever, long-term success or failure in the markets depends upon an investor's desire and ability to have an in-depth understanding of the risks embedded in an individual security, a portfolio as a whole, and assets relative to their liabilities.

In the early 1980s, sell-side firms began to embrace technology while engineering new types of financial instruments. The resulting explosion in securitization led to an exponentially more complex universe of investments. By the late 1980s, the rapidly mounting intricacies of the fixed income markets had caused a gulf between sell-side and buy-side investment technology. The concomitant emergence of low-cost computing created an opportunity for investment management firms to take advantage of newly created tools to develop complex valuation and risk-management methodologies that could be used to deliver consistent returns in excess of client benchmarks while assuming lower levels of risk. Extensive investment in and commitment to technology was required, but the potential value added was unquestionable.

Synthesis of theory and technology has always been an important driver of the asset management business. It underlies the performance equation and empowers both people and process. Savvy investment managers embrace the advances afforded by technology, while recognizing the associated costs and limits. Success, however, ultimately depends on how the technology and the information it provides are used. Even though platforms and environments in which investors operate have changed considerably over the last decade, firms that have been truly successful increasingly owe their achievements to a disciplined risk management orientation within a comprehensive asset/liability management paradigm.

Risk management practitioners continue to integrate complex academic ideas with ever-changing market realities. With the recent conceptual and technological advancement of the field of risk management, investment managers can now better implement their processes and better control their performance through the use of comprehensive risk and portfolio management systems. Clearly, the risk management revolution, both analytical and cultural, could not have been possible without advances in technology and data management that allowed the reverse engineering of the vast majority of fixed income securities, as well as without breakthroughs in option pricing theory, interest rate modeling, and prepayment modeling.

Compare today's risk management practices to those of 10 years ago. Back then, duration was the primary risk management technique; most analyses were deterministic and formulated as what-if scenarios; the notion of the likelihood of market events and information about comovements of market factors were ignored; and basis risks were not well understood, identified, measured, or explicitly managed. Dramatic advances in financial modeling and risk methodologies and the phenomenal improvements in computing price/performance ratios, data storage, and bandwidth have raised risk management to a whole new level. The concepts of exponentially weighted time series, 99% confidence losses, and Value-at-Risk trading limits have left academia and entered corporate boardrooms and management meetings. Once esoteric, these notions have been transformed into mainstream practices used by thousands of institutional investors, industry consultants, and regulators.

Today, we are witnessing another cycle of fundamental changes in the asset management industry, particularly among fixed income managers. The ability to navigate complex financial markets with comprehensive and relevant risk management information and systems has become absolutely crucial. With still-vivid memories of recent market catastrophes, investors are reluctant to entrust their assets to small boutiques that do not have, and may not care about, the operating scale required for sound risk management practices. As a result, asset management searches increasingly focus on a relatively small number of firms that offer a broad set of investment services and, even more importantly, have impressive track records of consistent risk-adjusted performance versus a wide array of liabilities. The implications for the industry are significant: We are witnessing unprecedented consolidation driven not by mergers and acquisitions, but by investors and their consultants, who are insisting upon proven risk management capabilities.

This book was written by risk management practitioners with whom I have worked for many years. The methodologies and ideas in this work represent an intriguing blend of finance, mathematics, statistics, computer science, and common sense. What makes them potentially even more interesting is that they were developed and continue to evolve in the context of supporting the risk management function of a global investment management and risk advisory firm. I am pleased that the authors have chosen to share these ideas with the broader financial and academic community and hope that this book will contribute to the ongoing dialogue among finance professionals and theorists that is essential to developing new ideas and raising the level of risk management practices for investors worldwide.

Laurence D. Fink
Chairman and CEO
BlackRock, Inc.

Preface

This book is a study of modern fixed income risk measurement and management. It represents several years of research, development, and practical application of risk management and financial modeling techniques to the every-day challenges of money management and risk advisory businesses. This work brings together numerous risk methodologies and practices currently in use, introduces a number of new ideas and models, and provides a broad perspective on the increasingly important role of risk management in all aspects of investment decision making, including enterprise-wide risk management, portfolio management, trading, and compliance. The book illustrates how risk management has evolved to unify different areas of modern finance, mathematics, statistics, and computer science and spurred application of progressively more sophisticated mathematical, statistical, and econometric methods. While describing a variety of theoretical, technical, computational, and organizational issues involving risk management, the book's recurring motif is that no single measure is capable of addressing all aspects of the ever-changing financial risks. Therefore, understanding assumptions and conceptual trade-offs made by the alternative risk methodologies becomes especially crucial.

This book contains precise but easy-to-understand descriptions and practical applications of various risk measurement and management techniques, including theoretical and empirical duration and partial duration measures, expected rate of return analysis, principal components analysis, Value-at-Risk, risk decomposition, stress testing, and portfolio optimizations. Despite the fact that parts of this book appeared in preliminary form as journal articles and chapters in finance books, it was written to be a cohesive work rather than a compilation of disjointed topics, so sequential reading is recommended.

Notwithstanding substantial reliance on financial and mathematical theory, the orientation of the book is an applied one. Even though the nature of the investigated problems requires application of rather advanced methods from linear algebra, calculus, and applied statistics, no specific knowledge of any particular body of mathematics is required for understanding the described concepts and making practical use of them. For instance, the study of the probability distributions of interest rate shocks and the subsequent derivation of the measures of historical plausibility in Chapter 3 are nontrivial. The nontechnical reader, however, may skip the derivation and proceed straight to the applications of these methods. Even without knowledge of the mathematical details, application of these results to scenario analysis, Monte-Carlo Simulation Value-at-Risk, and stress testing can be very beneficial. However, some basic knowledge of the mathematics of finance, matrix algebra, calculus, probability and statistics is desirable. The organization of the book is as follows.

Chapter 1 introduces the field of risk management and describes the challenges of this fascinating, "fashionable," and relatively young discipline. It acquaints the reader with the different stages of the market risk management process, illustrates the relationship between valuation and risk management problems, and portrays the evolution of risk management ideas over the last few decades. This chapter emphasizes that the vast majority of methodologies described in this book are equally applicable to measuring the absolute risk of fixed income securities and portfolios as well as the relative risk of portfolios vis-à-vis their benchmarks.

Chapter 2 presents parametric approaches to risk management. It includes a discussion of analytical and empirical durations and partial durations, scenario analysis, and expected rate of return analysis. Besides being useful in their own right, the parametric measures of market risk form the backbone of the more elaborate and comprehensive risk methodologies and techniques described later in the book.

Chapter 3 studies the stochastic dynamics of systematic risk factors. It contains an introduction to principal components analysis as well as an investigation of the probability distributions of interest rate shocks. In this chapter, the relationship between the first principal component and the term structure of volatility is explored, and the results are applied to the study of big market move days as well as the historical steepeners and flatteners of the U.S. Treasury curve.

Chapter 4 deals with the Variance/Covariance approach to Value-at-Risk (VaR). First, a deliberately unrealistic example is used to illustrate the distinction between parametric and probabilistic risk measures and motivate the need for Value-at-Risk. A nontechnical description of VaR and its increasingly important role in the life of a financial institution is then presented, followed by the description of the evolution of this measure, from RiskMetrics® cash flow maps to a modern formulation that uses partial durations. It is shown that the VaR framework enables investors to combine first-order exposures of fixed income portfolios and securities to interest rate, basis, and currency risks with correlations and volatilities of systematic risk factors. To provide intuition behind VaR, an approach to risk decomposition is then presented. The chapter concludes with a discussion of duration measures that capture the interest rate directionality of basis risks.

Chapter 5 deals with the problem of VaR modeling in its generality. First, the issues of value surface construction and estimation are discussed. Then, principal components analysis is used to approximate the distributions of systematic risk factors and reduce the dimensionality of the value surface. This enables us to arrive at an accurate representation of complex nonlinear value surfaces in a computationally feasible manner. The advantages of the proposed framework lie in its ability to quantitatively judge the trade-offs that are being made by alternative methodologies versus their computational costs. The detailed description of the Grid Monte-Carlo Simulation VaR that uses traditional and principal component scenario analysis then follows. In this chapter, the methods that incorporate the evolution of securities through time into VaR are also discussed, and the issues related to establishing the appropriate investment or trading horizon are highlighted. Finally, the ability of the existing formulations of VaR to measure catastrophic risks is investigated, and the importance of stress testing is revealed.

Chapter 6 uses the results of the previous chapters to present approaches to managing the market risk in fixed income portfolios via portfolio optimization techniques.

This book targets a broad audience of chief investment officers, corporate treasurers, portfolio managers, risk managers, traders, regulators, researchers, academics, compliance officers, and modelers. It is also suitable for undergraduate students as well as MBA and Ph.D. candidates majoring in finance or financial mathematics who would like to understand the concepts employed in fixed income risk management and gain hands-on experience in computing and applying various measures of risk in practice.

While the presented materials were developed in the course of our work at BlackRock, the contents of the book do not necessarily represent current or past practices of any organization. Needless to say, we are solely responsible for the errors that undoubtedly remain in the book.

Bennett W. Golub
Leo M. Tilman

Acknowledgments

The task of measuring and managing the risk of hundreds of complex and diverse fixed income portfolios offers the ideal setting for developing new ideas and applying them over a variety of economic cycles. The authors have been fortunate to work in precisely such an environment at BlackRock, Inc., a premier global asset management and risk advisory firm, which has served as our state-of-the-art "laboratory." This environment provided us with an ongoing and extremely focused demand for practical solutions to real-life problems and with sophisticated, knowledgeable, and experienced colleagues who gave us constant critique and feedback. The very nature of the problems we were dealing with – forecasting and mitigating potential financial losses – has created the sense of urgency to get things done.

BlackRock's risk management philosophy and culture require the constant development, enhancement, and validation of rigorous techniques for risk measurement and management in response to ever-changing financial markets. The firm's commitment to technology and proprietary analytics has provided significant resources for our work. At the same time, BlackRock's disciplined investment style and diversity of investment products and services, ranging from mutual funds and institutional accounts to hedge funds, REITs, and CLOs, have created a demand for methodologies that are theoretically sound, accurate, intuitive, and computationally feasible. On the other hand, the team approach to portfolio and risk management has led to empirical validation and enhancement of models through constant interaction between financial modelers, portfolio managers, traders, and analysts. This provided a unique opportunity for reconciling theory with reality. Simply put, nothing makes the mind focus better than being 20 feet from a trading desk during a financial market crisis!

The computational and conceptual challenges of risk measurement and management increase exponentially with the size of a financial institution and the diversity of asset classes in which it invests. BlackRock was founded in 1988 as a niche fixed income investment firm. It is now a global investment company that manages over $170 billion in assets and provides a wide range of risk management services to financial institutions with over $1 trillion in assets. This rapid growth has created unique challenges. It was not only critical to develop risk management methodologies universally pertinent to all classes of fixed income securities, portfolios, and benchmarks, but to ensure that these approaches were suitable for large-scale practical application in a computationally and operationally feasible manner.

The ever-changing nature of financial markets invariably adds challenges of its own to the tasks of risk measurement and management. Given that the initial work on this book dates back several years, new securities, new structures, and new systematic sources of risk have since emerged, and the financial markets have gone through a number of very distinct phases. We were fortunate to be a part of a diverse team that was capable of quickly adapting to market transformations and crises, constantly enhancing its understanding of market dynamics and incorporating this knowledge into risk management models.

We are greatly indebted to many colleagues who helped shape the concepts discussed in this book. First, we thank Larry Fink and Ralph Schlosstein, BlackRock's Chairman and President, respectively, for their encouragement, patience, and support of this project through its several-year long history. Second, we express deep gratitude to Charlie Hallac for his extraordinary talent in turning many of the ideas presented in the book into practical reality with robust implementation and infrastructure. Absent his efforts, everything we have done would have been primarily academic. Third, we thank Adam Wizon for his unique ability to assimilate and improve every aspect of the financial engineering process. Fourth, we are grateful to the tremendous inspiration we received from BlackRock's fixed income Portfolio Management Group for making real the problems on which we worked. In particular, Keith Anderson helped us over the years to focus in a practical and comprehensive way on risk management issues that mattered most, while Scott Amero provided us thoughtful advice that combined his market experience and knowledge of applied finance.

We would like to explicitly acknowledge the contributions of our present and past colleagues at BlackRock that were incorporated into this book and to apologize for any unintended omissions. We thank Bill De Leon for his idea on how to derive the spread directionality coefficient from the options markets, for his work on hedging the spread risk with Standard and Poors (S&P) Index futures, and for his analysis of the impact of time on risk characteristics of fixed income securities; Yury Geyman for his research on the properties of key rate and key treasury rate durations; Andrew Gordon for his insight with respect to risk of duration-neutral yield curve trades that led to the development of Monte-Carlo Simulation Value-at-Risk (VaR) using two principal components; Scott Peng for his discussion of the different types of hedging instruments; and Pavan Wadhwa for his analysis of duration drifts.

The book has benefited tremendously from conversations with and feedback from our colleagues, clients, and friends – Marlys Appleton, Max Baker, Mustafa Chowdhury, Nasir Dossani, Viola Dunne, George Evans, Imran Hussain, Yury Geyman, Richard Kushel, Michael Lustig, Steve Luttrell, Mark Paltrowitz, Glenn Perillo, Ehud Ronn, Joel Shaiman, Richard Shea, Irwin Sheer, Rajiv Sobti, Chris Turner, Fred Weinberger, Mark Winer, Adam Wizon, Sudha Yerneni, and so many others. An earlier attempt to compile some of the materials for this book was assisted by Edith Hotchkiss, although this version contains entirely new text and ideas.

We would like to express special gratitude to Raymond Ahn, Barbara Novick, Julie Park, Sue Wagner, and Dan Waltcher for their help in converting the manuscript into a published book. We thank BlackRock, Inc., for allowing us to use its analytic software in computing most of the numerical examples; however, any mistakes in the analyses are entirely ours. We are grateful to Mina Samuels, Jack Gaston, Janice Weisner, and everyone at John Wiley & Sons, Inc., for their enthusiasm, professionalism, and vision.

We are eternally indebted to the many reviewers of the original manuscript of the book. Our special thanks go to Bill De Leon, Philippe Jorion, and Irwin Sheer whose comments were particularly detailed and focused. We would like to express deep appreciation to Mark Abbott, Lev Borodovsky, T.J. Carlson, Michel Donegani, Lev Dynkin, Vladimir Finkelstein, Charles Grant, Harris Hwang, Ronald Kahn, Jim Lukens, Andrew Kalotay, Stewart Morrison, Greg Parseghian, Larry Pohlman, Richard Roll, Prashant Vankudre, Adam Wizon, Larry Wright, and Lauren Wright for reading the manuscript and making many insightful suggestions. We thank Rob Zellner for helping us develop some of the numerical examples in the text and Jill Greenfield, Alyssa Hong, and Goldie Silber for their administrative help.

Last but certainly not least, we thank our families for their unconditional love, devotion, and support. We dedicate this book to them.

New York   Bennett W. Golub
Summer 2000   Leo M. Tilman

1

The Art and Science of Risk Management

1.1 THE "BRAVE NEW WORLD" OF RISK MANAGEMENT

As any practitioner can attest, interest in risk management is highly correlated with large shocks to the financial system, their attendant dislocations, and the subsequent headlines and witch hunts. In fact, nothing focuses the mind better than surviving a brush with financial ruin or witnessing the demise of an institution similar to your own. Conversely, long periods of financial stability tend to make the life of a risk manager a lonely one, making him seek refuge in extracurricular activities, like starting a new hobby or writing a book. The evolution of the ideas presented in this work is a vivid illustration of this phenomenon. We started thinking about writing a book in 1996 when the market environment was characterized by optimism and confidence, high liquidity, tightening of credit spreads, and the "exuberant" rally in the stock markets of developed and emerging countries. Given the benign nature of basis risk factors at that time, interest rates accounted for the overwhelming majority of risk associated with investing in fixed income securities.

The Asia meltdown of October 1997 changed this tranquility, heightening attention to risk management. Besides interest rates, a host of other risk factors became significant, including emerging market credit

1

spreads, liquidity, and exchange rates. The events of that memorable month highlighted the impact of globalization on the capital markets' behavior. One year later, the credit and liquidity crisis of fall 1998 and the unprecedented turbulence in the financial markets became an even more persuasive illustration of the changed nature of financial risks. The financial near-demise of many well-respected practitioners and academics (e.g., Long-Term Capital Management) forced all market participants to take a deep and more focused look at their practices, procedures, and assumptions, hence revealing new intellectual and technological challenges facing risk management.

However, by early spring 1999, the Dow Jones Industrial Average (DJIA) was back at historical highs, interest rates reverted to more "normal" levels, and credit spreads tightened dramatically across most all spread-sensitive asset classes (Table 1.1). With the U.S. economy strong, stock markets rallied, emerging and high yield markets rebounded, liquidity improved, and the fears and concerns of fall 1998 seemed to be left behind. Some investors began wondering what the fuss was all about, fearing a different kind of risk this time around – the risk of *not having enough exposure* during a bull market. Nevertheless, the financial crises did teach market participants a number of valuable lessons. They highlighted the ever-changing nature of financial markets and taught investors to treat catastrophes not as *highly unlikely* but rather as *infrequent but on average regularly occurring* events. Taken in that light, the challenges facing modern risk management appear greater than ever before, and a deeper understanding of risk and the mechanisms by which financial markets are implicitly linked is vital.

The term *risk management* has been increasingly appropriated to incorporate the full range of potential problems with financial assets, such as administration, compliance, technology, and fraud control. While certainly acknowledging the extreme importance of these business risks, this book purposely limits the scope of risk management to

TABLE 1.1   DJIA, 10-year U.S. Treasury Yields, and 10-year Swap Spread (as of 10/5/98, 4/29/99, and 12/31/99)

	10/5/1998	4/29/1999	12/31/1999
DJIA	7,726	10,878	11,192
10-year OTR TSY (%)	4.18%	5.23%	6.11%
10-year Par TSY (%)	4.31%	5.40%	6.28%
10-year Swap Spread (basis points)	94	72	83

market risk management, focusing on the problems unique to applied financial modeling and its applications to portfolio management, trading, hedging, and other areas of financial decision making.

To illustrate the evolution of risk management as a discipline, let us compare and contrast the financial disasters that made the headlines in the 1980s and early 1990s versus the more recent ones. Consider some of the earlier landmark failures, all of which were characterized by missing knowledge or systems, a lack of models and analytics, oversight, or non-recognition of risk:

- S&L bailout – limited understanding of yield curve risks
- Orange County – leveraged risks without adequate monitoring and measurement
- Askin Capital Management – missing analytics
- Kidder Peabody – limited ability to manage risk of complex securities (e.g., Collateralized Mortgage Obligations: CMOs) through interest-rate cycles

More recent financial failures have been of a very different nature. They generally involved highly sophisticated financial entities who, despite their knowledge of their portfolio risk characteristics, were forced to simultaneously respond to unusually large and sudden market dislocations, including Russia's default, a widening of credit spreads, and a collapse in liquidity:

- Long-Term Capital Management (LTCM) – extremely complex leveraged positions stressed beyond equity capital[1]
- Laser Mortgage Management (LMM) – high leverage and large concentrations of risk combined with a loss of liquidity

Analysis of recent market catastrophes enables us to glimpse into the future of risk management. First and foremost, players today are much more analytical, knowledgeable, and conscious about quantitative analysis and risk management. Their increased sophistication is due to a variety of recent advances in technology as well as financial theory. On the technological front, tremendous improvements in computational capabilities and reduction in costs have allowed the pricing and analyzing of thousands of complex, path-dependent securities on a daily basis. Problems that were considered futuristic only a decade ago can now be solved. In addition, libraries of fixed income securities were reverse-engineered and made accessible to investors through software vendors such as Bloomberg, Bridge/EJV, Salomon Brothers' Yield Book, Trepp, and CMS Bond Edge. With basic "meat-and-potatoes" analytical capabilities in place, practitioners were able to move on to new and more exciting intellectual problems.

The fixed income investment universe has expanded dramatically over the last few years. As domestic markets were becoming increasingly efficient, investors began searching for excess return by expanding their holdings into more esoteric types of derivatives, illiquid securities, non-dollar and real estate debt, emerging market bonds, and other asset classes. While creating (at least in theory) diversification benefits on the portfolio level, this presented investors with "unfamiliar combinations of risk,"[2] dramatically complicating the task of measuring and managing financial risk. To adapt to the new realities, financial modelers and risk managers were forced to raise their analytical systems to a whole new level. Therefore, the news of BARRA's discontinuation of its existing line of domestic fixed income risk management products after almost 20 years of interesting work in this field is not at all surprising.[3] The costs of developing and maintaining risk management systems are increasing at an astonishing rate and are expected to intensify in the future. In today's competitive environment, a successful investment process must rely on analytical, risk management, and technological infrastructures as never before. The tasks of understanding a wide range of fixed income products and efficiently managing hundreds of portfolios against numerous customized benchmarks in a risk controlled fashion demand greater resources. The increased sophistication of clients and their awareness of risk management techniques present additional challenges. Understanding a client's investment objective and having systems in place that track positions, trades, and historical performance is no longer sufficient. In addition to these basic capabilities, client's risk preferences and utility functions must be translated into the language of risk management; sources of active return over the benchmark must be understood; and a variety of interest rate, currency, and basis risks must be measured and explicitly managed. Finally, the emergence of the World Wide Web has enabled investors to have continuous access to their investment portfolios, fundamentally altering the nature of communication between asset managers and their clients and creating the highest levels of transparency.

In his anti-utopian novel *Brave New World*, Aldous Huxley portrays a society that chooses to sacrifice feelings, emotions, and "high art" for the sake of *stability*. In some sense, the discipline of risk management is an analogous construct in the financial markets. Ironically, the individual pursuit of stability through the practice of risk management may have made financial markets *more directly susceptible* to market risk. This paradox has arisen because as financial markets became more global, dynamic, and intertwined, "standard" risk management practices began to propagate. As a result, traditional concepts of financial diversification (holding portfolios of assets with uncorrelated systematic sources of risk) are becoming undermined by common risk management practices of progressively similar capital pools. The use of similar risk management techniques by an increasing proportion of the financial system (asset managers, hedge funds, mutual funds, banks, insurance companies, etc.) leads, in times of crisis, to similar reactions by market participants to financial catastrophes:

- *Similar goals.* In times of turmoil, investors try to reduce total risk per unit of capital and/or raise cash to cover margin calls.
- *Similar response.* First, they naturally attempt to sell illiquid positions. After discovering "no bid" (huge and unrealistic spread widening on thin trading) for illiquid securities, liquid positions have to be sold, regardless of which market they are in.[4] This phenomenon may create correlations among asset classes that are fundamentally uncorrelated.
- *Vicious circle of liquidity.* Lenders increase "haircuts" on illiquid leveraged positions, thus forcing additional liquidations, further depressing the value of illiquid positions, and, in turn, exacerbating margin calls. At the same time, dealers become reluctant to take long or short positions of any significant size and widen bid/ask spreads.
- *Model risk.* Reliance on similar quantitative models can create dangers of its own since the behavior of financial markets changes fundamentally in times of crisis.[5]

The following examples illustrate how market dynamics changes due to adoption of similar risk management practices.

1. *Portfolio insurance in 1987.* Everyone is familiar with the impact that the infamous risk management technique, *portfolio insurance,* had on the stock market in 1987. The fact that "portfolio insurance caused the crash remains disputable; that it exacerbated the market movement is a certainty."[6] Instead of buying options outright, portfolio insurance attempted to use dynamic option replication strategies to mitigate market risks. Similar to *stop-loss* policies, portfolio insurance generated further selling as a result of lower market prices, only aggravating the sell-off.

2. *Hedging mortgages in the 1992 rally.* In 1992, interest rates fell dramatically after years of relatively high rates. Despite the fact that Wall Street had spent millions of dollars developing interest rate and prepayment models, the mortgage market did not trade to the durations predicted by their state-of-the-art option-adjusted spread models.[7] As a consequence, most mortgage investors sooner or later realized that rather than assuming that every financial problem has an analytical solution, subjective estimates must be created, managed, and incorporated into financial models. In the subsequent 1994 rally, lessons learned two years earlier manifested themselves in the fear of ever-shortening mortgage durations. This led to aggressive buying of U.S. Treasury securities that further strengthened the rally and exacerbated the shortening of mortgages.

3. *Credit spreads in fall 1998.* Russia's default on its sovereign debt created losses for many large financial institutions, the complete scope of which was not fully understood. The heightened credit risk aversion caused a dramatic widening of credit spreads, putting pressure on highly leveraged institutions, LTCM being the most prominent. As rumors spread and losses increased, risk management units uniformly started paring back positions and cutting credit lines. These actions, in turn, exacerbated the crisis that could have posed a serious threat to the entire financial system if not for the extraordinary initiative by the Federal Reserve to stabilize LTCM.

Financial markets constitute a complex, dynamic self-learning system. As a rigorous quantitative discipline that attempts to model this system and forecast its behavior, risk management has attracted a lot of brilliant people with academic backgrounds in physics, mathematics, and other natural sciences. While usually providing great insights into the analytical aspects of financial phenomena, these "rocket scientists" may oversimplify financial modeling problems by mapping the unchanging nature of most physical systems onto the evolving and adapting behavior of the nearly efficient financial markets. Since the underlying "truths" of financial markets (as determined theoretically or empirically) regularly change as more market participants learn about them, very few problems in other fields of human knowledge can compete in complexity with financial modeling. While the laws of physics do not change when an important relationship is discovered, fundamental characteristics of financial markets *do* change as knowledge about them is assimilated into the practice of market participants. The stochastic behavior of systematic risk factors and even their cause-and-effect relationships "mutate" because of investors' knowledge about them. Hence all risk management practices require frequent "reality checks" to verify that the forecasts of risk models are still consistent with actual market behavior. For instance, if a price movement is inconsistent with the predictions of a risk model, either the price is wrong,[8] the security has out- or underperformed the market, the model is broken, or the model's structure has become outdated. If the premise is accepted that the market teaches one about risk rather than risk being derivable from theory, then a concept of "objective risk criteria," bounced around longingly in the pension fund world, is fundamentally flawed. Because market risks continually change, the methodologies that measure them must evolve as well. By the time a risk becomes "objective," its characteristics may have changed materially.

Advancements in technology have made desecuritization an important trend influencing risk management. Back in the early 1980s, the emergence of powerful centralized computing and database capabilities enabled the introduction of various types of structured products, including mortgage-backed securities, credit card receivables, and the like. By securitizing large pools of individual loans, a spectrum of liquid securities was created, reducing costs and seemingly eliminating the need for significant informational and technical expertise. Explicitly or implicitly, the law of large numbers was invoked to persuade investors that they were getting securities with "average" characteristics. In practice, however, the provided information was often purposely limited in an attempt to enhance the liquidity of subsequent issues of sometimes dissimilar pools of assets. Today, technology is starting to reverse this trend as investors are able to efficiently pierce securitization shells and monitor pools of assets on a disaggregated basis. Massive data sets can now be stored and transferred at reasonable costs, and data mining and visualization techniques make it possible to manipulate gigantic amounts of data and interactively investigate multidimensional relationships on a computer screen. For example, when forecasting short-term prepayment characteristics of servicing portfolios, financial institutions can employ increasingly sophisticated modeling techniques to capture the information contained in detailed borrower-specific data, including mortgage application files, prepayment histories, credit card and bank account information, and so forth. While previously infeasible due to computational constraints, use of extensive data sets has improved the forecasting power of empirical models by an order of magnitude. This type of analysis is indicative of the future because technologically sophisticated investors will be positioned to add additional value by analyzing the data underlying complex structured securities.

In a world of pervasive analytical capabilities, modern risk management will be faced with challenges specifically related to applied financial modeling. Thus, portfolio-level analytics needs to identify common risk characteristics among diverse types of assets and quantify aggregate exposures through common denominators. In addition to interest rate risk and yield curve risk, which are well understood and modeled, systematic behavior of basis risks and their relationships with interest rates, currencies, and other systematic risk factors must be carefully studied. Increasingly sophisticated statistical, econometric, and financial methods need to be developed to estimate "fat tails" and unstable empirical relationships, including incorporating catastrophic events into business-as-usual distributions. In the absence of such models, the need for incorporating subjective judgement into risk management becomes even greater. Thus, since practitioners are taking on a more cautious view of the ability of statistical models to measure catastrophic risk, application of market knowledge and intuition in developing approaches to stress testing is critical.

Risk management is becoming more prominent in the life of financial institutions. No longer perceived by traders and portfolio management as a controlling or "policing" function that simply limits the upside, it is turning into an invaluable quantitative resource for all stages of the investment process. The risk-taking culture and the risk management culture are merging together, as the financial markets keep reminding investors that while one cannot make money without taking risks, the long-term viability of institutions is put in jeopardy if risks are not managed properly and relentlessly.

Predicting how the Brave New World of risk management will evolve in the future is difficult. The only certainty is that the tasks of measuring and managing risk will become even more complex and demanding, both conceptually and computationally. Given the rapid changes in the financial markets and products, it is the ability to successfully deal with these challenges that will determine long-term success or failure.

1.2 MARKET RISK MANAGEMENT PROCESS

Market risk management can be thought of as consisting of the following distinct stages:

1. Identification of relevant systematic risk factors
2. Measurement of market exposures
3. Estimation of joint probability distributions
4. Computation of risk measures and explicit risk mitigation and management

Risk management starts with the task of identifying all relevant *systematic risk factors*, exogenous variables that cause fluctuations of market prices of securities and portfolios. Some risk factors are *directly observable* and *measurable* macroeconomic variables, such as Gross Domestic Product (GDP), mortgage origination rates, yields on U.S. Treasury and other liquid securities, foreign exchange rates, swap spreads, and so forth. Other risk factors cannot be directly empirically observed. Among others, they include *composite* variables (spot and par rates, principal components, option-adjusted spreads, etc.) that can typically be derived from a set of directly observable risk factors. To fully understand the price behavior of a security or portfolio, all applicable risk factors have to be identified. For complex multicurrency fixed income portfolios containing derivatives and esoteric spread products, the number of relevant risk factors can be hundreds or even thousands. The "observable and measurable" criterion is crucial. For practical purposes, identifying a risk factor that cannot be accurately measured is useless. For instance, the behavior of certain types of mortgage derivatives (e.g., mortgage servicing rights, esoteric CMOs, Commercial Interest-Only Mortgage Backed Securities [CMBS IOs] etc.) as well as certain emerging market debt would be better understood if these markets were more liquid and the corresponding time series of nominal or option-adjusted spreads were available. Unfortunately, due to the illiquidity and lack of transparency in these markets, it is difficult to have confidence in their historical time series of credit spreads. This example illustrates that in practice it is necessary to identify fundamental risk factors that can be reliably measured. They sometimes serve as proxies for more relevant but unobservable risk factors.

Once the set of applicable risk factors has been identified, the second stage of risk management involves measuring exposures of securities to each risk factor and aggregating these exposures across securities in a portfolio. This problem can be solved in two different ways. A security's exposure to each risk factor can be measured in isolation, with all others being fixed. In mathematical terms, this is equivalent to taking a partial derivative of a security's price with respect to the given risk factor. Measures such as option-adjusted durations, key rate durations, spread durations, and others presented in Chapter 2 serve as examples of partial derivatives. Methods that use various partial derivatives are popular because of their simplicity. One drawback of these methodologies lies in their historical implausibility, since rarely does a risk factor move in isolation, with all others unchanged. Also, accurately predicting price movements with partial derivatives (*local* measures of price sensitivity) may not be always possible when the changes in the underlying risk factors are large. Last, this setting makes capturing the intricacies of interaction among various risk factors difficult, both conceptually and computationally. Irrespective of the traditional criticism of measuring market exposure using partial derivatives, they constitute a very useful portfolio and risk management tool by presenting price sensitivities in a simple and intuitive fashion. As an alternative to employing partial durations to measure risk associated with isolated movements of each risk factor, price sensitivity of securities and portfolios to the *simultaneous* change in several risk factors can be investigated. Approaches of this type include option-adjusted durations that capture the interest rate directionality of basis risks as well as principal components durations.

Even after (1) all relevant risk factors have been identified and (2) the exposure of securities and portfolios to them has been measured, the ability to judge market risk is still incomplete without knowledge of the joint probability distributions of systematic risk factors. For instance, adding a new (nonvolatile) security to a portfolio may have a diversification effect if the returns on this security are (substantially) negatively correlated with returns on the original portfolio, but may actually have a risk-amplifying effect if the returns on this security are highly volatile or if their correlation with returns on the existing portfolio is positive or not sufficiently negative. On a similar note, identical market exposure to two different risk factors does not imply the same level of risk because price volatility is a function of both market exposure and the volatility of the underlying risk factor. Insights into the risks of complex portfolios without information about the volatility of relevant systematic risk factors and knowledge about their interaction are limited. The third and crucial step of market risk management therefore involves estimation of the probabilistic distribution of risk factors. For the sake of tractability, risk management models commonly assume that *instantaneous changes in risk factors follow a joint normal distribution.* Normal distributions are fully defined by the vector of *volatilities* (standard deviations) and the matrix of *correlations* of the corresponding random variables. Recent advances in applied statistics, including ARCH/GARCH approaches and dynamic time series modeling, have enabled construction of sophisticated statistical models of financial time series data. Risk management employs these methods in estimating historical volatilities and correlations of changes in systematic risk factors.

While econometric models may fit historical data well and provide insights and intuition behind the historical behavior of financial markets, they often fail to accurately forecast future movements and relationships, which is not surprising. On July 31, 1998, for instance, based on the three years of historical swap spread data, extrapolation using time series models would have predicted that swap spreads would likely be nonvolatile in August–October 1998. Due to their exclusive reliance on historical data, these models were unable to forecast unexpected *exogenous* events, such as Russia's default and the dramatic widening of credit spreads in fall 1998. The swap spread widening in August–September 1998 constituted anywhere between a 7 and a 10 standard deviation event, depending on the methodology used to estimate the historical volatility on July 31, 1998. Under the normal distribution assumption, a 7 standard deviation event corresponds to the less than a 1-in-700,000,000,000 chance. Clearly, the methodology used to draw conclusions about the statistical magnitude of swap spreads in this example is unrealistic: either the normality assumption is inadequate, the standard deviation is misestimated, or approaches of this kind are too primitive to adequately address catastrophic events and structural breaks in the system. Thus, the majority of statistical models currently in use, while fitting historical data well, may often fail to predict fundamental changes in the behavior of risk factors and are unable to account for paradigm shifts. These include the sudden emergence of some economic variables (e.g., leverage or credit spreads) as key forces driving financial markets after long periods of subdued behavior. Conversely, some of the previously influential risk factors may temporarily or permanently become unimportant. For instance, the employment cost index and other economic indicators that greatly influenced the market in 1993–1997 as predictors of interest rate movements became virtually unnoticeable in mid-1998 when global markets, rather than the state of U.S. economy, influenced the Federal Reserve's decisions. Models based on historical information alone are unable, by construction, to capture these types of phenomena. This argues for an increasing incorporation of subjective judgement into risk management models, making it imperative to develop risk management models flexible enough to allow for the addition of new risk factors and the deletion of those that are no longer applicable.

After (1) risk factors have been identified and measured, (2) exposure of securities and portfolios to these factors has been determined, and (3) models that estimate the joint distribution of risk factors have been built, the fourth and final step in the risk management process involves the actual computation of risk measures. The vast majority of methodologies described in this book are designed to measure the absolute risk of fixed income securities and portfolios as well as the relative risk of portfolios vis-à-vis their benchmarks. Thus, we start by estimating exposure of individual securities to a particular type of systematic risk or to market risk as a whole. Then we aggregate risk across the portfolio's holdings. This enables measurement of the risk of portfolios (or *assets*) as well as the risk of their benchmarks (or *liabilities*) since the latter can usually be represented as portfolios of fixed income securities as well.[9] The *gap* between assets and liabilities can be thought of as a portfolio consisting of two positions: a long position in assets and a short position in liabilities. The relative risk of a portfolio of assets vis-à-vis its benchmark can therefore be computed as the risk of the gap.

In addition to risk measurement, this stage of the market risk management process also involves understanding the advantages and disadvantages of alternative risk methodologies, working with decision makers on translating their risk/return preferences into the language of risk management, and identifying a wide range of practical applications for portfolio and risk management. The ultimate success of risk management is achieved when quantitative tools are used not only to measure, monitor, and explicitly mitigate risk, but when they become a valuable resource in a variety of day-to-day investment activities, including asset allocation, portfolio management, and trading.

1.3 THEORY, PRACTICE, AND COMPUTATION: CHALLENGES SPECIFIC TO FIXED INCOME MARKETS

Fixed income investment management is characterized by the relationship among theoretical models and concepts, their practical implementation, and the role of computational resources. Problems that are trivial to solve theoretically are often impossible to apply in practice due to a variety of reasons, including an absence of historical information, the ever-changing composition of portfolios and their evolution through time, a large number of macroeconomic risk factors influencing asset prices, and so on.

The business of large-scale money management, as opposed to running a small trading book, adds complications of its own. Complex calculations have to be performed routinely for thousands of securities, hundreds of portfolios, and their benchmarks in a computationally and operationally feasible fashion. This creates yet another challenge. In order to meaningfully aggregate risk numbers across securities, portfolios, and benchmarks, one has to develop risk methodologies applicable to all types of fixed income securities, trading strategies, and portfolios. This implies creating a *superset* of systematic risk factors influencing all classes of fixed income securities and measuring risk with respect to all of them.

The art of managing risk in fixed income portfolios involves constantly making intelligent trade-offs. It entails finding the fine balance between theoretical knowledge, practical considerations, and computational feasibility. What makes risk management a fascinating discipline is the challenge of mathematically describing real-life phenomena and trying to develop an understanding of the assumptions and conscious trade-offs that are being made. Finally, after conjectures and models are built, it is then possible to test them in different market environments.

1.3.1 Price Discovery

To the uninitiated, it might seem that prices of fixed income securities are known and freely available in the market, just as stock prices are. If in addition to market prices, valuation models are also available to compute fair values of all securities in any given economic environment, numerous risk characteristics for portfolios and securities can be analyzed, including various duration measures and scenario analyses (Chapter 2), Variance/Covariance Value-at-Risk (VaR) (Chapter 4) and Monte-Carlo Simulation Value-at-Risk (Chapter 5). If, in addition to the current market prices, historical time series of prices are available as well, implied duration (Chapter 2) and Historical Simulation VaR (Chapter 5) can be computed as well.

Empirically observing market prices sounds easy in theory. However, since the vast majority of fixed income markets are over-the-counter and are not exchange-traded as stocks are, their *price discovery* is a burdensome operational task. To do a good job, a buy-side company would need to maintain a team of professionals dedicated to researching prices for thousands of fixed income securities with the help of the broker-dealer community. Table 1.2 presents the results of an experiment that illustrates the challenges of the price discovery process. First, several fixed income securities, characterized by varying degrees of liquidity and complexity, were identified. Then four different dealer firms were asked to price these instruments. The results were as expected. For liquid and less complex securities, price quote differentials among dealers were small. For structured or less liquid securities, price quotes varied dramatically across dealers or were unavailable altogether.

TABLE 1.2   Mid-Market Price Marks by Various Dealers for Different Security Types (as of 7/29/98)

Security Type	Description	Coupon	Maturity	Dealer 1	Dealer 2	Dealer 3	Dealer 4
US Treasury Note	Treasury Note	5.75	11/30/02	100.80	100.79	100.78	100.80
Generic MBS	FNMA 30 YR	8.00	05/01/22	104.13	103.90	103.69	104.14
US Corporate Bond	Ameritech Capital	6.55	01/15/28	99.10	98.94	99.22	99.48
Non-agency CMBS	RTC_94-C2-G	8.00	04/25/25	C/P	100.84	C/P	C/P
Whole Loan PAC CMO	BAMS_98-3-2A1	6.50	07/25/13	100.50	100.47	C/P	100.50
ABS - Prepay Sensitive	GT_97-1-B1	7.23	03/15/28	100.22	100.11	100.42	100.16

"C/P" = "Cannot Price"

Due to the fiduciary nature of their business, institutional money managers are required to use market data obtained from an independent third party, and therefore an approach to measuring the quality of market prices is needed. For each security, the historical change in price is decomposed into the components attributable to various risk factors: parallel and nonparallel movements in the yield curve, risk-free return, returns due to changes in credit spreads and implied volatility, and the like. If a substantial component of the price movement is not explained by the actual changes in the relevant risk factors, the following three possibilities exist. First, the security may have under- or outperformed the market. Second, there could have been pricing errors. Third, the parametric risk measures employed in estimating returns due to various systematic factors may have been incorrect. In practice, price discovery is a manual process subject to substantial human, operational, and data problems. Pricing errors have far-reaching consequences which can distort valuation models, impair relative value judgements, and lead to erroneous risk assessments. Regularly monitoring the quality of prices used in portfolio and risk management is therefore vital.

1.3.2 Dynamic Portfolio Characteristics

Dynamic portfolio characteristics tremendously complicate the tasks of measuring and managing risk of fixed income portfolios. Throughout this book, many results and conclusions are influenced by the following crucial considerations.

Impact of time. Risk characteristics of fixed income portfolios change, sometimes dramatically, as the underlying securities age. Irrespective of the market environment, options embedded in fixed income securities decay, durations decrease as bonds approach maturity, mortgage-backed securities and their derivatives become seasoned and experience burnout, becoming less sensitive to prepayments, etc.

Dependency on the economic environment. Risk characteristics of fixed income securities may be drastically different depending on the economic environment they are in. Imagine that interest rates suddenly increased by 100 basis points with all other risk factors being unchanged. First, all cash flows would now be discounted at higher rates. Second, the "in-the-moneyness" of the embedded options would change: options that used to be in-the-money may become out-of-the-money, securities with negative convexities may become positively convex, instruments that used to be highly risky may become virtually option-free (e.g., Planned Amortization Class [PAC] CMOs).

Reinvestment. While the vast majority of risk measures is concerned with analyzing changes in the values of fixed income securities resulting from unexpected market fluctuations, reinvestment risk should not be forgotten. Since, unlike most equities, fixed income securities generate substantial coupon payments subject to reinvestment, the expected total return on the portfolio may be substantially impaired if cash flows have to be reinvested at lower rates than originally planned. Expected rate of return analysis (EROR) (Chapter 2) allows us to measure the impact of time on risk characteristics of fixed income securities and portfolios and assess reinvestment risk.

Path dependency. As if things were not complicated enough, path dependency of certain classes of fixed income securities must be taken into account as well. Two identically structured instruments may have substantially different risk characteristics depending on the *historical path* of their market environments (e.g., barrier options, mortgage-backed securities, etc.).

1.3.3 New Securities, New Structures, and the Absence of Historical Information

Financial markets are constantly evolving. Not only do they become more efficient with advances in option pricing and technology, they are also being constantly extended by new security types and structures. In 1980, for example, mortgage-backed securities and their derivatives emerged. More recently, Brady bonds, U.S. Treasury Inflation-Protected securities (TIPS), various esoteric types of asset-backed securities, CMBS IOs, 144-As, and many other asset classes came to the market. Since newly introduced securities may offer additional return as compared to more developed markets, those who can keep up with recent market innovations may have a significant advantage. However, this entails immediately enhancing valuation models to accommodate the new structures and expanding risk management models to account for auxiliary systematic risk factors. Both valuation and risk management of new financial products are especially challenging given the absence of historical information about them. In the beginning, the tasks of determining the fair value of new securities as well as measuring their risk are more art than science, because traders and portfolio managers have yet to develop intuition regarding their market behavior and there is no historical information to perform any meaningful empirical analysis.

The fixed income risk management paradigm is very different from that employed in the stock market because of the constant introduction of new financial products, absence of relevant historical information, and challenges of price discovery. While the following discussion is closely related to Section 1.2 that deals with the market risk management process, a different angle is used here. The approach to modeling financial risk presented below has become second nature to fixed income practitioners. Thus, instead of attempting to measure the risk of a security directly, a factor-equivalent (replicating) portfolio is created, and its properties are subsequently analyzed. With varying degrees of accuracy that depend on the methodology, cash flow uncertainties and other characteristics of the factor-equivalent portfolio are tailored to resemble those of the original security. Replicating portfolios can be comprised of actual instruments with long and reliable price histories. For instance, the original formulation of RiskMetrics® Variance/Covariance Value-at-Risk (VaR) (Chapter 4) presented each fixed income security as a portfolio of zero-coupon bonds. Unfortunately, replicating fixed income instruments using actual securities is not always intellectually or computationally feasible. For this reason, many modern risk management methodologies use factor-equivalent portfolios, consisting of *imaginary* securities that represent systematic risk factors directly. For example, owning a corporate bond is, to the first-order approximation, equivalent to holding a portfolio of zero-coupon bonds as well as having the exposure to the appropriate corporate credit spread. The market risk of the original security is measured by integrating information about market exposures with estimates about volatilities and correlations of the instruments in the factor-equivalent portfolio.

1.4 STATISTICAL CHALLENGES: RISK MANAGEMENT VERSUS VALUATION

There are two distinct problems faced by investors: *valuation* and *risk management*. Valuation is concerned with determining the *fair value* of a security at a particular moment in time in a specified economic environment. Accurate computation of a security's fair value is contingent on the ability to reverse-engineer its cash flow structure (cash flow uncertainties, optionality, and path-dependency) as a function of systematic risk factors and time. Valuation models start with the current values of a variety of systematic risk factors and use stochastic processes to formulate conjectures about their evolution through time. This enables the generation of cash flow streams in a large number of hypothetical market environments and assessment of the probability associated with each scenario. According to modern option pricing theory, the *fair* price of a security is defined as a *mathematical expectation* of all conceivable discounted future payoffs.

Time series analysis has been widely used in economics and finance ever since it was discovered that univariate ARIMA models often have far better forecasting and explanatory power than extremely complicated multivariate macroeconomic models. For instance, technical analysis uses the past of a univariate time series to predict its future movements and judge relative value. Econometric prepayment models attempt to forecast mortgage prepayments as functions of borrower-specific factors, macroeconomic variables, and time. When describing the future evolution of systematic risk factors, some option-pricing models use time series analysis to statistically estimate parameters of the conjectured stochastic processes. Since valuation models compute the mathematical *expectation* of a price as a function of a large number of stochastic variables, they typically attempt to model as precisely as possible the *bulk* of the probabilistic distribution of future returns and are less concerned with the accuracy of modeling the *tails* of this distribution. Hence the use of less sophisticated time series methods when solving valuation problems.

The fact that valuation models use information about the current economic environment (yield curves, foreign exchange rates, observed market prices, implied volatilities, and various credit spreads) as input makes them *market-state dependent*. This observation provides the most direct and simplest explanation of the need for risk management: Because prices of fixed income securities change as valuation models' inputs fluctuate, the sensitivity of prices to various systematic risk factors as well as the probabilistic behavior of these sources of market risk need to be measured. Thus, once the fair value of a security is determined, traders use their views on the market as well as various relative value considerations to decide whether to go long or short this security. Risk management then comes into the picture in order to assess the risk associated with *unexpected* market moves. At this point, the knowledge of the probability associated with potential losses is combined with the estimates of their magnitude to arrive at a "worst-case loss." Notice that instead of attempting to model as accurately as possible the bulk of future distribution of price changes, risk management is concerned with measuring, mitigating, and controlling large financial losses, that is, modeling the left *tail* of the future distribution of random returns. This need for higher accuracy of modeling tails of probability distributions, in turn, spurred new interest in applied statistical modeling, including ARCH/GARCH, dynamic time series models, and the like.

1.5 EVOLUTION OF RISK MANAGEMENT IDEAS

Valuation and risk management problems are closely related. Many measures of risk rely on the ability to compute fair values of fixed income in a variety of historical and hypothetical economic environments. It is therefore not surprising that the emergence of risk management as a rigorous discipline has coincided with breakthroughs in different aspects of valuation – option pricing theory, interest rate modeling, prepayment modeling, and methods dealing with yield curve estimation. These intellectual advances in valuation, in turn, resulted from the application to finance of progressively sophisticated approaches from econometrics, computational mathematics, and stochastic calculus as well as the development of financial theory.

To set the stage for a more detailed discussion of various risk methodologies in the following chapters, this section provides an overview of the intellectual evolution of risk management. Although changes in prices of fixed income securities were known to have been influenced by dozens of systematic risk factors, as an analytical shortcut, price exposures to each risk factor were initially analyzed in isolation, with all other variables being fixed. This is equivalent to assuming that price fluctuations are driven by a single systematic risk factor. Let us utilize the language of fixed income markets and call this single source of systematic market risk "yield." In this setting, since the entire economic environment manifests itself in the relationship between the current price and the current yield, the ability to calculate the value of a security is equivalent to computing one point on the (unknown) price/yield function (Exhibit 1.1).

In contrast to valuation that deals with computing *fair* values of fixed income securities, risk management is concerned with estimating potential losses resulting from large unexpected market movements. This entails knowing how the price changes in response to *any* hypothetical change in yield. In other words, to be able to judge risk, the entire price/yield function of each instrument is needed. For a variety of computational and conceptual reasons, the timely and accurate construction of price/yield functions of all fixed income securities was not possible when investors first starting quantifying financial risks. Another method was needed to estimate risk without constructing the entire price/yield curve. The application of Taylor series expansions provided insight into the price sensitivity of fixed income securities. The first-order approximation of the price/yield function became known as *delta* or, converted into an elasticity measure, *duration,* while the second-order approximation was called *delta-gamma* or *duration-convexity* (Exhibit 1.2).

EXHIBIT 1.1   Ability to Compute Fair Price = One Point on the Price/Yield Curve

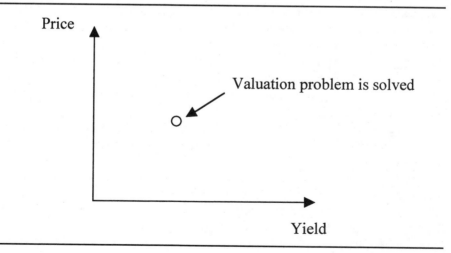

EXHIBIT 1.2   Duration and Convexity: Local Approximations of the Unknown Price/Yield Function

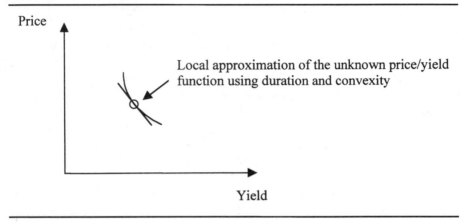

The first- and second-order approximations of the price/yield function may not be accurate predictors of price changes when the underlying changes in the systematic risk factors are large. In general, the more nonlinear the price/yield function is, the poorer the approximation. Unfortunately, judging the accuracy of the various approximations of the price/yield function without explicitly sketching its actual shape is difficult. Scenario analysis, an approach to constructing price/functions via numerous direct revaluations of a security in various economic environments, became an important step in the evolution of risk management ideas. While it can be difficult to perform scenario analysis when the number of risk factors is large, if price is assumed to be a function of a single risk factor, scenario analysis provides a rather comprehensive (deterministic) representation of market risk (Exhibit 1.3).

Knowledge about the nonstochastic price sensitivity of fixed income securities and portfolios to changes in systematic risk factors is, by itself, insufficient for understanding financial risk. Thus, price distributions of fixed income portfolios and securities can be constructed through combining deterministic parametric measures (Chapter 2) with forecasts of probability distribution of systematic risk factors (correlations and volatilities, Chapter 3). VaR and other probabilistic measures of risk discussed in Chapters 4 and 5 describe certain statistical

EXHIBIT 1.3   Scenario Analysis: Explicitly Constructing the Price/Yield Function

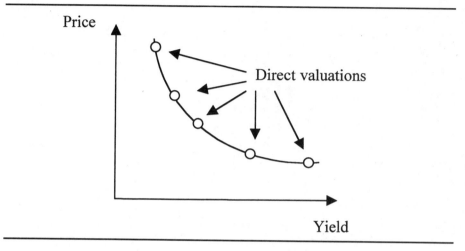

properties of probability density functions of price changes (Exhibit 1.4).

Exhibit 1.5 portrays the intellectual evolution of risk measures and methodologies. Using this diagram, the reader can track the application of progressively more sophisticated approaches to risk management as investors were coping with increasingly complex products and markets and gaining deeper understanding of financial risk. By presenting risk measures according to the way they emerged, we have attempted to help the reader develop a broad perspective on risk management as well as appreciation for its complexity and advancement over the years.

EXHIBIT 1.4   Price/Yield Function + Probability Distribution of Risk Factors = Comprehensive Risk Measures

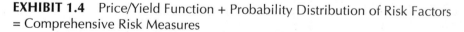

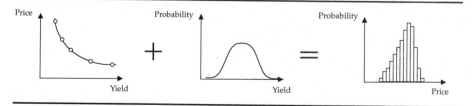

EXHIBIT 1.5 Evolution of Risk Management Ideas

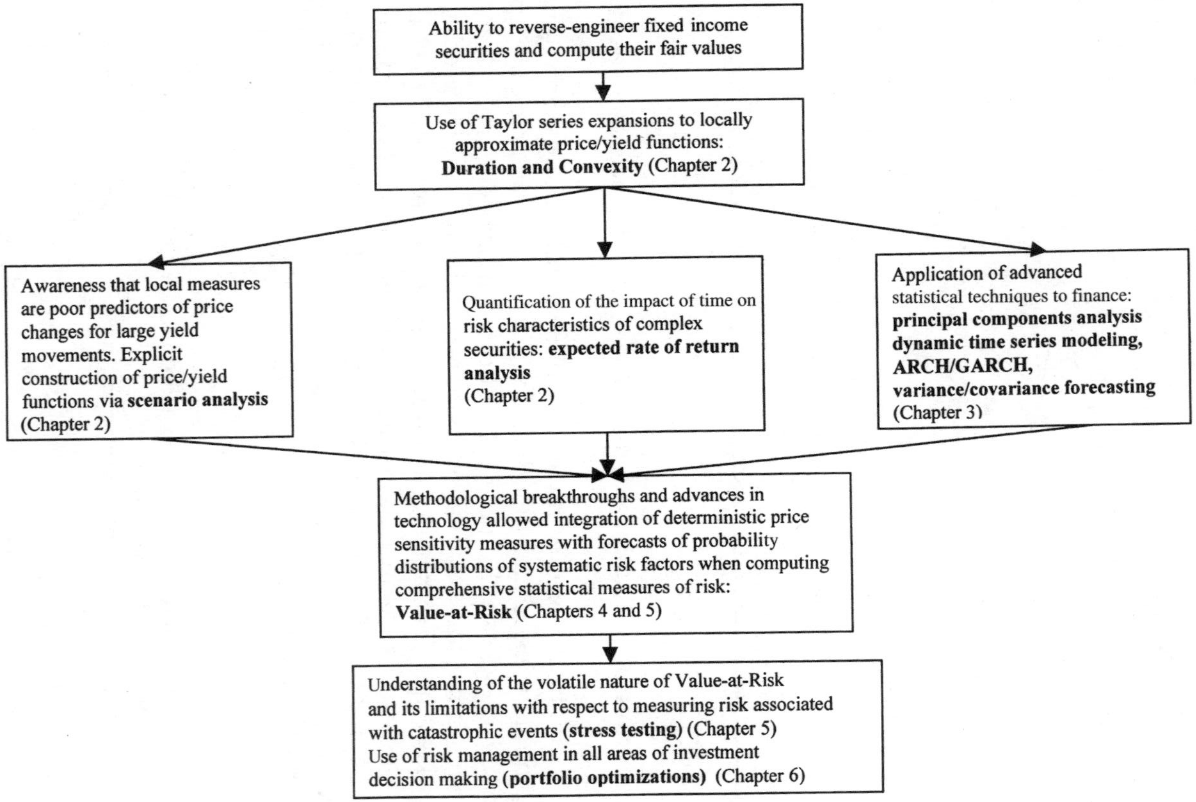

Ability to reverse-engineer fixed income securities and compute their fair values

Use of Taylor series expansions to locally approximate price/yield functions (Chapter 2)

Application of advanced statistical techniques to finance: **principal components analysis dynamic time series modeling, ARCH/GARCH, variance/covariance forecasting** (Chapter 3)

Quantification of the impact of time on risk characteristics of complex securities: **expected rate of return analysis** (Chapter 2)

Awareness that local measures are poor predictors of price changes for large yield movements. Explicit construction of price/yield functions via **scenario analysis** (Chapter 2)

Methodological breakthroughs and advances in technology allowed integration of deterministic price sensitivity measures with forecasts of probability distributions of systematic risk factors when computing comprehensive statistical measures of risk: **Value-at-Risk** (Chapters 4 and 5)

Understanding of the volatile nature of Value-at-Risk and its limitations with respect to measuring risk associated with catastrophic events (**stress testing**) (Chapter 5)
Use of risk management in all areas of investment decision making (**portfolio optimizations**) (Chapter 6)

ENDNOTES

1. See Jorion, 1999.
2. See Litterman and Winkelmann, 1996.
3. See "BARRA Refocuses Product Strategy" (BARRA, Inc. Press Release, April 19, 1999).
4. This claim may seem counterintuitive given that on-the-run (OTR) U.S. Treasury securities significantly outperformed off-the-run securities during the 1998 credit and liquidity crisis. Market participants typically buy off-the-run Treasuries for buy-and-hold purposes or as parts of asset swap strategies. Conversely, on-the-run securities are most typically used to quickly change duration. The extreme liquidity of on-the-runs made them particularly valuable during crises, since they permitted investors to rapidly adjust positions in size, which caused the outperformance of OTR Treasuries.
5. Some attribute LTCM's demise to its use of portfolio optimizations based on VaR that was computed over very recent historical data (see Jorion, 1999).
6. Discussion of portfolio insurance is based on Taleb, 1997.
7. Description of option-adjusted spread models is presented in Chapter 2.
8. See Section 1.3.1 on price discovery.
9. The absolute risk of a portfolio can be also thought of as the relative risk of a portfolio vis-à-vis a cash benchmark.

2

Parametric Approaches to Risk Management

2.1 INTRODUCTION

The price of a fixed income security can be thought of as a function of many interdependent systematic risk factors $F_1,\ldots,F_n$ and time:

$$P = P(F_1,\ldots,F_n,t) \tag{2.1}$$

Parametric approaches to risk management investigate the price sensitivity of securities and portfolios to each risk factor in isolation, with all others being fixed. This task can be best achieved by utilizing a Taylor series expansion of the price function around a point – a widely used mathematical technique that provides insights into the local properties of complex nonlinear relationships. Thus, if a function $P(\cdot)$ depends on a single variable x, the Taylor series expansion can be used to approximate the behavior of its percentage changes around an arbitrary point x_0 as follows:

$$\frac{P(x) - P(x_0)}{P(x_0)} = \frac{1}{P(x_0)} \cdot \frac{dP}{dx} \cdot (x - x_0) + \frac{1}{2!} \cdot \frac{1}{P(x_0)} \cdot \frac{d^2P}{dx^2} \cdot (x - x_0)^2 + \ldots \tag{2.2}$$

where the value of all derivatives is computed at x_0.

In a multivariate setting (Equation 2.1), expression of the Taylor series expansion becomes more involved because of the large number of possible interactions among systematic sources of risk:

$$\frac{dP}{P} = \sum_{i=1}^{n} \frac{1}{P} \cdot \frac{\partial P}{\partial F_i} \cdot dF_i + \frac{1}{P} \cdot \frac{\partial P}{\partial t} \cdot dt + \sum_{i=1}^{n} \sum_{j=1}^{n} \frac{1}{2 \cdot P} \cdot \frac{\partial^2 P}{\partial F_i \cdot \partial F_j} \cdot dF_i \cdot dF_j + ... \quad (2.3)$$

Expressions of the form $-\dfrac{1}{P} \dfrac{\partial P}{\partial F_i}$ are called partial durations. Option-adjusted duration, key rate durations, key treasury rate durations, volatility duration, spread duration, and prepayment duration (discussed later in this chapter) are well-known examples of partial durations of a security's price with respect to various risk factors. The great variety of partial duration measures is due to the large number of systematic sources of market risk that affect prices of fixed income securities as well as to a variety of ways to define them. For instance, this book will demonstrate that there are no significant conceptual differences between key rate durations, key treasury rate durations, and principal components durations: They simply correspond to alternative ways to describe yield curve dynamics. As far as dependency of prices on time $\left(\dfrac{\partial P}{\partial t} \right)$ is concerned, it is customary in the derivatives markets to directly compute such partial derivatives. Due to path dependency and other intricacies of fixed income securities with respect to their evolution through time, we present this aspect of market risk later in this chapter not in terms of partial durations, but within the expected rate of return framework (Section 2.7).

Liquidity risk has taken a prominent place among the most potent sources of market risk. Unfortunately, this type of risk is difficult to address via parametric approaches effective in quantifying the price sensitivity to interest rates, foreign currency exchange rates, basis risks, and other "traditional" systematic risk factors. In exchange-traded markets, players can and do attempt to quantitatively measure the price impact of contemplated transactions by analyzing open interest and daily volume data. However, due to the over-the-counter nature of the majority of fixed income markets, mechanisms for recording completed transactions do not exist. In the absence of relevant data or theoretical models, judgment and experience tend to be the best guides for fixed income investors in measuring the liquidity risk. Thus, bid/ask spreads for each asset class can be determined using the subjective judgment of traders. For instance, traders might believe that they could trade a large block (e.g., $50,000,000) of on-the-run U.S. Treasury securities at the 1/32 bid/ask spread, whereas the same size in a corporate bond may require 10/32 or more. After the bid/ask spreads are estimated either on the individual security or sector level, the absolute exposure of portfolios as well as relative exposure of portfolios vis-à-vis their benchmarks to their weighted average bid/ask spread can then be determined. Stress testing (Chapter 5) can offer a platform for measuring liquidity risk as well. Thus, various scenarios involving increased haircuts on leveraged positions, widening of bid/ask spreads, and margin calls may assist in determining the proportion of the assets that should be invested in illiquid versus liquid securities.

With respect to the more traditional (or tractable) sources of market risk, imagination and knowledge of financial markets are required to define the set of systematic risk factors $F_1,\ldots,F_n$ so that risk management calculations are intuitive and computationally feasible at the same time. In this chapter, a variety of ways to define systematic risk factors is studied and the corresponding first-order terms of the Taylor series expansion (durations) as well as second-order terms (convexities) are computed. First, the exposure of portfolios and securities to directional movements in interest rates, one of the most dominant sources of risk in fixed income markets, is analyzed.

2.2 MEASURING INTEREST RATE EXPOSURE: ANALYTICAL APPROACHES

2.2.1 Macaulay and Modified Duration, and Convexity

Duration and convexity are undoubtedly the most widely used measures of interest rate risk. They are used by traders in hedging and relative value decisions, portfolio managers when placing directional bets in portfolios relative to benchmarks, and clients and risk managers when formulating guidelines and compliance rules that regulate how closely assets must be managed against liabilities or portfolios against benchmarks. Performance attribution systems utilize durations and convexities when judging if a security has under- or outperformed the market. As discussed in Chapter 1, the first- and second-order terms of the Taylor series expansion are also important backtesting tools used in the price discovery process. While duration and convexity are concepts specific to fixed income, their analogs can be found in other markets as well. Since the future valuation of fixed income instruments depends on the evolution of interest rates and other economic variables over time, they can be thought of as derivative securities. For that matter, duration and convexity, measures of the price sensitivity to changes in interest rates, are the fixed income analogs of the "greeks" (delta and gamma) widely used in the derivatives markets.

In the most simplified setting, the price of a fixed income security is assumed to be a function of a single risk factor – yield-to-maturity (y):

$$P = P(y) \tag{2.4}$$

Exhibits 2.1 and 2.2 present the price/yield functions of selected instruments[1] and demonstrate that these relationships can be substantially nonlinear: The price functions of the 30-year on-the-run Treasury, a put on a U.S. Treasury future, and a swaption are visibly convex while the price functions for a 30-year MBS and a callable agency bond are moderately concave, or, as conventionally known in the fixed income world, *negatively convex*.

For a fixed income instrument whose cash flows are fixed, do not have any embedded options, and do not depend on the future evolution of interest rates and other risk factors, the price/yield function can be determined analytically. For example, the relationship between the price

EXHIBIT 2.1   Examples of Price Dependencies on Changes in Interest Rates (as of 12/31/98)

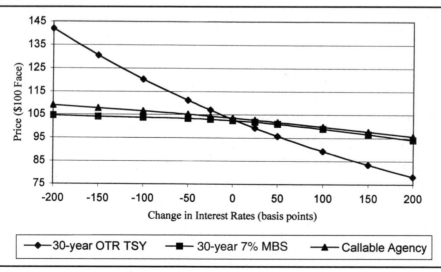

EXHIBIT 2.2   Examples of Price Dependencies on Changes in Interest Rates (as of 12/31/98)

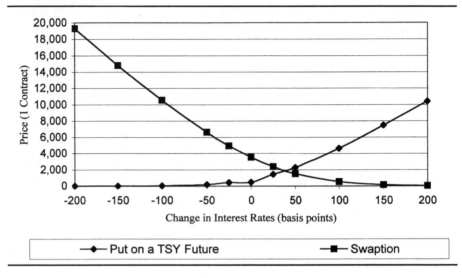

of an N-year bond that pays fixed annual cash flows $CF_1,...,CF_N$ and its yield-to-maturity is given by the following simple formula:

$$P = \sum_{t=1}^{N} \frac{CF_t}{(1+y)^t} \qquad (2.5)$$

where P is the current price, and y is the annually compounded yield-to-maturity. If the cash flows of a security are not fixed and are a function of interest rates and other risk factors, construction of the price/yield function entails solving the valuation problem. This involves application of rather elaborate numerical methods, including building yield curves, specifying stochastic processes that describe the future evolution of interest rates and other risks, valuing embedded options, forecasting prepayments, if any, and so forth. Explicit construction of price/yield functions for complex portfolios is known as *scenario analysis* and is discussed in detail later in this chapter. Even with today's ability to distribute complex calculations across networks of powerful computers, use of scenario analysis in mainstream risk management practices is sometimes limited because of the computational costs associated with the numerous direct revaluations of each security in a portfolio. Moreover, portfolio and risk managers find it difficult to manage fixed income portfolios using continuous representations of price/yield functions. While originally attempting to quantify market risk, practitioners realized the need for a simple and intuitive measure of price sensitivity to changes in interest rates. Hence, the introduction of duration.

Modified duration, a measure of price sensitivity of a fixed income security to changes in its yield-to-maturity, is linked to the first-order term of the Taylor series expansion (Equation 2.2). Modified duration is used to locally approximate the relationship between the price P and yield-to-maturity y as a linear function. It is defined as the negative of the percentage change in price, given a 100 basis point change in yield:

$$Modified\ Duration = -\frac{1}{P}\frac{dP}{dy} \tag{2.6}$$

It is easy to see that for securities with deterministic cash flows, modified duration can be derived analytically via Equations 2.5 and 2.6:

$$Modified\ Duration = \frac{1}{P\cdot(1+y)}\sum_{t=1}^{N}\frac{t\cdot CF_t}{(1+y)^t} \tag{2.7}$$

Equation 2.6 represents the way market participants currently view duration. Originally, however, a slightly different risk measure was created. Frederick Macaulay[2] is generally recognized as the first person to develop a formula that quantifies interest rate risk of fixed cash flow securities. His measure, which is now referred to as *Macaulay duration* (also known as unmodified duration), was defined as the average of individual cash flows' terms-to-maturity weighted by the present value of the corresponding cash flows:[3]

$$Macaulay\ Duration = \frac{1}{P}\sum_{t=1}^{N}\frac{t\cdot CF_t}{(1+y)^t} \tag{2.8}$$

It can be verified, both empirically and analytically, that Macaulay duration is directly linked to price volatility:[4] the larger Macaulay duration, the more volatile the price of the bond. This measure is also intuitive because it implies higher risks for securities whose cash flows are concentrated farther in the future. Clearly, Macaulay and modified durations are closely related:

$$Modified\ Duration = \frac{1}{(1+y)} \cdot Macaulay\ Duration \tag{2.9}$$

It turns out that if the price of a fixed cash flow bond is written as a function of the continuously compounded rather than annually compounded yield-to-maturity y_C:

$$P = \sum_{i=1}^{N} CF_i \cdot e^{-y_C \cdot t_i} \tag{2.10}$$

the formula for Macaulay duration is exactly the same as that for modified duration:[5]

$$Macaulay\ Duration = -\frac{1}{P}\frac{dP}{dy_C} \tag{2.11}$$

The straightforward verification of this fact is left to the reader.

As seen from Equations 2.2 and 2.6, modified duration enables the first-order approximation of the percentage change in price $\frac{\Delta P}{P}$ for a given change in yield Δy:

$$\frac{\Delta P}{P} \approx -Modified\ Duration \cdot \Delta y \tag{2.12}$$

For example, if a bond's modified duration is 10 years and interest rates rise by 100 basis points, the bond loses about 10% of its value.[6]

The accuracy of the first-order approximation of the price/yield function depends on the degree to which this dependency is convex or concave. In addition to the first term in the Taylor series expansion, the second term can be used to better capture the shape of the price/yield function:

$$\frac{dP}{P} \approx \frac{1}{P}\frac{dP}{dy} \cdot dy + \frac{1}{2} \cdot \frac{1}{P}\frac{d^2P}{dy^2} \cdot dy^2 \tag{2.13}$$

Convexity, the measure of interest rate risk linked to the second-order term in the Taylor series expansion in Equation 2.13, estimates the degree of nonlinearity of the price/yield relationship:

$$Modified\ Convexity = \frac{1}{P}\frac{d^2P}{dy^2} \qquad (2.14)$$

Similar to modified duration, modified convexity of fixed cash flow securities can be derived analytically as well:

$$Modified\ Convexity = \frac{1}{P\cdot(1+y)^2}\sum_{t=1}^{N}\frac{t\cdot(t+1)\cdot CF_t}{(1+y)^t} \qquad (2.15)$$

When used together, modified duration and modified convexity allow for a more precise approximation of changes in price for a given change in interest rates:

$$\frac{\Delta P}{P} \approx -Modifed Duration\cdot\Delta y + \frac{Modifed\ Convexity}{2}\cdot\Delta y^2 \qquad (2.16)$$

Table 2.1 presents modified durations of securities in the sample portfolio whose holdings are described in the Appendix (Table A.1).

Macaulay and modified durations and convexities were developed to provide accurate estimates of interest rate price sensitivity for instruments with deterministic cash flows. This limits their applicability to securities with cash flow uncertainties. Thus, in order to compute modified duration and convexity, stochastic cash flows of derivative securities need to be presumed fixed and generated using a predefined static interest rate scenario, which may lead to inadequate assessment of risk. In addition to that, by discounting cash flows using a single interest rate (Equation 2.5), modified duration and modified convexity assume that prices of fixed income securities depend solely on changes in a single risk factor – yield-to-maturity. When computing modified duration of a portfolio as a whole, it is therefore implicitly assumed that when interest rates change, irrespective of the maturities of the individual securities, their yields-to-maturity move in the same direction and by the same amount.

Because of these limitations, the increasing complexity of fixed income instruments created a need to generalize modified duration and modified convexity in a number of important directions:

TABLE 2.1 Duration Comparison Report for the Sample Portfolio (as of 12/31/98)

Position / Description	Coupon	Maturity	Strike	Mod Dur	OAS	OAD	OAC	Mtg/Tsy Dur	Vol Dur	Spd Dur	Dur-Neutral Steepeners			SEDUR	LEDUR
											0/2	2/10	10/30		
Treasury Bonds															
TREASURY NOTE (OTR)	4.63	12/31/00		1.89	-10	1.89	0.05			2.01	-47	47		94	
TREASURY NOTE (OTR)	4.25	11/15/03		4.33	-17	4.32	0.22			4.43		-3		138	
TREASURY NOTE (OTR)	4.75	11/15/08		7.78	-23	7.76	0.73			7.95		-194	186	4	
TREASURY BOND (OTR)	5.25	11/15/28		15.07	-21	14.93	3.34			15.29		1	-403	-2	-821
Agency Bonds															
FHLMC (callable)	6.33	02/13/06		5.54	46	3.25	-0.79		0.13	2.91	-21	12	1	106	
Futures															
MAR 10YR NOTE FUTURE		03/31/99				5.67	0.38				-3	-59		105	
MAR 30YR BOND FUTURE		03/31/99				9.47	0.89				-3	-18	-32	-2	-142
Options															
MAR 10 YR NOTE Put		02/20/99	117			-350.74	925.11		-29.73		203	3661		-6479	
10 YR NOTE FUTURE Call		02/20/99	119			266.42	452.59		-13.33		-154	-2780		4921	
Interest Rate Swaps															
US Swap	7.24	06/15/11				6.68	0.91			6.68	30	-156	94	-88	-52
Caps & Floors															
6.00 3M LIBOR CAP	6.00	02/19/02				-114.67	95.80		-8.89	-114.67	-623	-1887		-4288	847
6.40 5YR FLOOR (10YR CMT)	6.40	06/17/02				50.32	11.26		-0.99		70	-1125	911	-413	-250
OTC Derivatives															
Swaption 1	7.25	05/12/00	7.25			-195.71	284.47		-22.45	-195.71	-372	4575	-3914	1982	
Swaption 2	Float	06/23/99	5.85			148.11	132.62		-2.93	148.11	-117	-3478	3334	-364	-192
Non USD Government Securities															
SWEDEN GOVT	10.25	05/05/00		1.22	-110	1.23	0.02			1.26	-12	11		67	
JGB BD 174 (10 YR)	4.60	09/20/04		5.05	-44	5.18	0.31			5.23	1	-28		137	
UK TREASURY	9.00	10/13/08		6.94	-92	6.91	0.61			7.10	-1	-154	143	28	
CANADA GOVT	5.75	06/01/29		14.88	-3	14.78	3.30			15.13		1	-391	-2	-797

	Coupon	Maturity		Price											
Generic Pass-Throughs															
FGOLD 30YR	7.00	12/31/28		3.82	84	2.52	-2.59	-1.64	0.28	3.53	-3	20	-29	86	-22
FGOLD 30YR	8.00	12/31/28		2.73	138	1.85	-1.32	-1.51	0.17	3.04	-3	19	-20	75	-10
GNMA Construction Loans															
FHA CREEKWOOD GN/GN	7.30	11/30/38		11.68	144	3.57	-1.13			3.57		-62	56	8	-12
Non-Agency CMBS															
DLJMA_96-CF1 B1 144A	8.27	01/12/08		5.65	258	4.41	-0.54			5.68	-1	-52	19	77	
Inverse Floating Rate Mortgages															
CMOT13 Q	15.55	01/20/03		1.06	440	2.83	0.16	-0.17	0.00	1.12	-34	45	-4	157	
POs-Agency															
FNSTR_267 (FN 8.50)		10/01/24		2.47	-135	7.95	-4.02	4.70	0.08	2.69	3	-106		129	
IOs-Agency															
FHLMC_2043 (FG 7.00)	7.00	01/15/16		1.97	724	-45.94	-20.82	-43.24	1.37	2.39	10	832	-735	265	256
CMO Sequentials-Agency															
FNMA_93-178 (FN 7.00)	5.25	09/25/23		0.22	136	0.22	0.00		0.00	0.23	4			13	
Corporates - Finance															
BANKAMERICA CAPITAL II	8.00	12/15/26	Vary	11.73	133	8.72	0.05		0.39	8.31	-1	-49	-40	39	-171
Corporates - Industrial															
PROCTER & GAMBLE COMPANY (T	8.00	10/26/29	100	12.97	87	12.84	2.67		0.00	13.18		-10	-285	9	-606
Asset Backed - Prepay Sensitive															
CONHE_97-5 (Home Equity)	6.58	06/15/19		2.72	143	2.27	-1.00			2.73	-9	34		99	
Asset Backed - Non-Prepay Sensitive															
CHVAT_98-2 (Auto)	5.91	12/15/04		1.5	100	1.47	0.04			1.51	-11	20		71	
Total Assets	**7.02**			**6.19**		**6.82**	**0.81**	**-0.41**	**0.04**	**5.56**	**-6**	**-45**	**-21**	**58**	**-132**

- Incorporation of knowledge about the term structure of interest rates
- Ability to capture cash flow uncertainties with respect to interest rates and other economic variables

Extension of modified duration methodology in the first direction can be achieved by modifying Equation 2.5 to discount cash flows of a fixed income security using the appropriate spot rates[7] rather than yield-to-maturity:

$$P = \sum_{t=1}^{N} \frac{CF_t}{(1+r_t)^t} \qquad (2.17)$$

where r_t is the annualized spot rate at time t, and cash flows CF_t are obtained using a single hypothetical scenario that specifies evolution of interest rates and other risk factors over time. In this setting, it is typically assumed that volatility of interest rates is zero; interest rates evolve according to forward rates; and credit spreads, implied volatilities, and other basis risks stay constant. Clearly, the "fair" value obtained via this valuation technique may be different from that observed on the market because of the numerous assumptions built into the generation of static cash flows. To reconcile theoretical and empirical prices, practitioners introduced the concept of *zero volatility spread (ZVO)*, defined as an additional constant element of discounting (over the yield curve) that forces the "fair" value to equal the market price:[8]

$$P_{\text{market}} = \sum_{t=1}^{N} \frac{CF_t}{(1+r_t+ZVO)^t} \qquad (2.18)$$

2.2.2 Option-Adjusted Framework: OAV, OAS, OAD, OAC

Modified duration and convexity presume that cash flows of fixed income instruments are deterministic, do not have any embedded options, and are independent of the future evolution of interest rates and other risk factors. For many types of securities, this assumption is not realistic. For instance, cash flows of a mortgage-backed security depend on the borrowers' decision to prepay all or part of their mortgage loans early while some of the cash flows of callable corporate and agency bonds may not occur if these bonds are called. Thus, durations and convexities for the majority of derivative securities cannot be computed analytically and require application of elaborate numerical methods. Development of the price sensitivity measures that are applicable to all fixed income securities has been conceptually and computationally challenging. Before a financially sound and operationally feasible methodology could be created, a number of important developments needed to take place. First and foremost, numerical computation of durations and convexities for complex portfolios was contingent on the ability to reverse-engineer the vast majority of derivative fixed income securities, including collateralized mortgage obligations, asset-backed and mortgage-backed securities, commercial mortgage-backed securities, construction and project loans, futures, options, and so forth. Second, this methodology required dramatic advances in computational technology as well as breakthroughs in option pricing theory, numerical methods, as well as interest rate, yield curve, and prepayment modeling.

Option-adjusted measures – option-adjusted value (OAV), option-adjusted spread (OAS), option-adjusted duration (OAD), and option-adjusted convexity (OAC) – have become an important extension of the modified duration methodology. A rigorous description of option-adjusted spread methodology, which is a valuation rather than a risk management technique, is beyond the scope of this book.[9] The purpose of this section is to give an overview of the concepts underlying OAS framework and study their applications to risk management. Option-adjusted measures were developed in order to relax the assumption about the deterministic cash flow structure of fixed income securities. This was achieved by explicitly modeling the embedded options and other cash flow uncertainties across a large number of hypothetical interest rate environments. Among other things, implementation of the option-adjusted methodology involved:

- Obtaining information about the way a security is structured
- Estimation of yield curves and construction of interest rate trees
- Specification of the appropriate option valuation models, econometric prepayment models, stochastic processes that describe the evolution of interest rates and other systematic basis risks over time, and so forth

In the option-theoretic sense, *option-adjusted value* (OAV) is simply the fair value of a fixed income security. It is defined as the mathematical expectation of the discounted future cash flows given the assumption about the future evolution of interest rates and other systematic sources of risk. By virtue of requiring the specification of the current economic environment in addition to conjectures about future behavior of risk factors, OAVs of fixed income securities are *market-state dependent:* even if assumptions remain unchanged, theoretical values of instruments may vary dramatically with changes in the market environment.

The methods by which OAV is computed depend on the security type. The following are typical choices used by practitioners, although many instruments can be effectively valued using a variety of alternative approaches:

- For path-dependent instruments, including mortgages, mortgage derivatives, and certain OTC options, OAVs are ordinarily computed by sampling interest rate trees using Monte-Carlo simulation. Thus, a large number of interest rate scenarios or *paths* is created using random number generators or via stratified sampling (pseudo-random number generation) techniques. For each interest rate path, the present value of the corresponding cash flows is determined using the path-specific spot curve. OAV, which is computed as the average of pathwise prices, is a summary measure that encompasses a vast amount of information. While the entire distribution of pathwise prices can be analyzed directly, it is capable of providing only limited insights.

- To determine OAVs for path-independent, option-bearing securities (e.g., callable bonds, interest rate caps, floors, etc.), backward induction is typically used to value the option on every node of an interest rate tree, capturing a large number of possible interest rate environments generated by the interest rate model. The advantage of backward induction over Monte-Carlo simulation lies in substantially faster computations. This method is also not subject to the statistical imprecisions inherent in sampling of interest rate processes.

- When computing OAVs for interest rate swaps, floating rate notes, and other securities whose cash flows are option-free and path-independent, but interest rate dependent, the future evolution of interest rates first needs to be forecasted (via forward rates or otherwise). Given a conjecture about the future behavior of interest rates and other risk factors, cash flows are determined and subsequently discounted using the appropriate spot rates, arriving at OAV of an instrument.

- OAVs for short-term European options are typically computed using the Black-Scholes formula or its variants.[10]

The theoretical values of fixed income securities are often different from their actual prices observed in the market. Two alternative interpretations of this phenomenon exist. The first one argues that this discrepancy is caused by the inability of theoretical valuation models to fully account for the information contained in market prices due to the numerous assumptions and econometric estimation inaccuracies inherent in these models. Another school of thought interprets the difference between OAV and observed market prices as *market risk premium* embedded in market prices and not captured by theoretical valuation models.[11] The risk premium can be thought of as excess return demanded by investors as compensation for the perceived additional risk of holding a security. It combines market sentiment toward systematic asset class-specific risks as well as idiosyncratic security-specific risks. For instance, the risk premia of noncallable U.S. Treasuries (that are option- and default-free) measure the cost of liquidity and financing assumptions: as on-the-run issues exhibit increasingly different behavior from virtually identical off-the-run securities, their risk premia are becoming progressively negative.[12] For option-free fixed rate corporate bonds, risk premia reflect market sentiment toward credit risk in general, technical conditions, assessment of the issuer's creditworthiness, likelihood of credit quality deterioration or default, and implicit forecast of recovery rates in the event of a default. For default-free generic mortgage-backed securities, risk premia quantify the market's sentiment toward credit risk in general, technical conditions, uncertainty with respect to the valuation of the underlying prepayment options, and implied volatility risks.

Option-adjusted spread (OAS) can often be thought of as the risk premium associated with holding a fixed income security. OAS reconciles a theoretical model's assessment of fair price and the empirically observed market price. The concept of OAS is best illustrated via a security that employs Monte-Carlo simulation to construct a large number of interest rate paths, each corresponding to a stream of future cash flows $(CF_{i,t})$. OAS is defined as a constant spread over the path-specific spot curve $(r_{i,t})$ that equates the model-based OAV to the market price:

$$P_{\text{market}} = \frac{1}{K}\sum_{i=1}^{K}\sum_{t=1}^{N}\frac{CF_{i,t}}{(1+r_{i,t}+OAS)^t} \qquad (2.19)$$

where K is the number of interest rate paths employed in Monte-Carlo simulation, $CF_{i,t}$ and $r_{i,t}$ are the cash flows and the spot rates, respectively, corresponding to the ith path, and N is the maximum possible number of cash flows.

Option-adjusted spreads provide some basis for comparison of securities within and across asset classes. They can be used in risk management and as relative value tools. In risk management, unexpected changes in OAS are important risk factors that will be studied in Chapter 4. In portfolio management and trading, if two comparable securities have different OASs, relative value judgment may drive investors to bet on the security with the lower OAS cheapening in value relative to that with the higher OAS, or vice versa. Option-adjusted spreads[13] of securities in the sample portfolio are presented in Table 2.1. Notice that while OASs are positive for the vast majority of securities in the sample portfolio, they can also be negative for certain security types. Examples of instruments with negative OAS include on-the-run government securities in the United States and other markets as well as Principal-Only (PO) stripped MBS in some market environments.[14]

Once OAS is determined, option-adjusted duration (OAD) and option-adjusted convexity (OAC) can be computed. These measures of interest-rate risk constitute an important generalization of the modified duration methodology introduced earlier in this chapter. As demonstrated next, by using the OAS methodology when computing price sensitivities, option-adjusted risk measures capture many important properties of fixed income securities including various cash flow uncertainties and path-dependency. Recall that modified duration was defined in Equation 2.6 as the negative of the percentage change in price, given a 100 basis point change in yield-to-maturity. This concept was developed for option-free securities and is not generally applicable to instruments with cash flow uncertainties. For this reason, the option-adjusted framework departs from analyzing price sensitivity in terms of yields. Instead of assuming that prices are functions of yields-to-maturity on individual securities, it presumes that changes in prices are caused by *parallel shocks to the term structure of spot rates (r)*:

$$P = P(r) \tag{2.20}$$

By redefining the term *change in interest rates*, option-adjusted methodology introduces a more generalized risk management paradigm while preserving the assumption that price fluctuations of fixed income securities are driven by a single systematic risk factor.[15] Option-adjusted duration is defined as follows:

$$OAD = -\frac{1}{P}\frac{dP}{dr} \tag{2.21}$$

where dr is a parallel spot curve shock. It must be noted, however, that despite being the most widely used one-factor risk management model, approximating yield curve dynamics with parallel shocks is not the most historically plausible alternative. Later in this book (Chapter 3) we use principal components analysis to construct more empirically accurate representations of yield curve movements.

To illustrate the numerical computation of OAD, it is convenient to rewrite Equation 2.21 as follows:

$$OAD = -\frac{1}{P} \cdot \lim_{\Delta r \to 0} \frac{\Delta P}{\Delta r} \qquad (2.22)$$

When calculating OAD in practice using Equation 2.22, the following discretization is generally used:

$$OAD = -\frac{1}{P} \frac{P_{up} - P_{down}}{2 \cdot \Delta r} \qquad (2.23)$$

where P_{up} and P_{down} are OAVs directly recomputed by shifting the entire spot curve up and down, respectively, by a small parallel shock Δr and keeping option-adjusted spread constant.

Similar to modified duration (Equation 2.12), OAD can be used to approximate price changes resulting from small parallel yield curve movements:

$$\frac{\Delta P}{P} \approx -OAD \cdot \Delta r \qquad (2.24)$$

Depending on the security type, the size of the interest rate shock Δr used in Equation 2.23 may influence OAD estimates. This should be intuitive because the larger the shock, the more nonlinearity of the price function is captured when computing OAD. Table 2.2 illustrates the effect of different shock sizes on OAD estimates.

Similar to modified convexity, option-adjusted convexity (OAC) is linked to the second-order term of the Taylor series expansion:

$$OAC = \frac{1}{P} \frac{d^2 P}{dr^2} \qquad (2.25)$$

TABLE 2.2   Effect of Parallel Shock Size on OAD Estimates

Shock Size (basis points)	10-year Callable Corporate	Agency CMO	30-year MBS 6.00%	30-year MBS 7.00%	30-year MBS 8.00%	30-year MBS 9.00%	30-year MBS 10.00%
5	6.65	-4.65	6.17	5.36	3.89	2.29	2.31
10	6.65	-4.80	6.17	5.36	3.90	2.30	2.32
15	6.64	-4.93	6.17	5.36	3.90	2.30	2.33
20	6.64	-5.01	6.17	5.35	3.90	2.30	2.33
25	6.64	-5.04	6.17	5.34	3.90	2.29	2.34
30	6.64	-5.05	6.17	5.33	3.89	2.29	2.34
35	6.64	-5.07	6.17	5.32	3.89	2.29	2.34
40	6.64	-5.10	6.16	5.31	3.88	2.28	2.33
45	6.64	-5.10	6.16	5.30	3.88	2.27	2.33
50	6.64	-5.09	6.16	5.29	3.87	2.27	2.33

and can be computed using the following discretization:

$$OAC = \frac{1}{P} \frac{P_{up} + P_{down} - 2 \cdot P}{\Delta r^2}$$

(2.26)

Table 2.1 presents OADs and OACs of securities in the sample portfolio.

When computed via option-adjusted spread methodology, duration estimates are relatively stable for the majority of fixed income securities. However, OACs, being the second-order effects, are more difficult to measure accurately. Although in theory they can be computed by shocking the yield curve infinitesimally in either direction via Equation 2.26, this type of analysis depends, to a greater extent than duration, on the size of the spot curve shock. Too small a shock may lead to unstable estimates due to modeling limitations (e.g., valuation issues related to the discretization of continuous-time interest rate processes). Too large a shock may lessen the accuracy of duration estimates and may cause undesirable effects due to interest rate and prepayment models. Both too small and too large a shock may result in unreliable and unstable convexity estimates. These effects are greatly exacerbated by the optionality embedded in the security, especially if backward valuation is used.

By sampling interest rates above and below the current level and computing P_{up} and P_{down} (Equations 2.23 and 2.26), option-adjusted durations and convexities implicitly assume that irrespective of the direction of interest rates, comparable interest rate shocks of opposite signs cause comparable (in absolute value) changes in prices. However, this conjecture is not entirely correct for the so-called cuspy securities – those characterized by highly asymmetric price sensitivities to changes in interest rates (e.g., at-the-money European options that are close to expiration). In such cases, it is often useful to compute one-sided option-adjusted measures:

$$OAD_{up} = -\frac{1}{P}\frac{P_{up} - P}{\Delta r} \tag{2.27}$$

$$OAD_{down} = -\frac{1}{P}\frac{P - P_{down}}{\Delta r} \tag{2.28}$$

where, as before, P is the current price, P_{up} and P_{down} are option-adjusted values directly recomputed by shifting the entire spot curve by a small parallel shock Δr and keeping OAS constant. One-sided option-adjusted convexities can be computed in a similar fashion as well.

As compared to modified durations and convexities, option-adjusted measures have clear advantages because they explicitly model options and other cash flow uncertainties embedded in a security and account for its path-dependency and other characteristics. These measures are relatively accurate predictors of future price movements when yield curve movements are small. Needless to say, option-adjusted measures are computationally intensive, especially for complex path-dependent securities, and are sensitive to the assumptions underlying prepayment and interest-rate models. From now on, unless stated otherwise, we will use the terms *duration* and *option-adjusted duration* as well as *convexity* and *option-adjusted convexity* interchangeably.

The aggregate option-adjusted duration and convexity of a fixed income portfolio is computed as a weighted average of the durations and convexities, respectively, of the individual securities. The weight applied to each instrument's OAD (or, for that matter, OAC) depends on the asset type and is constructed to reflect the actual market exposure to a given systematic risk factor. For non-notional securities, the weight is simply the current market value of the security divided by the total market value of the portfolio. By convention, for notional securities (swaps, forwards, and futures), the weight is a function of the notional amount, the current price, and the premium paid, if any. Thus, the weight applied to parametric risk measures on swaps is $\dfrac{(1+P)\cdot Notional\ Value}{MV_{portfolio}}$ where P

is the current market price of the swap per \$1 of notional and $MV_{portfolio}$ is the total market value of the portfolio. For futures and forward contracts, the weight is $\dfrac{P \cdot Notional\ Value}{MV_{portfolio}}$. While the approach based on market values can be used for many derivatives as well, it breaks down for swaps with a market value of zero. Therefore, the method that utilizes notional values is more general.

Recall that OAS is a measure of the risk premium demanded by the market for holding a particular security. In OAD and OAC calculations (Equations 2.23 and 2.26), OAS is usually kept unchanged when prices P_{up} and P_{down} are directly recomputed by the valuation model. Therefore, typical formulations of the option-adjusted framework make an implicit assumption about the absence of *spread directionality*, the relationship between changes in OAS and changes in interest rates. While this dependency is not always stable, in the majority of market environments changes in credit spreads are inversely affected by changes in interest rates.[16] Similar to ignoring dependency of changes in spreads on changes in interest rates, many option-adjusted spread models also do not capture the relationship between implied volatility and interest rates *(volatility skew)*. Since implied volatility is a function of the in-the-moneyness of the option embedded in a security, implied volatility should change instead of being kept constant when interest rates are shocked and prices are recomputed. Assumptions about the absence of basis risk directionality have far-reaching consequences and will be addressed in Chapter 4.

2.2.3 Dynamic Nature of Local Risk Measures: Duration and Convexity Drift[17]

Option-adjusted duration and option-adjusted convexity measure the price sensitivity of fixed income securities to parallel changes in spot rates. Because OAD and OAC are linked to the first- and second-order terms, respectively, of the Taylor series expansion of the price function, they are, in the language of mathematics, *local* measures of risk. Thus, the accuracy of approximating price changes using duration and convexity (Equation 2.16) depends on the nonlinearity of the price/yield function. While accurately predicting price movements for small interest rate shocks, OAD and OAC may not be adequate for approximating highly nonlinear price/yield functions when changes in interest rates are large. Scenario analysis studied in the following section provides the most direct way to illustrate the *locality* of duration and convexity. As a useful exercise, the reader is encouraged to use OAD and OAC (Table 2.1) to approximate prices corresponding to the various changes in interest rates and then contrast them with the corresponding OAVs computed directly (see Table 2.4).

The locality of OAD and OAC can be directly measured by *duration and convexity drifts* – dependencies of these measures on interest rate movements. Hedging illustrates the importance of estimating duration drifts. Since duration (or delta) hedging is still by far the most common method of managing the interest rate risk (Chapter 6), OAD drift estimates the expected mismatch in duration between a portfolio and its hedges if interest rates change. Thus, measuring duration drift is a simple and effective approach to estimating costs associated with rebalancing of hedges.

Duration drift is defined as the negative of the first derivative of duration with respect to changes in interest rates. It is an estimate of the change in OAD for a 100 basis point parallel change in spot rates, that is,

$$OAD\ Drift = -\frac{dOAD}{dr} \tag{2.29}$$

where *dOAD* is the change in OAD and *dr* is a parallel shift in the spot curve. Convexity drift is defined in a similar fashion:

$$OAC\ Drift = -\frac{dOAC}{dr} \tag{2.30}$$

Positive duration drift is a desirable feature in a security since its duration will increase as markets rally, thereby lending itself to further gains as markets rally even further. Conversely, as markets sell off, a security with a positive duration drift shortens in duration, reducing the risk of losses if markets sell off even further. In hedging, positive duration drift is a desirable property of the hedged portfolio as well. Typically, due to the mismatch in duration drifts between a portfolio and its hedges, rebalancing is required when the interest rate environment changes. Assuming that the hedged portfolio with a positive duration drift is originally duration neutral, a market rally will result in a lengthening of its duration, and therefore rebalancing will imply selling securities at higher prices. Conversely, if markets sell off and duration of the hedged portfolio becomes negative, rebalancing will require purchasing supplemental hedges at lower prices. Being an additional protection against adverse market movements, positive duration drift will usually imply a give-up in *carry*.[18]

The derivation of expressions for duration and convexity drifts is straightforward. Differentiating duration (Equation 2.21) with respect to changes in interest rates gives:

$$\frac{d\,OAD}{dr} = -\frac{1}{P}\frac{d^2 P}{dr^2} + \frac{1}{P^2}\frac{dP}{dr}\frac{dP}{dr} \qquad (2.31)$$

resulting into the following expression for duration drift:

$$OAD\ Drift = -\frac{d\,OAD}{dr} = OAC - OAD^2 \qquad (2.32)$$

Duration drift is a function of both OAD and OAC.*

The duration drift of a noncallable Treasury security is always positive, regardless of the interest rate environment. The duration drifts of callable corporate bonds and generic mortgage-backed securities (MBS) are typically negative. However, as shown in Table 2.3, large positive interest rate shocks may result in the duration drifts of currently callable corporate bonds becoming less negative, or even positive. This happens because when rates rise dramatically, the call option embedded in corporate bonds becomes deep out-of-the-money, making its risk characteristics similar to those of a fixed cash flow security. Conversely, as rates fall sharply, the price of the currently callable corporate bond approaches the present value of its cash flows-to-call. Thus, until that point, its duration drift becomes increasingly negative due to declining convexity. After that point in the face of a further rally, the duration drift starts increasing, finally approaching zero when the call option becomes deep in-the-money. Similar to the case of callable corporate bonds, when the prepayment option of a current coupon mortgage-backed security is deep out-of-the-money, this leads the duration drift of this MBS to resemble that of a fixed cash flow security. In persistently low interest rate environments, MBS that have been exposed to extensive refinancing opportunities become much less sensitive to changes in interest rates as

---

* Because of fixed income markets' conventions of reporting duration and convexity (see footnote 2 in Appendix), the actual computations in Table 2.3 use the following formula for duration drift: $OAD\ Drift = \frac{1}{100}\cdot(OAC\cdot 100 - OAD^2) = OAC - \frac{OAD^2}{100}$.

TABLE 2.3 Duration Drifts of Selected Securities in Various Interest Rate Environments

		Base OAS (bps)	Parallel Interest Rate Shock (basis points)										
			+250	+200	+150	+100	+50	Base	-50	-100	-150	-200	-250
U.S. Treasury	OAV	-0.4	69.37	73.15	77.31	81.89	86.94	**92.52**	98.70	105.56	113.19	121.69	131.18
	OAD			10.86	11.30	11.76	12.23	**12.71**	13.21	13.73	14.25	14.78	
	OAC			2.04	2.17	2.30	2.45	**2.59**	2.75	2.91	3.08	3.25	
	Duration Drift			0.86	0.89	0.92	0.95	**0.97**	1.01	1.03	1.05	1.07	
Callable Corp	OAV	71	78.63	81.82	85.14	88.56	92.01	**95.38**	98.36	100.23	100.50	100.54	100.59
	OAD			7.95	7.92	7.77	7.42	**6.66**	4.93	2.13	0.31	0.08	
	OAC			0.65	0.47	0.18	-0.41	**-1.59**	-4.54	-6.37	-0.92	0.00	
	Duration Drift			0.01	-0.15	-0.43	-0.96	**-2.03**	-4.79	-6.42	-0.92	0.00	
Generic MBS	OAV	76	92.48	94.59	96.71	98.82	100.83	**102.64**	104.16	105.32	106.12	106.84	107.59
	OAD			4.47	4.38	4.17	3.78	**3.24**	2.57	1.86	1.44	1.37	
	OAC			0.09	-0.07	-0.42	-0.81	**-1.08**	-1.42	-1.33	-0.31	0.08	
	Duration Drift			-0.11	-0.26	-0.59	-0.95	**-1.19**	-1.48	-1.37	-0.33	0.06	
Notional PAC IO	OAV	81	23.49	22.72	22.11	21.65	21.28	**20.79**	19.62	16.91	11.58	7.40	5.97
	OAD			-6.06	-4.83	-3.85	-4.05	**-7.96**	-19.76	-47.57	-82.17	-75.85	
	OAC			2.89	2.62	1.66	-2.24	**-12.96**	-31.60	-61.90	39.61	149.22	
	Duration Drift			2.53	2.39	1.51	-2.40	**-13.59**	-35.50	-84.53	-27.92	91.69	
TAC PO	OAV	27	51.98	54.93	58.22	62.05	66.66	**72.66**	80.18	87.54	93.08	95.89	96.99
	OAD			11.36	12.22	13.59	15.92	**18.61**	18.56	14.74	8.96	4.08	
	OAC			2.48	3.66	5.08	8.33	**8.38**	-0.78	-8.34	-11.74	-7.09	
	Duration Drift			1.19	2.17	3.23	5.80	**4.91**	-4.23	-10.52	-12.54	-7.25	

the propensity to prepay "burns out." This results in their duration drifts becoming less negative and, finally, slightly positive. Duration drifts of highly leveraged securities such as IOs and POs fluctuate from positive to negative depending on the in-the-moneyness of the embedded options. Table 2.3 illustrates the above points numerically by presenting duration drifts of selected securities.

Although conceptually appealing, convexity drift is difficult to estimate accurately since it requires the computation of the third-order term of the Taylor series, which is even more difficult to measure precisely than convexity. Similar to the problems with stability and intuitiveness of convexity estimates, the accuracy of convexity drifts worsens with increasing optionality and depends substantially on the size of the utilized yield curve shift. Also, just like durations and convexities, their drifts are first-order approximations and may not be accurate predictiors of the actual price behavior when changes in interest rates are large.

2.2.4 Scenario Analysis

Scenario analysis directly measures the price sensitivity of fixed income securities to changes in interest rates. As opposed to duration and convexity, which make various local approximations of the price/yield function, scenario analysis sketches out its exact shape using direct revaluations (Exhibits 2.1 and 2.2). Until recently, despite its intuitive appeal, the uses of scenario analysis of complex securities has been rather limited primarily due to high computational costs. As emphasized earlier, market participants also find it difficult to make real-time portfolio and trading decisions using continuous representations of the price/yield functions, which explains the popularity of duration and convexity measures.

Typically, scenario analysis investigates the price dependency of fixed income securities on parallel changes in yield or the spot curve. First, a set of *instantaneous* interest-rate scenarios is specified. Examples in this book use parallel spot curve shocks of 0, ±25, ±50, ±75, ±100, ±150, and ±200 basis points. OAVs corresponding to each interest rate scenario are then computed using a valuation model. Similar to the computation of P_{up} and P_{down} in Equation 2.23 (OAD) and Equation 2.26 (OAC), OAS is kept constant in the majority of scenario analysis formulations, implicitly assuming the absence of spread directionality. Results of the scenario analysis of securities in the sample portfolio are presented in Table 2.4. Note, once again, that price/yield functions of fixed income securities with embedded options can be substantially nonlinear.

TABLE 2.4 Scenario Analysis Report for the Sample Portfolio (as of 12/31/98)

Security Description	Coupon	Maturity	Strike	-200	-150	-100	-50	-25	0	25	50	100	150	200
									Option-Adjusted Values for Various Parallel Interest Rate Shocks					
Treasury Bonds														
TREASURY NOTE (OTR)	4.63	12/31/00		104,034	103,047	102,072	101,108	100,631	100,156	99,685	99,216	98,287	97,369	96,462
TREASURY NOTE (OTR)	4.25	11/15/03		108,310	105,964	103,677	101,448	100,354	99,274	98,208	97,156	95,090	93,076	91,112
TREASURY NOTE (OTR)	4.75	11/15/08		118,637	114,000	109,579	105,361	103,326	101,338	99,396	97,499	93,835	90,338	86,999
TREASURY BOND (OTR)	5.25	11/15/28		141,976	130,474	120,251	111,148	106,973	103,027	99,295	95,765	89,261	83,421	78,168
Agency Bonds														
FHLMC (callable)	6.33	02/13/06		108,929	107,788	106,541	105,137	104,362	103,546	102,676	101,768	99,831	97,777	95,643
Futures														
MAR 10YR NOTE FUTURE		03/31/99		14,478	10,671	6,992	3,437	1,704	0	-1,675	-3,322	-6,534	-9,640	-12,643
MAR 30YR BOND FUTURE		03/31/99		27,359	19,827	12,779	6,181	3,040	0	-2,970	-5,904	-11,582	-16,964	-22,096
Options														
MAR 10 YR NOTE Put		02/20/99	117	0	2	26	186	411	469	1,421	2,281	4,635	7,468	10,395
10 YR NOTE FUTURE Call		02/20/99	119	14,579	10,788	7,202	4,051	2,771	1,328	1,017	534	106	13	1
Interest Rate Swaps														
US Swap	7.24	06/15/11		27,191	22,527	18,165	14,087	12,149	10,275	8,463	6,712	3,384	276	-2,627
Caps & Floors														
6.00 3M LIBOR CAP	6.00	02/19/02		21	63	155	325	449	604	795	1,027	1,634	2,432	3,376
10YR CMT, 5-YR TENOR 6.4%	6.40	06/17/02		11,445	9,776	8,170	6,654	5,938	5,255	4,610	4,006	2,937	2,079	1,458
OTC Derivatives														
Swaption 1	7.25	05/12/00	7.25	0	5	31	130	234	393	622	934	1,843	3,151	4,823
Swaption 2	Float	06/23/99	5.85	19,314	14,799	10,531	6,644	4,957	3,519	2,367	1,505	515	142	33
Non USD Government Securities														
SWEDEN GOVT	10.25	05/05/00		14,577	14,487	14,397	14,308	14,264	14,220	14,176	14,132	14,046	13,960	13,875
JGB BD 174 (10 YR)	4.60	09/20/04		1,130	1,102	1,074	1,047	1,034	1,021	1,008	995	971	947	924
UK TREASURY	9.00	10/13/08		264,714	255,362	246,425	237,883	233,753	229,715	225,765	221,903	214,432	207,283	200,442
CANADA GOVT	5.75	06/01/29		98,225	90,332	83,316	77,067	74,200	71,490	68,927	66,502	62,031	58,016	54,401
Generic Pass-Throughs														
FGOLD 30YR	7.00	12/31/28		104,599	104,116	103,732	103,333	102,999	102,521	101,876	101,045	98,994	96,639	94,167
FGOLD 30YR	8.00	12/31/28		106,788	106,179	105,593	104,958	104,594	104,167	103,660	103,031	101,420	99,412	97,243
GNMA Construction Loans														
FHA CREEKWOOD GN/GN	7.30	11/30/38		138,631	129,652	121,591	114,334	110,975	107,782	104,744	101,851	96,467	91,566	87,095
Non-Agency CMBS														
DLIMA_96-CF1 B1 144A	8.27	01/12/08		118,750	115,441	112,248	109,167	107,667	106,193	104,745	103,323	100,552	97,877	95,293
Inverse Floating Rate Mortgages														
CMOT13 Q	15.55	01/20/03		113,873	112,317	110,759	109,199	108,421	107,651	106,892	106,135	104,604	103,021	101,426
POs-Agency														
FNSTR_267 (FN 8.50)		10/01/24		97,248	95,941	94,221	91,898	90,499	88,813	86,947	84,834	80,539	76,462	72,818
IOs-Agency														
FHLMC_2043 (FG 7.00)	7.00	01/15/16		8,407	8,984	11,145	15,759	18,444	21,083	23,371	25,149	27,291	28,309	28,875
CMO Sequentials-Agency														
FNMA_93-178 (FN 7.00)	5.25	09/25/23		100,325	100,222	100,119	100,011	99,956	99,902	99,847	99,792	99,682	99,553	99,411
Corporates - Finance														
BANKAMERICA CAPITAL II	8.00	12/15/26	Vary	130,525	126,085	121,522	116,832	114,453	112,060	109,665	107,278	102,553	97,955	93,532
Corporates - Industrial														
PROCTER & GAMBLE COMPANY (T	8.00	10/26/29	100	166,712	154,889	144,304	134,806	130,423	126,264	122,316	118,566	111,612	105,315	99,601
Asset Backed - Prepay Sensitive														
CONHE_97-5 (Home Equity)	6.58	06/15/19		107,304	105,864	104,449	103,057	102,369	101,688	101,012	100,342	99,019	97,718	96,439
Asset Backed - Non-Prepay Sensitive														
CHVAT_98-2 (Auto)	5.91	12/15/04		103,735	102,957	102,189	101,432	101,057	100,685	100,315	99,947	99,220	98,501	97,793
Total Assets	**7.02**			**2,371,858**	**2,273,625**	**2,183,008**	**2,100,174**	**2,061,079**	**2,024,653**	**1,986,626**	**1,951,007**	**1,883,233**	**1,819,997**	**1,761,350**

Scenario analysis does not necessarily have to use parallel spot curve shocks. For instance, it could just as easily be performed in terms of parallel shocks to the par curve. Later in this book, we study other approaches to scenario analysis that use principal components and other nonparallel interest rate shocks. It must be noted that since evolution of securities through time is ignored by the traditional scenario analysis formulations, some of the conclusions can be misleading: Due to decay of embedded options, rolldown, and carry, the actual performance of fixed income securities in various interest rate environments can be substantially different from that predicted by scenario analysis, which uses instantaneous interest rate shocks. Later in this chapter (Section 2.7), the expected rate of return framework is used to present a more generalized approach to scenario analysis. This will allow the simultaneous exploration of the price sensitivity of fixed income securities to changes in interest rates as well as to the passage of time.

2.3 MEASURING INTEREST RATE EXPOSURE: EMPIRICAL APPROACHES

2.3.1 Coupon Curve Duration

Coupon curve duration (CCD) measures the price sensitivity of mortgage-backed securities to changes in interest rates. CCDs are conceptually very different from the previously described analytical measures of interest rate risk. They are perhaps the simplest durations to calculate since they are solely based on the *coupon curve*, the price dependency of MBS of the same agency and term on the coupon. Coupon curves of generic 30-year Fannie Mae (FNMA), Freddie Mac (FHLMC), and Ginnie Mae (GNMA) MBS are presented in Exhibit 2.3.

Similar to other interest rate duration measures, CCD is defined as the negative of the percentage change in price, given a 100 basis point change in interest rates (Equation 2.21) and is computed using the usual duration formula (Equation 2.23). The difference between CCD and other interest rate durations lies in the computation of P_{up} and P_{down}, which are derived directly from market prices as opposed to being computed by a valuation model such as OAVs. The rationale behind CCD is based on the "similarity" of mortgage-backed securities of the same agency and term in all risk characteristics (credit quality, types of underlying pools, origination guidelines, etc.) but one – coupon. When referring to the in-the-moneyness of the embedded prepayment option, it

EXHIBIT 2.3   Coupon Curves of Generic 30-year MBS (as of 12/31/98)

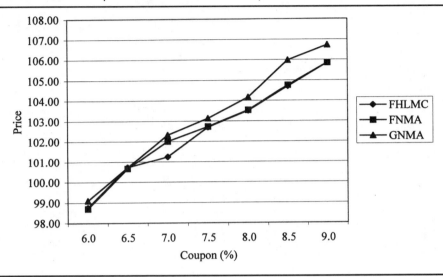

therefore can be argued that if interest rates increase by 50 basis points, the price of a 7.0% MBS should become equal to that of a 6.5% MBS. Conversely, if interest rates decrease by 50 basis points, the price of a 7.0% MBS should become equal that of a 7.5% MBS. Applying the above logic to P_{up} and P_{down} in Equation 2.23 yields:

$$CCD_{7.0} = -\frac{1}{P_{7.0}} \frac{P_{6.5} - P_{7.5}}{2 \cdot 0.005} \qquad (2.33)$$

where $P_{6.5}, P_{7.0}$, and $P_{7.5}$ are the current prices of 6.5%, 7.0%, and 7.5% MBS, respectively. CCDs of generic 30-year mortgage-backed securities are presented in Table 2.5.

CCDs have become an invaluable tool in reconciling analytical measures of risk with the market's perception of risk as reflected in prices of fixed income instruments. However, CCDs are only effective when measuring risk of fairly generic and homogeneous MBSs that are well priced and have similar weighted-average maturities. Extending this approach to other fixed income asset classes is difficult since identifying groups of instruments which are "similar" in all risk dimensions but one (coupon) is rare.

TABLE 2.5 Parametric Risk Measures for Generic 30-year MBSs (as of 12/31/98)

Agency	Coupon	Market Price	OAS	OAD	OAC	Spd Dur	Vol Dur	Prepay Dur	Mtg/Tsy Dur	OASCrv Dur	CpnCrv Dur	Imp Dur 10 Day	Imp Dur 30 Day	30 Day R²
FHLMC														
	6.00	98-24	74	4.58	-1.89	4.86	0.29	0.08	-0.76	4.58	6.08	3.46	3.69	85%
	6.50	100-23	74	3.12	-2.81	4.04	0.28	0.40	-1.26	2.80	3.22	2.76	2.87	85%
	7.00	101-30	84	2.52	-2.59	3.53	0.28	0.84	-1.64	1.38	2.28	1.84	1.84	68%
	7.50	102-22	106	1.81	-1.84	3.08	0.20	1.11	-1.60	0.23	2.04	0.84	0.89	43%
	8.00	103-16	138	1.85	-1.32	3.04	0.17	1.47	-1.51	0.91	1.90	0.53	0.53	36%
	8.50	104-22	130	1.15	-0.40	2.69	0.14	1.76	-1.77	1.15	2.67	0.30	0.34	12%
	9.00	105-27	139	1.09	-0.28	2.64	0.13	2.05	-1.78	1.09	2.71	** poor regression fit **		
	9.50	106-00	197	1.44	-0.53	2.69	0.13	2.31	-1.50	1.44	1.44	** poor regression fit **		
FNMA														
	6.00	98-22	72	4.18	-1.93	4.86	0.26	0.07	-0.78	4.18	5.71	3.46	3.72	86%
	6.50	100-21	71	3.10	-2.85	4.07	0.28	0.39	-1.31	2.96	3.33	2.72	2.88	85%
	7.00	102-00	77	2.40	-2.61	3.54	0.29	0.83	-1.76	1.40	2.40	1.96	1.98	75%
	7.50	102-23	101	1.77	-1.87	3.15	0.20	1.11	-1.71	1.35	1.94	0.83	0.99	42%
	8.00	103-17	135	1.80	-1.34	3.18	0.18	1.47	-1.61	1.80	1.77	0.53	0.55	37%
	8.50	104-24	127	1.11	-0.51	2.80	0.15	1.75	-1.90	1.11	2.64	0.51	0.45	22%
	9.00	105-27	135	1.12	-0.32	2.71	0.13	2.05	-1.82	1.12	2.68	** poor regression fit **		
	9.50	106-12	179	1.36	-0.55	2.76	0.13	2.31	-1.66	1.36	1.36	** poor regression fit **		
GNMA														
	6.00	99-03	67	5.73	-1.63	6.25	0.41	0.17	-1.11	5.73	5.71	3.64	3.94	85%
	7.00	102-10	82	2.57	-2.82	3.99	0.29	0.72	-1.61	1.88	2.31	2.40	2.20	71%
	7.50	103-04	96	1.82	-1.99	3.26	0.21	1.02	-1.58	0.69	1.84	1.33	1.17	43%
	8.00	104-05	116	1.85	-1.49	3.11	0.20	1.49	-1.56	1.30	2.33	1.05	0.75	29%
	8.50	105-31	107	1.43	-0.89	3.01	0.17	1.82	-1.78	1.43	2.63	0.14	0.22	10%
	9.00	106-23	139	1.62	-0.67	2.98	0.15	2.13	-1.58	1.62	2.23	** poor regression fit **		

2.3.2 OAS Curve Duration

Another measure of interest rate risk of mortgage-backed securities, OAS curve duration (OCD), is similar in spirit to CCD and represents a blend of analytical and empirical approaches. As opposed to employing coupon curves, OCD uses valuation models and OAS curves (Exhibit 2.4) when computing option-adjusted values P_{up} and P_{down} in Equation 2.23. This makes OCD significantly more computationally intensive and model-dependent than CCD.

The rationale behind OCD is as follows. If interest rates increase by 50 basis points, the in-the-moneyness of the prepayment option embedded in a 7.0% MBS becomes similar to that of a 6.5% MBS in the current market environment. Therefore, the risk premium (OAS) associated with investing in a 7.0% MBS in the "rates are 50 basis point higher" environment can be expected to become equal to the risk premium of a 6.5% MBS in the current market environment. Conversely, if rates fall by 50 basis points, OAS of a 7.0% MBS can be expected to become equal to OAS of a 7.5% MBS. This argues that when shocking spot curves and recomputing option-adjusted values P_{up} and P_{down} in the valuation model, OAS spread directionality should be accounted for as follows:

$$OCD_{7.0} = -\frac{1}{P_{7.0}} \frac{P_{7.0,up}(OAS_{6.5}) - P_{7.0,down}(OAS_{7.5})}{2 \cdot 0.005} \qquad (2.34)$$

EXHIBIT 2.4   OAS Curves of Generic 30-year MBSs (as of 12/31/98)

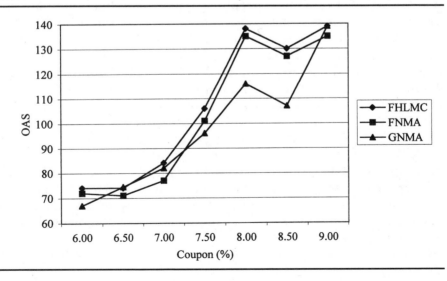

where $P_{7.0,up}$ ($OAS_{6.5}$) is the option-adjusted value of a 7.0% MBS in the "rates are 50 basis point higher" market environment computed using the current OAS of a 6.5% MBS. Similarly, $P_{7.0,down}$ ($OAS_{7.5}$) is the OAV of a 7.0% MBS in the "rates are 50 basis point lower" market environment computed using the current OAS of a 7.5% MBS. OAS curve durations of generic 30-year MBSs are presented in Table 2.5.

OAS curve duration does not assume that spreads remain unchanged when interest rates move. Therefore, this measure simultaneously captures the cash flow uncertainty and accounts for the spread directionality embedded in market prices. In market environments where spread movements are correlated with movements in interest rates, OCD is a very accurate measure of interest rate risk.[19] However, just like coupon curve durations, OCD is mostly applicable to the very homogeneous agency MBSs. In Chapter 4, alternative approaches to explicitly incorporating spread directionality into duration measures are presented.

2.3.3 Empirical (Implied) Duration

As an alternative to computing parametric risk measures by theorizing mechanisms underlying financial markets, econometric methods can be used to statistically estimate the price sensitivity of fixed income securities to a variety of systematic risk factors. Measures of interest rate risk obtained via applied statistical modeling techniques have become known as *empirical* or *implied* durations.[20] While econometrically sophisticated empirical duration formulations can be envisioned, this section illustrates this concept using the intellectually simplest and most direct approach. Like coupon curve duration, empirical duration estimates the interest rate risk through information embedded in market prices and yields. These two methodologies are also similar in not relying on the numerous assumptions built into interest rate, yield curve, and prepayment models. However, in contrast to CCD, empirical duration uses *historical time series* of prices and yields rather than the current market data.

Empirical duration methodology typically employs regression analysis. As opposed to analytically computing the first derivative of the price function with respect to yield, the statistical relationship between the dependent variable (percentage changes in prices) and the independent variable (changes in interest rates) is analyzed. As mentioned before, the term *change in interest rates* can be defined in many different ways. Thus, modified duration characterizes changes in interest rates as changes in yields-to-maturity of option-free bonds. OAD represents changes in interest rates as parallel movements in the spot curve. Empirical duration can be defined as the negative of the slope of the regression line of percentage changes in price $\left(\dfrac{\Delta P}{P}\right)$ of a bond with respect to changes in its yield-to-maturity (Δy):

$$\frac{\Delta P}{P} = \alpha - Empirical\ Dur \cdot \Delta y + \varepsilon \qquad (2.35)$$

where ε are normally distributed error terms. For the majority of fixed income instruments, the intercept α is typically statistically insignificant in virtually all market environments. Notice the similarity of Equation 2.35 with Equation 2.12 (modified duration). Obviously, Equation 2.35 represents the simplest possible formulation of empirical duration. While other formulations exist, some of them make it difficult to extract the isolated price sensitivity to interest rate movements because of the interaction between interest rates and other systematic risk factors.

A complication arises when computing empirical durations for derivative securities (e.g., mortgage-backed securities) whose yields-to-maturity cannot be meaningfully defined because of the embedded cash flow uncertainties. In this case, it is customary to assign to each derivative instrument a *benchmark fixed cash flow security* (usually a U.S. Treasury) whose yield-to-maturity is used as proxy for changes in interest rates (Δy) in Equation 2.35. The issues surrounding selection of benchmarks that adequately represent changes in interest rates merit a separate discussion. First, since empirical duration is defined in a univariate setting where price is a function of a single risk factor, selection of the appropriate benchmark should account for the fact that yield curves do not usually move in a parallel fashion. The benchmark must therefore be linked to the risk characteristics (e.g., OAD or weighted average life) of the derivative instrument whose empirical duration is to be measured. Table 2.5 shows 10- and 30-business-day empirical durations of generic MBS securities. Notice that empirical durations across all MBSs are substantially shorter than the corresponding OADs. Chapter 4 will show that the difference is due to the spread directionality of mortgage spreads and other basis risks ignored by OAD. Notice that the goodness-of-fit (as measured by R^2) is inversely related to the prices of MBSs.

Empirical duration methodology may not be directly applicable to all types of fixed income securities. In computing empirical durations, prices of securities with built-in forward contracts (e.g., generic to-be-announced [TBA] MBS) have to be adjusted for *carry:* since price movements of these instruments reflect both market fluctuations as well as price movements due to the embedded forward contract approaching expiration, the random component has to be isolated from the deterministic one. In addition to fluctuations attributed to interest rates, prices of complex fixed income securities may change due to a variety of other risk factors: credit spread movements, decay of embedded options, prepayments, time, etc. While captured in the time series of percentage price changes of derivative securities, these phenomena are not reflected in the yield-to-maturities of the corresponding U.S. Treasury benchmarks, biasing empirical duration estimates. Due to the market state-dependent nature of risk characteristics of fixed income securities, empirical durations may also lead to erroneous conclusions if the market environment used to compute them is substantially different from the market environment they are being applied to. For instance, if interest rates changed dramatically after empirical durations on mortgage-backed securities were computed, empirical results should be deemed outdated because in-the-moneyness of the embedded prepayment options has changed.

The goodness-of-fit measures (e.g., R^2) and tests for statistical significance of the regression coefficients may be used when judging the quality of empirical durations. If R^2 of the regression is high, the vast majority of the price variability is explained by movements of interest rates, and empirical duration therefore is an accurate measure of risk. Needless to say, empirical duration is very sensitive to pricing errors. They may also be biased due to purely statistical reasons, including the presence of autoregressive behavior, lags in price reaction to changes in yields, and nonnormality of residuals.

It is possible to test directly whether the empirical duration estimate is biased by the presence of spread directionality. By using multiple regressions, empirical duration calculation can be generalized to include various basis risks, for example,

$$\frac{\Delta P}{P} = \alpha - Empirical\ Dur \cdot \Delta y - Empirical\ Spread\ Dur \cdot \Delta OAS + \varepsilon \quad (2.36)$$

where *Empirical Dur* and *Empirical Spread Dur* denote empirical interest rate and spread durations, respectively. Since changes in credit spreads are rarely highly correlated with changes in interest rates, multicollinearity in Equation 2.36 is usually not a concern. Statistical significance of the empirical spread duration can be thought of as a test for the presence of spread directionality in a given market environment. Empirical duration calculations with and without the spread directionality term are presented in

TABLE 2.6 Empirical Durations with and without Spread Directionality for 30-year GNMA MBS (as of 12/31/98)

		10-day Regression							30-day Regression							60-day Regression						
		Avg	Impl	Avg	Impl	Spread Dir			Avg	Impl	Avg	Impl	Spread Dir			Avg	Impl	Avg	Impl	Spread Dir		
Coupon		OAD	Dur	Spd Dur	Spd Dur	t-value	p-value	R²	OAD	Dur	Spd Dur	Spd Dur	t-value	p-value	R²	OAD	Dur	Spd Dur	Spd Dur	t-value	p-value	R²
6.0	With Dir	5.76	4.09	6.29	1.48	-1.91	0.10	95	5.70	4.23	6.30	0.98	-1.69	0.10	86	5.70	4.82	6.32	3.14	-9.12	0.00	91
	Without		3.64					94		3.94					85		4.30					78
6.5	With Dir	3.55	3.52	5.06	1.01	-1.53	0.17	95	3.42	3.40	5.04	0.54	-1.17	0.25	86	3.42	3.69	5.07	2.21	-8.85	0.00	92
	Without		3.34					93		3.27					85		3.52					80
7.0	With Dir	2.82	2.56	4.07	1.02	-2.01	0.08	93	2.64	2.38	4.03	0.83	-2.06	0.05	75	2.61	2.29	4.05	1.30	-7.34	0.00	89
	Without		2.40					91		2.20					71		2.18					78
7.5	With Dir	2.06	1.55	3.34	0.73	-1.96	0.09	87	1.94	1.49	3.28	0.93	-2.80	0.01	56	1.96	1.22	3.29	0.90	-5.77	0.00	74
	Without		1.33					82		1.17					43		1.06					59
8.0	With Dir	2.03	1.31	3.16	0.72	-1.90	0.10	69	1.93	1.07	3.11	0.64	-2.79	0.01	46	1.94	0.73	3.09	0.71	-5.04	0.00	49
	Without		1.05					56		0.75					29		0.48					26
8.5	With Dir	1.53	0.28	3.07	0.19	-0.30	0.78	5	1.46	0.57	3.04	0.59	-1.67	0.11	12	1.55	0.39	3.03	0.44	-2.69	0.01	20
	Without		0.14					3		0.22					3		0.22					10
9.0	With Dir	1.70	0.30	3.03	0.00	0.00	1.00	7	1.67	0.40	3.01	0.23	-0.53	0.60	5	1.75	0.43	3.03	0.57	-2.34	0.02	11
	Without		0.10					8		0.19					4		0.12					2

55

Table 2.6. Note that these regression results may contain simultaneity bias since prices, yields, and spreads are determined at the same time.

Empirical duration is a simple, accurate, and intuitive measure of interest rate risk. By virtue of reflecting the actual empirically observed price behavior, empirical durations provide a valuable "sanity check" when judging the predictive power of option-adjusted and other analytical durations. During the credit and liquidity meltdown of fall 1998, mortgage spreads were widening as interest rates were declining. As a result, price gains resulting from the decrease in discount rates were offset by losses due to the widening of credit spreads and the increase in prepayments. At that time, empirical durations of generic mortgages were close to zero, reflecting the actual price behavior, while OADs exhibited only a moderate compression.

2.4 MEASURING YIELD CURVE RISK

2.4.1 Key Rate Durations[21]

Earlier in this chapter, several conceptually different approaches to measuring the price sensitivity of fixed income securities to changes in interest rates were identified. While the previously described measures of risk employ very different theoretical and computational tools, they all rely on the same unrealistic underlying assumption that prices of securities and portfolios are functions of a *single* systematic risk factor. Thus, changes in interest rates are represented as changes in yields-to-maturity in the computation of modified and empirical durations and as parallel changes in the spot curve in the calculation of option-adjusted measures. Not surprisingly, while being accurate predictors of price fluctuations resulting from small changes in the *level* of interest rates, modified, option-adjusted, and other durations fail to address risk associated with changes in the *shape* or *slope* of the yield curve. Consider the following example. When expecting an easing of short-term interest rates by the Federal Reserve, traders often bet on the steepening in the yield curve. To implement their view as a duration-neutral relative value trade, they may decide to buy the 2-year on-the-run (OTR) Treasury (TSY) security and sell the 30-year OTR TSY. Using duration to judge the interest rate risk of this trade (which has a duration of zero by construction) will erroneously indicate that it is risk-free. While this trade is insensitive to parallel movements[22] in the spot curve, it is exposed to a different kind of systematic market risk, that is, the flattening of the yield curve that cannot be measured by duration.

Another example of limitation of duration with respect to measuring yield curve risk comes from institutional asset management where a portfolio's investment guidelines typically specify a predefined *duration band*, the maximum allowed deviation of the portfolio's duration from that of the benchmark. Similar to the case of duration-neutral trades, an investment mandate may impose a very narrow duration band on a portfolio to limit the magnitude of duration bets, thus constraining an important source of risk (as well as limiting opportunities for outperformance). In search of active return, such a portfolio may be structured to hold longer instruments than those in its benchmark while the excess duration is hedged out using futures, swaps, or other derivatives. This may result in the *gap* between a portfolio and its benchmark having a yield curve bet that is not captured by duration. Obviously, this yield curve bet could be a major source of market risk. These examples demonstrate the need to generalize OAD methodology. In addition to investigating the price sensitivity to parallel changes in the entire term structure of interest rates, risk associated with nonparallel yield curve movements must be measured.

Key rate duration (KRD)[23] has become an important extension of the option-adjusted framework. The popularity of KRDs is generally attributed to their ability to describe yield curve risk in a visual and intuitive way. KRDs have also proven to be an effective hedging and yield curve risk management tool. They are typically implemented within the option-adjusted framework, and can be thought of as partial OADs corresponding to the movements of isolated regions of the yield curve. Key rate durations offer a visual depiction of yield curve exposure, both at the security and portfolio level. KRD profiles of selected securities are presented in Exhibit 2.5.

OAD measures the first-order price sensitivity to parallel changes in interest rates. KRDs generalize this approach. Instead of assuming that price P is a function of a single random variable (parallel spot curve shock as in Equation 2.20), KRDs present price as a function of n selected spot rates $r_1,\ldots,r_n$ that are known as *key rates*:

$$P = P(r_1,\ldots,r_n) \tag{2.37}$$

KRDs are partial durations that measure the first-order price sensitivity to the isolated movements of different segments of the spot curve:

$$krd_i = -\frac{1}{P}\frac{\partial P}{\partial r_i} \tag{2.38}$$

In this more general setting, because any yield curve movement can be represented as the vector of changes of properly chosen key rates

EXHIBIT 2.5   Key Rate Duration (KRD) Profiles of Selected Instruments (as of 12/31/98)

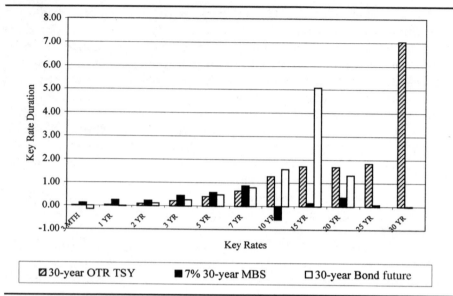

$(\Delta r_1,\ldots,\Delta r_n)$, a multivariate analog of Equation 2.24 can be used to approximate changes in price using the vector of KRDs:

$$\frac{\Delta P}{P} \approx -\sum_{i=1}^{n} krd_i \cdot \Delta r_i \qquad (2.39)$$

Equation 2.39 has far-reaching applications. It will be referred to on numerous occasions throughout the book, including with regard to its uses in stress testing and Value-at-Risk (VaR). KRDs can be computed via the direct analog of Equation 2.23:

$$krd_i = -\frac{1}{P}\frac{P_{i,\mathrm{up}} - P_{i,\mathrm{down}}}{2 \cdot \Delta r_i} \qquad (2.40)$$

Note that $P_{i,\mathrm{up}}$ and $P_{i,\mathrm{down}}$ in Equation 2.40 are directly computed by a valuation model after the appropriate KRD shock is applied to the spot curve. Just as in the case of OAD and OAC, OAS is kept constant in the calculation of KRDs, assuming the absence of spread directionality. Despite their conceptual similarity to OADs, the implementation of

KRDs within the OAS framework is nontrivial. The construction of KRD shocks therefore merits a separate discussion.

The partition of the yield curve into segments corresponding to different key rates runs the risk of being rather arbitrary, and its implementations vary across financial institutions that employ KRDs in portfolio and risk management. The most appropriate number of key rates and their positioning on the yield curve ultimately depend on the composition of a given portfolio. In the examples presented in this book, the key rates are defined as 3-month and 1-, 2-, 3-, 5-, 7-, 10-, 15-, 20-, 25-, and 30-year points on the spot curve. Alternatively, shorter-term portfolios might require a greater number of key rates at the shorter end of the yield curve. In the extreme case, one might imagine having a separate key rate for every annual, monthly, or even daily spot rate. Unfortunately, in practice this would be computationally infeasible and would lead to storing and processing vast amounts of information; but most importantly, only limited practical benefits could arise from this type of excessive granularity. Interestingly enough, identification of the key rate points on the yield curve and construction of the corresponding shocks are related to the issues of historical plausibility of interest rate shocks studied in Chapter 3. Thus, since certain points of the yield curve are highly correlated and exhibit similar volatilities, investigating the price sensitivity to their changes in isolation, with all other spot rates kept constant is unrealistic. From a mathematical viewpoint, recomputing OAD of a security when a single point on the spot curve is perturbed is also not meaningful: Price is similar to an integral; both are not sensitive to changes in the value of a continuous function at a single point.

Therefore, the following considerations are important for the construction of KRD interest rate shocks:

- Spot rates do not move in isolation. If a single spot rate is shocked, an entire *region* of the spot curve around this point should be shocked as well.
- For consistency and other reasons that will be apparent momentarily, KRD shocks should add up to the parallel shock, which leads to the intuitive concept that exposure to parallel changes in interest rates (OAD) is comprised of exposures to the different parts of the yield curve (KRDs).

When KRDs were first introduced, KRD shocks were constructed with the above-described rationale in mind. For instance, the 5-year KRD shock (Exhibit 2.6) was defined as having the value of zero basis points for all spot rates with terms less than 3 years, linearly rising to a

EXHIBIT 2.6   5-year KRD Spot Curve Shock and Its Effect on Forward Rates (as of 9/30/96)

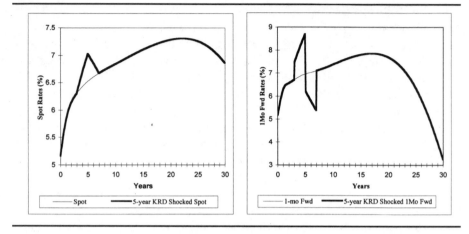

given number of basis points (Δr) at the 5-year point,[24] declining linearly back to zero at the next key rate (7-year), and staying at zero basis points for all maturities beyond 7 years. As the exception to this rule, the two boundary key rates (3-month and 30-year) were defined slightly differently: the 3-month KRD shock had a value of Δr between zero and 3-month points, linearly declining to zero at the 1-year key rate, and staying at zero for all maturities greater than 1 year. The 30-year KRD shock was defined as zero for all maturities less than or equal to 25 years, linearly increasing to Δr at the 30-year key rate, and staying at Δr for all maturities greater than 30 years.

The areas underneath the KRD shocks exactly add up to the parallel shock by construction (Exhibit 2.7). Unfortunately, this does not by itself guarantee that the sum of KRDs is exactly equal to OAD. For securities without cash flow uncertainties, the difference between OAD and the sum of KRDs is usually small. For complex derivative instruments, this difference may be substantial because of the nonlinearity of the value surface. This phenomenon is counterintuitive for practitioners. Imagine that Equations 2.24 and 2.39 are independently used to estimate the change in price resulting from a given parallel yield curve shock. If KRDs do not sum to OAD, the two methods will arrive at different results. To eliminate this inconsistency, the sum of KRDs can be forced to be equal to OAD. While different ad hoc methods exist, one approach simply adjusts KRDs proportionally by multiplying each KRD by the ratio of OAD and the original sum of KRDs. The authors are not aware

Exhibit 2.7   Key Rate Duration (KRD) Shocks Add Up to the Parallel Shock

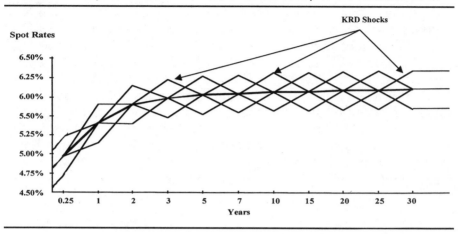

of any published empirical or theoretical validation (or, for that matter, critique) of this method. Throughout this book, KRDs will be scaled proportionally in the above-described fashion.

The KRD approach provides considerably more information than the single OAD statistic. The cost of this increased precision is directly reflected in the increase (sometimes by an order of magnitude) of the computational resources required to compute KRDs. The task of recomputing KRDs is a significant computational burden if the number of securities and portfolios is large. For practical purposes, an approximation is needed. Consistent with the discussion of duration drifts in Section 2.2.3, while OAD may change rather substantially as a result of market movements, the shapes of the KRD profiles of fixed income securities are relatively stable over short periods of time. Therefore, in practice, KRD can be recomputed on a less frequent basis than OAD. If KRDs are scaled to sum to OAD on a regular basis, they can reasonably reflect the latest changes in the market. Needless to say, this approach provides an accurate representation of yield curve exposures only in the absence of substantial yield curve movements. Finally, like OAD, the aggregate KRD profile of a fixed income portfolio can be computed as the weighted average of KRDs of the underlying securities.

Interpreting KRD profiles can be tricky because they simply measure the *sensitivities* to the different points on the spot curve and ignore the fact that spot rates of dissimilar maturities are not perfectly correlated and may exhibit sometimes dramatically different volatilities. Just like OAD, KRDs also exhibit duration drifts. Finally, the interest rate shocks used to compute KRD have historically implausible shapes and produce nondifferentiable points on the spot curve (Exhibit 2.6), implying discontinuous and sometimes even negative forward rates. This may result in rather different KRD profiles for very similar securities.

Despite some of these shortcomings, KRDs have proven to be a very popular risk management tool. They enable explicit quantitative representation of yield curve exposure and provide insights into absolute and relative yield curve risks embedded in securities and portfolios. In addition to being useful in their own right, KRDs are widely employed by other risk management methodologies described later in this book, including effective risk profile, Value-at-Risk (VaR), stress testing, and hedge optimizations. KRDs of securities in the sample portfolio are presented in Table 2.7.

2.4.2 Key Treasury Rate Durations[25]

Key treasury rate duration (KTRD) is often called KRD's "smaller and arguably more intuitive sibling."[26] While identical in spirit to KRDs, KTRDs have greater intuitive appeal to certain practitioners because they are tailored to the way portfolio managers and traders tend to think about the yield curve. Recall that KRDs are defined as price sensitivities to changes in the spot curve, a purely theoretical construct that cannot be directly observed in the market. Despite the wide use of spot curves in both valuation and risk management, few market participants (maybe with the exception of financial modelers and zero-coupon bond traders) think in terms of spot rates. Instead, investors tend to concentrate on on-the-run (OTR) or par curves that are more intuitive and directly observable. KTRDs measure the price sensitivity to changes in the par curve. If the liquidity premiums embedded in OTR U.S. Treasury securities are small in magnitude and can be assumed relatively constant over time, KTRDs can be thought of as price sensitivities to changes in the on-the-run curve as well. However, when OTR liquidity premiums are large (sometimes reaching as much as 40 basis points), due to the market state-dependent nature of valuation of fixed income securities, differences between price sensitivities to par versus OTR rates can be substantial. For the sake of simplicity and without loss of generality, this section will operate under the now obsolete assumption that *par curves* and *OTR curves* are interchangeable.

Just as in the case of KRDs, definition of key treasury rates is rather arbitrary. It is typically linked to the maturities of the on-the-run Treasury instruments, while additional rates are sometimes added for

TABLE 2.7 Key Rate Duration (KRD) Report for the Sample Portfolio (as of 12/31/98)

Position Description	Coupon	Maturity	Strike	OAD	OAC	KRD 3 MTH	KRD 1 YR	KRD 2 YR	KRD 3 YR	KRD 5 YR	KRD 7 YR	KRD 10 YR	KRD 15 YR	KRD 20 YR	KRD 25 YR	KRD 30 YR
Treasury Bonds																
TREASURY NOTE (OTR)	4.63	12/31/00		1.89	0.05	0.01	0.04	1.84								
TREASURY NOTE (OTR)	4.25	11/15/03		4.32	0.22	0.01	0.04	0.08	0.43	3.77						
TREASURY NOTE (OTR)	4.75	11/15/08		7.76	0.73	0.01	0.04	0.08	0.20	0.36	0.86	6.21				
TREASURY BOND (OTR)	5.25	11/15/28		14.93	3.34	0.01	0.04	0.09	0.21	0.40	0.65	1.27	1.71	1.68	1.83	7.03
Agency Bonds																
FHLMC (callable)	6.33	02/13/06		3.25	-0.79	0.01	0.05	0.85	0.57	0.52	1.20	0.04				
Futures																
MAR 10YR NOTE FUTURE		03/31/99		5.67	0.38	-0.16	-0.03	0.10	0.24	0.77	4.74					
MAR 30YR BOND FUTURE		03/31/99		9.47	0.89	-0.14	-0.01	0.11	0.26	0.48	0.79	1.58	5.07	1.33		
Options																
MAR 10 YR NOTE Put		02/20/99	117	-350.74	925.11	9.80	1.59	-6.35	-14.88	-47.54	-293.36					
10 YR NOTE FUTURE Call		02/20/99	119	266.42	452.59	-7.44	-1.20	4.82	11.31	36.11	222.82					
Interest Rate Swaps																
US Swap	7.24	06/15/11		6.68	0.91			-1.10	-0.54	0.49	0.79	4.12	2.93			
Caps & Floors																
6.00 3M LIBOR CAP	6.00	02/19/02		-114.67	95.80	8.47	22.12	23.51	-161.21	-7.56						
10YR CMT, 5-YR TENOR 6.4%	6.40	06/17/02		50.32	11.26	-0.42	-1.49	-2.40	-1.43	2.53	4.30	35.09	14.14			
OTC Derivatives																
Swaption 1	7.25	05/12/00	7.25	-195.71	284.47		22.39	10.41	-5.93	-10.82	-17.42	-146.44	-47.90			
Swaption 2	Float	06/23/99	5.85	148.11	132.62	-6.06	-1.67	2.10	4.89	8.92	14.36	114.71	10.86			
Non USD Government Securities																
SWEDEN GOVT	10.25	05/05/00		1.23	0.02	0.03	0.79	0.41								
JGB BD 174 (10 YR)	4.60	09/20/04		5.18	0.31	0.01	0.01	0.05	0.19	3.23	1.68					
UK TREASURY	9.00	10/13/08		6.91	0.61	0.02	0.06	0.12	0.27	0.51	1.17	4.78				
CANADA GOVT	5.75	06/01/29		14.78	3.30	0.01	0.05	0.09	0.22	0.40	0.65	1.27	1.77	1.82	1.76	6.74
Generic Pass-Throughs																
FGOLD 30YR	7.00	12/31/28		2.52	-2.59	0.13	0.25	0.23	0.45	0.58	0.87	-0.58	0.14	0.38	0.07	-0.01
FGOLD 30YR	8.00	12/31/28		1.85	-1.32	0.12	0.20	0.23	0.42	0.50	0.61	-0.48	0.02	0.22	0.03	-0.01
GNMA Construction Loans																
FHA CREEKWOOD GN/GN	7.30	11/30/38		3.57	-1.13	0.01	0.03	0.05	0.12	0.23	0.37	2.10	0.64	0.02		
Non-Agency CMBS																
DLJMA_96-CF1 B1 144A	8.27	01/12/08		4.41	-0.54	0.01	0.05	0.11	0.25	0.45	2.91	0.63				
Inverse Floating Rate Mortgages																
CMOT13 Q	15.55	01/20/03		2.83	0.16	0.20	1.06	1.38	0.36	-0.01	-0.01	-0.13	-0.02			
POs-Agency																
FNSTR_267 (FN 8.50)	8.00	10/01/24		7.95	-4.02	0.00	0.07	0.22	0.31	0.51	0.72	3.66	1.87	0.45	0.12	0.03
IOs-Agency																
FHLMC_2043 (FG 7.00)	7.00	01/15/16		-45.94	-20.82	1.27	1.79	-0.13	-0.96	-1.56	-3.13	-29.31	-13.47	-0.43		
CMO Sequentials-Agency																
FNMA_93-178 (FN 7.00)	5.25	09/25/23		0.22	0.00	0.20	0.02									
Corporates - Finance																
BANKAMERICA CAPITAL II	8.00	12/15/26		8.72	0.05	0.01	0.06	0.12	0.29	0.52	1.64	1.78	1.51	1.58	0.91	0.29
Corporates - Industrial																
PROCTER & GAMBLE COMPANY (THE)	8.00	10/26/29		12.84	2.67	0.01	0.05	0.11	0.26	0.47	0.75	1.40	1.81	1.68	1.59	4.71
Asset Backed - Prepay Sensitive																
CONHE_97-5 (Home Equity)	6.58	06/15/19		2.27	-1.00	0.01	0.05	0.39	1.60	0.21						
Asset Backed - Non-Prepay Sensitive																
CHVAT_98-2 (Auto)	5.91	12/15/04		1.47	0.04	0.08	0.30	0.48	0.53	0.09						
Total Assets	**7.02**			**6.82**	**0.81**	**0.03**	**0.16**	**0.30**	**0.30**	**0.63**	**1.16**	**1.70**	**0.86**	**0.47**	**0.32**	**0.91**

TABLE 2.8   10-year Key Treasury Rate Duration (KTRD) Shock: Conversion from OTR to Spot Curve Shock (as of 12/31/98)

	Actual OTR Points Used To Compute OTR Liquidity Premium			
	2-year	5-year	10-year	30-year
OTR Maturity (Years)	2.00	4.87	9.87	29.87
Par Yield(%)	4.65	4.72	4.89	5.31
OTR Yield(%)	4.54	4.54	4.66	5.10
Liq Premium(%)	0.11	0.18	0.23	0.21

	Original Rates				Rates After Applying Shock					
Key Rates	Spot Rates	Par Rates	Liquid Premium	OTR Rates	OTR Shock	OTR Rates	Par Rates	Spot Rates	Par Shock	Spot Shock
3-mo	4.76	4.76	0.01	4.74		4.74	4.76	4.76		
1-year	4.66	4.66	0.05	4.61		4.61	4.66	4.66		
2-year	4.65	4.65	0.10	4.54		4.54	4.65	4.65		
3-year	4.68	4.68	0.13	4.55		4.55	4.68	4.68		
5-year	4.73	4.72	0.18	4.54		4.54	4.72	4.73		
7-year	4.78	4.77	0.20	4.57	0.20	4.77	4.97	5.01	0.20	0.23
10-year	4.93	4.90	0.23	4.66	0.50	5.16	5.40	5.53	0.50	0.60
15-year	5.39	5.24	0.23	5.02	0.25	5.27	5.49	5.62	0.25	0.23
20-year	5.72	5.47	0.22	5.25		5.25	5.47	5.54		-0.18
25-year	5.53	5.40	0.22	5.19		5.19	5.40	5.39		-0.14
30-year	5.30	5.30	0.21	5.09		5.09	5.30	5.19		-0.11

the sake of analytical convenience or granularity. In the examples in this book, key treasury rates are defined as 1-, 2-, 3-, 5-, 10-, 20-, and 30-year points on the par curve.

Recall that KRDs are obtained by perturbing the spot curve around certain maturities and computing the percentage changes in the corresponding OAVs. When KRD shocks are applied to the region around each spot key rate, unless a security is forward looking (e.g., CMT cap), only the cash flows and discount rates with maturities that lie in this region are affected. KTRDs, on the other hand, are computed by perturbing a given segment of the par curve. Clearly, any movement of the par (or OTR) curve can be analytically translated into the corresponding change in the spot curve, and vice versa. Table 2.8 illustrates the computation involved in determining the spot curve shock implied by a 10-year KTRD par curve shock. It can be seen that all spot rates with terms greater than 10 years are affected, and all by different amounts. For instance, a 50 basis point change in the 10-year OTR rate will change the 10-year spot rate by more than 50 basis points, and will also change all spot rates with terms greater than 10 years.

The nontrivial connection between par curve shocks and spot curve shocks manifests itself in the complex relationship between KRD and KTRD profiles of fixed income securities (compare Exhibits 2.5 and 2.8). For instance, provided that the maturity of a zero-coupon bond (ZCB) falls exactly on one of the key rates, its KRD profile will be characterized

EXHIBIT 2.8   Key Treasury Rate Duration (KTRD) Profiles of Selected Instruments (as of 9/30/96)

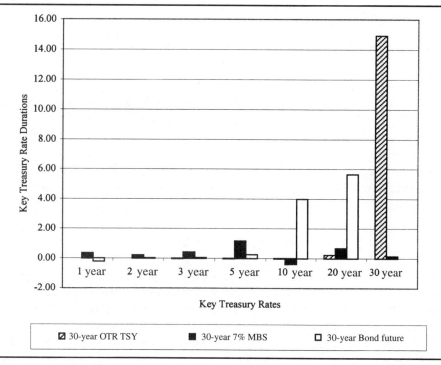

by a single nonzero KRD. On the other hand, KTRD of this zero-coupon bond will be distributed across several key treasury rates. From the KTRD perspective, a 30-year zero coupon bond is a leveraged position in the 30-year coupon-bearing bond financed by short positions in its coupon strips. Conversely, for a 30-year OTR bond whose entire KTRD exposure, as expected, is concentrated in the 30-year bucket, KRD profile is distributed along the entire spot curve (Exhibit 2.5). However, for securities with weighted-average lives less than 10 years, KRD and KTRD methodologies provide very similar results.

Similar to KRDs, KTRDs can be computed directly by changing different segments of the par curve and directly recomputing the resulting OAVs. This is an exact but rather computationally costly procedure. An alternative approach to computing KTRDs derives them analytically from KRDs. This shortcut illustrates the power and flexibility of measuring yield curve risk using KRDs. Section 2.4.1 described how KRDs can be used to approximate price change for a given change in the spot curve (Equation 2.39). Since KTRDs are defined as percentage changes in price resulting from given par curve shocks, and par curve shocks can, in turn, be translated into spot curve shocks (Table 2.8), KTRDs can be derived from KRDs as follows:

$$ktrd_j \approx \frac{\sum_{i=1}^{11} krd_i \cdot \Delta r_{i,j}}{\Delta r} \tag{2.41}$$

where $(\Delta r_{1,j},\ldots,\Delta r_{n,j})$ is the spot curve shock implied by the jth KTRD par curve shock and Δr is the overall magnitude of KTRD shocks (e.g., 50 basis points in Table 2.8). KTRDs of securities in the sample portfolio along with corresponding par curve durations (price sensitivities to parallel changes in the par curve) are presented in Table 2.9. Whether derived from KRDs or computed directly, KTRDs possess all conceptual advantages and disadvantages of KRDs.

2.4.3 Yield Curve Reshaping Durations

KRDs and KTRDs quantify yield curve positioning of fixed income portfolios and securities in an intuitive and visual fashion. Yield curve reshaping durations, short-end duration (SEDUR) and long-end duration (LEDUR), represent a variety of alternative approaches that directly measure the price sensitivity to changes in the slope of the yield curve.[27] As opposed to KRDs and KTRDs that measure first-order exposures to the isolated movements of different segments of the yield curve, yield curve reshaping durations present yield curve risks as summarized measures.

Yield curve reshaping durations are very appealing to portfolio managers and traders because they are explicitly linked to the commonly traded yield curve spreads. SEDUR, which is based on the hypothetical 2-to-10-year steepener in the on-the-run curve, measures the price sensitivity to changes in the shape of the short end of the yield curve. Similar to the option-adjusted measures and scenario analysis, SEDUR can be calculated directly using a valuation model. While keeping OAS constant, OAVs of a position can be recomputed using the following two *static hypothetical* scenarios:

1. The short end of the OTR curve, as measured by the 2-to-10-year spread, steepens by 50 basis points (Exhibit 2.9).
2. The short end of the OTR curve, as measured by the 2-to-10-year spread, flattens by 50 basis points.

Short-end duration (SEDUR) is defined as the percentage change in price, given a 100 basis point 2-to-10-year steepening in the OTR curve:

TABLE 2.9 Key Treasury Rate Duration (KTRD) Report for the Sample Portfolio (as of 12/31/98)

Position Description	Coupon	Maturity	Strike	OAD	OAC	ParCrv Dur	KTRD 1 YR	KTRD 2 YR	KTRD 3 YR	KTRD 5 YR	KTRD 10 YR	KTRD 20 YR	KTRD 30 YR
Treasury Bonds													
TREASURY NOTE (OTR)	4.63	12/31/00		1.89	0.05	1.89		1.89					
TREASURY NOTE (OTR)	4.25	11/15/03		4.32	0.22	4.33		-0.01	0.26	4.08			
TREASURY NOTE (OTR)	4.75	11/15/08		7.76	0.73	7.81			-0.01	0.17	7.65		
TREASURY BOND (OTR)	5.25	11/15/28		14.93	3.34	15.09			-0.01	-0.02	-0.02	0.23	14.91
Agency Bonds													
FHLMC (callable)	6.33	02/13/06		3.25	-0.79	3.26	0.02	0.83	0.53	1.28	0.59		
Futures													
MAR 10YR NOTE FUTURE		03/31/99		5.67	0.38	5.68	-0.23	0.02	0.04	3.69	2.16		
MAR 30YR BOND FUTURE		03/31/99		9.47	0.89	9.75	-0.20	0.02	0.05	0.25	3.98	5.65	
Options													
MAR 10 YR NOTE Put		02/20/99	117	-350.74	925.11	-351.42	14.55	-0.96	-2.59	-228.74	-133.68		
10 YR NOTE FUTURE Call		02/20/99	119	266.42	452.59	266.92	-11.05	0.73	1.97	173.74	101.53		
Interest Rate Swaps													
US Swap	7.24	06/15/11		6.68	0.91	6.82	-0.01	-1.18	-0.78	0.25	6.49	2.05	
Caps & Floors													
6.00 3M LIBOR CAP	6.00	02/19/02		-114.67	95.80	-114.73	32.63	29.31	-168.48	-8.19			
10YR CMT, 5-YR TENOR 6.4%	6.40	06/17/02		50.32	11.26	51.12	-2.10	-2.95	-2.96	-0.09	49.30	9.91	
OTC Derivatives													
Swaption 1	7.25	05/12/00	7.25	-195.71	284.47	-198.64	23.02	12.98	-0.21	-0.56	-200.33	-33.54	
Swaption 2	Float	06/23/99	5.85	148.11	132.62	149.45	-8.60	0.35	0.90	3.71	145.48	7.61	
Non USD Government Securities													
SWEDEN GOVT	10.25	05/05/00		1.23	0.02	1.23	0.80	0.43					
JGB BD 174 (10 YR)	4.60	09/20/04		5.18	0.31	5.18	-0.04	-0.04	-0.02	4.51	0.76		
UK TREASURY	9.00	10/13/08		6.91	0.61	6.96	0.02	0.03	0.09	0.68	6.13		
CANADA GOVT	5.75	06/01/29		14.78	3.30	14.95				-0.02	0.04	0.60	14.34
Generic Pass-Throughs													
FGOLD 30YR	7.00	12/31/28		2.52	-2.59	2.55	0.34	0.20	0.41	1.16	-0.38	0.67	0.14
FGOLD 30YR	8.00	12/31/28		1.85	-1.32	1.86	0.29	0.21	0.39	0.94	-0.37	0.34	0.06
GNMA Construction Loans													
FHA CREEKWOOD GN/GN	7.30	11/30/38		3.57	-1.13	3.61	0.01	0.01	0.04	0.16	2.91	0.48	

(continues)

TABLE 2.9 Continued

Position / Description	Coupon	Maturity	Strike	OAD	OAC	ParCrv Dur	KTRD 1 YR	KTRD 2 YR	KTRD 3 YR	KTRD 5 YR	KTRD 10 YR	KTRD 20 YR	KTRD 30 YR
Non-Agency CMBS													
DLJMA_96-CF1 B1 144A	8.27	01/12/08		4.41	-0.54	4.42	0.02	0.04	0.12	2.16	2.07		
Inverse Floating Rate Mortgages													
CMOT13 Q	15.55	01/20/03		2.83	0.16	2.83	1.22	1.41	0.39				
POs-Agency													
FNSTR_267 (FN 8.50)		10/01/24		7.95	-4.02	7.97	0.02	0.13	0.12	0.34	5.21	1.95	0.31
IOs-Agency													
FHLMC_2043 (FG 7.00)	7.00	01/15/16		-45.94	-20.82	-46.69	3.28	0.38	0.24	1.12	-41.57	-10.13	-0.01
CMO Sequentials-Agency													
FNMA_93-178 (FN 7.00)	5.25	09/25/23		0.22	0.00	0.22	0.22						
Corporates - Finance													
BANKAMERICA CAPITAL II	8.00	12/15/26	Vary	8.72	0.05	8.91	0.02	0.04	0.09	0.97	2.53	2.89	2.38
Corporates - Industrial													
PROCTER & GAMBLE COMPANY (THE)	8.00	10/26/29	100	12.84	2.67	13.02	0.01	0.02	0.04	0.18	0.70	1.22	10.85
Asset Backed - Prepay Sensitive													
CONHE_97-5 (Home Equity)	6.58	06/15/19		2.27	-1.00	2.27	0.02	0.35	1.67	0.23			
Asset Backed - Non-Prepay Sensitive													
CHVAT_98-2 (Auto)	5.91	12/15/04		1.47	0.04	1.47	0.36	0.47	0.55	0.10			
Total Assets	**7.02**			**6.82**	**0.81**	**6.90**	**0.13**	**0.24**	**0.16**	**1.00**	**2.44**	**0.83**	**2.10**

EXHIBIT 2.9   SEDUR Shock Applied to OTR Curve (as of 9/30/96)

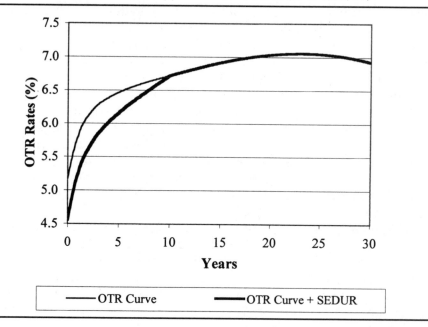

$$SEDUR = \frac{1}{P} \frac{P_{SEDUR,down} - P_{SEDUR,up}}{2 \cdot 0.5} \tag{2.42}$$

where $P_{SEDUR,down}$ and $P_{SEDUR,up}$ denote OAVs resulting from the steepening and flattening of the OTR curve, respectively. For instance, suppose SEDUR of a portfolio is 2.0 years, and SEDUR of its benchmark is 1.0 year. If the 2-to-10-year OTR spread steepens (widens) by 10 basis points, the portfolio will outperform its benchmark by $(2.0-1.0) \cdot 10 = 10$ basis points.

Long-end duration (LEDUR) measures the price sensitivity to changes in the shape of the long end of the yield curve. It is based on the hypothetical scenario of the 10-to-30-year steepening in the OTR curve. Computation of LEDUR within the OAS model framework is conceptually identical to that of SEDUR.

When approximating price changes resulting from relatively small yield curve shocks, KRDs provide an accurate and computationally less burdensome alternative (Equation 2.39) to computing OAVs directly. Similar to KTRDs that can be derived analytically using KRDs and the corresponding spot curve shocks, short-end and long-end durations can be derived from KRD and the appropriate spot curve shocks as well. Writing the analogs of Equation 2.41 for SEDUR and LEDUR is left to the reader.

Fixed income portfolio managers sometimes conceptually separate their duration bets from yield curve bets because decisions to lengthen or shorten a portfolio's duration relative to its benchmark versus decisions to implement yield curve steepeners or flatteners can be driven by different economic considerations and even executed by different traders. Unfortunately, without using analytical techniques (e.g., performance attribution methods, principal components decompositions, etc.), determining whether risks and subsequent returns were due to duration bets or yield curve bets can be difficult. A simple approach to solving this problem involves the construction of *duration-neutral* yield curve shocks that attempt to distinguish between duration bets and yield curve bets.[28]

The interest rate shocks used by SEDUR and LEDUR are not duration-neutral. This can be best illustrated using the following example. Suppose that a portfolio is long duration relative to its benchmark, and that this duration bet is implemented by buying 3- and 5-year bullet securities. Let us assume that in addition to the duration bet, the portfolio is positioned to have a short-end yield curve steepener relative to its benchmark. Recall that the SEDUR shock implies that the par yields of all maturities less than 10 years decline, while the yield curve steepens at the same time. Due to the interaction between duration and yield curve bets, if SEDUR of this portfolio relative to its benchmark is measured, it would come out to be a large positive number, indicating that the portfolio is positioned for a very large steepener. Clearly, SEDUR cannot separate duration bets from yield curve bets.

Visually, a *duration-neutral* yield curve shock is a change in the slope of the yield curve that can also be described as a twist or rotation of a portion of the yield curve around a duration-neutral focal point. Thus, duration-neutral shocks run *through* a yield curve as opposed to being positioned entirely above or below it (Exhibit 2.10). In order to differentiate between duration and yield curve bets, SEDUR and LEDUR shocks can be modified to be (somewhat arbitrarily) duration-neutral. Hence, as opposed to being below the yield curve as shown in the left-hand panel of Exhibit 2.10, SEDUR can cross the yield curve at the duration-neutral point (right-hand panel, Exhibit 2.10). Although still a rather ad hoc approach, this modification seems to isolate the portfolio's duration bet and focus on the exposure associated with changes in yield curve slope.

In addition to SEDUR and LEDUR, duration-neutral hypothetical interest rate shocks (0/2, 2/10, and 10/30), linked to the commonly

EXHIBIT 2.10 Duration Neutrality of Hypothetical Interest Rate Shocks

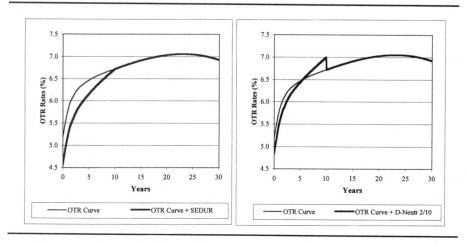

traded yield curve spreads, can be used in measuring yield curve risks (Table 2.1). Unfortunately, while simple and intuitively appealing, these static interest rate shocks are not characteristic of the empirically observed yield curve movements. In fact, constructing interest rate shocks that are intuitive and historically plausible at the same time is generally difficult. In Chapter 3, we introduce approaches to measuring historical plausibility of hypothetical interest rate shocks. Note that KRDs can be used in approximating returns due to hypothetical interest rate scenarios (Equation 2.39). They can therefore assist in stress testing, which is simply the deterministic measurement of potential losses associated with specific events. Hypothetical interest rate shocks constitute a special case of stress testing when the set of systematic risks is limited to interest rates. This subject will be discussed in its generality in Chapter 5.

KTRDs and yield curve reshaping durations provide, for some, more intuitive, user-friendly measures of yield curve risk. In general, many measures of risk, while providing conceptually similar information, resonate differently with different market participants. The goal of risk management is to mitigate and control risk. Risk management professionals are paid to understand the way decision makers (portfolio managers, traders, and other practitioners) think about the market and to develop risk measures that assist them in the day-to-day challenges of their work. Any conceptually viable approach that positively helps in achieving this goal is, by definition, the best alternative.

2.5 MEASURING BASIS RISKS

2.5.1 Volatility Duration

The recently renewed attention to measuring and explicitly managing risk associated with changes in implied volatility is not at all surprising. Considering that valuation of many derivative securities greatly depends on the assumed future volatility of interest rates and other risk factors, measuring *volatility duration,* the first-order price sensitivity to changes in implied volatility, is crucial. Readers familiar with derivative markets and option pricing theory will notice that the concept of volatility duration is not new and is a slight transformation of option *vega.*

Similar to other duration measures, volatility duration of interest rate derivatives valued via the Black-Scholes formula can be computed analytically. For fixed income securities with more complex types of cash flow uncertainties, volatility duration is typically estimated numerically within the OAS model framework via the usual partial duration formula:

$$Vol\ Dur = -\frac{1}{P}\frac{P_{\text{vol up}} - P_{\text{vol down}}}{2 \cdot \Delta vol} \tag{2.43}$$

Volatility durations of securities in the sample portfolios are presented in Tables 2.1 and 2.5. Since the value of an option increases with a rise in implied volatility, fixed income securities with embedded long options (e.g., options on futures, swaptions, caps, and floors) have by convention negative volatility durations, while securities with embedded short options (MBSs, callable corporates and agencies) have positive volatility durations. As expected, the more leveraged the embedded option is, the larger the price sensitivity is to changes in implied volatility. Volatility duration is also linked to the in-the-moneyness of the option embedded in a security. Thus, among comparable options on the same index and of the same maturity, the at-the-money (ATM) option has the largest volatility duration (exposure to misestimated as well as changing implied volatility) whereas deep in-the-money (ITM) and deep out-of-the-money (OTM) options have volatility durations that are very small. However, comparing volatility durations of options of different maturities can be misleading since the volatility duration of a short-term ATM option may be substantially smaller in magnitude than that of a long-term ITM or OTM option. Note a common misperception of the connection between positive volatility duration (resulting from an embedded short option) and negative convexity. While embedded short options often do cause fixed income securities to become negatively convex, it is not true that all negatively convex securities have embedded short options. For instance, premium-priced CMBSs (that are effectively prepayment protected) exhibit price compression as their prices rise. Hence, they are characterized by negative convexity but have no exposure to implied volatility whatsoever.

Computation of $P_{\text{vol up}}$ and $P_{\text{vol down}}$ in the implied volatility formula (Equation 2.43) depends on the valuation model. More precisely, volatility duration calculation is dictated by the extent to which the utilized interest rate model captures the term structure of volatility (TSOV). If an interest rate model (e.g., Black-Derman-Toy) is not calibrated to the derivatives market and requires a fixed implied volatility assumption, $P_{\text{vol up}}$ and $P_{\text{vol down}}$ are computed by shocking the user-specified implied volatility number by a small number of basis points and revaluing the security directly.

Interest rate models that incorporate the term structure of volatility (e.g., Black-Karasinski) enable more elaborate exploration of the price sensitivity with respect to changes in implied volatility. After the TSOV is derived from the interest rate derivatives' markets, the simplest approach to computing volatility duration entails shocking the entire term structure of volatility in a parallel fashion and computing $P_{\text{vol up}}$ and $P_{\text{vol down}}$. Notice the direct similarity to OAD. A more accurate approach to measuring volatility duration does not utilize the term structure of volatility, a theoretical and unobservable construct, but deals directly with the interest rate derivatives underlying the derivation of TSOV. Instead of shocking TSOV in a parallel fashion, implied volatilities of derivative securities used in the calibration are shocked up and down by a given number of basis points. The term structure of volatility is then reestimated, and finally $P_{\text{vol up}}$ and $P_{\text{vol down}}$ are directly recomputed by a valuation model.

Volatility duration is computed within the option-adjusted framework, and therefore all traditional advantages and disadvantages of partial duration measures apply. To that matter, volatility duration estimates are sensitive to the size of the volatility shock, volatility convexities may not be stable over time, and no relationship is assumed between changes in implied volatility and changes in OAS, which may not be the case in certain market environments. If shocking the term structure of volatility in a parallel fashion is insufficient, volatility KRDs can be computed to explore price sensitivities to the various parts of the volatility surface in isolation.

2.5.2 Spread Duration

The credit and liquidity crisis of 1998 yet again demonstrated the extreme importance of measuring the risk associated with systematic movements of credit spreads. As discussed in Section 2.2.2, credit spreads (as measured by option-adjusted spreads or nominal spreads) comprise several components, including the market's sentiment toward credit risk in general; asset class-, issuer-, and individual security-specific credit risk; various supply-and-demand factors; and valuation model inaccuracies. For instance, swap spreads reflect the price of interbank credit risk as well as numerous technical considerations, whereas mortgage option-adjusted spreads reflect the market's sentiment toward different aspects of systematic mortgage risks as well as uncertainty with respect to modeling prepayments and implied volatility. Traditional formulations of spread duration for MBS typically assume that changes in mortgage OASs do not cause prepayments, isolating discounting risk from prepayment risk. In Chapter 4, we analyze the validity of this assumption in detail and propose an alternative.

Spread duration measures the price sensitivity of fixed income securities to changes in credit spreads. Some practitioners interpret it as the price sensitivity to changes in discount factors, and others see it as the price sensitivity to changes in the market sentiment toward the risk of holding a particular asset class or individual security. Spread duration is computed in the exactly same manner as other option-adjusted partial durations:

$$Spd\ Dur = -\frac{1}{P}\frac{P_{\text{spread up}} - P_{\text{spread down}}}{2 \cdot \Delta s} \tag{2.44}$$

where $P_{\text{spread up}}$ and $P_{\text{spread down}}$ are computed by shocking the credit spread of a security by a small number of basis points (Δs) and computing the corresponding OAVs using a valuation model. Spread durations of securities in the sample portfolios are presented in Tables 2.1 and 2.5.

The definition of the term *spread* used to compute spread duration in Equation 2.44 is asset-class specific. For fixed income instruments that trade at a spread above a U.S. Treasury benchmark (option-free fixed rate corporate bonds, CMBS, ABS, high yield, etc.) *spread* is typically defined as the nominal credit spread (the difference between yield-to-maturity of an instrument and that of its Treasury benchmark). For option-bearing securities valued on the U.S. Treasury curve (MBSs and their derivatives, callable corporate and agency bonds, etc.) *spread* is defined as OAS. For interest rate swaps and their derivatives, *spread* is defined as swap spread. For Brady bonds, *spread* is defined as stripped spread. Sometimes market participants choose to calculate spread duration even on U.S. Treasury securities. In this context, spread duration measures the price sensitivity to changes in liquidity premiums (OASs) of the U.S. Treasury market.

For a fixed income security with deterministic cash flows, spread duration is typically close in value to OAD since shocking nominal spread or OAS is virtually equivalent to shocking the spot curve in a parallel fashion. The slight discrepancy between the two measures in these cases is generally caused by the different market conventions with respect to magnitude and compounding of the shocks utilized in option-adjusted duration versus spread duration calculations. Conversely, for fixed income securities with cash flow uncertainties (e.g., adjustable rate mortgages, floating rate notes, structured notes, IO, PO, etc.), spread durations may be substantially different from OADs. While spread duration estimates the price sensitivity to changes in discounting alone, OAD measures the simultaneous price sensitivity to changes in discounting as well as changes in cash flows due to interest rate movements.

Similar to other partial duration measures, it is a common practice to compute spread duration of a fixed income portfolio as a weighted average of spread durations of the individual securities without questioning the meaning of this aggregate measure. However, the similarity of spread duration to other partial durations is deceiving. As opposed to OADs, KRDs, and other parametric gauges that measure price sensitivity to systematic risk factors that are *universally* applicable to *all* fixed income securities, spread duration measures the exposure to risk factors that are partially systematic and partially idiosyncratic (asset class, issuer-, or security-specific). For instance, the value of a portfolio invested in U.S. Treasuries, swaps, and MBSs is sensitive to changes in a variety of basis risks: liquidity premiums of the U.S. Treasury market, swap spreads, and mortgage spreads, etc. Since these risk factors are not perfectly correlated and may exhibit drastically different volatilities, exposures to them must be managed separately rather than aggregated into a summarized number. This fact complicates the task of managing credit spread risk of fixed income portfolios. In Chapter 4, we present approaches to properly managing credit spread risk within Value-at-Risk (VaR) and generalized duration frameworks.

2.6 MEASURING MORTGAGE-RELATED RISKS

In this section, we digress from describing approaches dealing with universal risk factors and focus on systematic sources of market risk that are specific to mortgage backed securities (MBSs) and their derivatives. Given the fact that these instruments form the second largest fixed income market in the world, their unique characteristics merit special attention. Several approaches exist for measuring the exposure of portfolios and securities to prepayments and other mortgage-related risks. Similar to the measures of interest rate and yield curve risk described earlier in this chapter, all of these methods utilize partial durations to estimate the first-order price sensitivity to a given risk factor in isolation, while holding other variables unchanged.

2.6.1 Prepayment Duration

The homeowner's decision to prepay is typically influenced by various economic and borrower-specific variables and considerations, including the state of the domestic economy, prevailing mortgage origination rates, unemployment rates, the borrower's mortgage rate, credit card debt, age, profession, education, tax bracket, marital status, and the like. Given that econometric prepayment models attempt to model ultimately the sum of the individual decisions by millions of consumers, it is not surprising that they often fail to accurately predict the homeowner's prepayment behavior. Since fair values and risk measures of MBSs and their derivatives depend on prepayment models or assumed static vectors of prepayment speeds, the accuracy of these analytical methodologies is subject to the model risk that forecasts of future prepayments are *systematically* wrong.

Prepayment duration measures the risk associated with prepayment speeds being systematically slower or faster than those predicted by the user-specified or econometric prepayment model. Computed within the option-adjusted framework, prepayment duration is obtained via the standard duration formula:

$$Prepay\ Dur = -\frac{1}{P} \frac{P_{\text{speeds up}} - P_{\text{speeds down}}}{2 \cdot \Delta speeds} \tag{2.45}$$

where $P_{\text{speeds up}}$ and $P_{\text{speeds down}}$ require an agreed upon prepayment shock ($\Delta speeds$). One simple approach to computing prepayment duration is to scale the output of a prepayment model up and down by 25% and directly recompute the corresponding OAVs. Prepayment durations of generic 30-year MBSs are presented in Table 2.5. For example, prepayment duration of 30-year 8% FHLMC MBS is 1.47, implying that if prepayment speeds turn out to be twice as fast as those predicted by the model, this security is expected to lose 1.47% of its value. Faster prepayment speeds negatively impact premium and positively impact discount MBSs. The first part of this statement is consistent with Table 2.5, which shows that on 12/31/98, all premium MBSs have positive prepayment durations. It may seem counterintuitive that prepayment duration of the only discount MBS coupon (6%) is slightly positive rather than negative. This phenomenon can be explained by closely examining the Monte-Carlo simulation model used in computing OAVs of MBSs. Recall that the fair value of an MBS is computed by creating a large number of hypothetical interest rate paths. For each path, cash flows are generated using a prepayment model and subsequently discounted on the appropriate (path-specific) spot curve. OAV is the average of all pathwise prices. While almost all pathwise prices of premium mortgages are above par (implying negative sensitivity to prepayments), some of the pathwise prices of discount mortgages are positive and some are negative. This asymmetry results in prepayment duration being sometimes slightly positive for discount MBS coupons. Prepayment durations of all conventional 30-year 5.5% MBSs on that day (not shown) were in fact negative, confirming our intuition.[29]

2.6.2 Mortgage/Treasury Basis Duration

Mortgage/treasury basis (MTB) duration uses a different approach to measuring prepayment risk. As opposed to prepayment duration that estimates the first-order price sensitivity to changes in prepayment speeds as predicted by a prepayment model, MTB duration addresses the borrower's decision to prepay directly. MTB duration estimates the price sensitivity of MBSs to changes in one of the most influential causes of prepayments – the refinancing incentive measured as the spread between the current mortgage origination rate and the 10-year OTR Treasury rate. Description of prepayment risk in terms of spreads to Treasury rates as opposed to nominal mortgage origination rates is due to technical rather than conceptual reasons. Since MTB is an input to many of the existing econometric prepayment models, it is natural to use it in defining the prepayment sensitivity. Note that when practitioners discuss changes in mortgage spreads, they often implicitly refer to the simultaneous occurrence of two interconnected but not perfectly correlated phenomena: changes in nominal mortgage spreads and changes in mortgage OASs. MTB duration addresses the former phenomenon by measuring the price sensitivity to changes in nominal mortgage spreads. Spread duration deals with the latter type of mortgage risk by estimating the price sensitivity to changes in OASs. In Chapter 4, we study the relationship among changes in nominal and option-adjusted mortgage spreads in detail.

Formally, MTB is defined as the spread between the par coupon yield of a conventional (FNMA or FHLMC) MBS and that of the 10-year on-the-run TSY. Par coupon yield is the yield of a theoretical MBS priced at parity. Parity, in turn, is the price that implies the same yield regardless of prepayments while accounting for the MBS payment delay. MTB duration is computed by shifting this spread up and down by a small number of basis points and calculating the negative of the percentage change in price, given a 100 basis point change in the mortgage/treasury basis:

$$MTB\ Dur = -\frac{1}{P} \frac{P_{\text{MTB up}} - P_{\text{MTB down}}}{2 \cdot \Delta MTB} \tag{2.46}$$

MTB durations of 30-year generic MBSs are presented in Table 2.5.

It may seem counterintuitive that, as opposed to prepayment durations, which switch the sign approximately near the par coupon mortgage, MTB durations of both premium and discount securities are substantially negative (Table 2.5). This analytical result, which seems inconsistent with the theory that faster prepayment speeds negatively impact premium and positively impact discount MBSs, can be explained by exactly the same analysis of Monte-Carlo simulation of interest rate processes as described in Section 2.6.1. The dissimilarity between the two prepayment-related measures of risk (MTB duration is more asymmetric than prepayment duration) is due to prepayment duration capturing both the refinancing incentive and prepayments due to housing turnover, whereas MTB duration only addresses the former component. In addition to that, prepayment speeds are shocked directly in the prepayment duration calculation, whereas they are shocked indirectly when MTB is perturbed. The combination of these two effects results in the nonlinear and asymmetric price sensitivity to prepayments. More specifically, MTB duration becomes positive only for discount MBSs whose prepayment options are extremely deep out-of-the-money.

2.7 MEASURING IMPACT OF TIME

Changes in prices of fixed income securities due to their evolution through time $\left(\dfrac{\partial P}{\partial t} \right)$ can be measured within the expected rate of return (EROR) framework. As an explicit gauge of *ex ante* total return, EROR is a rare example of a methodology equally advantageous for portfolio management, risk management, and trading. The art of active portfolio management lies in finding optimal trade-offs between risk, return, and various market- and portfolio-specific constraints. As seen from the description of the different risk measures earlier in this chapter, the *risk* aspect of investment decisions is typically approached from a very quantitative angle. Conversely, methods that assess the expected return are usually qualitative in nature and are based on the trader's experience and intuition rather than financial models. In trading, expected rate of return can be combined with subjective judgments about richness and cheapness of individual securities or entire sectors when making relative value decisions. In risk management, EROR enables incorporating evolution of securities through time into Value-at-Risk (VaR, Chapter 5) and can also be effectively used in hedge optimizations (Chapter 6).

EROR analysis is representative of many fixed income risk management methodologies which despite being conceptually and theoretically straightforward, are computationally expensive and difficult to implement in practice. The idea behind EROR is simple. When holding a security over a specified *horizon*, its total return is solely determined by:

- Its current market value
- Its fair value at the horizon date
- The future value of cash flows that are generated by this security over the holding period and are subject to reinvestment

EROR is computed using the following formula:

$$EROR = \frac{MV_{\text{horizon}} - MV_{\text{today}} + Future\ Value\ of\ Cash\ Flows\ at\ Horizon}{MV_{\text{today}}} \qquad (2.47)$$

where MV denotes market value.

Despite its seeming "objectivity," EROR incorporates a great deal of subjective judgement and views on the market. It is also sensitive to interest rate and prepayment models used to compute the fair value of a security. Let us examine the assumptions underlying the EROR analysis in detail. To determine the fair market value ($MV_{horizon}$) of security at the horizon (Equation 2.47), the future economic environment, including yield curves, mortgage rates, implied volatilities, an so forth, must be specified, reflecting the user's intuition and views on the market. There are three alternative formulations of EROR – *forward, constant,* and *hypothetical.* The *forward* approach uses the *pure expectation hypothesis* to assume that interest rates between the valuation date and the horizon date evolve as predicted by forward rates. The *constant* method presumes that the economic environment at the horizon is exactly the same as it is today. While the *forward* approach is consistent with the assumption used by the vast majority of valuation models, empirical analyses of historical interest rate movements support the *constant* assumption rather than the pure expectation hypothesis.[30] Various theoretical models (e.g., Heath-Jarrow-Morton [HJM]) validate this empirical finding as well, demonstrating theoretically that the conjecture that forward rates are unbiased estimates of future spot rates is generally false. Without going into further detail, it suffices to note that when faced with the choice between the two assumptions, the majority of practitioners prefers the *constant* assumption to the *forward* one. Besides being more historically plausible, the *constant* assumption is very useful and intuitive for traders because it measures the return of securities associated with aging or "rolling down the yield curve." Finally, the *hypothetical* approach – a way for portfolio managers to explore various what-if market scenarios and their impact on total return – can be thought of as a generalized form of scenario analysis. Thus, in addition to measuring impact of time, evolution of credit spreads, interest rates, prepayments, implied volatilities, and other risk factors between the valuation date and the horizon date can be hypothesized, and the combined effect on price can be measured.

Once the economic environment at the horizon is determined, the path according to which the economy evolves between the date of the analysis and the horizon date needs to be specified. Despite its seeming simplicity, this is not a trivial exercise. However, this step is crucial because values of path-dependent securities as well as values of reinvested cash flows depend on the evolution of interest rates between the valuation date and the horizon. This path has to also be consistent with the assumed economic environment at the horizon. For instance, the following EROR scenario:

- At the horizon, interest rates are 100 basis points higher than they are on the valuation date
- Between the valuation and the horizon dates, interest rates evolve according to forward rates

will be inconsistent unless forward rates imply that spot rates are exactly 100 basis points higher at the horizon than they are today. EROR scenario analysis of securities in the sample portfolio is presented in Table 2.10.

EROR scenario analysis has clear advantages over the traditional, *instantaneous* scenario analysis. While both approaches provide accurate and comparable results for securities with embedded longer-term options, analysis of instantaneous sensitivities to changes in risk factors can create material financial illusions when applied to instruments with embedded shorter-term options (which are characterized by rapid decay).[31] The ability to capture the cost of carry as well as the time-dependent nature of risk characteristics can provide valuable insights into the price behavior of fixed income securities. Table 2.11 presents OAV of a (6-months + 1-day) call option on a 10-year interest rate swap as a function of both parallel changes in spot rates and time. As the swaption approaches its expiration, the decline in its base OAV *(negative carry)* reflects the progressively smaller probability of significant interest rate movements between the horizon date and the expiration date, and, hence, a lower upside of holding this security. Thus, with six months until expiration, gains corresponding to a sudden 25 basis point decline in interest rates are greater in magnitude than losses corresponding to a 25 basis point rise in interest rates. At this time, the probability of interest rates moving in either direction by 25 basis points or more is approximately 67% (Table 2.12).[32] However, with only one month until the expiration, the negative carry makes the total loss associated with an adverse 25 basis point movement in spot rates almost five times greater than the total gain associated with a comparable favorable interest rate move. The probability of interest rates moving in either direction by 25 basis points or more at that time is only 29%.

TABLE 2.10 EROR Scenario Analysis for the Sample Portfolio (as of 12/31/98)

Position Description	Coupon	Maturity	Strike	EROR Scenario Analysis (% per year)										
				-200	-150	-100	-50	-25	0	25	50	100	150	200
Treasury Bonds														
TREASURY NOTE (OTR)	4.63	12/31/00		6.54	6.04	5.55	5.06	4.81	4.57	4.33	4.09	3.61	3.13	2.66
TREASURY NOTE (OTR)	4.25	11/15/03		11.99	10.09	8.24	6.42	5.53	4.64	3.77	2.90	1.20	-0.47	-2.11
TREASURY NOTE (OTR)	4.75	11/15/08		20.66	16.50	12.52	8.71	6.86	5.05	3.28	1.55	-1.80	-5.02	-8.10
TREASURY BOND (OTR)	5.25	11/15/28		41.98	31.12	21.44	12.79	8.81	5.05	1.49	-1.89	-8.12	-13.73	-18.78
Agency Bonds														
FHLMC (collable)	6.33	02/13/06		8.57	8.01	7.39	6.63	6.16	5.65	5.06	4.41	2.94	1.29	-0.48
Futures														
MAR 10YR NOTE FUTURE		03/31/99		50.32	36.52	23.56	11.37	5.54	-0.10	-5.58	-10.89	-21.04	-30.60	-39.60
MAR 30YR BOND FUTURE		03/31/99		104.81	73.59	45.94	21.40	10.18	-0.39	-10.58	-20.61	-39.32	-57.12	-73.70
Options														
MAR 10 YR NOTE Put		02/20/99	117	-100.00	-100.00	-100.00	-100.00	-100.00	-100.00	-100.00	108.35	409.58	599.61	748.32
10 YR NOTE FUTURE Call		02/20/99	119	465.29	372.27	264.93	129.38	36.64	-100.00	-100.00	-100.00	-100.00	-100.00	-100.00
Interest Rate Swaps														
US Swap	7.24	06/15/11		16.94	12.64	8.58	4.75	2.92	1.14	-0.59	-2.26	-5.47	-8.50	-11.35
Caps & Floors														
6.00 3M LIBOR CAP	6.00	02/19/02		-100.00	-100.00	-99.97	-98.81	-95.08	-83.69	-55.22	5.07	324.55	1204.89	2377.74
10YR CMT, 5-YR TENOR 6.4%	6.40	06/17/02		132.27	102.14	72.29	42.73	28.08	13.56	-0.75	-14.73	-40.86	-62.48	-76.32
OTC Derivatives														
Swaption 1	7.25	05/12/00	7.25	-100.00	-100.00	-100.00	-100.00	-100.00	-100.00	-99.92	-98.20	67.97	2600.97	12860.50
Swaption 2	Float	06/23/99	5.85	614.49	448.43	290.01	138.84	65.87	89.14	-75.09	-100.00	-100.00	-100.00	-100.00
Non USD Government Securities														
SWEDEN GOVT	10.25	05/05/00		4.28	4.12	3.95	3.79	3.71	3.63	3.55	3.47	3.31	3.16	3.00
JGB BD 174 (10 YR)	4.60	09/20/04		11.38	9.10	6.87	4.70	3.63	2.58	1.54	0.51	-1.51	-3.47	-5.39
UK TREASURY	9.00	10/13/08		17.98	14.36	10.89	7.56	5.95	4.37	2.82	1.30	-1.65	-4.48	-7.19
CANADA GOVT	5.75	06/01/29		41.83	31.07	21.47	12.89	8.95	5.22	1.69	-1.66	-7.84	-13.40	-18.42

	Coupon	Date												
Generic Pass-Throughs														
FGOLD 30YR	7.00	12/31/28		6.47	6.43	6.53	6.72	6.86	6.64	6.21	5.58	3.90	1.90	-0.32
FGOLD 30YR	8.00	12/31/28		7.06	6.89	6.76	6.57	6.62	6.45	6.20	5.82	4.64	3.13	1.38
GNMA Construction Loans														
FHA CREEKWOOD GN/GN	7.30	11/30/38		34.98	26.83	19.51	12.90	9.84	6.92	4.15	1.50	-3.42	-7.91	-12.02
Non-Agency CMBS														
DLJMA_96-CF1 B1 144A	8.27	01/12/08		18.40	15.61	12.90	10.28	9.01	7.75	6.51	5.29	2.91	0.60	-1.64
Inverse Floating Rate Mortgages														
CMOT13 Q	15.55	01/20/03		13.04	12.19	11.33	10.48	10.05	8.31	9.20	8.81	7.99	7.13	6.26
POs-Agency														
FNSTR_267 (FN 8.50)		10/01/24		12.14	11.11	9.69	7.79	6.19	4.84	3.24	1.42	-2.45	-6.49	-10.26
IOs-Agency														
FHLMC_2043 (FG 7.00)	7.00	01/15/16		-51.48	-48.70	-40.81	-17.94	5.37	17.23	33.47	43.13	54.02	59.66	62.63
CMO Sequentials-Agency														
FNMA_93-178 (FN 7.00)	5.25	09/25/23		5.39	5.39	5.39	5.39	5.39	5.39	5.39	5.39	5.39	5.39	5.39
Corporates - Finance														
BANKAMERICA CAPITAL II	8.00	12/15/26	Vary	21.43	17.98	14.36	10.57	8.61	6.62	4.60	2.57	-1.48	-5.48	-9.35
Corporates - Industrial														
PROCTER & GAMBLE COMPANY	8.00	10/26/29	100	37.64	28.49	20.28	12.90	9.48	6.24	3.16	0.22	-5.22	-10.16	-14.64
Asset Backed - Prepay Sensitive														
CONHE_97-5 (Home Equity)	6.58	06/15/19		10.12	9.16	8.22	7.28	6.82	6.36	5.90	5.45	4.55	3.66	2.78
Asset Backed - Non-Prepay Sensitive														
CHVAT_98-2 (Auto)	5.91	12/15/04		7.09	6.71	6.33	5.96	5.77	5.59	5.40	5.22	4.86	4.50	4.15
Total Assets				**29.08**	**22.42**	**16.33**	**10.82**	**8.31**	**5.80**	**3.35**	**1.08**	**-3.24**	**-6.87**	**-8.91**

TABLE 2.11 EROR Scenario Analysis of a 6.83% (6-months + 1-day) × 10-year Call Swaption (as of 11/8/99)*

Option-Adjusted Value (Thousands of Dollars)

Time To Expiration	-200	-150	-100	-50	-25	0	25	50	100	150	200
6 Months + 1 day	15,233	11,118	7,322	4,138	2,896	1,923	1,209	720	217	54	11
5 Months + 1 day	15,439	11,301	7,440	4,137	2,838	1,827	1,101	620	161	33	6
4 Months + 1 day	15,545	11,389	7,475	4,055	2,700	1,660	937	484	99	15	2
3 Months + 1 day	15,699	11,527	7,568	4,012	2,576	1,486	762	345	49	5	1
2 Months + 1 day	15,871	11,685	7,697	4,005	2,460	1,298	573	209	16	1	0
1 Month + 1 day	16,026	11,828	7,821	4,015	2,303	1,005	304	60	1	0	0
1 day	16,213	12,001	7,979	4,137	2,281	486	0	0	0	0	0

Changes in Option-Adjusted Value (Thousands of Dollars)

Time To Expiration	-200	-150	-100	-50	-25	0	25	50	100	150	200
6 Months + 1 day	13,310	9,195	5,399	2,215	973	0	-714	-1,203	-1,706	-1,869	-1,912
5 Months + 1 day	13,516	9,378	5,517	2,214	915	-96	-822	-1,303	-1,762	-1,890	-1,917
4 Months + 1 day	13,622	9,466	5,552	2,132	777	-263	-986	-1,439	-1,824	-1,908	-1,921
3 Months + 1 day	13,776	9,604	5,645	2,089	653	-437	-1,161	-1,578	-1,874	-1,918	-1,922
2 Months + 1 day	13,948	9,762	5,774	2,082	537	-625	-1,350	-1,714	-1,907	-1,922	-1,923
1 Month + 1 day	14,103	9,905	5,898	2,092	380	-918	-1,619	-1,863	-1,922	-1,923	-1,923
1 day	14,290	10,078	6,056	2,214	358	-1,437	-1,923	-1,923	-1,923	-1,923	-1,923

* Notional Value = 100 Million Dollars

TABLE 2.12 Interest Rate Shocks Exceeding Given Thresholds: Cumulative Probability as a Function of Time (as of 11/8/99)

Time To Expiration	Parallel Spot Curve Shock (basis points)				
	+/-25	+/-50	+/-100	+/-150	+/-200
1 year	76.05%	54.20%	22.26%	6.74%	1.47%
6 months	66.64%	38.85%	8.46%	0.97%	0.06%
3 months	54.20%	22.26%	1.47%	0.03%	0.00%
2 months	45.52%	13.53%	0.28%	0.00%	0.00%
1 month	29.09%	3.47%	0.00%	0.00%	0.00%
1 week	2.88%	0.00%	0.00%	0.00%	0.00%

ENDNOTES

1. *Interest rates* can be defined in many different ways, including yields-to-maturity (if they can be meaningfully computed), parallel movements of the term structure of spot rates, etc. For the purposes of this discussion, price dependencies on parallel changes in interest rates are used to illustrate the shapes of price/yield functions.
2. See Macaulay, 1938, and Weil, 1973.
3. See Fabozzi, 1988.
4. In this book, the terms *price volatility* and *volatility of prices* are used interchangeably.
5. This interesting observation was pointed to us by our colleague Irwin Sheer.
6. It has become customary to say "10 years" when referring to duration of 10. It is due to the fact that the first measure of duration, Macaulay duration, was interpreted as the present value-weighted *term-to-maturity.*
7. For an excellent review of different types of yield curves, see Ilmanen, 1995, and Anderson et al., 1997.
8. Zero volatility spread is a special case of OAS discussed in detail in Section 2.2.2. The abbreviation ZVO is due to the fact that zero volatility spread is often referred to as *zero volatility option-adjusted spread.*
9. For an overview of OAS models, the reader is referred to the chapter by Audey et al., 1995, as well as Chapters 29 and 30 in Fabozzi, 1995a.
10. See Black and Scholes, 1973.
11. See Kao, 1999.
12. This purely technical phenomenon is due to the widely used practice of hedging the primary issuance of spread products with on-the-run Treasury securities as well as to the use of OTR TSY in implementing directional interest rate bets.
13. Throughout the book, unless stated otherwise, OASs are assumed to be continuously compounded and computed off of spot curves. Note that OAS numbers are sensitive to the methods by which spot curves are constructed as well as to the compounding conventions.

14. Since PO securities are essentially long the prepayment option, their "yields" in some market environments can become lower than those on the corresponding Treasury instruments, resulting in negative OASs. Of course, in the case of POs, negative OASs do not in any way imply that the risk of holding these instruments is less than that of holding Treasuries.

15. With respect to spread-sensitive securities, their price sensitivity to Treasury rates (OAD) should be distinguished from price sensitivity to credit spreads as measured by spread duration (Section 2.5.2). For instance, a floating rate note which resets on a quarterly basis has a large sensitivity to credit spreads and a very small sensitivity to Treasury rates.

16. See Kao, 1999.

17. We would like to thank our former colleague Pavan Wadhwa for his help with this section.

18. Carry is the total expected yield (or return) associated with holding a position. Carry incorporates the net coupon, the impact of time, and the cost of financing.

19. The presence of spread directionality in a given market environment can be measured via the statistical significance of the OAS term in the generalized empirical duration calculation (Section 2.3.3) or via other empirical methods (Kao, 1999).

20. See Breeden, D.T., 1994.

21. We would like to thank our colleague Yury Geyman for his contributions to the sections on KRDs and KTRDs.

22. Empirical studies indicate that OAD-neutral yield curve trades are not always entirely insensitive to the directional interest rate movements because parallel shocks can be correlated with various yield curve spreads in certain market environments. In order to eliminate sensitivity to directional market movements more effectively, yield curve trades should be constructed using the first principal component duration (Chapter 4) as opposed to OAD.

23. See Reitano, 1990, and Ho, 1992.

24. Δr_i is typically between 20 and 50 basis points.

25. The authors were introduced to KTRDs by Scott Peng (see Peng & Dattatreya, 1995).

26. We owe this expression to our colleague Yury Geyman.

27. See Klaffky et al., 1993.

28. This insight belongs to our colleagues E.G. Fisher and Stu Spodek.

29. Investigation of this interesting property of prepayment duration belongs to our colleagues Adam Wizon and Irwin Sheer.

30. See Ilmanen, 1995–1996.

31. Tables 2.11 and 2.12 as well as some of the conclusions in this section are based on research by Bill De Leon and Ben Golub.

32. Probability distributions of interest rate shocks (Chapter 3) were used to compute cumulative probabilities in Table 2.12.

3

Modeling Yield Curve Dynamics[1]

3.1 PROBABILITY DISTRIBUTIONS OF SYSTEMATIC RISK FACTORS

Changes in default-free interest rates are among the most influential forces affecting prices of fixed income securities. Fixed income risk management therefore must be highly concerned with analyzing, understanding, and forecasting yield curve movements. For simplicity and without loss of generality, this section limits the set of systematic risk factors to those representing interest rates, thus ignoring basis relationships and currency risks. Without substantial methodological changes, the majority of results presented here can be extended to include additional systematic risk factors. For reasons that will be apparent momentarily, this chapter will assume that interest rate movements are described by fluctuations of spot curves and, so will use the terms *yield curve* and *spot curve* interchangeably.

When estimating fair values of fixed income securities, valuation models use spot curves to compute present values of future payoffs (Equation 2.17). Different types of spot curves and methods by which they are constructed correspond to a variety of market conventions that assign the appropriate spot curve for each asset class. For instance, U.S.

Treasury securities, futures and options on U.S. Treasury securities, agency bonds, corporate and mortgage-backed securities use the spot curve constructed from the U.S. Treasury market. On the other hand, dollar-denominated interest rate derivatives, including swaps, swaptions, interest rate caps, and floors are usually valued on the spot curve bootstrapped from the markets linked to the London Interbank Offered Rate (LIBOR). Since pricing models need to discount cash flows of arbitrary maturities, representing spot curves as continuous functions is convenient.[2] However, such continuous representations seriously complicate the task of modeling yield curve dynamics, especially using statistical methods. To describe spot curve movements in a simpler and more intuitive setting, spot curves can be *discretized*, and their movements can be represented as vectors of changes of selected points, that is, *key rates* (see Section 2.4.1).

Deterministic measures of interest rate risk estimate the potential losses resulting from hypothetical what-if interest rate scenarios:

- Option-adjusted duration (OAD) estimates the price sensitivity to the 100 basis point parallel spot curve movement
- Scenario analysis explicitly sketches out price as a function of parallel changes in the spot curve
- Key rate durations (KRDs), key treasury rate durations (KTRDs), as well as short-end and long-end durations measure the price sensitivity to the various predefined, nonparallel changes in the spot curve

As an important extension of nonstochastic risk methodologies described in Chapter 2, statistical measures of risk synthesize information about market exposures with assumptions about the probability distributions of systematic risk factors. Of course, this entails the specification of the functional form of these probability distributions and the statistical estimation of their parameters. Recall that when computing fair values of fixed income securities, valuation models use stochastic processes to describe the evolution of interest rates[3] over time. Some of the earlier interest rate models (e.g., Ho-Lee, Hull-White) presumed changes in interest rates to be normally distributed. Since this assumption may cause interest rates to become negative under certain interest rate scenarios, the next generation of interest rate models (e.g., Black-Derman-Toy, Black-Karasinski) eliminated the possibility of negative interest rates by defining the probability distribution of changes in interest rates as log-normal.

In contrast to valuation models that need to project interest rates over the entire life of a fixed income security in order to compute the mathematical expectation of discounted future payoffs, risk management typically deals with much shorter horizons, for example, one day, one month, or one year. Over such shorter time frames, the normality assumption rarely leads to negative interest rates, even in catastrophic market environments. Similar to earlier interest rate models, it is often *analytically convenient* to assume for risk management purposes that changes in systematic risk factors are random variables that follow a joint multivariate normal distribution.[4] Consistent with the majority of interest rate models that presume interest rates to be mean-reverting, risk management typically postulates that the *population mean of changes in systematic risk factors is zero*, ignoring the actual sample mean of the data series that may be reflective of the recent market trends, if any.[5] However, while accurately modeling the business-as-usual part of the empirical probability distributions of interest rates, basis risk factors, and currencies, normal (and, for that matter, log-normal) distributions cannot capture *fat tails* present in the distributions of many financial time series. This limitation will be addressed throughout the book. *From now on, unless stated otherwise, changes in systematic risk factors are assumed to jointly follow a multivariate normal distribution with zero mean.* To fully define such a distribution, correlations and volatilities (or, equivalently, the covariance matrix) of changes in systematic risk factors need to be statistically estimated from the historical data. In this chapter, the set of risk factors will be limited to the set of key spot rates. Table 3.1 presents correlations and volatilities from the RiskMetrics® monthly dataset, which effectively uses 150 exponentially weighted daily observations with the decay factor of 0.97.[6]

A closer look at the distribution of U.S. key spot rates (Table 3.1) leads to a number of interesting observations. First, notice that the term structure of volatility (TSOV) of changes in spot rates is not flat: It sharply increases from the 3-month to the 2-year points, and then moderately declines between the 7-year and the 30-year points. Second, note that changes in key spot rates are generally highly correlated. Especially high correlations are exhibited within the following blocks: short (2- and 3-year), intermediate (5-, 7-, and 10-year), and long (10-, 15-, 20-, and 30-year). The 3-month rate is rather loosely correlated with the rest of the rates, while the 1-year rate is moderately correlated.

Yield curve dynamics can change dramatically over time. For instance, correlations and volatilities of changes in U.S. key spot rates on 12/31/98 paint a different picture. According to the data and consistent with intuition, the U.S. Treasury market was more volatile in December 1998 than it

TABLE 3.1 Correlations and Volatilities of U.S. Key Rates from RiskMetrics® Monthly Dataset (as of 9/30/96)

	3Mo	1Yr	2Yr	3Yr	5Yr	7Yr	10Yr	15Yr	20Yr	30Yr
Annualized yield volatility (%)	9.63	16.55	18.33	17.82	17.30	16.62	15.27	14.25	13.26	12.09
Vol of changes in spot rates (bps)	52	96	113	112	113	111	104	101	97	83
Correlation matrix										
3Mo:	1.00	0.80	0.72	0.68	0.65	0.61	0.58	0.54	0.51	0.46
1Yr:	0.80	1.00	0.91	0.91	0.89	0.87	0.85	0.81	0.78	0.76
2Yr:	0.72	0.91	1.00	0.99	0.97	0.95	0.93	0.89	0.85	0.84
3Yr:	0.68	0.91	0.99	1.00	0.99	0.97	0.96	0.92	0.90	0.88
5Yr:	0.65	0.89	0.97	0.99	1.00	0.99	0.98	0.96	0.93	0.92
7Yr:	0.61	0.87	0.95	0.97	0.99	1.00	0.99	0.98	0.96	0.95
10Yr:	0.58	0.85	0.93	0.96	0.98	0.99	1.00	0.99	0.98	0.97
15Yr:	0.54	0.81	0.89	0.92	0.96	0.98	0.99	1.00	0.99	0.98
20Yr:	0.51	0.78	0.85	0.90	0.93	0.96	0.98	0.99	1.00	0.99
30Yr:	0.46	0.76	0.84	0.88	0.92	0.95	0.97	0.98	0.99	1.00

Source: RiskMetrics® data has been produced and provided by the RiskMetrics Group, LLC at www.riskmetrics.com.

TABLE 3.2 Correlations and Volatilities of U.S. Key Rates from RiskMetrics® Monthly Dataset (as of 12/31/98)

		3Mo	1Yr	2Yr	3Yr	5Yr	7Yr	10Yr	15Yr	20Yr	30Yr
Annualized yield volatility (%)		14.25	14.27	28.93	28.32	28.74	27.12	25.29	22.19	19.31	16.11
Vol of changes in spot rates (bps)		68	66	135	133	136	130	125	120	110	85
Correlation matrix	3Mo:	1.00	0.51	0.21	0.18	0.11	0.11	0.11	0.10	0.09	0.02
	1Yr:	0.51	1.00	0.21	0.21	0.17	0.15	0.09	0.10	0.09	0.04
	2Yr:	0.21	0.21	1.00	0.98	0.90	0.88	0.83	0.81	0.76	0.43
	3Yr:	0.18	0.21	0.98	1.00	0.95	0.94	0.88	0.87	0.82	0.48
	5Yr:	0.11	0.17	0.90	0.95	1.00	0.99	0.93	0.92	0.88	0.56
	7Yr:	0.11	0.15	0.88	0.94	0.99	1.00	0.97	0.96	0.93	0.61
	10Yr:	0.11	0.09	0.83	0.88	0.93	0.97	1.00	0.99	0.96	0.67
	15Yr:	0.10	0.10	0.81	0.87	0.92	0.96	0.99	1.00	0.99	0.75
	20Yr:	0.09	0.09	0.76	0.82	0.88	0.93	0.96	0.99	1.00	0.84
	30Yr:	0.02	0.04	0.43	0.48	0.56	0.61	0.67	0.75	0.84	1.00

Source: RiskMetrics® data has been produced and provided by the RiskMetrics Group, LLC at www.riskmetrics.com.

was in September 1996 (Table 3.2). While the increase in the volatility of the long end of the spot curve was moderate, the volatility of the 3-month rate and the entire intermediate part of the yield curve increased dramatically. At the same time, interestingly enough, the volatility of the 1-year point declined substantially, becoming similar to that of the 3-month point. The correlation matrix reveals an even more drastic change in the market's dynamics. The very short end of the spot curve (3-month and 1-year) became uncorrelated with the rest of the curve and loosely correlated among each other. Note that during the liquidity and credit meltdown of 1998, correlations between the 3-month rate and other spot rates even reversed the sign and became temporarily negative. As seen from Tables 3.1 and 3.2, between 9/30/96 and 12/31/98, correlations among other key rates decreased as well. For instance, the correlation between the 30-year and the 20-year points became 0.84, down from 0.99.

The conceptual challenges of forecasting correlations and volatilities of systematic risk factors deserve a separate discussion since the statistical measures of risk are very sensitive to the methods used to estimate the parameters of probability distributions. Recent advances in time series analysis introduced a variety of approaches that offer tremendous methodological flexibility in computing covariance matrices, including detrending, exponential weighting of observations, variable time intervals over which distribution parameters are estimated, and so forth. However, the burden of choosing the most appropriate approach lies on the shoulders of the user and must reflect his or her views on several extremely crucial, almost *ideological,* issues:

- *Relevance of long-term history.* Long-term history (going back, say, 10 years) is applicable to forecasting of future events only if the market is believed to have remained fundamentally unchanged over this entire time period. In this context, permanent paradigm shifts (or structural breaks) should be distinguished from the shocks to the system that have only a temporary effect
- *Weighting of observations.* From a purely statistical perspective, more recent observations are better predictors of near-term future events than the more distant ones. By applying exponential weights to historical observations, transitions from one market regime to another can be captured very effectively and quickly

While not explicitly focusing on the issues of statistical estimation of correlations and volatilities, this book will discuss the far-reaching implications of different methodological choices made by risk managers. Nevertheless, the ideas presented in this chapter do not make any assumptions about the techniques used to estimate correlations and volatilities of changes in systematic risk factors.

3.2 PRINCIPAL COMPONENTS ANALYSIS: THEORY AND APPLICATIONS

3.2.1 Introduction

When yield curve risk is measured via deterministic approaches, characterizing interest rate movements in terms of key rates can be both intuitive and analytically appealing. However, due to their complex correlation and volatility structure, key rates are less efficient in describing the dynamics of interest rates from the statistical perspective. Having said that, historical correlations and volatilities can still provide useful inferences about the behavior of the different parts of the yield curve. For instance, the 20- and the 30-year key spot rates are typically highly correlated and exhibit similar volatilities (Tables 3.1 and 3.2). This knowledge can be effectively used in assessing the likelihood of a steepening or a flattening of the spot curve between the 20- and the 30-year maturities. Unfortunately, Tables 3.1 and 3.2 do not allow us to address a whole class of questions dealing with the dynamics of the yield curve as a whole, for example, what normally happens to the rest of the yield curve when the 10-year spot rate rallies by a given number of basis points.

Principal components analysis (PCA) is a statistical technique that examines, models, and explains the variance/covariance structures of the essentially multivariate real-life systems. Via a mathematical transformation, PCA substitutes a large number of the original interdependent variables with a small set of new uncorrelated *composite* variables called *principal components*, thus allowing for a more parsimonious description of the system's dynamics. Widely employed in geology, environmental, and other natural sciences for many decades, PCA was first applied to equity markets in the 1980s and to fixed income markets in the late 1980s–early 1990s and has been of interest to academics and practitioners ever since.[7] Due to the latent statistical nature of principal components and the inability to directly observe them in the market, their use in portfolio management and trading has been relatively limited.[8] However, the popularity of principal components in risk management has been rapidly increasing over the years.

In fixed income finance, principal components have a very intuitive interpretation of being the most dominant and characteristic yield curve shocks[9] (Exhibit 3.1). Using PCA, researchers discovered that the first three principal components, *level*, *steepness*, and *curvature*, typically explain anywhere between 95% and 99% of returns on fixed income securities over time. In the language of statistics, it is equivalent to saying that the first three principal components explain the vast majority of the total variability of the yield curve in virtually all market environments.

In this book, principal components are analytically derived from the variance/covariance matrix of changes in systematic risk factors. This streamlines computations (since no additional regressions or historical fittings are required) and enables principal components to incorporate the assumptions built into the estimation of the underlying covariance matrices. For instance, principal components can be based on covariance matrices computed using exponentially weighted observations, creating a tool that captures changes in the market environment virtually instantaneously. At the same time, the shapes of the

EXHIBIT 3.1   Annualized Principal Components Spot Curve Shocks (as of 9/30/96)

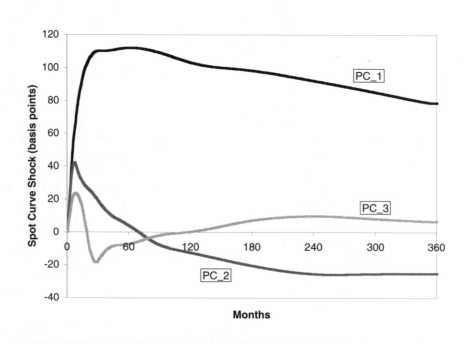

principal components' yield curve shocks are determined by the historical data instead of being postulated a priori. Namely, the first principal component is not assumed to be a parallel spot curve shock.[10] As demonstrated later in this chapter, the "humped" shape of the first principal component is an important piece of information that should not be ignored; it can be effectively used when placing yield curve bets or gaining intuition behind extreme market movements. Moreover, when not accompanied by the proper adjustment of other principal components, the assumption that the shape of the first principal component is parallel causes principal components to become correlated. Since in certain instances it is still analytically convenient to assume that the most dominant yield curve movement is parallel, there exists a way to properly transform the coordinate system, turning the first principal component into the parallel shock and adjusting the shapes of other principal components accordingly (Section 3.3).

In addition to providing insights into the dynamics of interest rates, principal components have become a powerful dimensionality reduction tool used in a variety of risk management methodologies, Monte-Carlo Simulation Value-at-Risk (VaR) being the most notable (see Chapter 5). This book makes an extensive use of principal components analysis. Readers less comfortable with this technique are urged to study it closely.[11]

3.2.2 Principal Components Analysis

Changes in systematic risk factors are assumed to follow a joint multivariate normal distribution with zero mean. To fully define such a distribution, it suffices to specify the covariance matrix Σ of changes in risk factors, which, for our purposes, are assumed to be exhausted by key spot rates. Principal components analysis (PCA) attempts to describe yield curve movements as parsimoniously as possible. It uses the original set of interdependent variables (key rates) to construct a set of new composite variables – principal components. Principal components are by construction the linear combinations of changes in the original key rates:

$$p_i = \sum_{j=1}^{n} p_{i,j} \cdot \Delta r_j \tag{3.1}$$

where p_i are principal components (random variables), Δr_j are changes in key rate points on the spot curve (random variables), and $p_{i,j}$ are the principal components' coefficients or *factor loadings*. Note that under the assumption that changes in key rates follow a multivariate normal distribution, principal components are normally distributed as well. Equation 3.1 can be rewritten in matrix terms as follows:

$$\begin{bmatrix} p_1 \\ \cdots \\ p_n \end{bmatrix} = \begin{bmatrix} p_{1,1} & \cdots & p_{1,n} \\ \cdots & \cdots & \cdots \\ p_{n,1} & \cdots & p_{n,n} \end{bmatrix} \cdot \begin{bmatrix} \Delta r_1 \\ \cdots \\ \Delta r_n \end{bmatrix} \tag{3.2}$$

or equivalently

$$\bar{p} = \Omega \cdot \bar{r} \tag{3.3}$$

where $\Omega = \{p_{i,j}\}$ is the matrix of principal components' factor loadings, and $\bar{p}$ and $\bar{r}$ are the vectors of principal components and changes in key spot rates, respectively. While practitioners often use the term *principal components* when referring to random variables p_i as well as factor loadings $(p_{i,1}, \ldots, p_{i,n})$, the meaning is usually clear from the context.

The system of yield curve movements is n-dimensional. Key spot rates fully describe any spot curve movement and therefore, in the language of mathematics, constitute the *basis* or *coordinate system*. Principal components form a different coordinate system in the space of spot curve changes. The process of constructing principal components can therefore be thought of as a geometrical transformation between the two coordinate systems, schematically presented in Exhibit 3.2.

Equations 3.1–3.3 show the transition from the basis of key spot rates to the coordinate system of principal components. Later in this chapter it will be shown that the matrix of principal components' factor loadings is orthogonal by construction, and therefore the equations below describe the reverse transformation, from principal components to key spot rates:

$$\Delta r_i = \sum_{j=1}^{n} p_{j,i} \cdot p_j \tag{3.4}$$

Equation 3.4 can be written in matrix terms as follows:

$$\begin{bmatrix} \Delta r_1 \\ \cdots \\ \Delta r_n \end{bmatrix} = \begin{bmatrix} p_{1,1} & \cdots & p_{n,1} \\ \cdots & \cdots & \cdots \\ p_{1,n} & \cdots & p_{n,n} \end{bmatrix} \cdot \begin{bmatrix} p_1 \\ \cdots \\ p_n \end{bmatrix} \tag{3.5}$$

EXHIBIT 3.2   Transition From One Coordinate System to Another:
Interdependent Key Rates versus Uncorrelated Principal Components

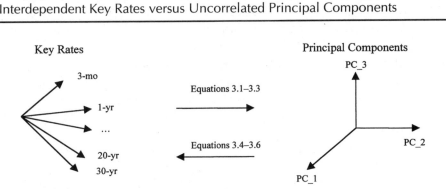

or equivalently,

$$\bar{r} = \Omega^T \cdot \bar{p} \qquad (3.6)$$

Before we proceed to the derivation of principal components' factor loadings, the following important concepts need definition:

- *The total variability* of a given dynamic system is a measure of how *jointly volatile* all the variables that belong to this system are. For instance, during the 1998 credit and liquidity crisis, the total variability of U.S. interest rates was high, while in July 1998 it was low. The formal definition of total variability will be presented later in this chapter. For now it suffices to note that total variability can be analytically computed from the covariance matrix Σ of key rate changes

- *The percentage of the total variability explained* by the given variable is the ratio of this variable's variance to the total variability of the system. By definition, this statistic can take on values between 0% and 100%. In this book, the terms the *percentage of the total variability* explained by a variable and the *explanatory power* of this variable will be used interchangeably.

Principal components can be obtained from the covariance matrix Σ via the following optimization problem. By repeatedly searching through all possible linear combinations of changes in key rates as shown in Equation 3.1:

1. The linear combination of key rate changes that explains the largest percentage of the total variability in the system is determined. The *unit-length vector* of factor loadings $(p_{1,1},...,p_{1,n})$ in this linear combination corresponds to the first principal component p_1.

2. The remaining variability in the system, not explained by the previously selected principal components, is computed. The next linear combination of length one is then found such that
   - It explains the largest percentage of the remaining variability in the system.
   - It is uncorrelated with all previously selected principal components.

3. Step 2 is continued until all principal components are determined. By construction, each principal component explains the largest percentage of variability in the system not explained by all previously selected principal components and is uncorrelated with all of them. As mentioned before, the principal components' factor loadings are constructed to be of length 1:

$$\sqrt{\sum_{j=1}^{n} p_{i,j}^2} = 1 \qquad (3.7)$$

While it is intuitive to think about principal components from the above-described optimization viewpoint, in practice principal components are typically analytically derived from the covariance matrix of key rate changes. It can be shown[12] that the principal components' factor loadings $(p_{i,1},...,p_{i,n})$ are the eigenvectors of the covariance matrix Σ or, equivalently, the unit-length solutions of the following equation:

$$\Sigma \cdot \begin{bmatrix} p_{i,1} \\ ... \\ p_{i,n} \end{bmatrix} = \lambda_i \cdot \begin{bmatrix} p_{i,1} \\ ... \\ p_{i,n} \end{bmatrix} \qquad (3.8)$$

The real numbers λ_i are, in turn, the solutions of the equation below:

$$\det(\Sigma - \lambda \cdot I) = 0 \qquad (3.9)$$

where I is the identity matrix and $\det(X)$ is the determinant of a matrix X.

The matrix notation can be used to rewrite Equation 3.8 as follows:

$$\begin{bmatrix} \lambda_1 & & 0 \\ & \cdots & \\ 0 & & \lambda_n \end{bmatrix} = \begin{bmatrix} p_{1,1} & \cdots & p_{1,n} \\ \cdots & \cdots & \cdots \\ p_{n,1} & \cdots & p_{n,n} \end{bmatrix} \cdot \Sigma \cdot \begin{bmatrix} p_{1,1} & \cdots & p_{1,n} \\ \cdots & \cdots & \cdots \\ p_{n,1} & \cdots & p_{n,n} \end{bmatrix}^T \qquad (3.10)$$

or equivalently,

$$\Lambda = \Omega \cdot \Sigma \cdot \Omega^T \qquad (3.11)$$

where Λ is a matrix with λ_i on the diagonal and zeros elsewhere, and Ω, as before, is the matrix of principal components' factor loadings. Since the rows of the matrix Ω are by construction linearly independent unit-length vectors, Ω is an orthogonal matrix:[13]

$$\Omega^{-1} = \Omega^T \qquad (3.12)$$

It can be shown that the eigenvalues λ_i of the covariance matrix Σ are the variances of the principal components p_i:

$$\lambda_i = \sigma^2(p_i) \qquad (3.13)$$

As already mentioned, under the assumption that changes in key spot rates follow a multivariate normal distribution, the entire knowledge about the historical behavior of interest rates is contained in the original covariance matrix Σ. PCA provides an alternative description of the yield curve dynamics, transforming the information contained in Σ into

- The vector $\lambda = (\lambda_1,\ldots,\lambda_n)$ of principal components' variances
- The matrix Ω of principal components' factor loadings

The two important concepts introduced earlier in this section can now be formally defined. Since any yield curve movement can be described by the set of *uncorrelated* principal components, the *total variability* of the system is the sum of the principal components' variances:

$$Total\ Variability = \sum_{j=1}^{n} \lambda_j \qquad (3.14)$$

As mentioned before, the percentage of the total variability explained by a given variable is the ratio of its variance to the total variability of the system. The percentages of the total variability of yield curve movements explained by principal components (or their "explanatory powers") can therefore be obtained from the following formula.

$$\zeta_i = \frac{\lambda_i}{\sum\limits_{j=1}^{n} \lambda_j} \tag{3.15}$$

Explanatory powers of principal components provide important information about the dynamics of interest rates. They can be used to determine how many risk factors are needed to approximate yield curve movements with a sufficient degree of accuracy. For instance, in market environments when the explanatory power of the first principal component is over 95%, describing interest rate movements with a single risk factor is adequate. On the other hand, when the explanatory power of the first principal component is low (e.g., fall 1998), two or even three principal components are required. As mentioned earlier, the first three principal components explain almost the entire yield curve variability in the majority of market environments.[14]

The principal components' factor loadings ($p_{i,1},...,p_{i,n}$) reflect the historical relationship among key spot rates and have a very intuitive interpretation. They visually depict the *shape* of the most dominant yield curve movements, that is, principal components. For reasons that will be described in Section 3.3, the principal components yield curve shocks can be obtained by multiplying the vectors of factor loadings ($p_{i,1},...,p_{i,n}$) by the one standard deviations $\sqrt{\lambda_i}$ of principal components.

Table 3.3 illustrates the derivation of principal components on 9/30/96 from the covariance matrix of changes in U.S. key spot rates obtained from the RiskMetrics® monthly dataset. On 9/30/96, nearly 93% of the spot curve variability was explained by the first principal component, 97% by the first two, and 99% by the first three. Needless to say, the explanatory powers of principal components are functions of the market environment. Table 3.4 demonstrates PCA on 12/31/98. Notice that the explanatory power of principal components has declined: The first principal component explains only 83%, while the first two principal components explain 90%, and the first three, 95%. Tables 3.3 and 3.4 also show the principal components' factor loadings ($p_{i,1},...,p_{i,n}$) as well as the corresponding annualized interest rate shocks. Notice the change in the shape of the first principal component between the two dates. As the front end of the spot curve became decoupled from the rest of the spot rates in fall 1998, the first principal component factor loadings corresponding to the 3-month and the 1-year rates dramatically declined.

TABLE 3.3 Principal Components Analysis of Spot Curve Movements (as of 9/30/96)

					Factor Loadings						PC Var	PC Vol	Var Expl	CVar Expl
	3Mo	1Yr	2Yr	3Yr	5Yr	7Yr	10Yr	15Yr	20Yr	30Yr				
Principal Components														
1:	11.1	28.5	35.9	36.4	36.9	36.3	34.0	32.4	30.3	25.6	9.1	3.0	92.8	92.8
2:	43.7	48.4	34.5	20.4	5.2	-9.4	-18.7	-30.1	-37.3	-37.1	0.5	0.7	4.8	97.6
3:	42.9	55.0	-44.9	-34.9	-20.6	-8.2	0.4	19.2	26.7	17.9	0.1	0.4	1.3	98.9
4:	76.7	-61.6	9.2	0.0	0.2	-2.0	-0.6	10.3	11.1	-0.3	0.1	0.2	0.6	99.5
5:	12.2	-5.1	-55.4	-2.0	38.7	46.6	32.9	-22.9	-36.3	-12.8	0.0	0.1	0.2	99.7
6:	8.7	0.3	17.6	-8.5	-13.9	-5.2	17.1	-44.4	-29.4	78.7	0.0	0.1	0.1	99.8
7:	2.1	-0.8	-38.2	51.4	43.6	-47.9	-30.5	-8.3	10.4	24.2	0.0	0.1	0.1	99.9
8:	3.0	-1.1	-24.0	65.7	-67.8	18.4	12.6	-0.3	-2.1	-2.2	0.0	0.1	0.1	99.9
9:	0.5	-0.4	-0.5	-2.0	0.2	60.5	-72.8	-19.7	19.8	15.9	0.0	0.1	0.0	100.0
10:	0.5	0.0	-2.5	1.3	-0.4	5.1	-27.0	68.0	-64.6	21.0	0.0	0.1	0.0	100.0

				Annualized One Standard Deviation Shocks (basis points)							Var Expl
	3Mo	1Yr	2Yr	3Yr	5Yr	7Yr	10Yr	15Yr	20Yr	30Yr	
PC_1 Spot Curve Shock	33	86	108	110	111	109	102	97	91	77	92.8
PC_2 Spot Curve Shock	30	33	24	14	4	-6	-13	-21	-25	-25	4.8
PC_3 Spot Curve Shock	15	19	-16	-12	-7	-3	0	7	9	6	1.3
PARALLEL Spot Curve Shock	92	92	92	92	92	92	92	92	92	92	87.9

PC Var = principal components' variances times 10,000;
PC Vol = principal components' volatilities times 100;
Var Expl = percentage of the variance explained;
CVar Expl = cumulative percentage of the variance explained.

TABLE 3.4 Principal Components Analysis of Spot Curve Movements (as of 12/31/98)

					Factor Loadings						PC Var	PC Vol	Var Expl	CVar Expl
Principal Components	3Mo	1Yr	2Yr	3Yr	5Yr	7Yr	10Yr	15Yr	20Yr	30Yr				
1:	3.0	3.4	37.6	38.7	40.4	39.1	36.9	35.4	31.7	17.0	10.8	3.3	83.3	83.3
2:	29.6	30.1	45.2	33.9	10.3	-1.0	-18.1	-25.8	-35.2	-51.9	1.0	1.0	7.5	90.8
3:	65.5	60.7	-14.8	-13.0	-13.3	-6.4	1.4	8.9	16.7	32.6	0.6	0.8	4.7	95.5
4:	7.8	-29.2	52.1	23.6	-31.3	-30.8	-27.9	-12.8	7.7	53.7	0.2	0.5	1.9	97.3
5:	65.5	-64.1	-4.1	-9.4	-9.6	1.1	24.4	11.7	0.3	-25.9	0.2	0.5	1.8	99.1
6:	21.6	-20.5	-25.4	2.3	64.8	19.9	-43.6	-30.1	-11.8	30.5	0.1	0.3	0.7	99.8
7:	2.1	-4.2	-35.8	53.1	-40.5	38.6	-43.5	24.2	11.6	-11.2	0.0	0.2	0.2	100.0
8:	0.1	-0.4	-28.0	41.4	30.5	-74.7	0.0	25.7	13.7	-12.1	0.0	0.0	0.0	100.0
9:	0.1	-0.2	29.7	-44.7	15.6	-3.8	-56.0	49.2	27.4	-23.7	0.0	0.0	0.0	100.0
10:	0.0	0.0	-0.8	0.9	-0.8	-0.2	-1.3	-56.0	78.8	-25.5	0.0	0.0	0.0	100.0

	Annualized One Standard Deviation Shocks (basis points)										Var Expl
	3Mo	1Yr	2Yr	3Yr	5Yr	7Yr	10Yr	15Yr	20Yr	30Yr	
PC_1 Spot Curve Shock	10	11	123	127	133	128	121	116	104	56	83.3
PC_2 Spot Curve Shock	29	30	45	33	10	-1	-18	-25	-35	-51	7.5
PC_3 Spot Curve Shock	51	47	-12	-10	-10	-5	1	7	13	25	4.7
PARALLEL Spot Curve Shock	94	94	94	94	94	94	94	94	94	94	67.7

PC Var = principal components' variances times 10,000;
PC Vol = principal components' volatilities times 100;
Var Expl = percentage of the variance explained;
CVar Expl = cumulative percentage of the variance explained.

102

3.2.3 The First Principal Component and the Term Structure of Volatility

The lack of intuition about principal components resulted in their limited use in portfolio management and trading. This section attempts to eliminate this obstacle by demonstrating that in the majority of market environments, the shape of the first principal component resembles that of the term structure of volatility (TSOV) of changes in U.S. spot rates. This phenomenon is a consequence of the fact that, except for the very short end of the yield curve, changes in U.S. Treasury spot rates are typically highly correlated during business-as-usual regimes (Tables 3.1 and 3.2). Interest rate movements tend to become even more synchronized during most market crises, resulting in even higher correlations.[15] Exhibit 3.3 compares the shape of the first principal component and that of the TSOV on 9/30/96. Notice that the two curves are almost identical near the most volatile part of the spot curve (2–10 years) and diverge moderately near both the short and the long ends of the spot curve.

Let $\sigma_i = \sigma(\Delta r_i)$ and $\sigma_j = \sigma(\Delta r_j)$ be the volatilities of changes in key spot rates r_i and r_j, respectively. Recall that by $p_{1,i}$ and $p_{1,j}$, we denoted the factor loadings of the first principal component corresponding to r_i and r_j.

EXHIBIT 3.3   The First Principal Component Shock and TSOV (as of 9/30/96)

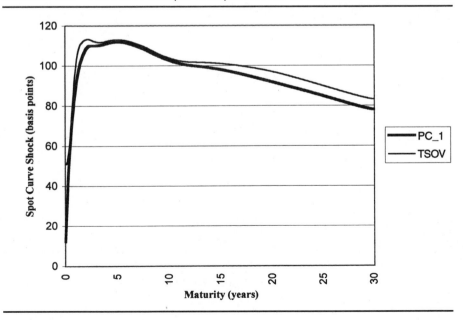

The statement "the shape of the first principal component resembles that of TSOV" can be written as the following approximate relationship:

$$\frac{\sigma_i}{\sigma_j} \approx \frac{p_{1,i}}{p_{1,j}} \tag{3.16}$$

It can be shown that the factor loadings $p_{1,i}$ and $p_{1,j}$ of the first principal component can be obtained via the following regression-like formula:[16]

$$p_{1,i} = \frac{\rho_{1,i} \cdot \sigma_i}{\sqrt{\lambda_1}} \tag{3.17}$$

$$p_{1,j} = \frac{\rho_{1,j} \cdot \sigma_j}{\sqrt{\lambda_1}} \tag{3.18}$$

where $\rho_{1,i}$ and $\rho_{1,j}$ are the correlations between the first principal component and the changes in key spot rates r_i and r_j, respectively.

Because the first principal component is constructed to explain the maximal percentage of the total variability in the system, the high correlation among changes in spot rates makes the first principal component highly correlated with them as well:

$$\rho_{1,i} \approx \rho_{1,j} \approx 1 \tag{3.19}$$

Combining Equations 3.16–3.19 yields

$$\frac{p_{1,i}}{p_{1,j}} = \frac{\dfrac{\rho_{1,i} \cdot \sigma_i}{\sqrt{\lambda_1}}}{\dfrac{\rho_{1,j} \cdot \sigma_j}{\sqrt{\lambda_1}}} = \frac{\rho_{1,i}}{\rho_{1,j}} \cdot \frac{\sigma_i}{\sigma_j} \approx \frac{\sigma_i}{\sigma_j} \tag{3.20}$$

Equation 3.20 illustrates that in market environments characterized by highly correlated spot rates, the shape of the first principal component resembles that of TSOV. Since correlations among spot rates typically increase during the periods of market turmoil, practitioners often witness large-move days reflecting "more of a level [*the first principal component and not parallel!*] shift in interest rates."[17] In other words, in the time of crisis all spot rates typically move in the same direction, and the relative magnitudes of their respective changes are determined by their historical volatilities.

Results obtained in this section argue that contrary to some of the existing practices,[18] the first principal component should not be assumed or explicitly forced to be a parallel spot curve shock. Principal components whose shapes are determined by historical data rather than specified a priori provide valuable insights into the historical movements of interest rates and also can assist in formulating yield curve bets.

3.2.4 Example: Historical Steepeners and Flatteners of the U.S. Treasury Curve

The similarity between the shape of the first principal component and that of TSOV has a number of implications. The most interesting among them deals with the interest rate directionality of changes in the shape of the yield curve. More specifically, the shape of the first principal component points to the market phenomenon very familiar to fixed income traders: when the market rallies, the yield curve often steepens, and when the market sells off, the yield curve flattens. In fact, this conclusion can be reached theoretically as well. Notice that according to the shape of the first principal component, the factor loading of the 2-year rate is larger than that of the 30-year rate. Therefore, if the market rallies, the 2-year rate will typically decrease more than the 30-year rate, causing the spot curve to steepen.

Two simple experiments dealing with spot and on-the-run U.S. Treasury curves were conducted to investigate whether the market data supports these theoretical results. Monthly changes in the level and slope of the U.S. spot and OTR curves were considered. In each experiment, the market was called *bull* if the 10-year key rate (spot or OTR, depending on the experiment) fell more than 20 basis points, *bear* if it rose more than 20 basis points, and *unchanged* otherwise. Likewise, a change in the slope of the yield curve (spot or OTR, depending on the experiment) was defined as a *steepening* if the spread between the 2- and the 30-year rates increased by more than 5 basis points, *flattening* if it decreased by more than 5 basis points, and *unchanged* otherwise. Exhibits 3.4 and 3.5 contain the results of these rudimentary empirical investigations.

Over the 4-year period (November 1992–November 1996), the ratio of bull steepenings to bull flattenings of the spot curve was 2.5 to 1, and

EXHIBIT 3.4   Relationship Between Changes in the Level and the Slope of the U.S. TSY Spot Curve

	FLATTEN	STEEPEN	UNCHANGED
BEAR	17	6	24
BULL	10	25	8
NEUTRAL	15	2	4

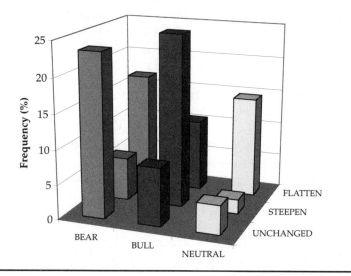

the ratio of bear flattenings to bear steepenings was 2.75 to 1. For the on-the-run curve, while bull steepening and bear flattening patterns seemed to dominate, the proportions were different: The ratio of bull steepenings to bull flattenings was 1.6 to 1, and the ratio of bear flattenings to bear steepenings was 6.5 to 1.

The empirical data seems to support the claim that changes in the slope of the yield curve are consistent with those implied by the shape of the first principal component. Therefore, if a large market movement is expected as a result of an economic data release or any other exogenous event, forecasting the change in the shape of the yield curve using the first principal component seems to be the most historically plausible alternative. However, since the first principal component only deals with the directional yield curve movements, twists and other types of changes in the shape of the yield curve (that correspond to the second and third principal components) were not accounted for by our experiments.

EXHIBIT 3.5   Relationship Between Changes in the Level and the Slope of the U.S. OTR TSY Curve Slope

	FLATTEN	STEEPEN	UNCHANGED
BEAR	27	4	6
BULL	10	17	17
NEUTRAL	8	4	6

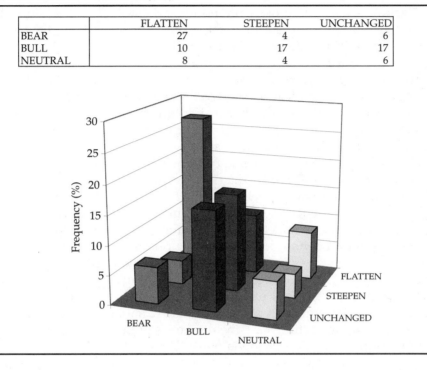

3.3 PROBABILITY DISTRIBUTIONS OF INTEREST RATE SHOCKS

Many areas of portfolio and risk management make extensive use of hypothetical what-if scenarios that describe the evolution of interest rates over time. Analyses of this type are often formulated in terms of spot curve shocks that are expected to occur instantaneously or over a specified horizon. The popularity of these methods is due to the fact that key rate durations (KRDs) of fixed income portfolios and securities allow for the approximation of potential losses associated with a given interest rate movement (Equation 2.39). Earlier in this book (Chapter 2), we discussed this class of approaches to measuring interest rate risk using static yield curve shocks, including yield curve reshaping durations, duration-neutral steepeners and flatteners, stress testing, and so on.

This section studies stochastic behavior of interest rate shocks using the framework inspired by PCA.[19] Operating under the assumption that changes in spot rates are normally distributed, it will be demonstrated that any spot curve movement is in one-to-one correspondence with a realization of a standard normal random variable.[20] This allows the likelihood associated with any movement of the yield curve to be judged. For instance, if it is determined that a given interest rate shock corresponds to a three standard deviation realization of the underlying standard normal variable, such a movement of interest rates will be deemed unlikely from a historical perspective. The ability to derive probability distributions of interest rate shocks of arbitrary shapes also enables the construction of coordinate systems other than principal components or key rates. Thus, the coordinate system of principal components can be rotated, turning the first principal component into a parallel shock. This knowledge can be utilized by the risk management methodologies (e.g., scenario analysis) that model the price sensitivity in terms of parallel spot curve movements or explicitly assume that the first principal component is parallel. Despite the fact that the mathematical tools used in deriving the probability distributions of interest rate shocks are rather complex, we urge the reader to bear with us: The results of this section are used extensively throughout the book, for example, in developing the measures of historical plausibility (Chapter 3) as well as in Monte-Carlo Simulation approach to Value-at-Risk (Chapter 5).

As studied in Section 3.2.2, the dynamics of interest rate movements can be equivalently described via two different coordinate systems: random changes in key spot rates (Δr_i) and random changes in principal components (p_i). In this section, we deal with both historical and hypothetical interest rate shocks – particular realizations of Δr_i and p_i. If key spot rates and principal components can be thought of as random variables spanning the respective coordinate systems, a given yield curve movement (a realization of Δr_i and p_i) corresponds to a vector of coefficients. We will adopt the following notation. From now on, the subscripts KR and PC next to a vector of coefficients will indicate that this interest rate shock is a realization of key spot rates or principal components, respectively. For instance,

$$\bar{z} = (z_1, ..., z_n)_{KR} \tag{3.21}$$

denotes an interest rate shock that is written in terms of changes in key rates, where the first key rate is shocked by z_1 basis points, the second key rate by z_2 basis points, and so forth. The *same* spot curve shock $\bar{z}$ can be represented as a realization of principal components as well:

$$\bar{z} = (v_1, ..., v_n)_{PC} \qquad (3.22)$$

Recall that Equations 3.1–3.6 describe the relationship between the coordinate systems of key rates and principal components. Thus, when applied to the interest rate shock $\bar{z}$, Equation 3.5 can be rewritten as follows:

$$\begin{bmatrix} z_1 \\ ... \\ z_n \end{bmatrix} = \begin{bmatrix} p_{1,1} & \cdots & p_{n,1} \\ ... & ... & ... \\ p_{1,n} & \cdots & p_{n,n} \end{bmatrix} \cdot \begin{bmatrix} v_1 \\ ... \\ v_n \end{bmatrix} = \sum_{i=1}^{n} \begin{bmatrix} p_{i,1} \\ ... \\ p_{i,n} \end{bmatrix} \times v_i \qquad (3.23)$$

Equation 3.23 reveals that any interest rate shock can be written as a sum of the principal components' factor loadings multiplied by the realization of the appropriate principal component. For any arbitrary change in key spot rates, there exists a unique set of realizations of principal components. Moreover, these realizations can be determined analytically. Conversely, any realization of principal components unequivocally implies a unique change in spot key rates.[21]

Another important corollary of Equation 3.23 lies in the ability to construct principal components' yield curve shocks. Thus, the one standard deviation change in the first principal component has the following representation in the (orthogonal) coordinate system of principal components:

$$One\ SD\ PC_1 = (\sqrt{\lambda_1}, 0, ..., 0)_{PC} \qquad (3.24)$$

where $\sqrt{\lambda_1}$, as before, is one standard deviation of the first principal component. When written in terms of changes in key rates, the first principal component shock has the following representation

$$One\ SD\ PC_1 = \begin{bmatrix} p_{1,1} & \cdots & p_{n,1} \\ ... & ... & ... \\ p_{1,n} & \cdots & p_{n,n} \end{bmatrix} \cdot \begin{bmatrix} \sqrt{\lambda_1} \\ ... \\ 0 \end{bmatrix} = (\sqrt{\lambda_1} \cdot p_{1,1}, ..., \sqrt{\lambda_1} \cdot p_{1,n})_{KR} \qquad (3.25)$$

When speaking about principal component yield curve shocks, practitioners typically refer to the expressions given by Equation 3.25. Since one standard deviation has a naturally embedded notion of horizon (daily, monthly, or annual standard deviation), the corresponding principal components shocks are defined for the same horizon as well. Annualized principal components of the U.S. Treasury spot curve are presented in Exhibit 3.1.

Before proceeding to deriving the probability distributions of interest rate shocks, consider the following definition. Suppose $\bar{z} = (z_1,\ldots,z_n)_{KR}$ and $\bar{x} = (x_1,\ldots,x_n)_{KR}$ are spot curve shocks represented as vectors of changes in key rates. Interest rate shocks $\bar{z}$ and $\bar{x}$ are said to be of the same shape if one can be obtained from the other via scaling by a real nonzero number c:

$$(z_1,\ldots,z_n)_{KR} = (c \cdot x_1,\ldots,c \cdot x_n)_{KR} \tag{3.26}$$

An example of the two shocks of the same shape is presented in Exhibit 3.6.

EXHIBIT 3.6   Interest Rate Shocks of the Same Shape

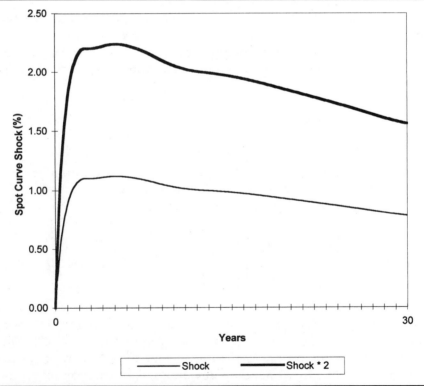

As mentioned earlier, the dynamic system of interest rate movements is n-dimensional. It is "spanned" by the vector of n key rates or, alternatively, by the vector of n principal components. While interdependent key rates form a nonorthogonal basis of the space of spot curve movements, uncorrelated principal components constitute an orthogonal basis. Clearly, in any n-dimensional space, there exists an infinite number of different coordinate systems, both orthogonal and nonorthogonal.

Suppose $\bar{z} = (z_1,...,z_n)_{KR}$ is a hypothetical interest rate shock presented in terms of key rates. In the beginning of this section, it was claimed that any interest rate shock corresponds to a particular realization of a standard normal random variable. Let us now establish the relationship between an arbitrary interest rate shock $\bar{z}$ and the realization of the underlying random variable. This will allow the probability of $\bar{z}$ occurring to be measured.

Recall that principal components' factor loadings are constructed to be of length 1. Let us start by analyzing the probability associated with $\bar{z}$ by constructing a vector $(\xi_1,...,\xi_n)$ of unit length whose shape is the same as that of $\bar{z}$:

$$\bar{z} = |\bar{z}| \cdot (\xi_1,...,\xi_n)_{KR} \qquad (3.27)$$

where $|\bar{z}| = \sqrt{\sum_{i=1}^{n} z_i^2}$ denotes the length of $\bar{z}$ as a vector.

Similarly to the definition of principal components (Equation 3.1), a new random variable ξ can be introduced as the following linear combination of key rates:

$$\xi = \sum_{i=1}^{n} \xi_i \cdot \Delta r_i \qquad (3.28)$$

where Δr_i are changes in key spot rates (random variables). Since ξ is a linear combination of several normal variables, its variance is given by the following formula:

$$\sigma^2(\xi) = (\xi_1,...,\xi_n) \cdot \Sigma \cdot (\xi_1,...,\xi_n)^T \qquad (3.29)$$

It is now possible to construct a new orthogonal basis of the space of spot curve changes that is different from the coordinate system of principal components. By design, we will make ξ the first element in this basis. This can be achieved by modifying the principal components' optimization procedure as follows:

1. The percentage of the total variability in the system explained by ξ is determined.
2. By repeatedly searching through all possible linear combinations of key rates, the next linear combination is found such that:
   - It explains the largest percentage of the remaining variability in the system, not explained by the previously selected variable(s).
   - It is uncorrelated with all previously selected variable(s).
3. Step 2 is repeated until the entire coordinate system is constructed. Each new element explains the largest percentage of the variability in the system not explained by all previously selected variables and is uncorrelated with all of them.

In the space of yield curve movements, the new orthogonal coordinate system (or basis) that is different from that of principal components has just been created. By construction, ξ is the first element in this basis. Just as any interest rate shock can be represented as a function of realizations of principal components (Equation 3.23), the analogous result for the newly constructed coordinate system can be obtained as well:

$$\begin{bmatrix} \Delta r_1 \\ \dots \\ \Delta r_n \end{bmatrix} = \begin{bmatrix} \xi_1 \\ \dots \\ \xi_n \end{bmatrix} \cdot \xi + \text{other elements of the basis} \tag{3.30}$$

or equivalently,

$$\begin{bmatrix} \Delta r_1 \\ \dots \\ \Delta r_n \end{bmatrix} = \begin{bmatrix} \sigma(\xi) \cdot \xi_1 \\ \sigma(\xi) \cdot \xi_n \end{bmatrix} \cdot \frac{\xi}{\sigma(\xi)} + \text{other elements of the basis} \tag{3.31}$$

It can be seen that

$$(\sigma(\xi) \cdot \xi_1, \dots, \sigma(\xi) \cdot \xi_n)_{KR} \tag{3.32}$$

is the one standard deviation shock whose shape is the same as that of $\bar{z}$, and $\dfrac{\xi}{\sigma(\xi)}$ is a standard normal variable.

Equations 3.30–3.31 deal with the representation of arbitrary changes in key spot rates (random variables) in the coordinate system whose first element is ξ. Below, we apply these general results to a particular realization of random key spot rates, that is, the shock $\bar{z}$. Due to the orthogonality, $\bar{z}$ is fully explained by the first element of the basis:

$$\bar{z} = \begin{bmatrix} z_1 \\ \cdots \\ z_n \end{bmatrix} = \begin{bmatrix} \sigma(\xi) \cdot \xi_1 \\ \cdots \\ \sigma(\xi) \cdot \xi_n \end{bmatrix} \cdot \frac{|\bar{z}|}{\sigma(\xi)} \tag{3.33}$$

where $\dfrac{|\bar{z}|}{\sigma(\xi)}$ is the realization of the standard normal variable corresponding to $\bar{z}$.

Equation 3.33 has a number of interesting applications, including the ability to compute a standard deviation of the parallel spot curve shock. This, in turn, allows us to impose probabilistic setting on scenario analysis (Section 2.2.4) and other methods that estimate the price sensitivity of fixed income portfolios and securities to parallel yield curve movements. Recall that the traditional approach to scenario analysis explicitly sketches out the shape of the price function by repeatedly shocking the spot curve by a given number of basis points and recomputing the resulting OAVs using a valuation model (Exhibits 2.1 and 2.2). While it is important to know the magnitude of the potential losses associated with, say, a 200 basis point increase in interest rates over one year, it is also useful to know the likelihood of such an event from a historical perspective. Let us illustrate how to compute the annualized one standard deviation of a parallel spot curve shock in a given market environment and then estimate the probability associated with a 200 basis point parallel movement in interest rates over one year.

Assuming that the entire set of systematic risk factors is represented as 10 key spot rates as shown in Table 3.1 ($n = 10$), a 200 basis point spot curve shock can be written as follows:

$$\bar{z} = (200, \ldots, 200)_{KR} \tag{3.34}$$

Clearly, the interest rate shock of unit length whose shape is the same as that of $\bar{z}$ is given by

$$(\xi_1, \ldots, \xi_{10}) = (\frac{1}{\sqrt{10}}, \ldots, \frac{1}{\sqrt{10}})_{KR} \tag{3.35}$$

Using the data from Table 3.1 and Equation 3.29, it can be shown that

$$\sigma\,(\xi) = (\xi_1,\ldots,\xi_{10}) \cdot \Sigma \cdot (\xi_1,\ldots,\xi_{10})^T = 291 \qquad (3.36)$$

and hence one standard deviation of a parallel spot curve shock on 9/30/96 is $291 \cdot \dfrac{1}{\sqrt{10}} = 92$ basis points per year (Table 3.3):

$$(\sigma\,(\xi) \cdot \xi_1,\ldots,\sigma(\xi) \cdot \xi_{10})_{KR} = (92,\ldots,92)_{KR} \qquad (3.37)$$

Analogous to Equation 3.33, a 200 basis point parallel spot curve shock can be written as follows:

$$\bar{z} = \begin{bmatrix} 200 \\ \ldots \\ 200 \end{bmatrix} = \begin{bmatrix} 92 \\ \ldots \\ 92 \end{bmatrix} \cdot \frac{200 \cdot \sqrt{10}}{291} = \begin{bmatrix} 92 \\ \ldots \\ 92 \end{bmatrix} \cdot \frac{200}{92} = \begin{bmatrix} 92 \\ \ldots \\ 92 \end{bmatrix} \cdot 2.17 \qquad (3.38)$$

Equation 3.38 demonstrates that on 9/30/96, the annualized 200 basis point parallel spot curve shock corresponded to a 2.17 standard deviation realization of the underlying standard normal variable. Since the probability of a continuous random variable taking a particular value is zero, we can use tables of *cumulative* normal distributions to describe the historical likelihood of a given interest rate shock. Thus, on 9/30/96, the probability of interest rates *increasing by 200 basis points or more* (or 2.17 standard deviations or more) over the course of one year was 0.015. In general, the magnitudes of annualized one standard deviation parallel shocks vary with market environments, ranging between 75 and 110 basis points, in our experience.

The ability to compute probabilities associated with various parallel spot curve movements can be used in a variety of instances. Thus, in analyzing the impact of time on dynamic risk characteristics of fixed income securities within EROR framework (Section 2.7), Table 2.12 presented probability of various interest rate movements as a function of time to option expiration. In Chapter 5, we use this capability in Grid Monte-Carlo Simulation Value-at-Risk. In the following sections, we utilize this technique to introduce the measures of historical plausibility of interest rate shocks.

3.4 HISTORICAL PLAUSIBILITY OF INTEREST RATE SHOCKS

The human mind can imagine all sorts of unusual interest rate shocks, and considerable time and resources may be spent investigating the price sensitivity of fixed income portfolios and securities to them. While concentrating on measuring as accurately as possible the magnitude of potential losses associated with various interest rate scenarios, rarely do risk methodologies address the issue of how *characteristic* of the recent yield curve dynamics a given hypothetical yield curve shock is. The goal of this section is to formally define *historical plausibility* of yield curve shocks, and describe the practical applications of the presented approach. The measures of plausibility described below introduce a historical perspective into a variety of methods that rely on hypothetical interest rate shocks. However, it is not true that historically "implausible" interest rate shocks should always be excluded from the consideration: stress testing is often concerned with investigating potential losses resulting from highly uncharacteristic market events. When used in conjunction with principal components decompositions and other tools, measures of historical plausibility can assist in generating plausible as well as deliberately implausible interest rate scenarios, allowing stress testing to become a meaningful and rigorous deterministic supplement of Value-at-Risk and other stochastic risk measures.

3.4.1 Explanatory Power

Earlier in this chapter, the notion of *explanatory power* – the percentage of the total variability in the system explained by a given interest rate shock – was introduced. Explanatory power is a measure of how *representative* or *characteristic* a shock is of the recent yield curve dynamics, and therefore can be thought of as the simplest measure of historical plausibility. High explanatory power implies that a large portion of historical changes in interest rates can be attributed to this particular yield curve movement. Among all interest rate shocks, the first principal component has the maximal explanatory power by construction. On 9/30/96, for instance, the first principal component explained 93% of the spot curve variability while the parallel shock explained 88% (Table 3.3). Explanatory power of interest rate shocks varies, sometimes dramatically, with the market environment. As shown in Table 3.4, the explanatory power of the first principal component on 12/31/98 was 83% while the explanatory power of the parallel shock was merely 67%, making practitioners question the accuracy of the risk measures that approximated changes in the yield curve as parallel shocks. The explanatory power of the hypothetical yield curve steepeners and flatteners employed by yield curve reshaping durations is typically low. Thus, on 9/30/96, the explanatory power of SEDUR was 38%.

3.4.2 Magnitude Plausibility

Section 3.3 has demonstrated that under the assumption that changes in interest rates are normally distributed, any interest rate shock $\bar{z}$ corresponds to a particular realization S of a standard normal variable (Equation 3.33):

$$\bar{z} \leftrightarrow S \tag{3.39}$$

This fact allows the second measure of historical plausibility, *magnitude plausibility* or *mpl($\bar{z}$)*, to be defined. As opposed to *explanatory power*, which estimates how *characteristic* a given yield curve shock is of the recent yield curve behavior, magnitude plausibility determines whether the *size* of a given interest rate shock is large from a historical perspective. For instance, low magnitude plausibility indicates that the shock is unusually large given the recent volatility of interest rates.

Since the probability of a normal random variable taking on any particular value is zero, magnitude plausibility is formulated in terms of cumulative probability distribution functions. In the example dealing with probability distributions of parallel shocks (Section 3.3), it was illustrated that on 9/30/96, one standard deviation of a parallel spot curve shock was 92 basis points per year. This allowed us to conclude that a 200 basis point shock corresponded to a 2.17 standard deviation event:

$$(200,\ldots,200)_{KR} \leftrightarrow S = 2.17 \tag{3.40}$$

When estimating magnitude plausibility, it appears to be convenient to make it a symmetric measure that is independent of the direction of interest rates. For that matter, when determining how plausible a 200 basis point parallel shock is from a historical perspective, we need to assess the joint probability of:

- Interest rates rallying by 200 basis points or more over the course of one year
- Interest rates selling off by 200 basis points or more over course of one year

In other words,

$$mpl(\bar{z}) = P(N(0,1) \le -2.17 \text{ or } N(0,1) \ge 2.17) = 3\% \tag{3.41}$$

where $P()$ denotes probability, and $N(0,1)$ denotes a standard normal random variable.

In a general setting, where S is a realization of a standard normal variable corresponding to a given interest rate shock $\bar{z}$, magnitude plausibility is computed via the following simple formula:

$$mpl(\bar{z}) = P(N(0,1) \leq -|S| \text{ or } N(0,1) \geq |S|) = 2 \cdot P(N(0,1) \geq |S|) \qquad (3.42)$$

The measure of magnitude plausibility introduced above implicitly assumes that irrespective of their current level, interest rates are as likely to rally as they are to sell off. This assumption may not be realistic in certain market environments. For instance, if interest rates are at their historical highs, the probability of them going down is arguably higher than that of them going up. In theory, the measure of magnitude plausibility can be enriched by employing conditional probabilities and thus accounting for the mean reversion of interest rates. It is important to note, however, that incorporation of any conjectures about mean-reversion into assessments of historical plausibility is only meaningful if the market is not believed to have gone through a permanent paradigm shift. The authors are not aware of any definitive results in this direction.

3.4.3 Shape Plausibility

In addition to measuring magnitude plausibility of an interest rate shock, it is useful to assess whether its *shape* is representative of the recent interest rate dynamics. The approach to measuring *shape plausibility* presented here appears to be somewhat unorthodox to some of our colleagues with financial economics backgrounds. It was inspired by applied modeling techniques frequently used in medicine, environmental and behavioral sciences, and other fields that make an extensive use of subjective judgment of experts. Instead of introducing a measure and then analyzing its properties, the desirable features of shape plausibility are first axiomatically defined and then one of the possible functional representations is identified.[22]

Principal components are the latent variables that depict the stochastic behavior of interest rates. The proposed measure of shape plausibility uses the following two important pieces of information obtained via principal components analysis:

- The representation of any interest rate shock as a set of realizations of principal components (Equation 3.23).
- The ranking of principal components by their explanatory powers ζ_i (Equation 3.15). Table 3.3 presents principal components analy-

sis of spot curve movements on 9/30/96. On that day, the first principal component explained 92.8% of the total variability of interest rates (ζ_1 = 92.8%), the second explained 4.80% (ζ_2 = 4.80%), and so forth.

Arguably, if a yield curve shock is truly *characteristic* of recent yield curve dynamics, its *decomposition* $(\theta_1,\ldots,\theta_n)$ into principal components should in some sense be consistent with the way the total interest rate variability is explained by principal components. We will say that an interest rate shock is the *most representative* of the given system if the *contribution* $(\theta_{M,i})$ of each principal component to this shock exactly equals to the percentage (ζ_i) of the total variability explained by this principal component. Continuing the example from Table 3.3, since the explanatory power of the first principal component is 92.80%, it seems logical to require the first principal component to "explain" exactly 92.80% of the *most representative* shock. By construction, the decomposition of the *most representative* shock into principal components is given by the vector of their explanatory powers (Table 3.3):

PC Decomposition of the Most Representative Shock

$$(\theta_{M,1},\ldots,\theta_{M,n}) = (\zeta_1,\ldots,\zeta_n) = (92.80,4.80,1.27,\ldots,0.03) \qquad (3.43)$$

In addition to the *most representative* shock, let us define the yield curve shock that is the *least representative* of the recent dynamics of interest rates. Since the last (*n*th) principal component has the smallest explanatory power by construction, we choose it to be the *least representative* interest rate shock. Clearly, the decomposition of the last principal component is as follows:

PC Decomposition of the Least Representative Shock

$$(\theta_{L,1},\ldots,\theta_{L,n}) = (0,\ldots,0,100) \qquad (3.44)$$

The measure of shape plausibility $spl(\bar{z})$ is defined as a mapping that assigns a number between 0% and 100% to a given interest rate shock:

$$spl : \bar{z} \to x \in [0\%, 100\%] \qquad (3.45)$$

The functional representation of $spl(\bar{z})$ is chosen so that shape plausibility of the most representative shock is 100% and that of the least representative shock is 0%. Clearly, there are many ways to define the measure of shape plausibility that possesses these properties. We present one of the possible approaches.

Write a hypothetical interest rate shock $\bar{z}$ in terms of realizations of principal components:

$$\bar{z} = (v_1, ..., v_n)_{PC} \qquad (3.46)$$

Due to the fact that $\bar{z}$ is a vector and in order to ensure that individual principal components' contributions add up to 1, we define the *contribution* of the ith principal component to $\bar{z}$ as the percentage of the squared length of $\bar{z}$ due to v_i:

$$\theta_i = \frac{v_i^2}{\displaystyle\sum_{j=1}^{n} v_j^2} \qquad (3.47)$$

It now remains to write a functional representation of shape plausibility. It should compare the principal component decomposition (Equation 3.47) of a given interest rate shock with those of the most representative and the least representative shocks (Equations 3.43 and 3.44, respectively). One of the approaches to contrast these different principal components' decompositions is presented here:

$$spl(\bar{z}) = 1 - \frac{\sqrt{\displaystyle\sum_{i=1}^{n} (\theta_i - \theta_{M,i})^2}}{\sqrt{\displaystyle\sum_{i=1}^{n} (\theta_{M,i} - \theta_{L,i})^2}} \qquad (3.48)$$

where, as before, θ_i, $\theta_{M,i}$, $\theta_{L,i}$ denote principal components decompositions of the given interest rate shock, the most representative shock, and the least representative shock, respectively. Equation 3.48 shows that shape plausibility of the most representative shock is 100%, and that of the least representative shock is 0% by construction.

All characteristics of a given interest rate shock, including its explanatory power, magnitude plausibility, and shape plausibility, may change substantially with the market environment. Thus, shape plausibilities of the first principal component and a parallel spot curve shock are typically between 80% and 90%, while the shape plausibilities of the yield curve reshaping durations shocks are between 30% and 45%, suggesting that these yield curve steepeners are not particularly plausible from a historical perspective.

3.4.4 Example: An Extreme Market Move During the 1998 Crisis

Consider an actual yield curve move – the dramatic increase in U.S. interest rates on 10/9/98 during the culmination of the credit and liquidity crisis of 1998. This interest rate shock was characterized by a 10 basis point move in the 3-month rate, approximately a 20 basis point move in the intermediate part of the spot curve, and a 7 basis point change in the 30-year spot rate (Exhibit 3.7).

Was this market event abnormal? Did the yield curve change its shape or level on this day in an uncharacteristic fashion? These questions are more difficult to answer rigorously than they first appear to be because, as emphasized on numerous occasions in this chapter, the yield curve is a rather large and complex dynamic system. It is difficult to directly study a system that depends on such a large number of interdependent variables. Results obtained earlier in this chapter allow us to parsimoniously describe the yield curve behavior and gain insights into the actual as well as hypothetical market movements by performing principal components analysis and applying the measures of historical plausibility.

Historical plausibility. According to Exhibit 3.7, shape plausibility (denoted by Sh) of the spot curve movement on 10/9/98 was 94%, while its explanatory power (denoted by Exp) was 82%, both indicating that the shape of this shock was characteristic of the dynamics of interest rates and historically plausible. However, low magnitude plausibility (denoted by Mgn) of 1% revealed that the magnitude of this steepening sell-off was unusually large from a historical perspective.

Principal components decomposition. Exhibit 3.7 also illustrates that 93% of the spot curve movement on 10/9/98 was attributed to the first principal component, 2% to the second, and 3% to the third. On the cumulative basis, the first three principal components explained 98% of this yield curve move. In addition to analyzing the percentage principal component decomposition, it is important to study the corresponding realizations of principal components in terms of standard deviations. It can be seen that on 10/9/98, the first principal component moved by 2.4 daily standard deviations, the second by 1.1, and the third by 2.6, confirming that this market move was probabilistically unlikely. Notice that this example supports the previous research[23] that discovered that for the majority of large market movements, changes in interest rates are almost entirely explained by the first principal component. In this particular case, principal components analysis also reveals that the large realization of the third principal component explains the unusual behavior of both the short and long ends of the yield curve.

EXHIBIT 3.7   Historical Interest Rate Shock (10/8/98–10/9/98): Principal Components Decomposition, Explanatory Power, and Historical Plausibility

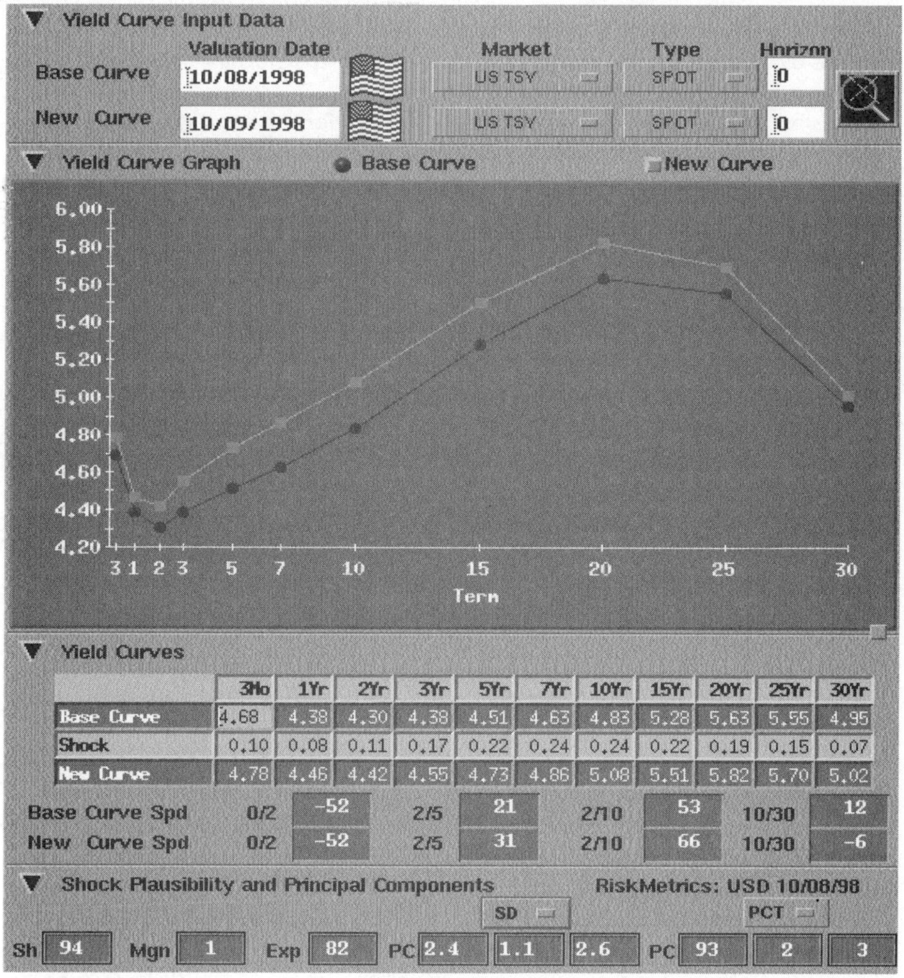

While useful in analyzing historical market movements, principal components and the measures of plausibility also enable the construction of hypothetical big market moves that can be used in stress testing and other risk methodologies.

ENDNOTES

1. Parts of this chapter are based on Golub and Tilman, 1997a.

2. Construction of well-behaved spot curves that fit data well and do not imply negative forward rates is a complex valuation rather than a risk management problem, which is beyond the scope of this book. For an excellent overview of this subject, the reader is referred to Anderson et al., 1997.

3. One-factor interest rate models typically specify the stochastic evolution of the *short rate* over time (see Cheyette, 1997).

4. This being said, many risk management applications can and do employ probability distributions other than normal.

5. Using the population mean of zero as opposed to the actual sample mean when computing historical correlations and volatilities is called *detrending*. For instance, if the 10-year spot rate increased by 10 basis points in each of the 10 consecutive days, the estimate of volatility of changes computed around the sample mean (of 10) would be zero, implying the absence of risk. If the dispersion around the population mean of zero were measured instead, it would properly reflect the actual volatility of the spot rate.

6. RiskMetrics® methodology is described in RiskMetrics®, 1996. This chapter excludes the 25-year spot key rate from the set of systematic risk factors because the dataset does not provide information about this maturity. While reporting both price and yield volatilities of key spot rates, RiskMetrics® only provides *correlations of returns* on zero-coupon bonds rather than *correlations of changes in key spot rates*. However, the two are the same to the first order approximation.

7. See Kuberek, 1990; Litterman and Scheinkman, 1991; and Barber and Copper, 1996.

8. The authors are aware of only a handful of proprietary and government trading desks that use principal components durations in weighting butterfly yield curve trades and in other portfolio management and trading decisions (see Weir, 1996).

9. When creating continuous principal components shocks, their values at the 0-month rate were extrapolated as zero.

10. It is customary to assume that a parallel spot curve is the most dominant yield curve movement and force the shape of the first principal component to be parallel (see Willner, 1996).

11. See Johnson and Wichern, 1982

12. See Johnson and Wichern, 1982.

13. Assuming that all eigenvalues of the covariance matrix Σ are distinct, orthogonality of principal components' factor loadings implies that principal components are statistically uncorrelated (see Johnson and Wichern, 1982).

14. It is not true, however, that any hypothetical spot curve shift can be explained by the first three principal components. For example, a one standard deviation move in the fourth principal component cannot be explained at all by the first three principal components.

15. See Ronn, 1996.

16. See Johnson and Wichern, 1982.

17. See Ronn, 1996.

18. See Willner, 1996.

19. A technique similar in spirit was also used by Barber and Copper, 1996.

20. By definition, a standard normal variable N(0,1) has a mean of zero and a standard deviation of 1.
21. If the number of principal components used to describe a given yield curve shock equals to the number of key rates, the decomposition is unique and can be obtained analytically. However, approximating an interest rate shock with a smaller number of principal components requires an optimization, and the solution is not necessarily unique.
22. See *measures of consistency* introduced by Brusilovskiy and Tilman, 1996.
23. See Ronn, 1996.

4

Measuring Interest Rate, Basis, and Currency Risks[1]

4.1 DETERMINISTIC VERSUS PROBABILISTIC RISK METHODOLOGIES

4.1.1 Introduction

The previous chapters have provided the foundation for introducing a substantially richer framework for measuring financial risk. As opposed to the purely deterministic what-if measures described earlier in the book, the methodologies presented here combine information about market exposures of fixed income securities and portfolios with assumptions about the joint probability distributions of the underlying sources of market risk. More specifically, this chapter constructs probabilistic measures of risk by integrating first-order price sensitivities to various interest rate, currency, and basis risks with empirical knowledge of historical volatilities of systematic risk factors and correlations among them. To motivate the need for Value-at-Risk (VaR) and illustrate the distinction between parametric approaches and those that integrate probability distributions, consider the following deliberately flawed financial example.

Suppose a risk-averse investor residing in New York owns the following investment portfolio with a current market value of one million dollars:

1. A 30-year New York State municipal zero-coupon bond valued at $500,000
2. An oceanfront condominium in the Hamptons, Long Island, New York, also valued at $500,000

From now on, we will refer to this portfolio of two assets as the New York portfolio. In pursuit of a risk-controlled investment style, this investor hires Parametric Measurement, Inc., a risk management consulting firm whose mandate is to estimate the total risk embedded in this portfolio. As the reader might surmise, Parametric Measurement specializes in parametric risk methodologies described in Chapter 2. Since the risk associated with holding a 30-year zero-coupon bond is well understood, the main complexity of the task lies in understanding the risks associated with owning the condominium and aggregating them with the bond's interest rate risk. As a first step, Parametric Measurement assembles a panel of real estate experts who, after a great deal of market research, come to a conclusion that due to the prime location, the price of the condominium is not typically affected by the real estate market fluctuations.[2] In the absence of market risks, it follows that this oceanfront property can only lose value in the event of natural disasters, that is, earthquakes and floods. According to the real estate experts,

- The condominium will lose 50% of its value in the event of an earthquake of 6 on the Richter scale.
- The condominium will lose 5% of its value per each day of flood.

In order to be consistent with conventional fixed income market practices, Parametric Measurement decides to employ duration (or *elasticity*) measures when analyzing the overall risk of this portfolio. Table 4.1 shows that there are three systematic sources of risk that affect this portfolio's value: municipal interest rates, earthquakes, and floods. Assuming that the option-adjusted duration of a 30-year zero-coupon bond (ZCB) is approximately 30 (Chapter 2), this bond would lose 30% of its value for each 100 basis point increase in municipal interest rates. According to the real estate experts, the condominium would lose 50% of its value after an earthquake of 6 on the Richter scale, so, its earthquake duration is 50. Analogously, since the price of the condominium would decline by 5% for each day of a flood, its flood duration is 5. Recall that partial duration of a portfolio is computed as the weighted average of the corresponding partial durations of the underlying assets. Since the portfolio's market value is equally divided among the bond and the condominium (which are exposed to different systematic risk factors), each

TABLE 4.1 Measuring Risk of the New York Portfolio Using Parametric Approaches

Risk Management Report

Portfolio: $500,000 NYS ZCB; $500,000 Hamptons Condominium

Asset	Risk Factor	Description	Risk Measure	Exposure
30-year NYS Muni ZCB	Interest Rates	Asset Loses 30% per 100 Basis Point Move	Interest Rate Duration	30.0
Hamptons Condominium	Earthquakes	Asset loses 50% per Earthquake of 6 on the Richter Scale	Earthquake Duration	50.0
	Floods	Asset Loses 5% per 1 Day of Flood	Flood Duration	5.0
Portfolio	Interest Rates	Portfolio Loses 15% per 100 Basis Point Move	Interest Rate Duration	15.0
Portfolio	Earthquakes	Portfolio Loses 25% per Earthquake of 6 on the Richter Scale	Earthquake Duration	25.0
Portfolio	Floods	Portfolio Loses 2.5% per 1 Day of Flood	Flood Duration	2.5
Portfolio	All	Total Loss	Aggregate Duration	42.5

portfolio-level partial duration can be obtained by dividing the individual assets' partial durations by 2 (Table 4.1). Thus, the portfolio's aggregate interest rate duration is 15, its earthquake duration is 25, and its flood duration is 2.5. By adding these three partial durations, Parametric Measurement arrives at the total portfolio's duration of 42.5.

Although deliberately unrealistic, this example highlights a number of crucial problems associated with parametric approaches to measuring market risk:

1. *Assuming that risk factors are perfectly correlated and exhibit similar volatilities.* The interest rate sensitivity of the New York portfolio is expressed per 100 basis point parallel movement in interest rates; the earthquake sensitivity is represented per an earthquake of 6 on the Richter scale; and the flood sensitivity is measured per one day of flood. Given the drastically different nature of these systematic risk factors, it should be obvious that risks in each of these dimensions need to be measured and managed separately rather than being aggregated into an overall sensitivity measure. By adding up the portfolio's interest rate, earthquake, and flood durations, it is implicitly assumed that a 100 basis point move in interest rates, an earthquake of 6 on the Richter scale, and a one-day flood *always happen simultaneously.* In the language of statistics, it is equivalent to postulating that these random events are *perfectly correlated and equally volatile.* Mistakes of this kind are made in risk management of real-life fixed income portfolios on a regular basis. For instance, a portfolio's overall spread duration (that is often viewed as an aggregate measure of sensitivity to changes in credit spreads) is computed as the weighted average of spread durations of individual securities. By doing so, price sensitivities to the quite different systematic risks – TSY liquidity premiums, mortgage option-adjusted spreads, corporate nominal spreads, emerging market spreads, etc. – are sometimes collapsed into one summary number. Another example comes from portfolio management, where the overall interest rate duration of a multicurrency portfolio is sometimes computed as the weighted average of interest rate durations of the underlying assets, implicitly assuming that yield curves in different markets are perfectly correlated and equally volatile. Ironically, this assumption contradicts the rationale for diversification that drives investors to multiple markets and currencies in the first place.

2. *Ignoring the likelihood of events.* Imagine that instead of the New York portfolio, a California portfolio – consisting of a California

municipal zero-coupon bond and a California waterfront property – was analyzed. Clearly, applying the duration approach to measuring the risk of the New York and California portfolios would lead to identical results because of the *deterministic* nature of this methodology. Due to the lack of the notion of likelihood (or probability), parametric techniques cannot assimilate important information, for instance, the fact that earthquakes in New York State are highly improbable or that floods are much more common in California than they are in New York.

3. *Failing to capture nonlinearity.* Defined as the first-order price sensitivity, duration is presented per unit of change in a risk factor. For instance, option-adjusted duration is the negative of the percentage change in price per a 100 basis point parallel movement in spot rates. Earthquake duration is the negative of the percentage change in price per an earthquake of 6 on the Richter scale. Via the analogs of Equation 2.24, duration is widely used to approximate price changes given any arbitrary realization of the underlying systematic risk factor. Thus, since the condominium's earthquake duration is 50 (per an earthquake of 6 on the Richter scale), by extrapolation, 25% and 100% losses can be inferred for earthquakes of 3 and 12 on the Richter scale, respectively. Clearly, such assessment of risk is fallacious since there may be no loss if the magnitude of an earthquake is less than 5, and the property might be completely demolished in the event of an earthquake of 7 on the Richter scale. This example highlights the significant limitations associated with linear approximations of price functions.

This chapter introduces Variance/Covariance Value-at-Risk (VaR), a summary risk measure that combines information about market exposures with assumptions about the probability distributions of systematic risk factors. VaR properly aggregates market exposures corresponding to the fundamentally different risk factors, making it especially useful in risk management of complex portfolios containing fixed income securities, equities, commodities, foreign currencies, and other asset classes. However, because of the linear measures of price sensitivity used in its computation, the Variance/Covariance approach to VaR cannot capture the nonlinearity of the value surface. Chapter 5 deals with the generalization of VaR methodology in this important direction.

Let us return to analyzing the risk of the portfolio consisting of a New York State municipal zero-coupon bond and a condominium in the Hamptons. As already mentioned, the following information is required to complete this analysis:

- *Forecasts of variability of municipal interest rates, earthquakes, and floods in New York.* According to Table 4.2, one annualized standard deviation ("Annualized Volatility") of New York State municipal interest rates was assumed to be 100 basis points per year, one standard deviation of earthquakes in New York was assumed to be zero, and one standard deviation of floods was assumed to be two days per year for coastal areas.[3]
- *Forecasts of correlations among risk factors.* Municipal interest rates, earthquakes, and floods in the state of New York were assumed to be completely uncorrelated with each other.

As discussed in Chapter 3, changes in systematic risk factors are assumed to follow a multivariate normal distribution with zero mean. Note that even when empirical probability density functions (PDF) of changes in systematic risk factors resemble normal distributions, the normality assumption has to be used with caution since PDFs of financial time series tend to exhibit fat tails. The normality assumption is entirely inadequate when a risk factor represents rare events, including earthquakes and other natural disasters, defaults of financial institutions, and the like. A multivariate normal distribution is fully defined by the vector of volatilities (standard deviations) and the correlation matrix (Table 4.2).

We are now ready to define a probabilistic framework for measuring financial risk. Consider the representation of the total percentage change in value of the New York portfolio as a sum of percentage gains or losses corresponding to each systematic risk factor in isolation:

$$\frac{\Delta V}{V} = \frac{\Delta V}{V}\bigg|_{\text{interest rates}} + \frac{\Delta V}{V}\bigg|_{\text{earthquakes}} + \frac{\Delta V}{V}\bigg|_{\text{floods}} \tag{4.1}$$

where the expressions on the right-hand side of Equation 4.1 denote the percentage changes in value due to interest rate movements, earthquakes, and floods, respectively. According to Table 4.1, the portfolio's aggregate partial durations with respect to interest rates, earthquakes, and floods are 15, 25, and 2.5, respectively. Given these price sensitivities, percentage changes in price can be approximated via partial durations and the corresponding changes in systematic risk factors (the analog of Equation 2.39):

$$\frac{\Delta V}{V} = -15 \cdot \Delta IntR - 25 \cdot \frac{\Delta EarthQ}{6} - 2.5 \cdot \Delta Flood \tag{4.2}$$

TABLE 4.2 Incorporating Probability Distribution Assumptions into Risk Measures (New York Portfolio)

Risk Management Report

Portfolio: $500,000 NYS ZCB; $500,000 Hamptons Condominium

Hypothetical Dynamics of Risk Factors (New York)

Annualized Volatility	Interest Rates	Earthquakes	Floods
	100 basis points	0 on Richter Scale	2 days
Correlations			
Interest Rates	1	0	0
Earthquakes	0	1	0
Floods	0	0	1

Asset	Risk Factor	Risk Measure	Exposure To Factor	Factor Volatility	Exposure (%/year)
30-year NYS Muni ZCB	Interest Rates	Interest Rate Duration	30.0	100	30
Hamptons Condominium	Earthquakes	Earthquake Duration	50.0	0	0
	Floods	Flood Duration	5.0	2	10
Portfolio	Interest Rates	Interest Rate Duration	15.0	100	15
Portfolio	Earthquakes	Earthquake Duration	25.0	0	0
Portfolio	Floods	Flood Duration	2.5	2	5
Portfolio	All	Price Volatility	N/A	N/A	15.8
Portfolio	All	95% Loss (VaR)	N/A	N/A	26.1

where $\Delta IntR$ is a change in municipal interest rates, $\Delta EarthQ$ is the magnitude of an earthquake (it is divided by 6 since earthquake duration is measured per an earthquake of 6 on the Richter scale), and $\Delta Flood$ is the length of a flood.

For the sake of convenience, denote these three systematic risk factors as F_1, F_2, F_3 and the corresponding partial durations as $pdur_1$, $pdur_2$, and $pdur_3$. Then Equation 4.2 can be rewritten as follows:

$$\frac{\Delta V}{V} = -\sum_{i=1}^{3} pdur_i \cdot \Delta F_i \tag{4.3}$$

Since all risk factors are assumed to be normally distributed, their linear combination – the percentage change in price – is implicitly assumed to be normal as well:

$$\frac{\Delta V}{V} \sim N(0,\sigma) \tag{4.4}$$

where $N(0,\sigma)$ is the normal distribution with zero mean and standard deviation σ. Recall that the standard deviation of a linear combination of normal random variables can be computed using the following simple formula (element-wise analog of Equation 3.29):

$$\sigma = \sigma(\frac{\Delta V}{V}) = \sqrt{\sum_{i=1}^{3}\sum_{j=1}^{3} pdur_i \cdot \sigma(\Delta F_i) \cdot pdur_j \cdot \sigma(\Delta F_j) \cdot \rho(\Delta F_i, \Delta F_j)} \tag{4.5}$$

where $\sigma(\Delta F_j)$ is the standard deviation of changes in jth risk factor and $\rho(\Delta F_i, \Delta F_j)$ is the correlation between changes in risk factors F_i and F_j.

Define the vector of one standard deviation price exposures as:

$$\bar{e} = \left[pdur_1 \cdot \sigma(\Delta F_1), \quad pdur_2 \cdot \sigma(\Delta F_2), \quad pdur_3 \cdot \sigma(\Delta F_3) \right] \tag{4.6}$$

Combining Equations 4.5 and 4.6 yields:

$$\sigma = \sigma(\frac{\Delta V}{V}) = \sqrt{\bar{e} \cdot \rho \cdot \bar{e}^T} \tag{4.7}$$

where ρ is the correlation matrix of changes in systematic risk factors.

If the market exposures of the New York portfolio as well as correlations and volatilities of interest rates, earthquakes, and floods from Table 4.2 are entered into Equation 4.7, it can be easily verified that one standard deviation of the portfolio's value in the example above is 15.8% per year:

$$\sigma = \sigma(\frac{\Delta V}{V}) = \sqrt{[15 \quad 0 \quad 5] \cdot \begin{bmatrix} 1 & 0 & 0 \\ 0 & 1 & 0 \\ 0 & 0 & 1 \end{bmatrix} \cdot [15 \quad 0 \quad 5]^T} = 15.8\% \qquad (4.8)$$

where [15 0 5] is a vector of standard deviation dollar exposures obtained via Equation 4.6.

As already mentioned, the assumption about normality of changes in systematic risk factors implies normality of percentage changes in price. Estimating *price volatility* (one standard deviation) is therefore the first step in understanding the risk of fixed income portfolios since it allows us to analytically obtain any percentile of the distribution of their price changes. If a random variable is normally distributed, 68% of its realizations are expected to fall between −1 and +1 standard deviations.[4] If applied to constructing one-sided confidence intervals, this implies that if the annualized price volatility of the New York portfolio is 15.8%, then in one out of every 6.25 years (16% of years), the portfolio should be expected to lose 15.8% of its current value or more.

4.1.2 Value-at-Risk

"Once esoteric," the concept of Value-at-Risk (VaR) has become one of the most popular "mainstream practices used by thousands of institutional investors, industry consultants, and regulators."[5] Over the past few years, significant advances in measuring VaR and understanding its strengths and weaknesses were made, which led to its acceptance as one of the key measures of business-as-usual financial risk. VaR has "emerged as a key component of capital adequacy for commercial banks."[6] Firmwide risk management departments have begun using it to set trading risk limits. Financial institutions whose assets are managed by external money managers have begun employing VaR in implementing duration overlay strategies. Finally, methodologies underlying portfolio optimization and asset allocation systems have started minimizing risk as measured by VaR.

The very interpretation of VaR has evolved over the years as market participants became more familiar with the assumptions underlying this measure, its advantages and limitations, and the false sense of comfort it may provide.[7] Shortly after its introduction, VaR was understood as a *maximal* and (with a high degree of confidence) *improbable* loss that a position or portfolio may incur over a specified horizon. VaR numbers were typically presented to the upper management as follows: "At the 99% (or 95%) confidence level, the portfolio is not expected to lose more than its Value-at-Risk over a given horizon." The concept of *confidence level*, a purely statistical construct, became widely used in the everyday communication among portfolio managers, traders, risk managers, executives, and boards of directors. In statistics, a 99% confidence level implies that there is a 1% chance that the losses will exceed VaR. However, when 99% is used colloquially, it is sometimes heard as meaning *never*. Inevitably, when *never* showed up during 1997–1998 market crises as an adverse realization of P/L, the appeal of VaR sank. Many investors became disillusioned with this risk measure and ruled it useless altogether. Later, it was realized that the existing formulations of VaR were neither designed to nor capable of measuring catastrophic risks.

Over the recent years, investors' attitude toward VaR has gone through a phase of maturation. A more balanced view on what can and cannot be achieved by using VaR now seems to be adopted. VaR has even gained a different interpretation – a *large loss corresponding to infrequent, but, on average, regularly occurring events* (rather than simply a *large improbable loss*). VaR is no longer "one number from a black box [which] provides little understanding of risk".[8] Market participants have gained intuition behind the properties of this measure in various market environments. Numerous supplemental analyses have been developed to provide insights into VaR estimates, including risk decomposition, marginal VaR, and so forth. Many practitioners, portfolio managers, executives, compliance officers, and boards of directors have become increasingly comfortable with the concept of VaR. Since then, the acceptance of VaR has proceeded almost too well.

In some cases, market participants have taken usage of VaR to the extreme. In their attempt to be vigilant, some risk management departments have begun imposing rigid VaR limits on portfolios and positions. Unfortunately, these policies may do more harm than good unless volatility of VaR is taken into account. For example, during the 1998 market crisis, historical volatility of interest rates increased while correlations between the 3-month spot rate and spot rates corresponding to longer maturities became temporarily negative.[9] As a result, VaRs of leveraged portfolios that were invested in longer securities and financed via short maturity instruments increased dramatically. At financial institutions with corporate risk limits, portfolio managers suddenly found themselves out of compliance and were obliged to adjust their positions in the middle of the crisis in order to reduce VaR. Given the distressed market environment at the time, this resulted in larger losses than those incurred by investors who did not have predefined corporate VaR limits and were in a position to wait until the markets rebounded. VaR limits would have forced many market participants to adjust their positions in the middle of the crisis, only exacerbating the selloff and causing devastating losses.

In this book, we will review a variety of VaR methodologies. While focusing on the applied financial modeling aspects, we will address the conceptual, operational, and even political challenges facing financial institutions that manage risk via VaR. VaR is by far the most comprehensive measure of financial risk since it combines information about the price/yield functions with knowledge about the probability distributions of systematic risk factors. Yet, while being an invaluable risk management tool, VaR needs to be accompanied by stress testing, backtesting, and, even more importantly, an understanding of its statistical nature and knowledge of its underlying assumptions. The concept of VaR illustrates a very important point that has become the recurring motif of this book: No single measure of risk *alone* will suffice in the evolving financial markets.

VaR provides a conceptual framework for presenting financial risk as a single, intuitive summary measure. It is concerned with estimating unusually high losses resulting from large market events. Value-at-Risk analysis starts with specifying the VaR *horizon* (e.g., one month) and the *confidence level* (e.g., 95%). As mentioned earlier, VaR has the following two equivalent interpretations:

- *Worst case loss.* Over one month, there is a 95% probability that a portfolio will not lose more than its VaR.
- *An unlikely, but on average, regularly occurring event.* On average, in one out of every 20 months, the portfolio should be expected to incur a loss greater than or equal to its VaR.

For confidence levels other than 95% and different horizons, VaR is defined as the worst case loss that can be expected to occur over the given horizon with the probability of (100 − *confidence level*)%.

Under the assumption that changes in a portfolio's value follow a normal distribution, VaR can be obtained analytically just as any other percentile of a normal distribution. Thus, the 95% VaR (in percent) can be computed using the following formula (Exhibit 4.1):

EXHIBIT 4.1   Variance/Covariance Value-at-Risk

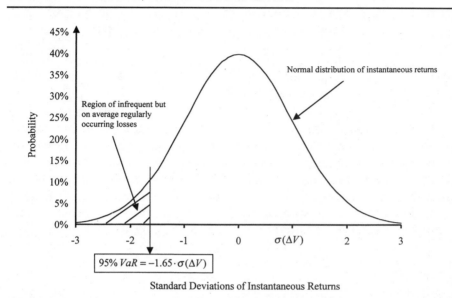

Standard Deviations of Instantaneous Returns

$$95\%\ VaR = 1.65 \cdot \sigma\left(\frac{\Delta V}{V}\right) \tag{4.9}$$

Similarly, VaR can be expressed in dollars as well:

$$95\%\ VaR = 1.65 \cdot \sigma(\Delta V) \tag{4.10}$$

If Equations 4.8, 4.9, and 4.10 are applied to the example from the previous section, VaR of the New York portfolio can be computed as 15.8% · 1.65 = 26.1% or $261,000 per year.

When compared with deterministic approaches, the VaR framework has clear advantages. By virtue of utilizing information about the dynamics of underlying systematic risk factors, VaR may arrive at substantially different risk estimates even if the static market exposures of two portfolios are identical. Let us illustrate this point by modifying the example dealing with the New York portfolio. Instead of a portfolio consisting of a New York State municipal zero-coupon bond and a waterfront Hamptons condominium, consider the California portfolio containing a 30-year Sonoma County municipal zero-coupon bond and a waterfront Russian River condominium in Sonoma County, California.[10]

Assume that all price sensitivities of this portfolio (interest rate duration, earthquake duration, and flood duration) as well as the market value split between fixed income and real estate assets are exactly the same as those of the New York portfolio. Since parametric approaches (Table 4.1) do not utilize any information other than market values and durations, from a deterministic perspective the California and New York portfolios can be erroneously deemed equally risky.

Obviously, such assessment of risk is unrealistic since the likelihood of floods and earthquakes in Sonoma County may be incomparably greater than in New York. Consider the hypothetical correlations and volatilities of municipal interest rates, earthquakes, and floods in Sonoma County presented in Table 4.3. While variability of municipal interest rates is assumed to be the same as that in New York (100 basis points per year), the assumed standard deviations of earthquakes and floods are substantially larger (3 on the Richter scale and 5 days per year, respectively). Moreover, the correlation matrix is not trivial anymore: It was assumed that there is a small correlation of 0.2 between earthquakes and floods (since earthquakes may cause floods), and there is a correlation of 0.7 between interest rates and both earthquakes and floods (since natural disasters may impair the county's ability to meet its financial obligations).[11] Under these assumptions, using Equations 4.8, 4.9, and 4.10, it can be shown that the price volatility of the California portfolio is 33.5% and its VaR is 55.3%, more than twice as large as that of the identical New York portfolio.

4.2 MEASURING U.S. INTEREST RATE RISK

4.2.1 Variance/Covariance Value-at-Risk and Ex Ante Tracking Error

The concept of Variance/Covariance VaR was inspired by portfolio mean variance theory, and its analogs have been widely used in the equity markets for decades. The term itself was introduced by J.P. Morgan and was first used in the original publication of RiskMetrics® methodology.[12] Along with BARRA's tracking errors, RiskMetrics® VaR was one of the earlier attempts to approach fixed income risk from an empirical probabilistic perspective. The overwhelming majority of risk in a typical high quality fixed income portfolio arises from changes in the term structure of interest rates. This might explain why initial VaR formulations analyzed financial risk only along the interest rate dimension. In this section, we present the original definition of Variance/Covariance VaR in order to

TABLE 4.3 Incorporating Probability Distribution Assumptions into Risk Measures (California Portfolio)

Risk Management Report

Portfolio: $500,000 Sonoma County (CA) ZCB; $500,000 Russian River Condominium (Sonoma County, CA)

		Hypothetical Dynamics of Risk Factors (Sonoma County, CA)		
		Interest Rates	Earthquakes	Floods
		100 basis points	3 on Richter Scale	5 days
Annualized Volatility				
Correlations				
	Interest Rates	1	0.7	0.7
	Earthquakes	0.7	1	0.2
	Floods	0.7	0.2	1

Asset	Risk Factor	Risk Measure	Duration Exposure	Volatility	Exposure (%/year)
30-year Sonoma Muni ZCB	Interest Rates	Interest Rate Duration	30.0	100	30
Hamptons Condominium	Earthquakes	Earthquake Duration	50.0	3	= 3/6 * 50 = 25
	Floods	Flood Duration	5.0	5	25
Portfolio	Interest Rates	Interest Rate Duration	15.0	100	15.0
Portfolio	Earthquakes	Earthquake Duration	25.0	3	12.5
Portfolio	Floods	Flood Duration	2.5	5	12.5
Portfolio	All	Price Volatility	N/A	N/A	33.5
Portfolio	All	95% Loss (VaR)	N/A	N/A	55.3

demonstrate the intellectual evolution of stochastic measures of risk and their relationship with the previously described deterministic (parametric) risk methodologies.

Similar to Equation 4.1, original RiskMetrics® methodology considered the following representation of the portfolio's return as the sum of returns on the underlying assets:

$$\Delta V = \Delta V|_{\text{asset 1}} + \Delta V|_{\text{asset 2}} + \ldots + \Delta V|_{\text{asset n}} \qquad (4.11)$$

By making the assumption that changes in values of the individual assets follow a multivariate normal distribution, VaR of a portfolio of n assets was defined as the 5th percentile of its distribution of returns:

$$VaR = 1.65 \cdot \sigma(\Delta V) = 1.65 \cdot \sqrt{\sum_{i=1}^{n}\sum_{j=1}^{n} V_i \cdot \sigma_i^P \cdot V_j \cdot \sigma_j^P \cdot \rho(i,j)} \qquad (4.12)$$

where V is the total value of the portfolio; V_i is the market value of the ith asset, σ_i^P is price volatility[13] of the ith asset, and $\rho(i, j)$ is correlation between the returns on assets i and j.

The initial release of RiskMetrics® VaR methodology presented fixed income securities as replicating portfolios of zero-coupon bonds (ZCBs). This was done via the so-called *cash flow mappings* that explicitly allocated the present value of each cash flow among a predefined set of key rate maturities. Once a security was replicated as a collection of zero-coupon bonds, ZCB historical correlations and volatilities were used to compute the security's price volatility and its VaR (Equation 4.12). However, this method was directly applicable only to fixed cash flow instruments. Despite this significant limitation, practitioners quickly realized the potential of the proposed approach and generalized it to properly handle cash flow uncertainties embedded in fixed income securities. Thus, instead of cash flow mappings, investors began using key rate durations (Section 2.4.1) to construct risk-equivalent (replicating) zero-coupon bond portfolios. The advantage of such a representation lies in its applicability to all types of securities, including those with cash flow uncertainties.

Suppose that krd_i is the ith key rate duration of a fixed income security, and *Mod Dur$_i$* is modified duration of the zero-coupon bond whose maturity corresponds to the ith key rate. The position in ZCB that has the same interest rate exposure as that implied by the ith key rate duration of the security can be obtained via the dollar duration hedging argument:[14]

$$V_i = \frac{V \cdot krd_i}{Mod\ Dur_i} \qquad (4.13)$$

Recall that the percentage price changes of a fixed cash flow bond can be approximated using its modified duration and changes in its yield-to-maturity. Computing one standard deviation of both sides of Equation 2.12 gives

$$\sigma\left(\frac{\Delta P}{P}\right) = Mod\ Dur \cdot \sigma(\Delta y) \qquad (4.14)$$

We can now substitute expressions from Equations 4.13 and 4.14 into Equation 4.12:

$$VaR = 1.65 \cdot V \cdot \sqrt{\sum_{i=1}^{n}\sum_{j=1}^{n} krd_i \cdot \sigma(\Delta y_i) \cdot krd_j \cdot \sigma(\Delta y_j) \cdot \rho(\Delta y_i, \Delta y_j)} \qquad (4.15)$$

Changes in ZCB yields-to-maturity can be thought of as changes in spot rates, and therefore Equation 4.15 can be rewritten as follows:

$$VaR = 1.65 \cdot V \cdot \sqrt{(krd_1, ..., krd_n) \cdot \Sigma \cdot (krd_1, ..., krd_n)^T} \qquad (4.16)$$

where $(krd_1,...,krd_n)$ is a vector of key rate durations (KRDs), and Σ is the *covariance* matrix of changes in spot rates. Notice that while Equation 4.15 presents VaR in terms of KRDs, standard deviations of changes in key spot rates, and correlations among them, Equation 4.16 is a simplified expression for VaR that uses KRDs and the *covariance* matrix of changes in key spot rates.

Table 4.4 demonstrates the process of constructing replicating ZCB portfolios for two fixed income securities, an on-the-run U.S. Treasury and a MBS. The results obtained via cash flow mappings are denoted by JPM, and those computed via key rate durations are denoted by KRD. It can be seen that for fixed cash flow securities (e.g., an OTR TSY), the JPM and KRD replicating portfolios and the corresponding VaR numbers are virtually identical.

We presented a rather lengthy derivation of Equation 4.16 in order to illustrate the intellectual transition from cash flow mappings to partial durations. Starting with VaR written in terms of price volatilities of the

TABLE 4.4 Selected Securities, Their Replicating (Risk-Equivalent) ZCB Portfolios, and Value-at-Risk

Sec Type	VaR	OAD	MV	Cash	3-mo	1-year	2-year	3-year	5-year	7-year	10-year	15-year	20-year	30-year
Zero Coupon Bonds														
Yields					5.35	5.81	6.14	6.31	6.53	6.67	6.84	7.10	7.28	6.86
Prices					98.69	94.43	88.61	83.00	72.52	63.17	51.04	35.12	23.93	13.22
Durations					0.24	0.97	1.94	2.91	4.84	6.77	9.67	14.49	19.30	29.01
30-year OTR TSY														
KRD	18.67	12.42	$100	$0.0	0.01	0.06	0.12	0.27	0.48	0.74	1.36	1.73	1.82	5.82
Equiv Port (JPM)	18.53	12.42	$100	$0.3	$2.6	$5.8	$6.0	$8.4	$10.0	$10.6	$13.6	$12.3	$11.5	$19.6
Equiv Port (KRD)	18.67	12.42	$100	-$3.6	$5.9	$6.0	$6.0	$9.2	$9.9	$11.0	$14.1	$12.0	$9.5	$20.1
30-year 7% FNMA MBS														
KRD	9.24	5.42	$100		0.01	0.05	0.29	0.57	0.87	0.86	1.33	0.88	0.41	0.15
Equiv Port (KRD)	9.24	5.42	$100	-$1.4	$5.6	$5.3	$15.1	$19.5	$18.0	$12.6	$13.7	$6.1	$2.1	$0.5

MV = Market Value.

individual assets in a portfolio, by a series of transformations VaR was turned into a function of KRDs and correlations and volatilities of changes in key spot rates. A more modern proof simply involves taking one standard deviation of both sides of Equation 2.39.

Performance of fixed income portfolio managers is typically measured using an ex post measure of risk-adjusted excess return called *Information Ratio (IR)*:

$$IR = \frac{\dfrac{\Delta P}{P} - \dfrac{\Delta B}{B}}{\sigma\left(\dfrac{\Delta P}{P} - \dfrac{\Delta B}{B}\right)} \qquad (4.17)$$

where $\dfrac{\Delta P}{P}$ and $\dfrac{\Delta B}{B}$ are the historical percentage returns on a portfolio

and its benchmark, respectively. The standard deviation $\sigma\left(\dfrac{\Delta P}{P} - \dfrac{\Delta B}{B}\right)$ of

the excess return, also known as *tracking error*, has been a part of fixed income vocabulary for several decades:[15]

$$TE = \sigma\left(\frac{\Delta P}{P} - \frac{\Delta B}{B}\right) \qquad (4.18)$$

Therefore, a natural extension of VaR for money managers is to think about market risk in units of standard deviations. We define interest-rate risk *(IntRR)* of a fixed income security as the *a priori component of the total risk arising solely from the variability of default-free spot rates*. More specifically, *IntRR* is one standard deviation of returns solely due to changes in interest rates:

$$IntRR = \sigma\left(\frac{\Delta V}{V}\right) \qquad (4.19)$$

As seen from Equation 4.9, Variance/Covariance VaR and *IntRR* are closely related:

$$VaR = 1.65 \cdot \sigma\left(\frac{\Delta V}{V}\right) = 1.65 \cdot IntRR \qquad (4.20)$$

and therefore

$$IntRR = \sqrt{(krd_1, ..., krd_n) \cdot \Sigma \cdot (krd_1, ..., krd_n)^T} \qquad (4.21)$$

Equations 4.18 and 4.19 indicate that *IntRR* provides an ex ante estimate of the tracking error under the assumption that the set of systematic risk factors is exhausted by interest rates. In market environments characterized by benign behavior of basis risks, *IntRR* can be used to forecast tracking errors. Assuming that $(krd_{P,1}, ..., krd_{P,n})$ and $(krd_{B,1}, ..., krd_{B,n})$ are the KRD profiles of the portfolio and its benchmark, respectively, let us denote the KRD profile of the *gap* between the portfolio and the benchmark as follows:

$$(\Delta krd_1, ..., \Delta krd_n) = (krd_{P,1} - krd_{B,1}, ..., krd_{P,n} - krd_{B,n}) \qquad (4.22)$$

Combining Equations 4.18–4.22 yields

$$TE = \sqrt{(\Delta krd_1, ..., \Delta krd_n) \cdot \Sigma \cdot (\Delta krd_1, ..., \Delta krd_n)^T} \qquad (4.23)$$

Note that Equation 4.23 measures the ex ante tracking error arising solely from changes in interest rates and does not account for other systematic risks or idiosyncratic (security-specific) risks, which can be significant for portfolios with few holdings.

4.2.2 Principal Components Durations, Key Rate Durations, and Value-at-Risk

When measuring the risk along the interest rate dimension, many traditional approaches to risk management estimate the price sensitivity of fixed income portfolios and securities to hypothetical yield curve shocks. Option-adjusted duration (OAD) methodology, for instance, computes the first-order exposure to parallel changes in the spot curve. Short-end and long-end durations estimate potential losses associated with hypothetical steepeners of the OTR Treasury curve (see Section 2.4.3). Since principal components are by construction the most dominant yield curve shocks, the first-order price sensitivity to changes in principal components can be computed as well.[16] Similar to the discussion in Chapter 2, a pricing model can be used to directly reestimate the value of each security after the spot curve is shocked up and down by principal com-

ponents shocks. Consistent with all previously described partial duration methodologies, OAS is kept constant in all calculations, implying
the absence of spread directionality.

The ith principal component duration $(pcdur_i)$ is defined as the negative of the percentage change in price for each one standard deviation
change in the ith principal component:

$$pcdur_i = -\frac{1}{P}\frac{P_{i,\text{up}} - P_{i,\text{down}}}{2} \tag{4.24}$$

where $P_{i,\text{up}}$ and $P_{i,\text{down}}$ are option-adjusted values obtained by shifting
the yield curve up and down, respectively, by the ith principal compo-
nent shock. Note that while option-adjusted duration and modified
duration are defined for each 100 basis point change in interest rates,
principal components durations are formulated for each one standard
deviation change in principal components. As discussed in Chapter 3,
principal components vary with market environments. Thus, the magnitude as well as the shape of the principal components yield curve
shocks fluctuate daily, reflecting the changes in correlations and
volatilities of key rates.

Let us now write an analog of Equations 4.1 and 4.11 that deals with
attributing changes in market value to changes in principal components.
Instead of presenting the percentage changes in value as a sum of partial
returns due to gains and losses on individual assets in a portfolio, the
decomposition of returns is done in terms of systematic risk factors, that
is, principal components:

$$\frac{\Delta V}{V} = \frac{\Delta V}{V}\bigg|_{PC,1} + \dots + \frac{\Delta V}{V}\bigg|_{PC,n} \tag{4.25}$$

where $\dfrac{\Delta V}{V}\bigg|_{PC,i}$ is the percentage value change due to movements in the

ith principal component. Because they are measures of the first-order
price sensitivity, principal components durations (PCD) allow for
approximation of each term on the right-hand side of Equation 4.25:

$$\frac{\Delta V}{V} = -pcdur_1 \cdot \frac{p_1}{\sqrt{\lambda_1}} - \dots - pcdur_n \cdot \frac{p_n}{\sqrt{\lambda_n}} \tag{4.26}$$

where $p_1,\ldots,p_n$ are principal components, and $\sqrt{\lambda_1},\ldots,\sqrt{\lambda_n}$ are their standard deviations. The need for the normalization of the principal components' realizations $\dfrac{p_i}{\sqrt{\lambda_i}}$ is due to principal components durations being defined per one standard deviation change in principal components.

Principal components are uncorrelated random variables by construction, therefore taking the variance of both sides in Equation 4.26 yields

$$IntRR^2 = \sigma^2\left(\frac{\Delta V}{V}\right) = pcdur_1^2\,\frac{\sigma^2(p_1)}{\lambda_1} + \ldots + pcdur_n^2\,\frac{\sigma^2(p_n)}{\lambda_n} \qquad (4.27)$$

where, by definition, $\sigma^2(p_i) = \lambda_i$ (Equation 3.13). We finally arrive at the following representation of *IntRR* in terms of principal components durations:

$$IntRR = \sqrt{\sum_{i=1}^{n} pcdur_i^2} \qquad (4.28)$$

Equation 4.28 implies that any fixed income portfolio can be characterized by a *risk vector* whose coordinates are principal component durations and whose length is *IntRR*. This result may seem counterintuitive since all principal components durations have equal weights in the computation of *IntRR* irrespective of their explanatory power (Equation 4.28) and look as if they contribute equally to the overall risk. However, this is not the case. Recall that volatility of the first principal component is almost an order of magnitude greater than that of the second principal component. This implies that while computing the first principal component duration, the interest rate shock applied to the spot curve will be much larger than that corresponding to the second principal component. Therefore, the first principal component duration will be much larger in magnitude than that of the second principal component, resulting in greater contribution to *IntRR*.

We conclude this section by establishing an analytical relationship between key rate durations (KRDs) and principal component durations (PCDs). As shown later in this chapter, this result has a number of interesting theoretical and practical applications. Rewrite Equation 4.28 in the following form:[17]

$$IntRR = \sqrt{(\frac{pcdur_1}{\sqrt{\lambda_1}},...,\frac{pcdur_n}{\sqrt{\lambda_n}}) \cdot \Lambda \cdot (\frac{pcdur_1}{\sqrt{\lambda_1}},...,\frac{pcdur_n}{\sqrt{\lambda_n}})^T} \qquad (4.29)$$

where Λ is the diagonal matrix of principal components' variances. Combining Equations 3.11 and 4.29 yields

$$IntRR = \sqrt{(\frac{pcdur_1}{\sqrt{\lambda_1}},...,\frac{pcdur_n}{\sqrt{\lambda_n}}) \cdot \Omega \cdot \Sigma \cdot \Omega^T \cdot (\frac{pcdur_1}{\sqrt{\lambda_1}},...,\frac{pcdur_n}{\sqrt{\lambda_n}})^T} \qquad (4.30)$$

where Ω is the matrix of principal components' factor loadings (Equation 3.3), and Σ is the covariance matrix of changes in key rates. Equation 4.30 can be simplified even further by employing the basic linear algebra rules:

$$IntRR = \sqrt{\left[(\frac{pcdur_1}{\sqrt{\lambda_1}},...,\frac{pcdur_n}{\sqrt{\lambda_n}}) \cdot \Omega\right] \cdot \Sigma \cdot \left[(\frac{pcdur_1}{\sqrt{\lambda_1}},...,\frac{pcdur_n}{\sqrt{\lambda_n}}) \cdot \Omega\right]^T} \qquad (4.31)$$

Equations 4.21 and 4.31 illustrate that *IntRR* can be approached from two different angles. The reader can easily verify that the two alternative representations of *IntRR* establish a theoretical relationship between KRDs and PCDs:

$$(krd_1,...,krd_n) = (\frac{pcdur_1}{\sqrt{\lambda_1}},...,\frac{pcdur_n}{\sqrt{\lambda_n}}) \cdot \Omega \qquad (4.32)$$

Due to the fact that Ω is an orthogonal matrix, Equation 4.32 can be rearranged as follows:

$$(\frac{pcdur_1}{\sqrt{\lambda_1}},...,\frac{pcdur_n}{\sqrt{\lambda_n}}) = (krd_1,...,krd_n) \cdot \begin{bmatrix} p_{1,1} & \cdots & p_{n,1} \\ \cdots & \cdots & \cdots \\ p_{1,n} & \cdots & p_{n,n} \end{bmatrix} \qquad (4.33)$$

This allows expressing each principal component duration as a function of KRDs and the principal components' factor loadings:

$$pcdur_i = \sum_{j=1}^{n} krd_j \cdot \sqrt{\lambda_i} \cdot p_{i,j} \qquad (4.34)$$

PCDs can be obtained by multiplying KRDs by the one standard deviation shock corresponding to the appropriate principal component.

In practice, KRDs computed directly via a valuation model may be slightly different from those implied analytically by PCDs, and vice versa (Table 4.5). The minor dissimilarities can be typically attributed to the effects of convexity, path-dependency, as well as sensitivity of certain asset classes to nondifferentiable points on the forward curve caused by KRD shocks (Exhibit 2.6). In rows marked *KRD* in Table 4.5, KRDs are computed directly, while PCDs are derived analytically via Equation 4.34, and *IntRR* is obtained via Equation 4.21. Conversely, in rows marked *PC*, PCDs are computed directly while KRDs and *IntRR* are obtained analytically. Notice that both KRDs and PCDs arrive at virtually identical estimates of *IntRR*. Also note that for all securities, the value of the first PCD is very similar to *IntRR*. This is because on the date when the experiment was performed, the first principal component explained the vast majority of the historical yield curve variability.

Unlike KRD interest rate shocks, which are analytically convenient but historically implausible, principal components are characteristic of the recent yield curve behavior and do not cause forward rates to become negative. PCDs, therefore, are better measures of interest rate risk than KRDs are, especially when used in hedging. While exactly matching KRDs of a security or portfolio to those of the hedge instruments certainly works well (Chapter 6), such hedging strategies are not parsimonious and may result in excessive transaction costs. In effect, principal components hedges may be thought of as immunization strategies,[18] while KRD hedges resemble dedication strategies (when the number of key rates is large). Unfortunately, many market participants find principal components and their durations unintuitive. Equation 4.34 demonstrates that hedging interest rate risk via KRDs is equivalent to hedging it via PCDs. This result also allows us to analytically derive KRDs from PCDs. Thus, a historically more plausible approach to measuring yield curve risk (PCDs) can be used to compute a more appealing measure (KRDs), helping those practitioners that find KRDs useful in measuring yield curve risk or implementing yield curve trades.

TABLE 4.5 Comparison of Key Rate Duration (KRD) and Principal Component Duration (PCD) Profiles of Selected

Sec	Method	IntRR	OAD	Key Rate Durations										PC Durations		
				3-mo	1-year	2-year	3-year	5-year	7-year	10-year	15-year	20-year	30-year	1	2	3
TSY	KRD	11.32	12.42	0.01	0.06	0.12	0.27	0.48	0.74	1.36	1.73	1.82	5.82	11.04	-2.41	0.56
	PC	11.38	12.42	0.01	0.07	0.07	0.30	0.47	0.62	1.47	1.80	2.36	5.25	11.10	-2.42	0.59
CORP	KRD	8.97	9.30	0.02	0.07	0.13	0.30	0.53	1.15	1.58	1.74	1.71	2.09	8.85	-1.48	0.30
	PC	9.09	9.30	0.00	0.08	0.07	0.35	0.47	1.11	1.71	1.85	2.25	1.43	8.96	-1.49	0.32
MBS	KRD	5.60	5.42	0.01	0.05	0.29	0.57	0.87	0.86	1.33	0.88	0.41	0.15	5.58	-0.35	-0.08
	PC	5.66	5.42	0.00	0.08	0.19	0.65	0.85	0.83	1.44	0.91	0.43	0.09	5.65	-0.37	-0.07

TSY = U.S. Treasury; CORP = Corporate Bond; MBS = Mortgage-Backed Security;

4.2.3 Effective Risk Profile and Other Practical Applications

This section describes practical applications of the results obtained earlier in this chapter to portfolio management and risk management of fixed income portfolios. It also presents a simple approach to risk decomposition applicable in special cases when the vast majority of a system's variability can be explained by the first principal component. Rewrite Equation 4.21 as follows:

$$IntRR = \sqrt{\sum_{i=1}^{n}\sum_{j=1}^{n} krd_i \cdot krd_j \cdot \sigma^2(\Delta r_i, \Delta r_j)} \qquad (4.35)$$

where krd_i are KRDs of a security or portfolio, and $\sigma^2(\Delta r_i, \Delta r_j)$ denotes covariance between changes in key spot rates r_i and r_j.

Presenting each key rate as a linear combination of principal components via Equation 3.4 yields

$$\sigma^2(\Delta r_i, \Delta r_j) = \sigma^2\left(\sum_{u=1}^{n} p_{u,i} \cdot p_u, \sum_{v=1}^{n} p_{v,j} \cdot p_v\right) \qquad (4.36)$$

Covariance between two linear combinations of random variables is equal to the linear combination of covariances, and therefore

$$\sigma^2(\Delta r_i, \Delta r_j) = \sum_{u=1}^{n}\sum_{v=1}^{n} p_{v,j} \cdot p_{u,i} \cdot \sigma^2(p_u, p_v) \qquad (4.37)$$

Recall that principal components are uncorrelated by construction, and their variances are given by Equation 3.13:

$$\sigma^2(p_u, p_v) = \begin{cases} \sigma^2(p_u) = \lambda_u, & if\ u = v \\ 0, & otherwise \end{cases} \qquad (4.38)$$

Substituting Equations 4.37 and 4.38 into Equation 4.36 yields

$$\sigma^2(\Delta r_i, \Delta r_j) = \sum_{v=1}^{n} p_{v,i} \cdot p_{v,j} \cdot \lambda_v \qquad (4.39)$$

Equation 4.39 allows us to obtain yet another alternative expression for *IntRR*:

$$IntRR = \sqrt{\sum_{i=1}^{n}\sum_{j=1}^{n}\sum_{v=1}^{n}(krd_i \cdot p_{v,i} \cdot \sqrt{\lambda_v})(krd_j \cdot p_{v,j} \cdot \sqrt{\lambda_v})} \qquad (4.40)$$

Equation 4.40 identifies an interesting relationship between *IntRR*, KRDs, and the principal components' factor loadings. It pinpoints the exact components of risk, that is, expressions of the form $krd_i \cdot p_{v,i} \cdot \sqrt{\lambda_v}$ whose units are basis points per year and which can be thought of as the potential gains or losses of a security due to its exposure to the *i*th key spot rate. It can be seen from Equations 3.25 and 4.40 that *IntRR* is a function of KRDs multiplied by the one standard deviation principal components shocks.

We will now describe an interesting corollary of these results. Recall that in market environments when the first principal component explains the vast majority of the yield curve variability, the magnitude of the first PCD is much greater than those corresponding to other principal components. Because of that, Equations 4.28 and 4.40 lead to the following approximation of *IntRR* via KRDs and the one standard deviation first principal component shock:

$$IntRR = \sqrt{\sum_{i=1}^{n} pcdur_i^2} \approx |pcdur_1| \approx \left|\sum_{i=1}^{n} krd_i \cdot p_{1,i} \cdot \sqrt{\lambda_1}\right| \qquad (4.41)$$

Equation 4.41 enables us to introduce the following important concept. For a fixed income security or portfolio, define *effective risk profile (ERP)* to be the element-wise product of its KRDs $(krd_1,...,krd_n)$ and the one standard deviation first principal component shock $(\sqrt{\lambda_1} \cdot p_{1,1},..., \sqrt{\lambda_1} \cdot p_{1,n})$:

$$(krd_1 \cdot p_{1,1} \cdot \sqrt{\lambda_1},..., krd_n \cdot p_{1,n} \cdot \sqrt{\lambda_1}) \qquad (4.41)$$

Elements of effective risk profile can be thought of as the instantaneous returns of a security under the first principal component spot curve shock. First, notice that in market environments when the first principal component explains the majority of the yield curve variability, elements of ERP approximately add up to *IntRR* (Equation 4.41). ERP therefore enables the *risk decomposition* of *IntRR*, identifying the yield curve exposures that contribute the most to the overall risk. Before elaborate risk decomposition methodologies were introduced (Chapter 5), practitioners have experienced difficulties in using VaR because it presented the risk as a single, probabilistic summary measure.[19] The introduction of ERP[20] was one of the earlier attempts to supplement VaR with a sound risk decomposition technique even though it was accurate only in one special case. In addition to being an approach to risk decomposition, ERP provides a visual representation of the price sensitivity to the different points on the spot curve. ERP is arguably a better measure of yield curve risk than KRDs since it combines knowledge of market exposures, information about the shape of the most dominant yield curve movement, and the estimate of the recent historical variability of interest rates. A hypothetical example in Table 4.6 uses effective risk profile to describe the yield curve risk of a portfolio with a flat KRD exposure. Notice that contrary to the KRD profile, the risk associated with this position is not equally distributed along the yield curve but reflects the "humped" shape of the first principal component.

We hope that the theoretical and experimental results described in this section will assist the reader in developing a perspective on the arsenal of measures of yield curve risk. By comparing various methodologies and establishing connections among them, we intended to illustrate that risk management is often faced with making trade-offs between measures that are superior from a theoretical perspective and those that have a greater intuitive appeal to decision makers. Equation 4.34 is an example of a rare circumstance when one can analytically transform a more plausible measure into a more intuitive one, thus preserving the existing intellectual paradigm. Next, we summarize a variety of practical applications arising from the methods described in the preceding sections.

Yield curve risk management. There are several alternative approaches to measuring yield curve risk: *IntRR* (or equivalently, VaR), ERP, PCDs,

TABLE 4.6 Comparison of KRD and Effective Risk Profiles of a "KRD-Flat" Position

	IntRR	Sum	3-mo	1-year	2-year	3-year	5-year	7-year	10-year	15-year	20-year	30-year
KRD Profile (yrs)	185	2.00	0.20	0.20	0.20	0.20	0.20	0.20	0.20	0.20	0.20	0.20
Effective Risk (bp/yr)		185	7	17	22	22	22	22	20	19	18	15

KRDs, and a variety of measures based on hypothetical yield curve shocks. While all of these methodologies explore the first-order price sensitivity of fixed income instruments to interest rate movements, PCDs, VaR, IntRR, and ERP take into account both market exposures and knowledge of the recent historical interest rate dynamics. Both effective risk profile and KRDs provide a visual representation of interest rate risk. In situations when the first principal component explains the vast majority of the yield curve variability, ERP also decomposes IntRR, identifying yield curve regions with the highest concentrations of risk.

Hedging. Hedging interest rate risk via VaR or PCDs is superior to traditional duration hedging (Chapter 6).

Extreme market movements. Dramatic changes in the yield curve can typically be attributed entirely to the first principal component. If duration neutrality is to be maintained when preparing for the market environments with potentially high interest rate volatility, being duration-neutral with respect to the first principal component is superior to being duration-neutral with respect to a parallel shift in the yield curve. Instead of matching dollar OADs (Chapter 6), the first principal component dollar durations need to be matched.

4.2.4 Application: Managing a Large Number of Portfolios Against Different Benchmarks

Asset management firms are typically retained by institutional investors and high net worth individuals to earn consistent active returns over assigned benchmarks in a risk-controlled fashion. When managing portfolios on behalf of their clients, money managers have the fiduciary responsibility not to give preferential treatment to any single client vis-à-vis the others. In other words, portfolios with similar investment mandates must have comparable tracking errors and similar active returns. In order to ensure that, investment strategies and risk management practices have to be consistently implemented across analogous portfolios.

When a money manager is selected for a particular assignment, a variety of *investment guidelines* (or *compliance rules*) is specified to ensure that the portfolio will be managed according to the objectives and risk preferences of the client. These typically include

- *Duration bands* that constrain the magnitude of directional interest rate bets, for instance, "the duration gap between the portfolio and its benchmark should be no more than one year in absolute value" or "the duration gap between the portfolio and its benchmark should not exceed 20% of the benchmark's duration."

- *Security selection,* which defines the types of securities that can be owned in the portfolio. Guidelines of this type include various restrictions on shorting securities, investing in certain classes of derivative instruments, emerging markets, or high yield debt. They may also include constraints with respect to credit quality, prepayment and volatility risks, etc.

- *Asset allocation limits.* Some compliance rules impose various issue- and issuer-specific constraints, for example, "no more than 5% of the portfolio's equity should be invested in a single security" or "the maximum percentage allocation to asset-backed securities cannot exceed 10% of the portfolio's net asset value."

- *VaR constraints,* while theoretically appealing, may lead to excessive transactions and even losses if the volatile nature of VaR is not properly taken into account (see Section 4.1.2). Nevertheless, some financial institutions have recently begun formulating compliance rules in terms of Value-at-Risk.

This section illustrates how ex ante tracking errors (Equation 4.23) can be used to consistently manage directional interest rate bets of fixed income portfolios with comparable investment mandates. In this context, we say that two portfolios have comparable investment mandates if their guidelines and risk/return objectives vis-à-vis the respective benchmarks are similar. This task is complicated because portfolios with similar mandates are often managed against benchmarks that exhibit very different risk characteristics. The results presented next demonstrate that while OAD is still the most commonly used tool for placing directional bets, it may incorrectly estimate risk if not considered in conjunction with ex ante tracking errors.

Consider the expression for ex ante tracking error discussed earlier in this chapter (Equation 4.23):

$$TE = \sqrt{(\Delta krd_1, ..., \Delta krd_n) \cdot \Sigma \cdot (\Delta krd_1, ..., \Delta krd_n)^T} \qquad (4.43)$$

where Σ is the covariance matrix of changes in key rates, and Δkrd_i are differences in KRDs between the portfolio and its benchmark.

For the purposes of this discussion and without loss of generality, let us assume that we start with a portfolio *(P)* that is perfectly matched with its benchmark *(B)* in terms of KRDs.

$$krd_{P,i} = krd_{B,i} \tag{4.44}$$

Equations 4.43 and 4.44 imply that before a duration bet is implemented, ex ante tracking error of this portfolio is zero. Let OAD_B denote option-adjusted duration of the benchmark, and OAD_{gap} that of the gap between the portfolio and its benchmark (i.e., OAD_{gap} is the magnitude of the active duration bet). For simplicity, also assume that a lengthening of the portfolio by a given number of duration years is implemented by evenly distributing the duration bet among all KRDs:

$$krd_{P,i} = krd_{B,i} \cdot \frac{OAD_{gap} + OAD_B}{OAD_B} \tag{4.45}$$

Substituting assumptions from Equation 4.45 into Equation 4.22 results in the following simple representation of the KRD gap between the port-folio and its benchmark:

$$\Delta krd_i = krd_{P,i} - krd_{B,i} = \frac{OAD_{gap}}{OAD_B} \cdot krd_{B,i} \tag{4.46}$$

Combining Equations 4.43–4.46 yields:

$$TE = \frac{OAD_{gap}}{OAD_B} \sqrt{(krd_{B,1}, ..., krd_{B,n}) \cdot \Sigma \cdot (krd_{B,1}, ..., krd_{B,n})^T} \tag{4.47}$$

Equation 4.21 enables us to simplify Equation 4.47 even further:

$$TE = \frac{OAD_{gap}}{OAD_B} IntRR_B \tag{4.48}$$

Equation 4.48 indicates that tracking error associated with an active duration bet is a function of the following three factors: (1) the magnitude (OAD_{gap}) of the duration bet itself, (2) duration of the benchmark (OAD_B), and (3) interest rate risk of the benchmark ($IntRR_B$).

In Table 4.7, we explore the relationship between directional interest rate bets and tracking errors in the following three dimensions:

TABLE 4.7 Relationship Between Directional Interest Rate Bets and Tracking Errors

Benchmark	OAD	IntRR	Duration of the Gap					% Duration Lengthening					
			+.2	+.4	+.6	+.8	+1	10%	20%	40%	60%	80%	100%
ML 1-3Yr	1.72	2.05	0.24	0.48	0.72	0.95	1.19	0.21	0.41	0.82	1.23	1.64	2.05
LEH_INT_GOV_CORP	3.24	4.00	0.25	0.49	0.74	0.99	1.23	0.40	0.80	1.60	2.40	3.20	4.00
ML_3-5Yr	3.38	4.39	0.26	0.52	0.78	1.04	1.30	0.44	0.88	1.76	2.63	3.51	4.39
SAL_MTG	4.14	4.87	0.24	0.47	0.71	0.94	1.18	0.49	0.97	1.95	2.92	3.90	4.87
LEH_AGG	4.68	5.40	0.23	0.46	0.69	0.92	1.15	0.54	1.08	2.16	3.24	4.32	5.40
LEH_GOV_CORP	4.95	5.68	0.23	0.46	0.69	0.92	1.15	0.57	1.14	2.27	3.41	4.54	5.68
COMPOSITE 1	7.08	7.98	0.23	0.45	0.68	0.90	1.13	0.80	1.60	3.19	4.79	6.38	7.98
LEH_LONG_GOV_CORP	9.53	10.35	0.22	0.43	0.65	0.87	1.09	1.04	2.07	4.14	6.21	8.28	10.35
COMPOSITE 2	16.80	16.27	0.19	0.39	0.58	0.77	0.97	1.63	3.25	6.51	9.76	13.02	16.27

Benchmark	OAD	IntRR	Tracking Error (% per year)									
			0.10	0.20	0.30	0.40	0.50	0.60	0.70	0.80	0.90	1.00
ML_1-3Yr	1.72	2.05	0.08	0.17	0.25	0.34	0.42	0.50	0.59	0.67	0.76	0.84
LEH_INT_GOV CORP	3.24	4.00	0.08	0.16	0.24	0.32	0.41	0.49	0.57	0.65	0.73	0.81
ML 3-5Yr	3.38	4.39	0.08	0.15	0.23	0.31	0.38	0.46	0.54	0.62	0.69	0.77
SAL_MTG	4.14	4.87	0.09	0.17	0.26	0.34	0.43	0.51	0.60	0.68	0.77	0.85
LEH AGG	4.68	5.40	0.09	0.17	0.26	0.35	0.43	0.52	0.61	0.69	0.78	0.87
LEH_GOV_CORP	4.95	5.68	0.09	0.17	0.26	0.35	0.44	0.52	0.61	0.70	0.78	0.87
COMPOSITE 1	7.08	7.98	0.09	0.18	0.27	0.35	0.44	0.53	0.62	0.71	0.80	0.89
LEH_LONG_GOV_CORP	9.53	10.35	0.09	0.18	0.28	0.37	0.46	0.55	0.64	0.74	0.83	0.92
COMPOSITE 2	16.80	16.27	0.10	0.21	0.31	0.41	0.52	0.62	0.72	0.83	0.93	1.03

1. The portfolio is lengthened or shortened relative to its benchmark by a fixed number of duration years.
2. The portfolio is lengthened or shortened relative to its benchmark by a fixed percentage of the benchmark's duration.
3. The portfolio is lengthened or shortened relative to its benchmark by a fixed number of basis points of tracking error.

For the purposes of this illustration, the following commonly used fixed income benchmarks are employed:

- Merrill Lynch 1–3-year Treasury Index (ML_1–3Yr)
- Lehman Intermediate Government/Corporate Index (LEH_INT_GOV_CORP)
- Merrill Lynch 3–5-year Treasury Index (ML_3–5Yr)
- Salomon Mortgage Index (SAL_MTG)
- Lehman Aggregate Index (LEH_AGG)
- Lehman Government/Corporate Index (LEH_GOV_CORP)
- Customized Index 1: 14% Lehman Mortgage, 27% Lehman Corporate/ABS, 59% Lehman TSY 5.5–30-year Index (Composite 1)
- Lehman Long Government/Corporate Index (LEH_LONG_GOV_CORP)
- Customized Index 2: 50% LEH_LONG_GOV_CORP and 50% May 15, 2021 U.S. TSY ZCB (Composite 2)

Consistent with the way directional interest rate bets are usually implemented in practice, the upper left portion of Table 4.7 (labled "Duration of the Gap") presents tracking errors of portfolios that are made longer than their respective benchmarks by a given number of duration years (0.2, 0.4, 0.6, 0.8, and 1.0). Assessing interest rate risk in these cases is very relevant to investors since the vast majority of compliance rules constrain duration gaps in terms of duration years. Table 4.7 indicates that independent of the risk characteristics of their benchmarks, lengthening different portfolios by the same number of duration years results in similar ex ante tracking errors. Consider two fixed income portfolios that are perfectly matched to Lehman Long Government/Corporate Index and Merrill Lynch 1–3-year Treasury Index, respectively. Clearly, despite the drastic difference in the risk characteristics of these indices, lengthening each portfolio by 0.6 years vis-à-vis its respective benchmark results in very comparable tracking errors (65 and 72 basis points per year).

Another popular practice is to formulate duration bets and compliance rules in terms of percentages of the benchmarks' durations. The upper right portion of Table 4.7 deals with this representation of directional bets. It shows that lengthening the portfolios from the previous example by 10% of their benchmarks' durations results in the drastically different ex ante tracking errors of 104 and 21 basis points per year, respectively. While the ratio of *IntRR* to duration is relatively constant across different benchmarks, tracking errors are proportional to the absolute magnitude of duration bets. These results suggest that compliance rules regulating the investment process in terms of percentages of the benchmarks' durations may imply very different interest rate risk limits for portfolios with similar mandates.

The analyses described above deal with the estimation of ex ante tracking errors resulting from various duration bets. In certain situations, it is also useful to answer the opposite question: For portfolios managed against different benchmarks, what are the directional interest rate bets that correspond to a predefined risk tolerance? The lower panel of Table 4.7 answers this question for a variety of benchmarks. As expected, a fixed level of interest rate risk (as measured by ex ante tracking error) implies very similar duration bets across different portfolios. For instance, if all portfolios are tailored to have exactly the same tracking error of 0.3% per year, the implied duration bets will range in magnitude from 0.25 to 0.31 years, depending on the benchmark.

Since tracking errors are symmetric measures of risk, conclusions dealing with the lengthening of portfolios relative to their benchmarks are also applicable to cases when portfolios are to be shortened.

4.3 MEASURING NONDOLLAR INTEREST RATE, BASIS, AND CURRENCY RISKS

4.3.1 Global Variance/Covariance Value-at-Risk

Up until now, we have studied a variety of methodologies that assume that the vast majority of risk in fixed income portfolios is caused by the variability of U.S. default-free interest rates. Among these approaches, Variance/Covariance VaR was shown to be the most comprehensive measure of interest rate risk since it properly combines information about market exposures with knowledge about the recent probabilistic dynamics of U.S. Treasury key spot rates. Clearly, it is unrealistic to the measure the U.S. interest rate risk alone as a proxy for the overall price volatility of portfolios containing credit spread-sensitive instruments and securities issued in currencies other than U.S. dollars (USD). VaR methodology therefore needs to be extended in the following four dimensions:

- Incorporation of nondollar interest rate risks
- Incorporation of foreign currency risks
- Incorporation of basis risks
- Elimination of the assumption that the value surface is linear in all variables

This section introduces *Global Value-at-Risk*, a risk measure that uses Variance/Covariance VaR framework to combine interest rate risks across different markets, foreign currency risks, and basis risks into one summarized number. While extending interest rate risk-only VaR in these three dimensions, Global VaR still presumes that price is a linear function of systematic risk factors. Later in this book we relax this assumption and introduce several VaR approaches that properly account for the nonlinearity of the value surface (Chapter 5).

Consider a multicurrency portfolio containing fixed income securities denominated in U.S. dollars (USD) and British pounds (GBP). Similar to Equation 4.1, let us write the following representation of changes in the market value of this portfolio resulting from changes in all applicable systematic risk factors:

$$\Delta V = \Delta V|_{IntRR,\text{US}} + \Delta V|_{IntRR,\text{UK}} + \Delta V|_{fx,\text{GBP/USD}} + \Delta V|_{\text{basis risks}} \qquad (4.49)$$

where $\Delta V|_{IntRR,\text{US}}$ is the change (in USD) of the portfolio's value due to movements of the U.S. Treasury spot curve, $\Delta V|_{IntRR,\text{UK}}$ is the change (in USD) of the portfolio's value due to changes in U.K. government interest rates, $\Delta V|_{fx,\text{GBP/USD}}$ is the change (in USD) of the portfolio's value due to fluctuations in the GBP/USD exchange rate, and $\Delta V|_{\text{basis risks}}$ is the change (in USD) of the portfolio's value due to changes in basis risk factors. As mentioned earlier, Global VaR extends Variance/Covariance VaR (Equation 4.16) to account for nondollar, currency, and basis risks. It is therefore important to study each term in Equation 4.49 in detail.

4.3.2 Nondollar Interest Rate Risks

Interest rate-related returns on fixed income securities can be approximated via key rate durations and the underlying changes in key spot rates (Equation 2.39). Write the following representation of the change in portfolio's market value due to U.S. interest rate movements:

$$\Delta V|_{IntRR,\,US} = -V_{USD} \cdot \sum_{i=1}^{n} krd_{USD,i} \cdot \Delta r_{USD,i} \tag{4.50}$$

where V_{USD} is the market value of the USD sub-portfolio, $krd_{USD,i}$ are key rate durations of the USD subportfolio computed using USD government curve, and $\Delta r_{USD,i}$ are changes in key rates on the U.S. Treasury spot curve. Recall that aggregate (portfolio-level) partial durations of a fixed income portfolio are computed as weighted-averages of partial durations of the individual securities and presented in terms of the *market value* of the portfolio (Section 2.2.2). In the case of the USD subportfolio, if the ith key rate increases by 100 basis points, the entire USD subportfolio is expected to lose $krd_{USD,i}$ percent of its market value V_{USD}.

Expressed in U.S. dollars, the change in the portfolio's value due to changes in U.K. government interest rates can be presented in a similar fashion:

$$\Delta V|_{IntRR,\,UK} = -\frac{V_{GBP} \cdot \sum_{i=1}^{n} krd_{UK,i} \cdot \Delta r_{UK,i}}{fx_{GBP/USD}} \tag{4.51}$$

where V_{GBP} is the market value of the GBP subportfolio, $krd_{UK,i}$ are KRDs of the GBP subportfolio computed using the U.K. government curve, and $\Delta r_{UK,i}$ are changes in U.K. government spot key rates.

Notice that the representation of risk in Equation 4.51 assumes that the foreign exchange rate is nonstochastic, ignoring the interest rate/exchange rate cross-product term. In other words, since change in market value corresponding to U.K. interest rates is presented in U.S. dollars, the foreign currency risk associated with converting into U.S. dollars interest rate-related gains and losses $\Delta V|_{IntRR,UK}$ is not accounted for. For the majority of fixed portfolios and securities, such changes-on-changes are second-order effects that can be ignored. However, for certain notional instruments (e.g., swaps, futures, and forward contracts) these cross-product terms are first-order effects that have to be properly modeled. This leads us to an interesting observation. When nonlinearity of the value surface is discussed in this book, we typically refer to nonlinearity of the value surface along the interest rate dimension (convexity). The argument above demonstrates that some fixed income instruments have value surfaces that are substantially nonlinear with respect to the interaction between interest rates and foreign currency exchange rates. In these cases, Variance/Covariance VaR methodology based on local parametric measures of risk may not be sufficient, and the application of more elaborate approaches to measuring VaR may be required.

We can now estimate the overall interest rate risk embedded in the portfolio from the example above. Similar to Equation 4.12,

$$VaR_{IntRR} = 1.65 \cdot \sigma(\Delta V|_{IntRR,US} + \Delta V|_{IntRR,UK}) \qquad (4.52)$$

For simplicity, let us denote the vector of all dollar KRDs as follows:

$$\$krd = (V_{USD} \cdot krd_{US,1}, ..., V_{USD} \cdot krd_{US,n}, \frac{V_{GBP} \cdot krd_{UK,1}}{fx_{GBP/USD}}, ..., \frac{V_{GBP} \cdot krd_{UK,m}}{fx_{GBP/USD}}) \qquad (4.53)$$

where n and m are the numbers of key rates identified on U.S. and U.K. government curves, respectively.

As a straightforward but useful exercise, we leave to the reader to verify that combining Equations 4.50–4.53 yields the following expression for the interest rate portion of Global VaR:

$$VaR_{IntRR} = 1.65 \cdot \sqrt{\$krd \cdot \Sigma \cdot \$krd^T} \qquad (4.54)$$

where $\$krd$ is the vector of dollar KRDs, and Σ is the $(n + m) \times (n + m)$ covariance matrix of changes in U.S. and U.K. government rates.

4.3.3 Foreign Currency Risks

The analytical representation of the market risk associated with isolated fluctuations of foreign currency exchange rates is different from that of interest rate risk. For a portfolio invested in U.S. and U.K. securities, write the expression for the change in its market value (in USD) due to changes in the GBP/USD exchange rate ($fx_{GBP/USD}$) as follows:

$$\Delta V|_{fx,GBP/USD} = \frac{V_{GBP}}{fx_{new}} - \frac{V_{GBP}}{fx_{old}} \tag{4.55}$$

where V_{GBP} is the market value (in GBP) of the GBP subportfolio, and fx_{new} and fx_{old} are the GBP/USD foreign currency exchange rates after and before the change, respectively. Via a series of simple mathematical transformations applied to the right-hand side of Equation 4.55, the expression for the foreign currency component of Global VaR in Equation 4.49 can be written as follows:

$$\Delta V|_{fx,GBP/USD} = V_{GBP} \cdot \frac{fx_{old} - fx_{new}}{fx_{new} \cdot fx_{old}} = -\frac{V_{GBP}}{fx_{old}} \cdot \frac{fx_{new} - fx_{old}}{fx_{new}} \tag{4.56}$$

where $\dfrac{V_{GBP}}{fx_{old}}$ is the original market value of the GBP subportfolio expressed in U.S. dollars and $\dfrac{fx_{new} - fx_{old}}{fx_{new}}$ is the percentage change in the GBP/USD exchange rate. For the purposes of VaR, volatility of the random variable $\dfrac{fx_{new} - fx_{old}}{fx_{new}}$ and its correlations with other systematic risks can be either directly statistically estimated or approximated by those of the more commonly computed statistic $\dfrac{fx_{new} - fx_{old}}{fx_{old}}$.

The ability to measure market value sensitivity to changes in the GBP/USD exchange rate allows us to incorporate foreign currency risks into the Global VaR calculation. Recall that the set of systematic risk factors relevant for the considered portfolio consists of $n + m + 1$ variables: n U.S. key spot rates, m U.K. key spot rates, and the

GBP/USD foreign currency exchange rate. For reasons that will become apparent momentarily, denote by $\bar{e} = (e_1,...,e_{n+m+1})$ the vector of one standard deviation exposures (Equation 4.6) of the portfolio to the set of risk factors :

$$1 \le i \le n: \qquad e_i = -V_{\text{USD}} \cdot krd_{\text{USD},i} \cdot \sigma(\Delta r_{\text{US},i}) \qquad (4.57)$$

$$n+1 \le i \le n+m: \qquad e_i = -\frac{V_{\text{GBP}}}{fx_{\text{GBP/USD}}} \cdot krd_{\text{UK},i} \cdot \sigma(\Delta r_{\text{UK},i}) \qquad (4.58)$$

$$i = n+m+1: \qquad e_i = -\frac{V_{\text{GBP}}}{fx_{\text{GBP/USD}}} \cdot \sigma(fx_{\text{GBP/USD}}) \qquad (4.59)$$

where $\sigma(\Delta r_{\text{US},i})$ and $\sigma(\Delta r_{\text{UK},i})$ are volatilities of changes in U.S. and U.K. key spot rates, respectively, and $\sigma(fx_{\text{GBP/USD}}) = \sigma(\frac{fx_{\text{new}} - fx_{\text{old}}}{fx_{\text{new}}})$ is volatility of percentage changes in the GBP/USD foreign currency exchange rate as per Equation 4.56.

It can be easily verified that the formula for the portion of Global VaR that accounts for all interest rate risks and foreign currency risks is as follows:

$$VaR = 1.65 \cdot \sigma(\Delta V|_{IntRR,US} + \Delta V|_{IntRR,UK} + \Delta V|_{fx,GBP/USD}) = 1.65 \cdot \sqrt{\bar{e} \cdot \rho \cdot \bar{e}^T} \qquad (4.60)$$

where ρ is the correlation matrix of changes in interest rates and percentage changes in foreign currency exchange rates.

A closer look at historical correlations and volatilities of changes in U.S. and U.K. government key spot rates and percentage changes in the GBP/USD foreign currency exchange rate leads to a number of interesting observations (Table 4.8). First, notice that in both the U.S. and U.K. government markets on 12/31/98, spot rates corresponding to shorter maturities were loosely correlated with those of longer maturities, while correlations among key rates of maturities greater than 10 years were high. At the same time, U.S. and U.K. government rates of comparable maturities were at best moderately correlated (the highest correlation of 0.51 was observed between the 10-year spot rates). As far as historical volatilities are concerned, it is noteworthy that while the term structure of volatility of U.S. spot key rates had a "humped" shape, TSOV of U.K.

TABLE 4.8 Correlations and Volatilities of USD and GBP Interest Rates and the GBP/USD Exchange Rate (as of 12/31/98)

		USD 3-mo	USD 1-yr	USD 2-yr	USD 3-yr	USD 5-yr	USD 7-yr	USD 10-yr	USD 15-yr	USD 20-yr	USD 30-yr	GBP 3-mo	GBP 1-yr	GBP 2-yr	GBP 3-yr	GBP 5-yr	GBP 7-yr	GBP 10-yr	GBP 15-yr	GBP 20-yr	GBP FX*
Ann Vol		68	66	135	133	136	130	125	120	110	85	64	74	82	84	86	85	87	88	88	7.77
Correlation	USD 3-mo	1.00	0.51	0.21	0.18	0.11	0.11	0.11	0.10	0.09	0.02	0.30	0.29	0.29	0.27	0.26	0.22	0.19	0.14	0.11	-0.14
Matrix	USD 1-yr	0.51	1.00	0.21	0.21	0.17	0.15	0.09	0.10	0.09	0.04	0.17	0.32	0.37	0.32	0.29	0.19	0.17	0.21	0.12	0.19
	USD 2-yr	0.21	0.21	1.00	0.98	0.90	0.88	0.83	0.81	0.76	0.43	-0.09	-0.04	0.29	0.37	0.36	0.37	0.38	0.28	0.27	0.10
	USD 3-yr	0.18	0.21	0.98	1.00	0.95	0.94	0.88	0.87	0.82	0.48	-0.09	-0.03	0.29	0.37	0.36	0.39	0.40	0.30	0.29	0.11
	USD 5-yr	0.11	0.17	0.90	0.95	1.00	0.99	0.93	0.92	0.88	0.56	-0.10	-0.03	0.27	0.35	0.35	0.40	0.41	0.33	0.32	0.13
	USD 7-yr	0.11	0.15	0.88	0.94	0.99	1.00	0.97	0.96	0.93	0.61	-0.07	-0.02	0.27	0.37	0.37	0.44	0.45	0.37	0.36	0.10
	USD 10-yr	0.11	0.09	0.83	0.88	0.93	0.97	1.00	0.99	0.96	0.67	-0.07	-0.03	0.26	0.39	0.40	0.50	0.51	0.43	0.42	0.06
	USD 15-yr	0.10	0.10	0.81	0.87	0.92	0.96	0.99	1.00	0.99	0.75	-0.06	-0.02	0.25	0.38	0.40	0.50	0.52	0.44	0.44	0.04
	USD 20-yr	0.09	0.09	0.76	0.82	0.88	0.93	0.96	0.99	1.00	0.84	-0.04	-0.01	0.23	0.36	0.38	0.49	0.51	0.45	0.44	0.01
	USD 30-yr	0.02	0.04	0.43	0.48	0.56	0.61	0.67	0.75	0.84	1.00	0.01	0.02	0.11	0.22	0.25	0.38	0.40	0.38	0.38	-0.07
	GBP 3-mo	0.30	0.17	-0.09	-0.09	-0.10	-0.07	-0.07	-0.06	-0.04	0.01	1.00	0.83	0.25	0.16	0.12	0.04	-0.04	-0.06	-0.07	-0.10
	GBP 1-yr	0.29	0.32	-0.04	-0.03	-0.03	-0.02	-0.03	-0.02	-0.01	0.02	0.83	1.00	0.46	0.33	0.26	0.14	0.03	-0.01	-0.07	0.00
	GBP 2-yr	0.29	0.37	0.29	0.29	0.27	0.27	0.26	0.25	0.23	0.11	0.25	0.46	1.00	0.95	0.88	0.71	0.58	0.44	0.34	0.20
	GBP 3-yr	0.27	0.32	0.37	0.37	0.35	0.37	0.39	0.38	0.36	0.22	0.16	0.33	0.95	1.00	0.97	0.84	0.74	0.60	0.51	0.15
	GBP 5-yr	0.26	0.29	0.36	0.36	0.35	0.37	0.40	0.40	0.38	0.25	0.12	0.26	0.88	0.97	1.00	0.91	0.85	0.70	0.65	0.11
	GBP 7-yr	0.22	0.19	0.37	0.39	0.40	0.44	0.50	0.50	0.49	0.38	0.04	0.14	0.71	0.84	0.91	1.00	0.97	0.83	0.81	0.07
	GBP 10-yr	0.19	0.17	0.38	0.40	0.41	0.45	0.51	0.51	0.51	0.40	-0.04	0.03	0.58	0.74	0.85	0.97	1.00	0.86	0.88	0.09
	GBP 15-yr	0.14	0.21	0.28	0.30	0.33	0.37	0.43	0.44	0.45	0.38	-0.06	-0.01	0.44	0.60	0.70	0.83	0.86	1.00	0.93	0.02
	GBP 20-yr	0.11	0.12	0.27	0.29	0.32	0.36	0.42	0.44	0.44	0.38	-0.07	-0.07	0.34	0.51	0.65	0.81	0.88	0.93	1.00	0.00
	GBP FX	-0.14	0.19	0.10	0.11	0.13	0.10	0.06	0.04	0.01	-0.07	-0.10	0.00	0.20	0.15	0.11	0.07	0.09	0.02	0.00	1.00

*Ann Vol is annualized yield volatility in basis points (interest rates) and annualized price volatility in percent (exchange rates)

Source: Risk Metrics® data has been produced and provided by the Risk Metrics Group, LLC at www.riskmetrics.com.

spot rates was almost monotonically upward sloping. Finally, notice that the GBP/USD foreign currency exchange rate was poorly correlated with both the U.S. and UK yield curves.

4.3.4 Overview of Systematic Basis Risks

For those investors who were conveniently ignoring basis risks during the years of their benign behavior, the market crises of 1997–1998 served as persuasive illustrations of the potency of these systematic risk factors. It became apparent that explicit measurement and management of interest rate risk alone is insufficient for portfolios invested in asset classes whose values depend on changes in implied volatility, mortgage prepayments, credit spreads, and other basis risks. In fall 1998, devastating financial losses resulting from a dramatic widening of credit spreads forced risk managers to focus on incorporating basis risks into the existing risk methodologies. Not only was it important to identify relevant and reliably measurable systematic sources of basis risks, the unstable relationships among basis risks, interest rates, and other risk factors needed to be understood and quantified. Exhibit 4.2 shows the evolution of the 10-year USD swap spread between March 1992 and May 1999. A trading strategy consisting of a 10-year interest rate swap perfectly duration-hedged with a 10-year U.S. Treasury would have incurred huge losses during the technically driven credit and liquidity crisis of fall 1998.

Basis risk factors that are relevant to fixed income markets can be divided into the following three categories (Table 4.9): implied volatilities, nominal and option-adjusted mortgage spreads, and credit spreads. This allows us to write a more detailed expression for the basis risk component of Global VaR (Equation 4.49):

$$\Delta V|_{\text{basis risks}} = \Delta V|_{\text{volatility}} + \Delta V|_{\text{mortgages}} + \Delta V|_{\text{credit spreads}} \qquad (4.61)$$

In Chapter 2, we discussed a variety of duration measures that estimate the price sensitivity of fixed income securities to each group of systematic basis risk factors. The following sections will incorporate this information into the Variance/Covariance VaR framework.

4.3.5 Implied Volatility Risks

Volatility duration *(Vol Dur)* was defined in Section 2.5.1 as a measure of the price sensitivity of securities with embedded options to changes in

EXHIBIT 4.2   10-year USD Swap Spread (3/1992–5/1999)

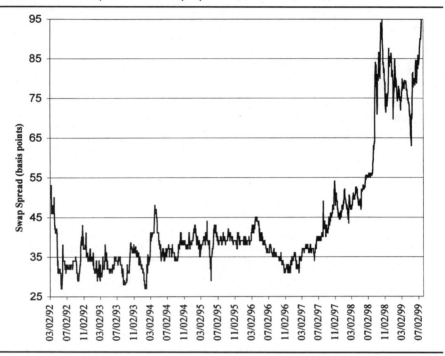

implied volatility assumptions. The component $\Delta V|_{\text{volatility}}$ of Global VaR corresponding to implied volatility risk can be therefore written as follows:

$$\Delta V|_{\text{volatility}} = -V_{\text{vol}} \cdot Vol\,Dur \cdot \Delta vol \qquad (4.62)$$

where V_{vol} is the market value of the subportfolio exposed to changes in implied volatilities, *Vol Dur* is volatility duration of this subportfolio, and Δvol is a change in implied volatility.

For the sake of simplicity, Equation 4.62 assumes that all basis risks associated with changes in implied volatility are driven by a single systematic risk factor. To capture the nonparallel movements in term structures of implied volatilities (volatility "smiles" and "frowns"), the approach presented above can be extended for multiple implied volatility risk factors, exposures to which can be measured by volatility key rate durations.

TABLE 4.9 Selected Systematic Basis Risk Factors

Category	Basis Risk Factors	Industry/Region	Rating	Maturity	Structure	Country	In-The-Moneyness	Proxy
Volatility	Implied Volatility			varies		varies	varies	
Mortgages	Mortgage/TSY Basis			15, 30		US		
	Mortgage OAS			15, 30	MBS, IO, PO	US	100 OTM, 50 OTM, ATM, 50 ITM, 100 ITM	
Credit Spreads	Agency Spreads			2, 5, 10		US		
	Swap Spreads			2, 5, 10, 30		varies		
	Investment Grade	Finance, Industrials, Utilities, Yankees	AAA, A, A, BBB	2, 3, 5, 10, 30		varies		
	Corporate Spreads							
	High Yield Spreads		BB, B, CCC			US		
	CBO/CLO Spreads	Senior, Subordinate	AAA, AA, A, BBB, BB and below	10	Cash, Zero	US		ABS, CMBS, High Yield
	Emerging Markets	Brady Bonds, Latin America, Eastern Europe, Asia		varies	varies	varies		EMBI+, Brazil C, Poland PDI, Korea 2008
	ABS Spreads	Auto		2		US		
		Credit Cards		2,5,10				
		Home Equity Fixed		2, 5, 10				
		Home Equity Float		3				
		HELOC*		3				
		Manufact. Housing		2, 5, 10				
		Student Loans		2,7				
		Stranded Cost		2, 5, 10				
	CMBS		AAA	5, 7, 10	CMBS, IO	US		
			AA, A, BBB	10				
			BBB-, BB, B	10				

* "HELOC" denotes "Home Equity Line of Credit"

165

4.3.6 Mortgage Basis Risks

As briefly mentioned in Chapter 2, when practitioners allude to changes in mortgage spreads, they implicitly refer to the occurrence of two interconnected but not perfectly correlated phenomena: changes in nominal mortgage spreads and changes in mortgage option-adjusted spreads (OASs). The former is a fundamental basis risk factor that causes mortgage prepayments: if mortgage origination rates rise, economic incentives to refinance existing mortgages decline, causing mortgage prepayments to slow down. Conversely, if mortgage origination rates fall, it becomes advantageous to refinance existing mortgage loans, forcing mortgage prepayments to speed up. The second phenomenon, changes in mortgage OASs, is a technical (related to supply and demand) basis risk factor. It reflects changes in the market sentiment (expressed as risk premium or OAS) toward holding mortgages. Cause-and-effect relationships among changes in nominal mortgage spreads and changes in mortgage OASs can be illustrated analytically. For instance, if mortgage origination rates decline, mortgage prepayments intensify, implying higher prepayment risk in the mortgage market and, hence, higher mortgage OASs. In Section 4.5.1, we show that changes in mortgage OASs cause nominal mortgage spreads to change as well. While these causalities empirically manifest themselves in nominal mortgage spreads and mortgage OASs typically moving in the same direction, these basis risks are not perfectly correlated and exhibit different volatilities. This argues that changes in nominal mortgage spreads and changes in mortgage OASs have to be represented as separate systematic sources of basis risk:

$$\Delta V|_{\text{mortgages}} = \Delta V|_{MTB} + \Delta V|_{OAS} \qquad (4.63)$$

where MTB denotes mortgage/treasury basis, a measure of change in nominal mortgage spreads (Section 2.6.2). Using the results from Chapter 2, we obtain the following first-order approximation for the risk associated with changes in nominal mortgage spreads:

$$\Delta V|_{MTB} = -V_{Mtg} \cdot MTB \, Dur \cdot \Delta MTB \qquad (4.64)$$

where V_{Mtg} is the market value of all mortgage backed securities and mortgage derivatives in a portfolio, and $MTB \, Dur$ is their aggregate mortgage/treasury basis duration.

Depending on the structure, the OAS sensitivity of MBS and their derivatives to changes in nominal mortgage spreads may be dramatically different. It is due to the fact that a shift in prepayment expectations implies drastically different risks for deep discount mortgages versus deep premium mortgages versus interest-only and principal-only securities, and so forth. This argues that it may not be sufficient to measure mortgage OAS risks using a single risk factor. Here are some possible approaches to defining OAS risk factors that differentiate MBSs by their structure (generic MBS, IO, PO, etc.) as well as the in-the-moneyness of the embedded prepayment options:

- OAS of a 100 basis point out-of-the-money generic MBS (MBS-100)
- OAS of a 50 basis point out-of-the-money generic MBS (MBS-50)
- OAS of an at-the-money generic MBS (MBS-0)
- OAS of a 50 basis point in-the-money generic MBS (MBS+50)
- OAS of a 100 basis point in-the-money generic MBS (MBS+100)
- OAS of a 50 basis point out-of-the-money (new) PO security (PO–50)
- OAS of an at-the-money (new) PO security (PO–0)
- OAS of a 50 basis point in-the-money (new) PO security (PO+50)
- OAS of a 50 basis point out-of-the-money (new) IO security (IO–50)
- OAS of an at-the-money (new) IO security (IO–0)
- OAS of a 50 basis point in-the-money (new) IO security (IO+50)

Determination of whether the prepayment option underlying a MBS is in-the-money, at-the-money, or out-of-the-money should reflect the actual incentive of mortgage borrowers to prepay their outstanding loans. For any point in time, we define the at-the-money (ATM) mortgage rate to be the gross weighted-average coupon (WAC) of then newly originated conventional mortgages. In order to compute historical time series of OASs corresponding to each of the listed mortgage basis risk factors, the following simple algorithm can be used. On each day, after separate OAS curves are constructed for generic mortgages, IOs, and POs, OASs corresponding to each in-the-moneyness point are determined (Exhibit 4.3). Then historical correlations and volatilities of mortgage basis risk factors are computed, and their relationship with other systematic sources of risk is investigated (Table 4.10).

EXHIBIT 4.3   Computation of OAS Basis Risk Factors for MBS of Different In-the-Moneyness

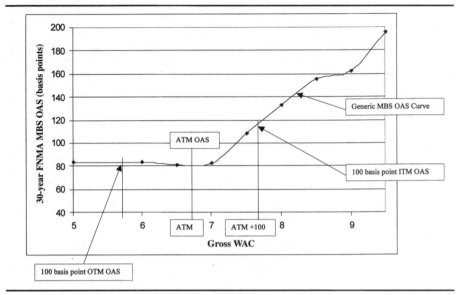

We are now ready to write the functional representation of the overall risk associated with movements in mortgage OASs:

$$\Delta V|_{OAS} = -\sum_{i=1}^{k} V_{Mtg,i} \cdot Spd\,Dur_{Mtg,i} \cdot \Delta OAS_{Mtg,i} \qquad (4.65)$$

where k is the number of different mortgage basis risk factors, $V_{Mtg,i}$ is the market value of the subportfolio exposed to the ith mortgage basis risk, $Spd\,Dur_{Mtg,i}$ is spread duration of the ith subportfolio, and $\Delta OAS_{Mtg,i}$ is a change in the corresponding OAS.

For instance, the change in the portfolio's value due to a movement in OASs of generic mortgages whose prepayment option is 100 basis points in-the-money is as follows:

$$\Delta V|_{MBS+100} = -V_{MBS+100} \cdot Spd\,Dur_{MBS+100} \cdot \Delta OAS_{MBS+100} \qquad (4.66)$$

where $V_{MBS+100}$ is the aggregate market value of all 100 basis point ITM mortgages in the portfolio, $Spd\,Dur_{MBS+100}$ is the aggregate spread dura-

TABLE 4.10 Correlations and Volatilities of Selected Interest Rates and Basis Risks

	3-mo	10-year	30-year	MTB	MBS -100	MBS -50	MBS 0	MBS 50	MBS 100	PO -50	PO 0	PO 50	Impl. Vol	Swap 2-year	Swap 5-year	Swap 10-year	Agency 2-year	Agency 5-year	Agency 10-year
Ann Vol (bp)	68	125	85	47	57	57	57	64	80	208	208	236	415	38	32	29	45	44	42
Correlations																			
3-mo TSY	1.00	0.11	0.02	-0.15	-0.32	-0.32	-0.30	-0.22	-0.21	0.11	0.11	0.01	0.02	-0.19	-0.07	0.06	-0.17	-0.17	-0.04
10-year TSY	0.11	1.00	0.67	-0.20	-0.21	-0.21	-0.18	-0.05	-0.14	0.19	0.19	0.07	-0.14	-0.25	-0.41	-0.40	-0.08	-0.08	-0.04
30-year TSY	0.02	0.67	1.00	-0.09	-0.17	-0.17	-0.14	0.00	-0.06	-0.06	-0.06	-0.11	-0.02	-0.17	-0.21	-0.22	-0.05	0.04	-0.16
MTB	-0.15	-0.20	-0.09	1.00	0.70	0.70	0.69	0.67	0.60	-0.20	-0.20	-0.18	0.10	0.27	0.27	0.30	0.14	0.16	0.22
MBS -100	-0.32	-0.21	-0.17	0.70	1.00	1.00	1.00	0.95	0.83	-0.32	-0.32	-0.29	-0.21	0.07	-0.04	0.00	-0.14	-0.09	0.19
MBS -50	-0.32	-0.21	-0.17	0.70	1.00	1.00	1.00	0.95	0.83	-0.32	-0.32	-0.29	-0.21	0.07	0.07	0.00	-0.14	-0.09	0.19
MBS 0	-0.30	-0.18	-0.14	0.69	1.00	1.00	1.00	0.97	0.82	-0.33	-0.33	-0.29	-0.22	0.05	0.05	0.00	0.14	-0.14	0.20
MBS +50	-0.22	-0.05	0.00	0.67	0.95	0.95	0.97	1.00	0.87	-0.34	-0.34	-0.34	-0.22	0.02	0.02	0.00	-0.14	-0.10	0.21
MBS +100	-0.21	-0.14	-0.06	0.60	0.83	0.83	0.82	0.87	1.00	-0.35	-0.35	-0.48	-0.22	0.07	-0.08	-0.01	-0.01	-0.13	0.13
PO -50	0.11	0.19	-0.06	-0.20	-0.32	-0.32	-0.33	-0.34	-0.35	1.00	1.00	0.90	0.10	-0.15	-0.01	-0.01	0.17	0.20	0.03
PO 0	0.11	0.19	-0.06	-0.20	-0.32	-0.32	-0.33	-0.34	-0.35	1.00	1.00	0.90	0.10	-0.15	-0.01	0.00	0.17	0.20	0.03
PO +50	0.01	0.07	-0.11	-0.18	-0.29	-0.29	-0.29	-0.34	-0.48	0.90	0.90	1.00	0.20	-0.08	0.11	0.10	0.16	0.24	0.07
Impl. Vol	0.02	-0.14	-0.02	0.10	-0.21	-0.21	-0.22	-0.22	-0.22	0.10	0.10	0.20	1.00	0.10	0.25	0.21	0.27	0.11	0.16
Swap 2-year	-0.19	-0.25	-0.17	0.27	0.07	0.07	0.05	0.02	0.07	-0.15	-0.15	-0.08	0.10	1.00	0.61	0.53	0.29	0.31	0.27
Swap 5-year	-0.07	-0.41	-0.21	0.27	-0.04	0.07	0.05	0.02	-0.08	-0.01	-0.01	0.11	0.25	0.61	1.00	0.89	0.27	0.56	0.38
Swap 10-year	0.06	-0.40	-0.22	0.30	0.00	0.00	0.00	0.00	-0.01	-0.01	0.00	0.10	0.21	0.53	0.89	1.00	0.21	0.43	0.30
Agency 2-year	-0.17	-0.08	-0.05	0.14	-0.14	-0.14	0.14	-0.14	-0.01	0.17	0.17	0.16	0.27	0.29	0.27	0.21	1.00	0.20	0.27
Agency 5-year	-0.17	-0.08	0.04	0.16	-0.09	-0.09	-0.14	-0.10	-0.13	0.20	0.20	0.24	0.11	0.31	0.56	0.43	0.20	1.00	0.32
Agency 10-year	-0.04	-0.04	-0.16	0.22	0.19	0.19	0.20	0.21	0.13	0.03	0.03	0.07	0.16	0.27	0.38	0.30	0.27	0.32	1.00

tion, and $\Delta OAS_{MBS+100}$ is a change in the corresponding OAS. Thus, if a $100 million subportfolio of MBSs that are 100 basis points in-the-money has an aggregate spread duration of 2.5, a 100 basis point widening in mortgage OAS will result in a $2.5 million loss.

4.3.7 Credit Spread Risks

The extreme widening of credit spreads across all spread-sensitive asset classes became one of the most notable characteristics of the 1998 credit and liquidity crisis. In late August 1998, Russia's default on its sovereign debt drastically changed credit risk aversion in fixed income markets around the world, reducing tolerance of investors to credit risk. While all credit spreads dramatically increased in August–October 1998, some asset classes incurred losses greater than others. For instance, the widening of spreads on commercial MBSs was much more severe than that of swap spreads (Exhibit 4.4), while emerging market and high yield securities were hit much harder than U.S. high grade corporate bonds. This served as a vivid illustration of the following important phenomenon: While typically moving in the same direction in the time of crisis as well as during the business-as-usual market environments, credit spreads on different asset classes are imperfectly correlated and exhibit different volatilities. It became readily apparent to risk managers that the common practice of measuring a portfolio's overall credit spread exposure as the weighted average of individual securities' spread durations was inadequate. Instead, exposures to different systematic basis risks needed to be measured separately and then properly aggregated within the Global VaR framework.[21]

There is virtually an infinite granularity with which fixed income securities can be classified into asset groups characterized by relatively homogeneous spread movements. Practitioners typically think about the following systematic credit spread risk factors (Table 4.9):

1. Spreads on bonds issued by U.S. governmental agencies, which are typically differentiated by maturity. Callability can be taken into account as well.

2. 2-, 5-, 10-, and 30-year points are usually selected by practitioners to represent movements of terms structures of swap spreads in each interest rate derivatives market (United States, Japan, Great Britain, Europe, etc.).

3. Credit spreads on U.S. investment grade corporate securities are typically divided into four main industries (Finance, Utilities,

EXHIBIT 4.4   Differential Spread Between 10-year AAA CMBS and 10-year USD Swaps (5/97–5/99)

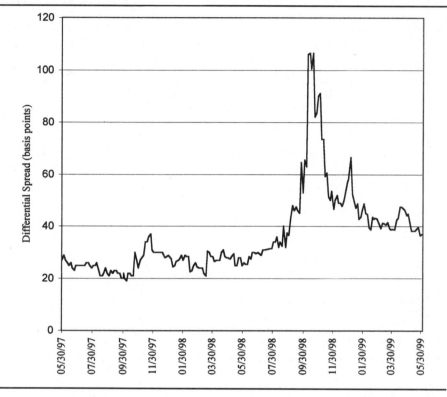

Industrials, and Yankees). For each industry, spreads corresponding to different credit ratings and maturities are followed.

4. According to high yield traders, credit spreads in these markets
   are not commonly differentiated by maturity or industry. Instead,
   they are tracked for each credit rating, structure (cash bond or
   zero), and subordination level.

5. Time series of CBO/CLO credit spreads are not currently available. To assess risk associated with a widening in these spreads,
   historical dynamics of different CBO/CLO tranches is typically
   approximated by ABS credit spreads (for AAA- and AA-rated
   tranches), by CMBS spreads (for A- and BBB-rated tranches), and
   by high yield spreads for all others.

6. EMBI+ Index is typically used as the systematic basis risk factor
   relevant to Brady Bonds and other types of emerging market debt.

Sector		FIN	FIN	FIN	FIN	FIN	FIN	FIN	FIN	FIN	FIN	FIN	FIN	FIN
Rating		AAA	AAA	AAA	AAA	AAA	AA	AA	AA	AA	AA	A	A	A
Term		2	3	5	10	30	2	3	5	10	30	2	3	5
Volatility (bp/year)		21	20	17	27	36	32	27	31	48	43	34	31	37
Sector	Rating	Term						CORRELATIONS						
FIN	AAA	2	1.00	0.96	0.78	0.69	0.67	0.76	0.81	0.56	0.48	0.67	0.82	0.81	0.61
FIN	AAA	3	0.96	1.00	0.86	0.66	0.64	0.77	0.84	0.57	0.49	0.65	0.87	0.86	0.64
FIN	AAA	5	0.78	0.86	1.00	0.65	0.61	0.70	0.75	0.57	0.52	0.60	0.76	0.77	0.61
FIN	AAA	10	0.69	0.66	0.65	1.00	0.79	0.64	0.68	0.56	0.61	0.74	0.61	0.62	0.52
FIN	AAA	30	0.67	0.64	0.61	0.79	1.00	0.53	0.64	0.29	0.44	0.93	0.60	0.61	0.42
FIN	AA	2	0.76	0.77	0.70	0.64	0.53	1.00	0.84	0.44	0.61	0.60	0.86	0.85	0.76
FIN	AA	3	0.81	0.84	0.75	0.68	0.64	0.84	1.00	0.60	0.60	0.73	0.93	0.93	0.76
FIN	AA	5	0.56	0.57	0.57	0.56	0.29	0.44	0.60	1.00	0.44	0.39	0.49	0.51	0.60
FIN	AA	10	0.48	0.49	0.52	0.61	0.44	0.61	0.60	0.44	1.00	0.47	0.42	0.45	0.53
FIN	AA	30	0.67	0.65	0.60	0.74	0.93	0.60	0.73	0.39	0.47	1.00	0.69	0.71	0.55
FIN	A	2	0.82	0.87	0.76	0.61	0.60	0.86	0.93	0.49	0.42	0.69	1.00	0.98	0.73
FIN	A	3	0.81	0.86	0.77	0.62	0.61	0.85	0.93	0.51	0.45	0.71	0.98	1.00	0.74
FIN	A	5	0.61	0.64	0.61	0.52	0.42	0.76	0.76	0.60	0.53	0.55	0.73	0.74	1.00
FIN	A	10	0.11	0.26	0.44	0.38	0.36	0.27	0.42	0.30	0.38	0.46	0.39	0.41	0.40
FIN	A	30	0.63	0.61	0.61	0.75	0.84	0.62	0.73	0.50	0.46	0.95	0.69	0.72	0.61
FIN	BBB	2	0.60	0.63	0.66	0.64	0.58	0.72	0.82	0.47	0.53	0.67	0.75	0.80	0.60
FIN	BBB	3	0.59	0.62	0.66	0.64	0.57	0.71	0.81	0.46	0.52	0.65	0.73	0.79	0.60
FIN	BBB	5	0.28	0.31	0.40	0.41	0.29	0.26	0.52	0.62	0.45	0.40	0.33	0.38	0.67
FIN	BBB	10	0.47	0.54	0.63	0.53	0.36	0.67	0.62	0.50	0.64	0.40	0.54	0.58	0.80
IND	AAA	2	0.82	0.85	0.80	0.70	0.70	0.81	0.89	0.52	0.64	0.73	0.82	0.84	0.64
IND	AAA	3	0.77	0.82	0.81	0.71	0.69	0.81	0.88	0.48	0.63	0.71	0.82	0.85	0.62
IND	AAA	5	0.73	0.77	0.79	0.70	0.70	0.78	0.85	0.47	0.65	0.74	0.77	0.81	0.60

* "FIN" and "IND" denote Financials and Industrials, respectively.

If a finer gradation of emerging market risks is desired, various liquid bonds can serve as proxies for sovereign and regional exposures (Brazil C-bonds for Latin America, Korea 2008 for Southeast Asia, and Poland PDI for Eastern Europe).

7. Credit spreads on asset-backed securities are defined for each collateral type and maturity. The distinction is typically made between prepayment-sensitive and prepayment-protected instruments.

8. Spreads on commercial MBSs are differentiated by credit rating, maturity, and structure (traditional versus interest-only).

Tables 4.10 and 4.11 present historical correlations and volatilities of selected basis risk factors and interest rates. Notice the high correlation between nominal mortgage spreads (mortgage/treasury basis) and mortgage OASs of different in-the-moneyness. Moderately strong correlation can also be observed within each group of risk factors: interest rates, swap spreads, PO spreads, agency spreads, and corporate spreads of the same maturity and rating.

After all systematic credit spread risk factors are identified and their historical correlations and volatilities are estimated, all securities in a portfolio are grouped into homogeneous cohorts, each corresponding to a separate credit spread risk. As a generalization of Equation 4.65, credit spread-related changes in a portfolio's market value can be written as a function of market values and aggregate spread durations of these cohorts:

$$\Delta V\big|_{credit\ spreads} = -\sum_{i=1}^{N} V_i \cdot Spd\ Dur_i \cdot \Delta s_i \qquad (4.67)$$

where V_i is the market value of the subportfolio exposed to the ith credit spread risk factor, $Spd\ Dur_i$ is the aggregate spread duration of this subportfolio, and Δs_i is a change in the corresponding credit spread.

We finally arrive at the final expression for Global VaR that integrates all interest rate risks, foreign currency risks, and basis risks into one summary number:

$$VaR = 1.65 \cdot \sigma(\Delta V) = 1.65 \cdot \sqrt{\bar{e} \cdot \rho \cdot \bar{e}^T} \qquad (4.68)$$

where ρ is the correlation matrix of changes in systematic risk factors, and, analogous to Equation 4.60, $\bar{e}$ is the vector of annualized one standard deviation U.S. dollar exposures:

Interest rates: $e_i = -V_i \cdot krd_i \cdot \sigma(\Delta r_i)$ (4.69)

Foreign currencies: $e_i = -V_i \cdot \sigma(fx_i)$ (4.70)

Credit spreads: $e_i = -V_i \cdot Spd\ Dur_i \cdot \sigma(\Delta s_i)$ (4.71)

Implied volatility: $e_i = -V_i \cdot Vol\ Dur \cdot \sigma(\Delta vol)$ (4.72)

Mortgage/treasury basis: $e_i = -V_i \cdot MTB\ Dur \cdot \sigma(\Delta MTB)$ (4.73)

Table 4.12 presents a series of VaR measures of the sample portfolio. US IR denotes VaR that only captures U.S. interest rate risk. The next column to the right, US IR+B, presents VaR that captures both U.S. interest rate risks and U.S. basis risks. The third column, IR+B presents VaR that incorporates interest rate risks and basis risks across all markets. Finally, the IR+B+FX column incorporates foreign currency risks to the calculations, presenting the overall Global VaR. Notice that VaR of notional securities (options on futures, caps, floors, and swaptions) is greater than 100%. This is a consequence of the fact that Variance/Covariance VaR methodology uses linear approximations of price functions, implying that the probability distribution of price changes is symmetric.

Global VaR as well as a variety of other risk methodologies rely on the covariance matrix of systematic risk factors being positive definite. Violations of this assumption may lead to principal components having negative variances and VaR hedge optimizations having no solutions (Chapter 6). While extensive research on the more robust covariance matrix estimation is available,[22] the authors discovered that many practitioners enforce positive definiteness of covariance matrices by arbitrarily turning all negative eigenvalues into small positive numbers. Needless to say, the impact of such a procedure on individual covariances is unpredictable.

There seems to be a better alternative to force covariance matrices to be positive definite while retaining intuition behind the underlying historical correlations and volatilities. Note that covariance matrices of systematic risk factors are constructed from a large number of different time series. Each of these historical time series has a different data source, observation frequency, potential data problems, and so forth. It is typically the case that even before covariance matrix construction begins, practitioners know a priori that some of the individual covariances will

TABLE 4.12 Global Variance/Covariance VaR Report for the Sample Portfolio (as of 12/31/98)

Position / Description	Coupon	Maturity	Strike	Market Value	OAD	OAC	Variance/Covariance Value-at-Risk (% per year)			
							US IR	US IR+B	IR+B	IR+B+FX
DOLLAR BLOCK										
Canada										
CANADA GOVT	5.75	06/01/29		71	14.78	3.30			15.74	20.53
CAD Total				**71**	**14.78**	**3.30**			**15.74**	**20.53**
United States										
TREASURY NOTE (OTR)	4.63	12/31/00		100	1.89	0.05	4.09	4.09	4.09	4.09
TREASURY NOTE (OTR)	4.25	11/15/03		99	4.32	0.22	9.51	9.51	9.51	9.51
TREASURY NOTE (OTR)	4.75	11/15/08		101	7.76	0.73	15.87	15.87	15.87	15.87
TREASURY BOND (OTR)	5.25	11/15/28		103	14.93	3.34	22.68	22.68	22.68	22.68
FHLMC (callable)	6.33	02/13/06		104	3.25	-0.79	6.80	6.32	6.32	6.32
MAR 10YR NOTE FUTURE		03/31/99			5.67	0.38	12.51	12.51	12.51	12.51
MAR 30YR BOND FUTURE		03/31/99			9.47	0.89	18.97	18.97	18.97	18.97
MAR 10 YR NOTE Put		02/20/99	117	0	-350.74	925.11	774.72	774.72	774.72	774.72
10 YR NOTE FUTURE Call		02/20/99	119	1	266.42	452.59	588.42	588.42	588.42	588.42
US Swap	7.24	06/15/11		10	6.68	0.91	13.91	13.80	13.80	13.80
6.00 3M LIBOR CAP	6.00	02/19/02		1	-114.67	95.80	312.42	300.15	300.15	300.15
10YR CMT FLOOR, 5-YR TENOR 6.4%	6.40	06/17/02		5	50.32	11.26	106.85	106.85	106.85	106.85
Swaption 1	7.25	05/12/00	7.25	0	-195.71	284.47	444.64	431.30	431.30	431.30
Swaption 2	Float	06/23/99	5.85	4	148.11	132.62	318.70	312.20	312.20	312.20
FGOLD 30YR	7.00	12/31/28		103	2.52	-2.59	4.49	4.05	4.05	4.05
FGOLD 30YR	8.00	12/31/28		104	1.85	-1.32	3.32	2.98	2.98	2.98
FHA CREEKWOOD GN/GN	7.30	11/30/38		108	3.57	-1.13	7.20	6.71	6.71	6.71
DLJMA_96-CF1 B1 144A	8.27	01/12/08		106	4.41	-0.54	9.22	8.28	8.28	8.28
CMOT13 Q	15.55	01/20/03		108	2.83	0.16	4.05	3.90	3.90	3.90
FNSTR_267 (FN 8.50)		10/01/24		89	7.95	-4.02	15.75	15.33	15.33	15.33
FHLMC_2043 (FG 7.00)	7.00	01/15/16		21	-45.94	-20.82	99.06	99.39	99.39	99.39

(continues)

175

TABLE 4.12 *Continued*

Position Description	Coupon	Maturity	Strike	Market Value	OAD	OAC	Variance/Covariance Value-at-Risk (% per year)			
							US IR	US IR+B	IR+B	IR+B+FX
FNMA_93-178 (FN 7.00)	5.25	09/25/23		100	0.22	0.00	0.23	0.25	0.25	0.25
BANKAMERICA CAPITAL II	8.00	12/15/26	Vary	112	8.72	0.05	16.13	14.96	14.96	14.96
PROCTER & GAMBLE COMPANY (THE)	8.00	10/26/29	100	126	12.84	2.67	20.20	19.07	19.07	19.07
CONHE_97-5 (Home Equity)	6.58	06/15/19		102	2.27	-1.00	4.84	4.55	4.55	4.55
CHVAT_98-2 (Auto)	5.91	12/15/04		101	1.47	0.04	2.50	2.35	2.35	2.35
USD Total	**6.95**			**1,708**	**5.42**	**0.62**	**11.73**	**11.17**	**11.17**	**11.17**
DOLLAR BLOCK TOTAL	**6.89**			**1,780**	**5.73**	**0.71**	**11.26**	**10.72**	**11.23**	**11.18**
NON-EURO BLOCK										
Sweden										
SWEDEN GOVT	10.25	5/5/2000		14	1.23	0.02			1.33	21.07
Total SEK	**10.25**			**14**	**1.23**	**0.02**			**1.33**	**21.07**
United Kingdom										
UK TREASURY	9	10/13/2008		230	6.91	0.61			9.52	16.70
Total GBP	**9**			**230**	**6.91**	**0.61**			**9.52**	**16.70**
NON-EURO BLOCK TOTAL	**9.63**			**244**	**6.58**	**0.58**			**8.97**	**16.08**
JAPAN										
Japan										
JGB BD 174 (10 YR)	4.6	9/20/2004		1	5.18	0.31			15.48	34.89
TOTAL JAPAN	**4.6**			**1**	**5.18**	**0.31**			**15.48**	**34.89**
TOTAL PORTFOLIO	**7.02**			**2,025**	**5.82**	**0.69**	**9.90**	**9.42**	**10.47**	**10.63**

be less accurate and less reliable than others. Any method that modifies covariance matrices to be positive definite should use this knowledge, making sure that reliable covariances remain unchanged and those whose accuracy is questionable are altered to the minimum extent possible. It appears that this problem can be best solved via a simple optimization-like procedure where the unreliable covariances are perturbed by small amounts until the matrix becomes positive definite.

4.3.8 Applications of VaR to Portfolio and Risk Management

Value-at-Risk and ex ante tracking errors can be effectively used in both portfolio management and risk management. In Section 4.2.4, we demonstrated how they can be employed in implementing consistent directional interest rate bets across a large number of portfolios. In this section, we show how Global VaR can assist in gaining insights into asset allocation risks as well as in tracking risk characteristics of fixed income portfolios over time.

Consider a fixed income portfolio managed against the Lehman Brothers U.S. Aggregate Bond Index. For simplicity, assume that we start with this portfolio exactly replicating its benchmark. In the course of our experiment, two different sectors of the portfolio, corporates and mortgages, are being over- and underweighted by various percentages in duration-neutral fashion. In order to implement these hypothetical trades, the U.S. Treasury sector is under- or overweighted accordingly. Table 4.13 shows ex ante tracking errors resulting from various active asset allocation bets.[23] We chose to present risk in terms of tracking errors rather than VaR to reflect the way portfolio managers typically think about these issues. It can be seen from the upper left panel of Table 4.13 that a 20% underweight in Treasuries and a 20% overweight in corporates results in a 41 basis point per year ex ante tracking error. A 20% underweight in Treasuries and a 20% overweight in mortgages results in a 37 basis point tracking error. A 20% underweight in Treasuries and a 10% overweight in each corporates and mortgages results in a 34 basis point per year tracking error. Notice that a 34 basis point tracking error is smaller than the individual tracking errors of 41 and 37 basis points due to diversification effects. In order to provide an even more intuitive representation of the asset-allocation risks, we identified directional interest rate bets ("Equiv. Dur Extension" column in Table 4.13) that have the same risk as the asset allocation bets studied above. It is shown that being 20% underweight in Treasuries and 10% overweight in both corporates and mortgages is risk-equivalent to having a 0.4 year duration bet on.

TABLE 4.13   Analyzing Risk of Asset Allocation Bets Using Ex Ante Tracking Errors

Treasury Underweight	Tracking Errors (%/year)			Risk-Equivalent Duration Bet
	Corporate Overweight	Mortgage Overweight	Corp & Mtg Overweight	
1%	0.02	0.02	0.02	0.04
2%	0.04	0.04	0.03	0.06
5%	0.11	0.09	0.09	0.12
10%	0.21	0.19	0.17	0.24
15%	0.31	0.30	0.27	0.31
20%	0.41	0.37	0.34	0.40
25%	0.52	N/A*	0.45	0.50
30%	0.55	N/A*	0.51	0.64

* Unable to compute due to duration-neutral constraint.
Source: Lehman Sunbond System.

Global VaR is also valuable in tracking the risk of portfolios over time. Exhibit 4.5 depicts the evolution of VaR numbers of a static hypothetical portfolio containing U.S. Treasuries and 10-year swaps through fall 1998. The upper line of the graph corresponds to VaR that measures exposure to interest rates alone. The lowest line corresponds to VaR that measures exposure to basis risks alone. Finally, the middle line corresponds to the overall Global VaR. Since swap spreads were negatively correlated with interest rates during the time inverval considered, interest rate risk and credit spread risk partially diversified each other. While the portfolio maintained relatively constant market exposures to both interest rates and swap spreads over this period, its VaR was fluctuating drastically as the market environment was changing. Thus, due to the unprecedented widening of swap spreads, the portfolio's basis risk increased almost five-fold between July and September 1998. Due to the spike in interest rate volatility in October 1998, the portfolio's interest rate risk rose dramatically despite the constant duration.

4.4 RISK DECOMPOSITION

If a fixed income portfolio is invested in multiple currencies and a variety of spread-sensitive asset classes, its VaR is a summary measure that

EXHIBIT 4.5   Tracking Evolution of Risk Using Global Value-at-Risk

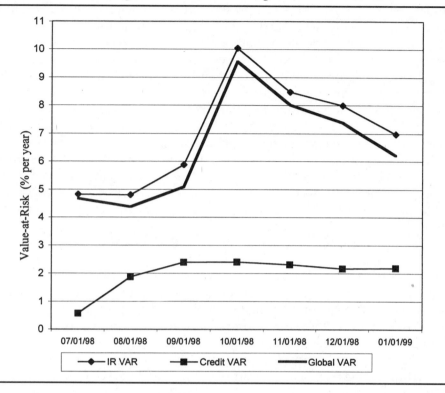

encompasses a vast amount of information. Unfortunately, while convenient and intellectually appealing, synthesizing hundreds of market values, partial durations, correlations, and volatilities into one black box
presents difficulties with respect to the interpretation of VaR and its
practical applications. Because of this obstacle, many investors were
originally skeptical about VaR and pessimistic about the future of this
risk management technique. This caused risk managers to realize that
further popularization and advancement of VaR was impossible without
developing rigorous and intuitive approaches to *risk decomposition*. Introduction of the effective risk profile (ERP) method (Section 4.2.3) was one
of the earlier attempts to decompose VaR, supplementing this summary
measure with the description of its most dominant components. Unfortunately, applications of effective risk profile were limited to measuring
interest rate risk alone since ERP relied on the fact that the vast majority
of the variability in the system is explained by the first principal component. In 1996–1997, a variety of more general risk decomposition frame-

works were introduced, Goldman Sachs' Hot Spots™ being one of the most well-known.[24] This book presents an approach to risk decomposition independently developed by the authors around the same time.

Our risk decomposition methodology was inspired by the applied statistical technique called stepwise regression. Typically employed in modeling complex systems that depend on a large number of interdependent explanatory variables,[25] stepwise regression attempts to build the most parsimonious model that explains the dynamics of a given explanatory variable. By repeatedly searching through all variables, on each iteration, stepwise regression identifies the exogenous variable whose addition to or deletion from the model improves the model's goodness-of-fit the most.[26] Besides explaining the variance of the dependent variable very effectively, stepwise regression ranks exogenous variables according to their explanatory power and explicitly investigates how they interact among each other.[27]

VaR presents the variability of a portfolio's value as a summary number, and therefore risk decomposition has the same objectives as stepwise regression. First, all relevant systematic risk factors need to be grouped into *risk clusters*, each corresponding to a group of *similar* sources of risk. Second, risk clusters with the largest contribution to VaR must be identified.[28] Third, interaction among various risk clusters needs to be analyzed, in order to reveal the diversification effects.

The definition of *risk clusters* used in risk decomposition depends on the nature of the portfolio. If a portfolio is invested in U.S. Treasury securities, it is important to investigate the contribution of each point on the yield curve to the overall risk, and therefore each risk cluster should contain a single key rate. If a portfolio is invested in G7 government securities, defining each key rate and exchange rate as a separate risk cluster would lead to an unmanageable amount of information. In this case, each country's yield curve (all key rates grouped together) as well as each exchange rate should be represented as a separate risk cluster. If a portfolio is invested in a large number of spread-sensitive asset classes, each risk cluster should correspond to a different asset class. However, when dealing with a portfolio invested solely in U.S. corporate bonds, this granularity would be insufficient, and distinction between different industries, credit ratings, and even maturities may be required. In addition to depending on the composition of the portfolio, the definition of risk clusters also depends on the goals of risk decomposition: Risk clusters that can assist portfolio managers in understanding risk in their portfolios are different from those useful for upper management in making asset allocation decisions.

The risk decomposition methodology can be best illustrated by example. Let us identify groups of systematic factors with the largest contribution to Global VaR of the sample portfolio (10.63% per year on 12/31/98, Table 4.12). Recall that each risk cluster is a collection of systematic risk factors, exposure to which is measured either by partial durations (e.g., Equations 4.69, 4.71–4.73) or by market values (e.g., Equation 4.70). If exposures to all systematic risks except for a given risk cluster are set to zero in Equation 4.68, the risk associated with a given risk cluster in isolation can be computed. This can be applied to a collection of risk clusters as well. As previously mentioned, the risk decomposition procedure repeatedly identifies risk clusters that explain the maximal amount of risk not accounted for by all previously selected risk clusters.

Step 1. Separately measuring the risk of each cluster. The columns Individual Contribution in Table 4.14, show VaR resulting from exposures to each risk cluster in isolation. For instance, being exposed to U.S. interest rates alone results in a 9.90% per year VaR, whereas being exposed to all U.S. basis risks alone results in a 1.39% per year VaR. When considered in isolation, exposure to U.S. interest rates is the most influential risk cluster, followed by the GBP/USD exchange rate, U.S. basis risks, and U.K. interest rates.

In addition to estimating exposures to each risk cluster in isolation, risk decomposition is concerned with analyzing interaction among various groups of systematic risk factors.

Step 2. By virtue of having the largest "individual" VaR, the cluster of U.S. interest rates is the most influential component of risk in the sample portfolio (Table 4.14). The next step of risk decomposition deals with identifying the second most influential risk cluster. Consider a set of different hypothetical portfolios that in addition to U.S. interest rates are exposed to one more risk cluster. By definition, the second most influential component of risk is supposed to amplify or diversify U.S. interest rate risk to the maximum extent possible. According to Table 4.14, the cluster of U.K. interest rates (GBP GOV) is the second most influential risk factor. While it is not the risk cluster with the second largest individual VaR, when combined with exposure to U.S. interest rates, this set of risk factors increases VaR of the sample portfolio by 0.57% per year (see Marginal Contribution columns), bringing cumulative VaR to 10.46% per year (Cumulative Contribution columns). While U.K. interest rates have the individual VaR of 1.08% per year, when combined with U.S. interest rates they only contribute 0.57%. The difference between the two numbers (0.51% per year, Diversification VaR column) is a benefit of diversification.

Step 3. After having determined the first two most influential risk clusters (U.S. interest rates and U.K. interest rates), the algorithm contin-

TABLE 4.14 Executive-Level VaR Decomposition for the Sample Portfolio

Total VaR: 10.63% per year

Ranking	Currency	Market	Individual Contribution		Marginal Contribution		Cumulative Contribution		Diversification
			VaR	% of Total	VaR	% of Total	VaR	% of Total	VaR
1	USD	GOV	9.90	93%	9.90	93%	9.90	93%	0.51
2	GBP	GOV	1.08	10%	0.57	5%	10.46	98%	1.84
3	USD	ALL BASES	1.39	13%	-0.45	-4%	10.02	94%	0.10
4	CAD	GOV	0.56	5%	0.45	4%	10.47	98%	1.25
5	GBP	FX	1.46	14%	0.20	2%	10.68	100%	0.50
6	CAD	FX	0.45	4%	-0.05	0%	10.63	100%	0.15
7	SEK	FX	0.15	1%	0.00	0%	10.63	100%	0.01
8	JPY	GOV	0.01	0%	0.00	0%	10.63	100%	0.01
9	SEK	GOV	0.01	0%	0.00	0%	10.63	100%	0.02
10	JPY	FX	0.02	0%	0.00	0%	10.63	100%	

* Diversification VaR = Individual VaR – Marginal VaR.

182

ues searching through all remaining group of risk factors, looking for the third risk cluster that would produce the highest risk diversification or amplification effect. According to Table 4.14, the set of all U.S. basis risks (USD ALL BASES) is the third most influential risk cluster. On 12/31/98 basis risks were negatively correlated with U.S. and U.K. interest rates, decreasing the cumulative VaR by 0.45% per year.

Step 4. Following the procedure in step 3, the fourth most influential risk cluster was identified as Canadian government interest rates (CAD GOV). Exposure to this group of systematic factors increases the overall VaR by 0.45% per year, yielding the cumulative VaR of 10.47% per year. Finally, it can be shown that the GBP/USD foreign exchange rate (GBP FX) brought the cumulative VaR number to 10.68% per year, demonstrating that all other systematic risks were not material.

Because it provides a meaningful interpretation of VaR estimates, risk decomposition can play an important role in a variety of trading, portfolio management, and risk management tasks. This section has demonstrated that by breaking down Global VaR of the sample portfolio into its components, we were able to explicitly investigate benefits of diversification and reveal areas with the largest concentration of risk. Results of risk decomposition can assist in identifying the actual bets embedded in a trade or portfolio and can be reconciled with the bets that portfolio managers *believe* were implemented, ensuring that market views are consistent with the actual structure of portfolios and trading strategies. This practical application of risk decomposition is related to *implied views*.[29] Finally, when performed on a security level, risk decomposition measures *marginal VaR* – the contribution of an individual security to the overall risk of the portfolio. However, if the number of holdings in a portfolio is large, the approach to risk decomposition presented in this section becomes a very computationally costly way to compute marginal VaR, creating a need for alternative analytical methods.[30]

4.5 GENERIC BASIS RISKS AND THEIR INTEREST RATE DIRECTIONALITY

While Global VaR and its risk decomposition provide valuable insights into many portfolio management and trading tasks, they are most often used for reporting of risk exposures and other risk management activities. Real-time asset allocation and trading decisions are difficult to make in terms of VaR since they would require the use of optimization (Chapter 6). In contrast, duration, a single number, is a widely used portfolio management and trading tool. Unfortunately, duration is a partial derivative of price with respect to a single systematic source of risk and does not capture the interaction among different risk factors. In Section 4.5.1, we use knowledge obtained in studying Global VaR to create duration measures specifically designed to account for empirically observed market relationships. This section will develop comprehensive duration measures that capture the simultaneous price sensitivity of fixed income securities and portfolios to a variety of systematic risk factors. We start with the discussion of swap spread duration, a measure of the first-order price sensitivity to changes to the market sentiment toward generic credit risk. We then proceed to incorporating information about the interest rate directionality of credit spreads and other basis risks into option-adjusted duration.

4.5.1 Swap Spread Duration

Spread duration measures the price sensitivity of fixed income securities to changes in credit spreads (Chapter 2). Depending on the security type, spread duration is computed by shocking either option-adjusted or nominal spread up and down by a given number of basis points and recomputing the resulting percentage change in price using a valuation model. While providing accurate estimates of the price sensitivity of individual securities, spread duration is not meaningful on a portfolio level since credit spreads of different asset classes are not perfectly correlated and exhibit different volatilities. Global VaR is an approach to properly account for dissimilarities in credit spread movements. Thus, securities characterized by reasonably similar credit spread behavior can be grouped into relatively homogeneous subportfolios, the aggregate spread duration of each subportfolio can be estimated, and the total portfolio's credit spread exposure can then be computed by combining spread durations with correlations and volatilities of the corresponding systematic basis risk factors. Unfortunately, in the authors' experience, practical management of credit spread risk in fixed income portfolios via VaR is somewhat unintuitive and conceptually dissimilar to the more traditional techniques currently used by practitioners. This prompted introduction of *swap spread duration*, a simple and effective measure of generic credit spread risk equally applicable to securities, portfolios, as well as portfolios vis-à-vis their benchmarks.[31] Swap spread duration was one of the earlier attempts to measure credit spread risk within a theoretically justifiable single-factor approach.[32]

In Chapter 3, we emphasized that dramatic yield curve movements are typically explained by the first principal component. Section 3.2.3

established the relationship between this phenomenon and the fact that correlations among various points on the U.S. spot curve tend to increase during periods of market turmoil. Swap spread duration is based on the analogous observation with respect to the credit spread-sensitive markets. In fact, large shocks to the financial system are often characterized by a dramatic increase in correlations among changes in credit spreads of different structured products (swaps, corporate bonds, asset-backed securities, mortgage-backed securities, emerging markets, high yield debt, etc.). In such market environments, the vast majority of systematic credit spread movements are often driven by a single amorphous systematic risk factor representing a generic market sentiment toward credit risk. After Russia's default in August 1998, for instance, there was no fundamental reason to believe that mortgage prepayments would accelerate. Yet option-adjusted spreads (OASs) on all MBSs and their derivatives widened substantially along with other asset classes for a purely technical reason – a decline in investors' desire to hold spread products.[33]

Because of liquidity considerations and the increasing importance of swaps (see Chapter 6), the 10-year swap spread can be selected to measure the generic sentiment of market participants toward credit spread risk. Thus, a swap spread widening can be thought of as a heightening in the risk aversion toward credit spread risk, and therefore credit spreads on other credit-sensitive asset classes should be expected to widen as well. Conversely, a swap spread tightening may suggest an increased appetite of investors for credit spread risk, and spreads on other spread products should be expected to tighten as well. As should be expected with any gross generality, these assumptions may not be always realistic because credit spreads of each asset class are driven by a variety of factors, only one of which is the sentiment toward the generic credit spread risk (Exhibit 4.4). For instance, swap spread changes can be decomposed into generic and idiosyncratic components, as do changes in credit spreads of other asset classes.

Swap spread duration methodology is an attempt to explicitly quantify credit spread risk in fixed income portfolios. By analyzing empirical relationships among credit spread movements of various spread products, the goal of this approach is to bring spread durations of individual securities to a *common denominator*, that is, changes in swap spreads. Swap spread duration uses individual spread durations (that measure sensitivity to different systematic risk factors) to estimate the overall price sensitivity to changes in generic sentiment toward credit spread risk. The transformation from spread duration to swap spread duration is achieved via *betas* – explicit forecasts of the relationship between changes in option-adjusted or nominal spreads of a given asset class

(ΔOAS) and changes in 10-year swap spread (Δs). These forecasts can be judgmental or can be based on analytical or empirical methods, the simplest being the following regression:

$$\Delta OAS = \alpha + \beta \cdot \Delta s + \varepsilon \qquad (4.74)$$

where α and β are the regression coefficients, and ε are the normally distributed error terms.

Consider the following example. Even if we assume the perfect correlation between changes in the 10-year AAA CMBS spread and the 10-year swaps spread (which is generally not true), these systematic risk factors do not move one for one due to the difference in their respective volatilities (Exhibit 4.4). Swap beta (β) as given by Equation 4.74 measures the magnitude of change in CMBS spreads for a given change in swap spreads. Suppose that this beta is empirically estimated to be 1.5, implying that CMBS spreads will be expected to widen by 15 basis points when swap spreads widen by 10. If a CMBS has a spread duration of 5 years, a 10 basis point swap spread widening will then imply a $5 \cdot 1.5 \cdot 0.10\% = 0.75\%$ loss. Of course, this calculation assumes that there are no changes in the CMBS market in addition to those caused by the swap spread movement.

Swap spread duration (*SwSpd Dur*) is defined as the product of a security's spread duration (*Spd Dur*) and β between changes in the security's credit spread and changes in the 10-year swap spread:

$$SwSpd\ Dur = \beta \cdot Spd\ Dur \qquad (4.75)$$

Clearly, since government securities are assumed to have no exposure to generic credit risk, their β's are zero by definition. Swap spread duration methodology *isolates* the generic (or systematic) component of credit spread risk from the asset-class-specific risk, creating a way to reasonably aggregate credit exposures across different instruments in a portfolio. By mapping exposure to a particular credit spread onto sensitivity to swap spreads, effective and consistent management of absolute and relative credit risks of fixed income portfolios becomes possible.

However, while providing adequate estimates of generic credit spread risk for the vast majority of spread-sensitive asset classes, swap spread duration as defined by Equation 4.75 fails to address the following important cause-and-effect relationship specific to MBSs and their derivatives. In these markets, a credit sentiment-driven change in OASs affects prices of MBSs in the secondary market, causing banks and mortgage servicers to change existing mortgage origination rates (or mortgage treasury basis) and therefore influencing prepayments. This argues for the extension of swap spread duration methodology that accounts for the relationship between generic credit events and mortgage prepayments.

As discussed in Chapter 2, OAS models presume the absence of spread directionality. Thus, when interest rates are shocked during the OAD calculation, both mortgage/treasury basis and OAS are kept constant. On the other hand, spread duration and mortgage/treasury basis durations are partial derivatives of the price, each computed with all other inputs being fixed. The reader can therefore verify that the following relationship must hold to the first-order approximation:

$$OAD \approx Spd\ Dur + MTB\ Dur \tag{4.76}$$

where OAD, $Spd\ Dur$, and $MTB\ Dur$ are option-adjusted duration, spread duration, and mortgage/treasury basis duration, respectively.

As mentioned earlier, both OAS and mortgage/treasury basis can be assumed to be implicit functions of swap spreads, allowing us to write the following first-order approximations:

$$dOAS\big|_{\text{swaps}} = \frac{\partial OAS}{\partial s} \cdot ds \tag{4.77}$$

$$dMTB\big|_{\text{swaps}} = \frac{\partial MTB}{\partial s} \cdot ds \tag{4.78}$$

where $dOAS\big|_{\text{swaps}}$ and $dMTB\big|_{\text{swaps}}$ are swap spread-driven changes in mortgage OASs and mortgage/treasury basis, respectively, and ds is a swap spread change. Clearly, Equation 4.77 can be rewritten using the definition of swap spread beta (β):

$$dOAS\big|_{\text{swaps}} = \frac{\partial OAS}{\partial s} \cdot ds = \beta \cdot ds \tag{4.79}$$

Consider a current coupon MBS whose swap spread-related changes in price can be expressed as follows:

$$\frac{dP}{P}\bigg|_{\text{swaps}} = -Spd\ Dur \cdot dOAS\big|_{\text{swaps}} - MTB\ Dur \cdot dMTB\big|_{\text{swaps}} \tag{4.80}$$

Combining Equations 4.78–4.80 yields

$$\left.\frac{dP}{P}\right|_{swaps} = -Spd\,Dur \cdot \beta \cdot ds - MTB\,Dur \cdot \frac{\partial MTB}{\partial s} \cdot ds \qquad (4.81)$$

Any change in price corresponds to a change in yield. By recalling that change in yield on a current coupon mortgage is the change in mortgage/treasury basis, we can write the following approximation of change in price of a current coupon MBS, given a change in swap spreads:

$$\left.\frac{dP}{P}\right|_{swaps} = -OAD \cdot dy = -OAD \cdot dMTB\big|_{swaps} \qquad (4.82)$$

Equating the two representations of $\left.\dfrac{dP}{P}\right|_{swaps}$ yields:

$$OAD \cdot \frac{\partial MTB}{\partial s} = Spd\,Dur \cdot \beta + MTB\,Dur \cdot \frac{\partial MTB}{\partial s} \qquad (4.83)$$

By taking into account Equation 4.76, the relationship between changes in mortgage/treasury basis and changes in swap spread can be determined:

$$\frac{\partial MTB}{\partial s} = \frac{Spd\,Dur \cdot \beta}{OAD - MTB\,Dur} = \frac{Spd\,Dur \cdot \beta}{Spd\,Dur} = \beta \qquad (4.84)$$

Equation 4.84 is intuitive to mortgage market traders since changes in mortgage/treasury basis caused by changes in generic credit sentiment are typically similar in magnitude of changes in OASs on current coupon mortgages. Rewrite Equation 4.81 as follows:

$$\left.\frac{dP}{P}\right|_{swaps} = -Spd\,Dur \cdot \beta \cdot ds - MTB\,Dur \cdot \beta \cdot ds \qquad (4.85)$$

Recalling that swap spread duration measures the overall price sensitivity to changes in swap spreads, Equation 4.85 yields:

$$SwSpd\ Dur \cdot ds = Spd\ Dur \cdot \beta \cdot ds + MTB\ Dur \cdot \beta \cdot ds \qquad (4.86)$$

This allows us to arrive at a more generalized expression for swap spread duration that is applicable to MBSs as well as other asset classes:

$$SwSpd\ Dur = \beta \cdot (Spd\ Dur + MTB\ Dur) \qquad (4.87)$$

Despite the conceptual simplicity of swap spread beta, its estimation in practice is nontrivial. First, the term structure of volatility of credit spreads is not flat.[34] Second, credit spreads corresponding to maturities other than 10-year tend to be more correlated to swap spreads of comparable maturities rather than the 10-year swap spread. Regressing credit spreads against swaps spreads of comparable maturities and then taking into account the shape of TSOV of changes in swap spreads improves the forecasting accuracy of swap spread betas:[35]

$$\beta_{5-year,10-year} = \beta_{5-year,5-year} \cdot \frac{p_{1,5-year}}{p_{1,10-year}} \qquad (4.88)$$

where $\beta_{5-year,10-year}$ is the beta of changes in spread of a 5-year instrument and those of the 10-year swap, $\beta_{5-year,5-year}$ is the beta of changes in spread of a 5-year instrument and those of the 5-year swap, and $p_{1,5-year}$ and $p_{1,10-year}$ are the factor loadings of the first principal component of changes in swap spreads corresponding to 5- and 10-year swaps, respectively.

The impact of technical (supply and demand) factors on the accuracy of this methodology has been increasingly noticeable as well. Due to the fact that U.S. swap spreads are quoted versus yields on on-the-run (OTR) Treasury securities, recent dramatic fluctuations in OTR liquidity premiums (or specialness) have caused an additional volatility of swap spreads. At the same time, wider use of swaps in hedging as an alternative to U.S. Treasury securities (Chapter 6) caused dissimilarities in their behavior versus other spread-sensitive asset classes. For instance, during the extraordinarily high corporate debt issuance in summer 1999, many market participants hedged upcoming corporate supply by shorting swaps, causing swap spreads to widen even more dramatically than in fall 1998 (Exhibit 4.2). Finally, practical applications of swap spread duration to managing credit spread risk in fixed income portfolios must take into account the unstable nature of empirical relationships among various credit spreads, suggesting usage of shorter time series when estimating empirical relationships. Due to a variety of technical factors as well as data problems, purely empirical determination of swap spread betas often leads to counterintuitive results. Empirically determined regression betas must therefore be reconciled with intuition and experience of portfolio managers and traders. When doing so, keep in mind that the vast majority of market participants tends to think about spread relationships in terms of levels and not changes. Swap spread betas and swap spread durations of securities in the sample portfolio are presented in Table 4.15.

4.5.2 Generalized Duration

When duration measures are used to address various aspects of market risk in fixed income portfolios, the price sensitivity to each systematic risk factor is typically investigated separately, with all other factors being fixed. This allows us to *isolate* market exposure in each relevant risk dimension. OAD, for instance, measures price sensitivity to parallel changes in interest rates while keeping all basis risks constant; swap spread duration estimates the price sensitivity to changes in swap spreads alone; volatility duration measures exposure solely due to changes in implied volatility. While providing very valuable information about market risks, partial durations tremendously complicate the tasks of portfolio and risk management since the market exposure in each relevant dimension has to be measured, tracked, and explicitly managed separately. This, in turn, may lead to excessive transactions (Chapter 6). An alternative to a VaR approach that combines various partial durations with information about the empirical behavior of the corresponding systematic risk factors thus seems desirable. *Generalized duration* methodology enables construction of comprehensive risk measures that incorporate the interest rate directionality of basis risks into OAD framework.

When speaking about OAD, practitioners sometimes implicitly assume that it is a measure of the *total* price sensitivity of fixed income securities and portfolios to parallel changes in interest rates. Clearly, this is not correct since changes in interest rates are often inversely correlated with changes in credit spreads. Existence of this phenomenon (that is, *spread directionality*) argues that OAD is not always capable of accurately forecasting performance: It simply measures change in price for a given interest rate move and does not account for any additional gains or losses resulting from interest-rate-related changes in various basis risks. Recall that option-adjusted duration framework assumes that price P of a fixed income security is a function of parallel spot curve movements (r):

TABLE 4.15 Swap Spread Duration and Generalized Duration Report for the Sample Portfolio (as of 12/31/98)

Position Description	Coupon	Maturity	Strike	Mtg/Tsy Dur	Vol Dur	Spd Dur	Swap Beta	SwSpd Dur	OAD	Gen Dur
Treasury Bonds										
TREASURY NOTE (OTR)	4.63	12/31/00				2.01			1.89	1.89
TREASURY NOTE (OTR)	4.25	11/15/03				4.43			4.32	4.32
TREASURY NOTE (OTR)	4.75	11/15/08				7.95			7.76	7.76
TREASURY BOND (OTR)	5.25	11/15/28				15.29			14.93	14.93
Agency Bonds										
FHLMC (callable)	6.33	02/13/06			0.13	2.91	0.95	2.77	3.25	2.90
Futures										
MAR 10YR NOTE FUTURE		03/31/99							5.67	5.67
MAR 30YR BOND FUTURE		03/31/99							9.47	9.47
Options										
MAR 10 YR NOTE Put		02/20/99	117		-29.73				-350.74	-332.90
10 YR NOTE FUTURE Call		02/20/99	119		-13.33				266.42	274.42
Interest Rate Swaps										
US Swap	7.24	06/15/11				6.68	1	6.68	6.68	6.01
Caps & Floors										
6.00 3M LIBOR CAP	6.00	02/19/02			-8.89	-114.67	0.65	-74.54	-114.67	-101.88
10YR CMT, 5-YR TENOR 6.4%	6.40	06/17/02			-0.99		0.65	0.00	50.32	50.91
OTC Derivatives										
Swaption 1	7.25	05/12/00	7.25		-22.45	-195.71	0.65	-127.21	-195.71	-169.52
Swaption 2	Float	06/23/99	5.85		-2.93	148.11	0.65	96.27	148.11	140.24
Generic Pass-Throughs										
FGOLD 30YR	7.00	12/31/28		-1.64	0.28	3.53	0.95	3.35	2.52	2.02
FGOLD 30YR	8.00	12/31/28		-1.51	0.17	3.04	0.90	2.74	1.85	1.47

(continues)

TABLE 4.15 Continued

Position Description	Coupon	Maturity	Strike	Mtg/Tsy Dur	Vol Dur	Spd Dur	Swap Beta	SwSpd Dur	OAD	Gen Dur
FHA CREEKWOOD GN/GN	7.30	11/30/38				3.57	0.95	3.39	3.57	3.23
Non-Agency CMBS										
DLJMA_96-CF1 B1 144A	8.27	01/12/08				5.68	1.26	7.19	4.41	3.69
Inverse Floating Rate Mortgages										
CMOT13 Q	15.55	01/20/03		-0.17	0.00	1.12	0.75	0.84	2.83	2.75
POs-Agency										
FNSTR_267 (FN 8.50)		10/01/24		4.70	0.08	2.69	0.90	2.42	7.95	7.66
IOs-Agency										
FHLMC_2043 (FG 7.00)	7.00	01/15/16		-43.24	1.37	2.39	0.75	1.79	-45.94	-46.94
CMO Sequentials-Agency										
FNMA_93-178 (FN 7.00)	5.25	09/25/23			0.00	0.23	0.65	0.15	0.22	0.21
Corporates - Finance										
BANKAMERICA CAPITAL II	8.00	12/15/26	Vary		0.39	8.31	1.25	10.39	8.72	7.45
Corporates - Industrial										
PROCTER & GAMBLE COMPANY (T	8.00	10/26/29	100		0.00	13.18	1.16	15.22	12.84	11.32
Asset Backed - Prepay Sensitive										
CONHE_97-5 (Home Equity)	6.58	06/15/19				2.73	0.58	1.6	2.27	2.11
Asset Backed - Non-Prepay Sensitive										
CHVAT_98-2 (Auto)	5.91	12/15/04				1.51	0.58	0.88	1.47	1.38
Total Assets	**7.02**			**-0.41**	**0.04**	**5.56**		**2.87**	**6.82**	**6.51**

$$P = P(r) \tag{4.89}$$

and therefore

$$OAD = -\frac{1}{P}\frac{dP}{dr} \tag{4.90}$$

The presence of spread directionality requires the introduction of a richer setting. Let us now assume that price P is a function of two systematic risk factors – parallel spot curve movements (r) and changes in swap spreads $(s(r))$ that are, in turn, a function of interest rates:

$$P = P(r, s(r)) \tag{4.91}$$

This allows us to define *generalized duration (Gen Dur)* – an attempt to measure the total price sensitivity to changes in interest rates:

$$Gen\ Dur = -\frac{1}{P}\frac{dP(r, s(r))}{dr} = -\frac{1}{P}\frac{\partial P}{\partial r} - \frac{1}{P}\frac{\partial P}{\partial s}\frac{ds}{dr} \tag{4.92}$$

where $-\dfrac{1}{P}\dfrac{\partial P}{\partial r}$ is option-adjusted duration (OAD), and $-\dfrac{1}{P}\dfrac{\partial P}{\partial s}$ is swap spread duration (*SwSpd Dur*).

We define *swap spread directionality coefficient (SSDir)* to be an estimate of changes in swap spreads resulting from parallel changes in the spot curve:

$$SSDir = \frac{ds}{dr} \tag{4.93}$$

For example, on 12/31/98 changes in swap spreads were negatively correlated with directional spot curve movements. At that time, historical swap spread directionality coefficient was estimated as –0.1, implying that a 100 basis point increase in interest rates was expected to cause swap spreads to tighten by 10 basis points. Combining Equations 4.92 and 4.93 yields the following expression for generalized duration:

$$Gen\ Dur = OAD + SSDir \cdot SwSpd\ Dur \tag{4.94}$$

In addition to swap spreads and generic credit-related prepayments, generalized duration allows for incorporation of a variety of other basis risks into interest rate duration. Thus, Equation 4.94 can be extended to capture price dependency on numerous systematic risk factors that could, in turn, be functions of interest rates, basis risks, etc. This involves axiomatic specification of cause-and-effect relationships in financial markets that the user expects to persist over a given horizon. Exhibit 4.6 shows one such possible causality diagrams where interest rates are assumed to affect both swap spreads and implied volatilities. Swap spreads, in turn, are presumed to influence OASs and credit-related prepayments in a way consistent with swap spread duration calculation (upper branch of Exhibit 4.6). Similar to how the relationship between interest rates and swap spreads is depicted by swap spread directionality coefficient *SSDir*, interest rate directionality of implied volatility can be described by volatility directionality coefficient *VOLDir*:

$$VOLDir = \frac{dvol}{dr} \qquad (4.95)$$

This enables us to extend the generalized duration formulation as follows:

$$Gen\ Dur = OAD + SSDir \cdot SwSpd\ Dur + VOLDir \cdot Vol\ Dur \qquad (4.96)$$

where *Vol Dur* is volatility duration.

Table 4.16 presents the details of the generalized duration computation for a 30-year 7.0% FNMA MBS that uses the cause-and-effect relationships among systematic risk factors as shown in Exhibit 4.6. Notice that generalized duration (1.61) is much closer in magnitude to implied duration (1.63) than is OAD (1.78), suggesting that generalized duration may be more predictive of the actual price behavior than OAD. The advantages of the generalized duration methodology became apparent during the 1998 credit and liquidity crisis. At that time, interest rates were falling while credit spreads were widening, causing implied durations of mortgages to become virtually zero. By combining various empirical relationships among interest rates, credit spreads, and implied volatilities within the generalized duration approach, insights into the actual price behavior of various asset classes could be gained. Having no knowledge about movements of credit spreads, OAD was incapable of capturing these phenomena. Table 4.15 compares generalized durations and OADs of securities in the sample portfolio.

Given the inherently unstable nature of relationships among interest rates and various basis risks, the task of forecasting directionality

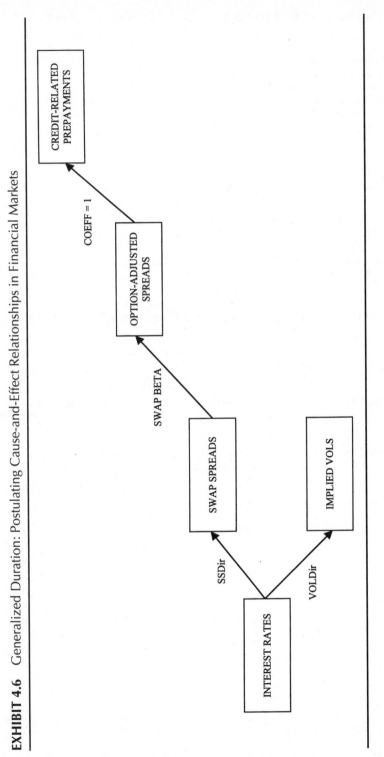

EXHIBIT 4.6 Generalized Duration: Postulating Cause-and-Effect Relationships in Financial Markets

TABLE 4.16   30-year 7% FNMA MBS: Generalized Duration Is Much Closer to Implied Duration than OAD

Sensitivity Components	Sensitivity Measure	Num Expression	Result	Implied Dur
Interest Rates Only	Option-Adjusted Duration	1.78	1.78	
Effect of Interest Rates on Swap Spreads	SSDir · Swap Spread Duration	-0.1 · 2.17	-0.22	
Effect of Swap Spreads on MTB	SSDir · MTB Duration	-0.1 · -1.48	0.15	
Effect of Interest Rates on Implied Vols	VOLDir · Volatility Duration	-0.6 · 0.17	-0.10	
Total			**1.61**	**1.63**

coefficients is nontrivial. According to Exhibits 4.7 and 4.8, directionality coefficients tend to increase in absolute value during financial crises. While even the sign of these regression betas can change as a function of market environments, they are rarely zero, explaining why OAD is typically dissimilar to implied duration. While swap spread and implied volatility directionality coefficients are usually measured

EXHIBIT 4.7   Historical Swap Spread Directionality Coefficient Over Time

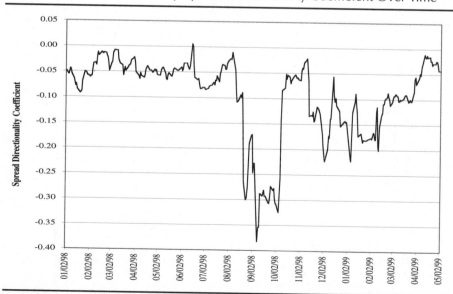

EXHIBIT 4.8   Implied Volatility Directionality Coefficient Over Time

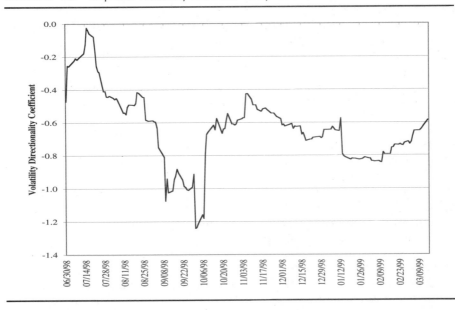

as regression coefficients,[36] they can be implied by the options markets as well. Derivation of swap spread directionality coefficient via
implied volatilities of swaptions and options of U.S. Treasury securities is shown in Table 4.17.[37]

TABLE 4.17   Forecasting Swap Spread Directionality Coefficient Using
Options Markets

	Normalized Implied Volatility (basis points)		Implied SSDir (relative to 10-year TSY)	
	1-month	**3-month**	**1-month**	**3-month**
2-year TSY	133	131		
5-year TSY	137	136		
10-year TSY	135	137		
30-year TSY	93	99		
2-year Swap	117	116	−0.13	−0.15
5-year Swap	120	119	−0.11	−0.13
10-year Swap	125	123	−0.07	−0.10

ENDNOTES

1. Parts of this chapter are based on the paper by Golub and Tilman, 1997b, reprinted in Nawalkha and Chambers, 1999.
2. We ask those readers who viscerally object to this assumption to grant us this liberty for pedagogical purposes.
3. Correlations and volatilities of municipal interest rates, earthquakes, and floods used in this section are purely hypothetical.
4. See Johnson and Wichern, 1982.
5. We owe this expression to Laurence Fink (see Foreword to this book).
6. See Jorion, 1999.
7. Just think of VaR optimizations by LTCM as described by Jorion, 1999.
8. See Litterman, 1996.
9. This observation is based on correlations from the RiskMetrics® monthly dataset.
10. The choice of this geographical location is purely pedagogical. Sonoma County was selected as an example of an area, parts of which, to the best of the authors' knowledge, are generally susceptible to natural disasters: mud slides, floods, and earthquakes.
11. Technically speaking, natural disasters are correlated with credit risk factors rather than interest rates. For the sake of simplicity, this example assumes that credit events manifest themselves as changes in yields on municipal bonds and need not be modeled as separate risk factors.
12. See RiskMetrics, 1996.
13. Recall that the terms *volatility* and *standard deviation* of price changes are used interchangeably.
14. Readers not familiar with dollar duration hedging are referred to Chapter 6.
15. See Jensen, 1969
16. See Willner, 1996.
17. The brute-force verification of the fact that Equations 4.28 and 4.29 are equivalent is left to the reader.
18. See Barber and Copper, 1996.
19. See Linsmeier and Pearson, 1996.
20. See Golub and Tilman, 1997a.
21. Credit spreads change for technical as well as fundamental reasons. The alternative to the Global VaR approach to measuring the credit risk uses probability transition matrices of credit ratings (see CreditMetrics™, 1997).
22. See Ledoit, 1996, 1998, and 1999; Michaud, 1998; and Jorion, 1996.
23. We thank Lehman Brothers for allowing us to use their SunBond software package in constructing the example dealing with asset allocation risks. Even though the risk methodology underlying SunBond package is different from Global VaR, it illustrates important applications of risk measures that capture both interest rate and basis risks.
24. See Litterman, 1996.
25. When referring to explanatory variables in this section, we use the terms *independent, exogenous,* and *explanatory* interchangeably. This by no means implies that these variables are statistically independent.

26. See Neter et al., 1986.
27. Since explanatory variables are selected sequentially in a path-dependent fashion, the resulting model does not necessarily have best goodness-of-fit among all models of the same complexity.
28. Groups of systematic risk factors with the largest contribution to the overall VaR became known as *Hot Spots*™ (see Litterman, 1996).
29. See Litterman, 1996.
30. See Ho et al., 1996.
31. Our experience with swap spread duration originated with BlackRock's portfolio managers who were looking for a tractable tool that would estimate aggregate absolute and relative exposures to spread risk.
32. See Schumacher, 1998.
33. Following the bond market jargon, we call economics-related market events *fundamental* and supply-and-demand-related events *technical*.
34. See Kao, 1999.
35. We owe this result to our colleagues Ming Yan and Roland Villacorta.
36. See Dunlevy, 1999.
37. We owe this idea to our colleague Bill De Leon. Note that this method is only capable of estimating ratios of implied volatilities and assumes that changes in swap spreads are perfectly negatively correlated with changes in interest rates.

5

Value-at-Risk
Methodological Trade-offs

5.1 GENERAL FORMULATION OF VALUE-AT-RISK

This chapter studies the concept of Value-at-Risk (VaR) in its generality and illustrates that VaR modeling involves making a number of crucial methodological trade-offs. By introducing elaborate and comprehensive measures of market risk, it brings together a variety of seemingly unrelated risk management models and approaches discussed in the previous chapters. First, partial durations and scenario analyses (Chapter 2) are employed to describe prices of fixed income securities as functions of various systematic sources of market risk. Second, principal components and parallel shocks (Chapter 3) are used to reduce the dimensionality of the VaR problem and enable application of simulation-based (or nonparametric) statistical methods. Third, expected rate of return (EROR) analysis (Chapter 2) is utilized to incorporate evolution of fixed income instruments through time into VaR. It is then shown that nonparametric approaches to VaR may not be computationally feasible for certain types of complex fixed income portfolios that depend on a large number of loosely correlated systematic risk factors. This motivates introduction of a VaR methodology that captures the nonlinear dependency of price on changes in interest rates and accounts for the first-order exposures to basis, foreign currency, and other systematic risks at the same time.

Finally, Historical and Monte-Carlo Simulation VaR methods are compared, the importance of establishing the appropriate VaR horizon is discussed, and the necessity to supplement VaR with stress testing while measuring losses associated with catastrophic events is demonstrated.

In Chapter 2, we indicated that the price (P) of a fixed income security can be thought of as a function of many interdependent stochastic systematic risk factors $F_1,\ldots,F_n$ and time:

$$P = P(F_1,\ldots,F_n,t) \tag{5.1}$$

For instance, the price of an option is a function of the price on the underlying asset, the risk-free interest rate, and implied volatility. The price of a U.S. Treasury bond depends solely on the values of key rates on the U.S. Treasury spot curve. The price of a Canadian mortgage held by a U.S. investor is a function of Canadian key spot rates, CAD/USD foreign currency exchange rate, Canadian mortgage spreads, and implied volatility. Using the language of geometry, we define *value surface* as a graphical representation of the multidimensional dependency of a security's price on changes in relevant risk factors.[1]

Risk management is concerned with forecasting potential gains and losses resulting from changes in systematic risk factors (random variables). As functions of random variables (Equation 5.1), prices of fixed income securities and portfolios are random variables as well, and their *probability density functions* (PDFs) can be obtained via analytical as well as simulation-based statistical techniques. Knowledge of PDFs allows investors to gain insights into the nature of market risks embedded in a security or portfolio. VaR, *IntRR*, and other statistical measures simply describe particular characteristics of price distributions, including their means (expected returns), standard deviations (tracking errors), large but infrequent losses (VaR), upside versus the downside, and so forth. When PDFs are constructed using analytical methods, risk measures typically correspond to the various analytically derived confidence intervals. Whenever nonparametric risk measurement approaches are employed, risk measures cannot be obtained analytically and are formulated in terms of percentiles of probability distributions instead.

5.2 TRADITIONAL VaR TRADE-OFF: NONLINEARITY VERSUS COMPUTATIONAL TIME

After a variety of VaR methodologies were developed and implemented in 1995–1996, academics and practitioners were faced with a new set of conceptual and technical challenges. In addition to knowing the mechanics of VaR computations, numerous assumptions underlying VaR needed to be studied, and their implications needed to be fully understood. In 1997–1998, research interests included studies of the consequences of approximating nonlinearity of the value surface, definition and measurement of basis risk factors, analysis of the relationship between confidence levels and accuracy of VaR forecasts,[2] influence of historical correlations and volatilities estimation on VaR,[3] connection between VaR horizons and styles of money management, and the like. In addition to technical and econometric aspects of computing VaR that were undoubtedly quite complex, the need to understand the nature of methodological trade-offs made by various VaR methodologies became apparent.

Let us assume that valuation models are available and fair values of all fixed income securities can be computed in any given market environment. Provided that the joint probability distribution of systematic risk factors has been conjectured and its parameters have been estimated from the historical data, a large number of samples can be drawn from this joint distribution using a random or pseudo-random number generator.[4] For each joint realization of systematic risk factors (or new market environment), valuation models can be used to directly recompute fair values of all securities in a portfolio. By drawing a histogram of differences between simulated prices and the current price, the empirical PDF of price changes can be created, fully characterizing the market risk embedded in the portfolio. This most general approach to constructing PDFs has become known as *Full Monte-Carlo Simulation.* First, notice that this methodology is flexible enough to allow for arbitrary distribution assumptions about the stochastic dynamics of systematic risk factors. It can be used to simulate changes in interest rates, basis risks, and currencies using probability distributions other than normal, creating a richer setting than Variance/Covariance VaR, which relies on normality assumption. Exhibit 5.1 presents the PDF of annualized price changes of a generic MBS on 1/27/98.[5] Because of the embedded short interest rate option (created by the right of mortgage borrowers to prepay their loans at any time without a penalty), the value surface of this instrument is negatively convex (i.e., concave) along the interest rate dimension (Chapter 2). As seen in Exhibit 5.1 and for reasons that will become apparent later in this chapter, negative convexity manifests itself in the distribution of value changes being skewed to the left and having fat tails. Therefore, the assumption made by the Variance/Covariance VaR methodology (Chapter 4) about changes in prices being normally distributed may not be realistic for fixed income securities whose value surfaces are substantially nonlinear.

EXHIBIT 5.1 Distribution of Annualized Price Changes of Generic MBS Obtained Using Monte-Carlo Simulation

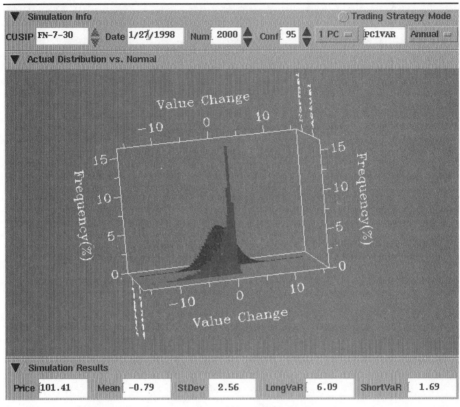

While intellectually appealing and straightforward to implement in practice, *Full Monte-Carlo Simulation* VaR may not always be computationally feasible because every security in a portfolio needs to be directly revalued for each sampled joint realization of systematic risk factors. This task is especially time-consuming for fixed income portfolios containing a large number of complex path-dependent derivatives (mortgages and their derivatives, path-dependent options, etc.) whose valuation itself requires a Monte-Carlo simulation. Even with today's capability to distribute complex computations across extensive networks of powerful computers, *Full Monte-Carlo Simulation* of certain types of fixed income portfolios may take hundreds of machine days. Therefore, this methodology may not be inadequate for the needs of financial institutions that manage the risk of thousands of securities and hundreds of portfolios in a productionized setting on a daily basis.

As opposed to *Full Monte-Carlo Simulation VaR*, which fully captures the shape of the value surface via direct revaluations, Variance/Covariance VaR[6] is relatively computationally inexpensive because it makes the most rudimentary assumption about the shape of the value surface – that it is linear in all systematic risk factors. As studied in Chapter 4, Variance/Covariance VaR employs partial durations to account for cash flow uncertainties of fixed income securities. When value surfaces are substantially nonlinear, the *locality* of partial durations employed by this methodology may result in significant inaccuracies in forecasting losses resulting from large changes in systematic risk factors. This limitation of Variance/Covariance VaR – one of the most analytically convenient and computationally inexpensive measures of market risk – may have far-reaching, adverse consequences. By approximating prices as linear combinations of normally distributed systematic risk factors, Variance/Covariance VaR presumes that random changes in prices are normally distributed as well. This may lead to the erroneous conclusions that a long position in a non-notional security can lose more than 100% of its value or that it is equally risky to hold a derivative security as it is to short it. Moreover, as seen from Exhibit 5.1, risk may be vastly underestimated if symmetric normal price distributions are assumed for securities whose actual price distributions are highly skewed to the left because of embedded short options or other characteristics that cause negative convexity.

Practitioners have devoted a lot of thought to understanding the nature of trade-offs between capturing nonlinearity of the value surface and computational time.[7] In this setting, since no approximations are made with respect to the probability distribution of systematic risk factors, computational feasibility must be achieved by sacrificing accuracy in approximating the nonlinearity of the value surface. The entire spectrum of approaches to constructing PDFs of price changes and estimating VaR represents the different trade-offs that are made in order to approximate the unknown PDFs (which could have been obtained via Full Monte-Carlo Simulation if it were computationally feasible). On the opposite ends of the spectrum are Full Monte-Carlo Simulation VaR, which directly models the shape of the value surface, and Variance/Covariance VaR, which assumes that it is linear in all variables. In between, there is a variety of parametric and nonparametric approaches, which, while accurately modeling the distribution of systematic risk factors, make more or less rudimentary assumptions about the nonlinearity of the value surface. Similar in spirit to Variance/Covariance VaR, Delta-Gamma VaR[8] and its numerous variants use different Taylor series approximations of the value surface. Even though higher-order derivatives (local risk measures) are employed, Delta-Gamma VaR is still incapable of capturing nonlinearity when the underlying market movements are large. Unfortunately, it is precisely these large changes in systematic risks that cause many rare but, on average, regularly occurring losses that VaR is designed to measure. Between Delta-Gamma and Full Monte-Carlo Simulation approaches on the methodological spectrum of VaR methodologies, a variety of nonparametric methods (e.g., Grid Monte-Carlo Simulation VaR, presented later in this chapter) simulate random price fluctuations using a number of direct revaluations that are smaller than those used by Full Monte-Carlo Simulation VaR. For the same reason that makes Full Monte-Carlo Simulation VaR computationally infeasible, these methodologies suffer from "a curse of dimensionality problem since the number of direct valuations needed grows exponentially with the number of [systematic risk] factors."[9] As investors venture into new markets and become exposed to unusual combinations of systematic risks, application of the vast majority of nonparametric methods becomes extremely computationally expensive.

5.3 ADDITIONAL TRADE-OFF DIMENSION: NONLINEARITY VERSUS DISTRIBUTION OF RISK FACTORS

Approximating nonlinearity of the value surface is not the only way to improve the computational feasibility of nonparametric VaR methods. This section introduces another decision-making dimension in VaR modeling – *approximation of the distribution of systematic risk factors*. Principal components analysis and other methodologies discussed in the previous chapters enable a more parsimonious description of the joint probability distribution of systematic risk factors, reducing the dimensionality of the value surface, eliminating the need for numerous limiting assumptions about its shape, and making construction of empirical probability density functions via Monte-Carlo simulation less computationally expensive. VaR modeling requires, as Barber and Copper put it,[10] to choose between "parsimony and explanatory power." While the researchers typically interpret "explanatory power" as the approximation of nonlinearity, this section uses a more conventional treatment of this term – the explanatory power of principal components that are used to approximate the joint dynamics of systematic risk factors. Trade-offs of a different nature are thus created between parsimony in value surface modeling and the degree to which probability distributions of systematic risks are approximated. More accurate estimates of VaR for complex portfolios consisting of instruments with very nonlinear payoffs can thus be derived within a reasonable time frame. The advantage of the presented here framework also lies in its ability to quantitatively judge the trade-offs that are being made by alternative risk methodologies versus their computational costs. The degree to which different methods capture the richness in the dynamics of risk factors can also be estimated. The approach introduced next may be supplemented by the existing empirical methods that determine whether the obtained VaR estimate is a reasonable approximation of the unknown *true* VaR.[11]

This section presents a detailed discussion of the Grid Monte-Carlo Simulation approach to measuring VaR. First, we discuss the issues of the value surface construction and estimation using traditional and principal component scenario analysis. Grid Monte-Carlo Simulation VaR is an example of a risk management methodology that allows for more precise value surface modeling by approximating the distribution of systematic risk factors. Without substantial loss of generality, the following discussion limits analysis of nonlinearity of the value surface to the interest rate dimension alone. In Section 5.3.5, we use principal components constructed in the return space to generalize this approach for portfolios that are exposed to a variety of basis, currency, and other types of market risks.

Assume that changes in default-free interest rates (key spot rates) are the sole source of risk in a given fixed income portfolio. As before, key spot rates are assumed to follow a multivariate normal distribution with zero mean. Table 5.1 uses results from Chapter 3 to present alternative ways to portray the probabilistic dynamics of this system using principal components and other orthogonal coordinate systems, the one utilizing parallel spot-curve shocks being most notable.

TABLE 5.1   Alternative Ways to Describe Yield Curve Movements (as of 1/9/97)

Description of Risk Factors	Number	Explanatory Power
Key Rates	11	100%
Three Principal Components	3	99%
Two Principal Components	2	98%
One Principal Component	1	95%
Parallel Spot Shock	1	87%

TABLE 5.2 Value-at-Risk Trade-offs: Value Surface Nonlinearity, Dynamics of Risk Factors, and Computational Costs

Value-at-Risk Methodology	Modeling of Nonlinearity	Modeling of Distribution	Computational Costs
Variance/Covariance	Poor	100%	Low
Delta-Gamma	Fair	100%	Low
Grid Monte-Carlo Simulation Using Parallel Shock	Good	87%	Moderate
Grid Monte-Carlo Simulation Using First Principal Component	Good	95%	Moderate
Grid Monte-Carlo Simulation Using Two Principal Components	Excellent	99%	High
Grid Monte-Carlo Simulation Using Three Principal Components	Excellent	100%	Very High
Full Monte-Carlo Simulation	100%	100%	Infeasible

For each representation of yield curve movements, the dimensionality of the corresponding value surface is measured by the number of different systematic risk factors. At the same time, the concept of explanatory power (Chapter 3) quantifies the degree to which yield curve dynamics is sacrificed for the sake of dimensionality reduction. Table 5.2 indicates that the "curse of dimensionality" can be mitigated by employing principal components and other composite sets of systematic factors with high cumulative explanatory power. On 1/9/97, for instance, only 1% of the yield curve dynamics was unaccounted for by three principal components, 2% by two principal components, and 5% and 13% by the first principal component and a parallel spot curve shock, respectively. Needless to say, the actual percentages of the total variability in the system explained by the different sets of risk factors vary over time. In the majority of volatile market environments, the explanatory power of both the first principal component and the parallel shock is typically high, making one-dimensional value surfaces sufficient. However, these approaches would have arrived at inaccurate VaR estimates on 12/31/98 when the explanatory power of the first principal component was 83% and that of the parallel shock was merely 67% (Table 3.4). At that time, value surface modeling arguably required at least two risk factors. Explanatory power of interest rate shocks provides a basis for rational methodological trade-offs: depending on the market environment, practitioners can determine how many systematic risk factors are needed to adequately capture the yield curve dynamics. For many real-life complex systems, one or two principal components are typically sufficient. This may reduce the value surface dimensionality by almost an order of magnitude, enabling application of Monte-Carlo simulation methods. Table 5.2 demonstrates trade-offs made by various approaches to VaR. As emphasized earlier, Variance/Covariance VaR is incapable of accounting for the nonlinearity of the value surface while fully modeling the dynamics of interest rates and being computationally trivial. Full Monte-Carlo Simulation VaR captures both the shape of the value surface and the richness in the behavior of systematic risk factors but is computationally infeasible for complex portfolios. Other VaR methods approximate both the dynamics of risk factors and value surface nonlinearity with various degrees of accuracy. Grid Monte-Carlo Simulation VaR, described in Section 5.3.2, seems to make the most effective trade-off between modeling value surface nonlinearity and yield curve dynamics versus computational costs.

5.3.1 Traditional and Principal Components Scenario Analysis

As illustrated in Exhibit 1.4, VaR modeling starts with the measurement of market exposures and subsequently combines them with information about the joint probability distribution of risk factors. In this setting, knowledge of market exposures is typically represented in the form of the value surface – the price dependency on changes in systematic risk factors. As opposed to local measures of risk like duration, scenario analysis (Chapter 2) is designed to reveal the actual shape of value surface separately in each dimension, enabling the estimation of potential gains and losses resulting from large changes in risk factors. With all other systematic risk factors kept constant, scenario analysis investigates the price sensitivity to movements in a given risk factor directly using a valuation model. Unfortunately, estimating the shape of the value surface along each axis alone is insufficient. If the number of risk factors is greater than 1, interactions among different systematic sources of risk have to be investigated directly. This involves recomputing option-adjusted values corresponding to various cross-product changes in risk factors (*grid points*) and interpolating between them. Clearly, the number of direct valuations needed to gain insight into the shape of a multidimensional value surface grows exponentially with the number of risk factors. Hence the need for effective dimensionality reduction tools.

Typical fixed income scenario analysis assumes that the (one-dimensional) value surface is a function of parallel changes in the spot curve (Chapter 2). In practice, interest rates are typically shocked in a parallel fashion up and down by various amounts (±25, ±50, ±100, ±200 basis points) and the corresponding OAVs are directly computed. Table 5.3 presents the results of traditional scenario analysis of a derivative mortgage-backed security (FHLMC 181 CMO IOette). For instance, a 200 basis point decline in interest rates reduces the price of this security to 1,496, down from the current price of 2,113.[12] Conversely, a 200 basis point increase in interest rates causes only a moderate gain (2,306 versus 2,113). This rather esoteric security is characterized by very large negative duration and very large negative convexity, making it a perfect example of an instrument with a highly asymmetric probability distribution function.

Scenario analysis investigates the price sensitivity of fixed income portfolios and securities to deterministic yield curve shocks without any assessment of their historical likelihood. Under the assumption that changes in interest rates are normally distributed, Chapter 3 established that an interest rate shock corresponds to a realization of a normal random variable, enabling the construction of one standard deviation shocks of arbitrary shapes. Thus, on 1/9/97, the annualized one standard deviation parallel spot curve shock was 77.5 basis points (Table 5.4). Therefore, the probability associated with each parallel interest rate shock used in scenario analysis could be measured. For instance, a 200 basis point increase in interest rates over one year cor-

TABLE 5.3   Traditional Scenario Analysis of FHLMC 181 CMO IOette (as of 1/9/97)

Scenarios	One Std Dev	OAV
–200 BPS	–2.58	1,496
...	...	...
–25 BPS	–0.32	2,043
0 BPS	0.00	2,113
25 BPS	0.32	2,169
...	...	...
200 BPS	2.58	2,306

TABLE 5.4 Principal Components of U.S. Treasury Spot Curve Movements (as of 1/9/97)

	3Mo	1Yr	2Yr	3Yr	5Yr	7Yr	10Yr	15Yr	20Yr	30Yr
Ann Vol of Changes(bp):	29	58	82	88	93	98	95	94	91	80

Correlation Matrix

	3Mo	1Yr	2Yr	3Yr	5Yr	7Yr	10Yr	15Yr	20Yr	30Yr
3Mo:	1.00	0.59	0.52	0.49	0.46	0.43	0.42	0.41	0.40	0.39
1Yr:	0.59	1.00	0.94	0.94	0.92	0.90	0.89	0.87	0.86	0.83
2Yr:	0.52	0.94	1.00	0.99	0.97	0.94	0.93	0.91	0.90	0.86
3Yr:	0.49	0.94	0.99	1.00	0.99	0.98	0.93	0.95	0.93	0.91
5Yr:	0.46	0.92	0.97	0.99	1.00	0.99	0.99	0.97	0.96	0.94
7Yr:	0.43	0.90	0.94	0.98	0.99	1.00	1.00	1.00	0.97	0.95
10Yr:	0.42	0.89	0.93	0.93	0.99	1.00	1.00	0.99	0.99	0.97
15Yr:	0.41	0.87	0.91	0.95	0.97	0.99	0.99	1.00	1.00	0.98
20Yr:	0.40	0.86	0.90	0.93	0.96	0.97	0.99	1.00	1.00	0.99
30Yr:	0.39	0.83	0.86	0.91	0.94	0.95	0.97	0.98	0.99	1.00

Principal Components

	3Mo	1Yr	2Yr	3Yr	5Yr	7Yr	10Yr	15Yr	20Yr	30Yr	PC Vol	Var Exp	CVar Exp
1:	5.26	20.60	30.49	33.53	35.90	38.06	36.75	36.16	34.70	29.90	2.57	95.28	95.28
2:	29.53	38.76	49.01	33.38	15.18	-3.31	-15.32	-27.29	-35.30	-40.52	0.44	2.80	98.08
3:	81.94	29.35	-17.12	-20.54	-18.26	-16.40	-6.16	7.95	17.21	26.65	0.26	0.96	99.04
4:	47.80	-66.38	-10.20	0.63	21.34	35.25	22.94	-5.20	-16.80	-25.91	0.17	0.41	99.44
5:	8.74	-52.43	57.79	19.50	-20.14	-36.30	-23.76	3.47	17.08	29.36	0.15	0.35	99.79
6:	1.96	0.63	11.36	-12.39	-21.32	2.18	-14.82	50.98	42.30	-68.16	0.09	0.13	99.92
7:	3.64	-7.46	-40.50	36.37	60.26	-39.52	-36.49	14.02	14.53	-6.01	0.06	0.05	99.97
8:	2.90	-0.53	-33.50	73.29	-56.39	7.38	9.66	9.06	-9.21	-1.99	0.04	0.02	99.99
9:	0.13	0.16	6.18	-9.26	4.19	-39.26	33.09	61.30	-58.81	2.31	0.02	0.01	99.99
10:	0.06	0.47	-0.86	5.09	1.79	-50.48	67.43	-34.78	33.71	-23.00	0.02	0.01	100.00

Annualized One StDev Shocks (bps):	3Mo	1Yr	2Yr	3Yr	5Yr	7Yr	10Yr	15Yr	20Yr	30Yr	%Exp
PC_1 Spot Curve Shock	14	53	78	86	92	98	94	93	89	77	95.28
PC_2 Spot Curve Shock	13	17	22	15	7	-1	-7	-12	-16	-18	2.80
PC_3 Spot Curve Shock	21	8	-4	-5	-5	-4	-2	2	4	7	0.96
PARALLEL Spot Shock	77	77	77	77	77	77	77	77	77	77	86.65

PC Vol = Volatility * 100, Var Exp = Percentage of Variance Explained, CVar Exp = Cumulative Percentage of Variance Explained responded to a 200/77.5 = 2.58 standard deviation event (column 2, Table 5.3). Practitioners often look at scenario analysis profiles to determine if they represent an acceptable exposure to changes in interest rates. Alternatively, they may treat one or two scenarios as critical and, if necessary, restructure their portfolios to meet certain scenario requirements. Incorporation of the notion of likelihood enables scenario analysis not only to pinpoint market events leading to large losses but also provide an estimate of probability associated with such market movements.

Principal components can be employed in scenario analysis as well. Thus, the price sensitivity can be investigated for various realizations of principal components measured in standard deviations. This type of scenario analysis, at least conceptually, is even more straightforward than that utilizing parallel shocks since it does not require the extra step of converting basis points into standard deviations. Due to the fact that principal component shocks are formulated in units of standard deviations and not basis points, principal components scenario analysis is defined in a probabilistic setting to begin with.

Table 5.5 investigates the shape of the value surface of the same IOette in the dimensions corresponding to the first three principal components. Thus, for ±0.25, ±0.5, ±1, ±2, ±3 standard deviation changes in each of the first three principal components in isolation, option-adjusted values (OAVs) are directly computed by a valuation model. The magnitudes of price movements due to these isolated changes in principal components vary dramatically, with the range of price fluctuations attributed to the first principal component being by far the largest. This confirms that the first principal component (which

TABLE 5.5 Principal Components Scenario Analysis of FHLMC 181 CMO IOette (as of 1/9/97)

Scenarios	PC_1	PC_2	PC_3
−3.00 SD	1,326	2,107	2,012
...	...	...	...
−0.25 SD	1,935	2,015	2,006
0.00 SD	2,005	2,005	2,005
0.25 SD	2,063	1,996	2,005
...	...	...	...
3.00 SD	2,210	1,883	1,995

explained 95% of the yield curve movements on 1/9/97), accounted for
the majority of price variability as well.

As mentioned in the beginning of this section, investigating the
shape of the value surface along each dimension in isolation is not
always adequate. Despite the fact that principal components are independent random variables, the individual principal components' scenario values are additive only if the value surface is assumed linear. This
assumption, however, is illogical since we are using Monte-Carlo simulation in order to capture the nonlinearity in the first place. Therefore,
OAVs corresponding to the various cross-products (simultaneous realizations) of principal components need to be directly computed as well,
creating a number of technical nuances. For instance, in order to sketch a
reasonably accurate three-dimensional value surface (Monte-Carlo simulation with two principal components), a rather dense grid covering the
possible outcomes of the two independent variables must be created.
However, since every grid point requires what might be a computationally expensive direct valuation, the challenge is to determine a relatively
small number of grid points without significantly sacrificing precision.[13]
Exhibit 5.2 presents two possible sets of grid points that can be
employed in sampling three-dimensional value surfaces. It can be seen
that irrespective of the method used to identify the grid points, the
required computational resources are significant and grow exponentially
with the dimensionality (number of systematic risk factors). Later in this
chapter, two-dimensional simulation is used to measure VaR of duration-neutral yield curve trades (Section 5.3.3).

EXHIBIT 5.2   Grid Points (Direct Valuations) Needed for Constructing Three-
Dimensional Value Surfaces

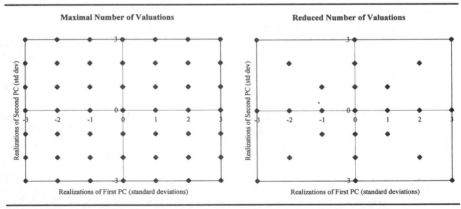

5.3.2 Grid Monte-Carlo Simulation VaR

Construction of empirical probability density functions (PDFs) relies on the ability to determine price changes resulting from arbitrary joint realizations of systematic risk factors. This implies that continuous representations of value surfaces must be created by interpolating and extrapolating discretely sampled one- or multidimensional scenario analysis values. Exhibit 5.3 presents value surfaces of FHLMC 181 CMO IOette obtained by interpolating traditional and first principal component scenario analysis OAVs (Tables 5.3 and 5.5).[14] The similarity between the two value surfaces arises because the explanatory power of the first principal component (95%) in that market environment was comparable to that (86%) of the parallel spot curve shock (Table 5.4).

Once the continuous value surface is constructed, Monte-Carlo Simulation is used to draw a large number of joint realizations of systematic risk factors. For each random drawing, the appropriate point on the value surface is identified, and the gain or loss is computed, defining the PDF of annualized value changes (Exhibit 5.4).

EXHIBIT 5.3   Value Surface of FHLMC 181 CMO IOette: Traditional versus Principal Component Scenario Analysis (as of 1/9/97)

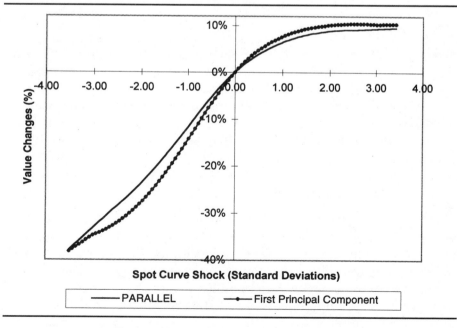

EXHIBIT 5.4   Distribution of Value Changes of FHLMC 181 CMO: Grid Monte-Carlo Simulation versus Variance/Covariance

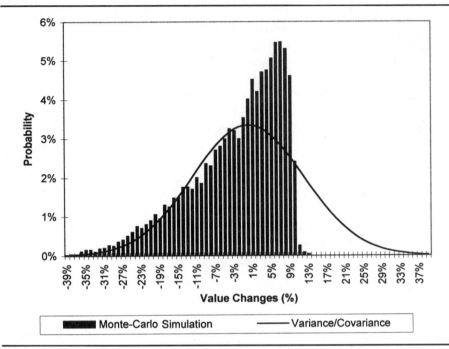

As stated in Chapter 3, the majority of examples in this book assume that changes in systematic risk factors are normally distributed. Chapter 4 has shown that within Variance/Covariance VaR methodology, the assumption about the normality of changes in systematic risk factors implies the normality of price changes. In drastic contrast with distributions of risk factors that are relatively symmetric but may exhibit fat tails, price distributions of securities with very nonlinear payoffs are highly asymmetric, making the normality assumption completely inadequate. By capturing nonlinearity of value surface via scenario analysis and (reasonably) accurately approximating the dynamics of risk factors, Grid Monte-Carlo Simulation enables construction of much more realistic PDFs. Exhibit 5.4 depicts the PDF of FHLMC 181 CMO IOette, showing that potential losses associated with holding this security are much larger in magnitude than potential gains. In theory, in absence of arbitrage opportunities, this adverse upside/downside asymmetry should manifest itself in the higher risk premium and higher coupon demanded by investors for owning this security. The presented formulation of VaR is only concerned with the risk aspect of the risk/return trade-off. In Section 5.3.4, we present a way to incorporate expected return and other evolution-through-time characteristics of fixed income securities into probability distribution functions.

After the distribution of price changes has been constructed, its statistical properties can be analyzed. As opposed to parametric methods where VaR can be analytically derived from standard deviation, simulation-based methods estimate VaR and other important characteristics in terms of percentiles of empirical distribution functions. Table 5.6 describes the properties of the empirical PDF of FHLMC 181 CMO IOette. A number of interesting observations can be made with regard to the effect of large negative convexity on the distribution of value changes. First, notice that the mean of the distribution is negative (–2.44%). For positively convex instruments, the mean is usually positive. Of course, as previously mentioned, this estimate of the mean does not capture the *carry* associated with holding this instrument. Second, note that negative convexity causes the distribution to be skewed to the left, whereas positive convexity causes it to be skewed to the right. In this particular case, negative convexity manifests itself in the distribution of price changes being highly skewed to the left and having fat tails. Thus, the 5th percentile is –20.35% while the 95th percentile is only 8.29%, implying that for the same level of confidence, potential losses are substantially higher than potential gains. Departure from the assumption of the normality of returns allows one to illustrate that a long position in this security has a drastically different risk than a short position. Table 5.7 compares the results of Full Monte-Carlo Simulation, Grid Monte-Carlo Simulation, and Variance/Covariance approaches. As expected, using first principal component in Grid Monte-Carlo Simulation as opposed to parallel shock leads to a more accurate approximation of Full Monte-Carlo VaR. Among the four methods, Variance/Covariance VaR is the least effective in capturing the nonlinearity. Table 5.8 compares standard deviations of price changes as well as VaRs obtained via Variance/Covariance and Grid Monte-Carlo Simulation methods for a wide range of fixed income securities. Notice that while estimates of standard deviation obtained via these methods differ by as much as 30%, VaR estimates can differ by as much as 300%. Notice another oddity of the Variance/Covariance VaR approach – it may arrive at the conclusion that a long nonnotional security (e.g., an interest rate floor) may lose more than 100% of its value over one year.

Grid Monte-Carlo Simulation VaR is not additive across securities in a portfolio. In order to compute it for a fixed income portfolio, the value surface of the entire portfolio has to be estimated by aggregating value

TABLE 5.6 Monte-Carlo Simulation of FHLMC 181 CMO IOette (as of 1/9/97)

Basic Input Information

DATE:		1/9/97
DESCRPTION:		IOette
1SD Parallel		77.47 bps

BPS	SD	OAV
-200	-2.58	1,496
-150	-1.94	1,625
-100	-1.29	1,784
-50	-0.65	1,961
-25	-0.32	2,043
0	0.00	2,113
25	0.32	2,169
50	0.65	2,213
100	1.29	2,271
150	1.94	2,299
200	2.58	2,306

Moments: dV (%dV)

N	:	10000		Min	:	-774.1	(-36.64%)
Mean	:	-51.55	(-2.44%)	Max	:	206.51	(9.77%)
StdDev	:	189.88	(8.99%)	Range	:	980.61	(46.41%)
Skew.	:	-0.90	(-0.9)	Kurtos.	:	0.18	(0.18)

Percentiles: dV (%dV)

1%	:	-574.82	(-27.20%)	25%	:	-166.62	(-7.89%)
2%	:	-520.77	(-24.65%)	Median	:	-3.78	(-0.18%)
3%	:	-484.73	(-22.94%)	75%	:	100.41	(4.75%)
5%	:	-429.98	(-20.35%)	90%	:	156.07	(7.39%)
10%	:	-335.37	(-15.87%)	95%	:	175.16	(8.29%)

TABLE 5.7   Comparison of VaR Methodologies: Full Monte-Carlo, Grid Monte-Carlo, and Variance/Covariance

	VaR (long position)				VaR (short position)			
Security Description	Full Sim	1 PC Sim	Paral Sim	Var/ Covar	Full Sim	1 PC Sim	Paral Sim	Var/ Covar
FHLMC_181 (CMO, IOette)	27.4	24.8	20.7	21.1	12.9	10.2	9.3	21.1
FNMA 7% 30-year (MBS)	6.5	6.7	5.3	7.6	5.6	5.9	5.6	7.6

Full Sim = Full Monte-Carlo Simulation; 1 PC Sim = Grid Monte-Carlo Simulation Using First Principal Component; Paral Sim = Grid Monte-Carlo Simulation Using Parallel Shock; Var/Covar = Variance/Covariance.

surfaces of individual securities. Then, Monte-Carlo simulation has to be performed using this portfolio's value surface. Of course, just as with Global VaR, tracking errors, and other measures of risk presented in the previous chapters, Grid Monte-Carlo Simulation VaR only addresses the systematic component of the portfolio's risk and ignores the nonsystematic risks of the individual securities.[15] Table 5.9 presents Grid Monte-Carlo Simulated VaR for the U.S. dollar portion of the sample portfolio. Notice that the total portfolio's annualized VaR of $164,171 constitutes 9.61% of its current value. Comparing this VaR estimate with 11.73% obtained for the USD subportfolio via the Variance/Covariance method (USD Total line for US IR column in Table 4.12, Chapter 4) illustrates that for portfolios with positive convexities Variance/Covariance VaR typically overestimates the magnitude of potential losses.

5.3.3 Example: Measuring Risk of Duration-Neutral Yield Curve Bets

As mentioned earlier, two types of interest rate-related bets in fixed income portfolios can typically be identified: directional (or duration) bets and yield curve bets. The trades of the former type involve betting on the general direction of interest rates (i.e., yield curve moving in a particular direction in a parallel fashion). These strategies are typically implemented by changing the duration of a portfolio either in absolute terms or relative to the assigned benchmark. The trades of the latter category bet on yield curve becoming steeper or flatter without changing its level. As opposed to duration bets whose risk/return profiles are generally well understood, it is considerably harder to measure risk as well as performance of yield curve strategies. Traditional approaches to isolating and measuring yield

TABLE 5.8 Comparison of Monte-Carlo Simulated VaR and Variance/Covariance VaR (as of 1/9/97)

Security Description	OAD	OAC	One Standard Deviation			VaR (long position)			VaR (short position)		
			V/C	Sim	%Diff	V/C	Sim	%Diff	V/C	Sim	%Diff
10YR OTR TSY	7.0	0.6	6.6	5.5	20.4	10.9	8.3	31.4	10.9	9.7	11.9
30YR TREASURY STRIP	23.6	5.6	19.9	18.8	5.5	32.8	25.4	29.1	32.8	36.1	-9.2
10YR CMT FLOOR 07/15/1996	106.5	111.6	112.9	106.8	5.7	186.3	70.7	163.5	186.3	256.0	-27.2
10YR CMT FLOOR 06/15/1997	102.0	93.7	116.3	99.2	17.3	191.9	71.2	169.5	191.9	232.5	-17.4
10YR CMT CAP 12/12/1995	-83.1	44.6	85.7	65.2	31.5	141.5	72.8	94.4	141.5	134.5	5.2
GENERIC FGOLD 30YR MBS TBA	3.7	-1.5	3.3	2.8	18.2	5.5	5.6	-2.8	5.5	3.3	66.5
FNSTR_251 1; TRUST PO	13.9	6.8	13.3	10.4	28.7	22.0	13.1	68.0	22.0	20.9	5.3
FNSTR_251 2; TRUST IO	-18.5	-20.1	18.9	14.8	27.5	31.1	35.5	-12.3	31.1	11.5	171.6
FNMA_94-26 G TAC PO	31.4	20.6	30.8	26.5	16.2	50.8	26.0	95.7	50.8	62.7	-18.9
FHLMC_181 F IOette	-11.9	-9.9	11.9	9.0	32.4	19.6	20.4	-3.5	19.6	8.3	136.9
MTG SERVICING CONV 30YR <6.50	-7.5	-2.8	7.2	7.0	3.2	11.9	14.0	-15.0	11.9	7.8	51.7
MTG SERVICING CONV 30YR 6.50-6.99	-6.9	-5.1	6.9	8.0	-14.3	11.4	17.3	-34.3	11.4	5.9	92.4
MTG SERVICING CONV 30YR 7.00-7.49	-9.1	-7.8	9.1	10.6	-14.3	15.0	24.9	-39.9	15.0	7.2	106.9
MTG SERVICING CONV 30YR 7.50-7.99	-13.0	-11.7	12.9	13.8	-6.3	21.3	34.3	-37.7	21.3	9.9	115.3
MTG SERVICING CONV 30YR 8.00-8.49	-18.5	-18.0	18.4	16.6	10.9	30.3	40.0	-24.1	30.3	13.7	120.9
MTG SERVICING CONV 30YR 8.50-8.99	-18.7	-13.9	18.4	14.9	23.8	30.3	32.8	-7.4	30.3	15.0	102.3
MTG SERVICING CONV 30YR 9.00-9.49	-20.2	-9.9	19.7	15.2	29.6	32.6	31.1	4.8	32.6	18.2	79.5
MTG SERVICING CONV 30YR 9.50-9.99	-16.9	-6.8	16.6	13.0	27.5	27.3	25.5	7.0	27.3	16.8	62.4
MTG SERVICING CONV 30YR >=10.00	-13.2	-6.4	12.9	10.6	22.2	21.4	21.0	1.6	21.4	13.7	55.7

OAD = Option Adjusted Duration; OAC = Option Adjusted Convexity; V/C = Variance/Covariance; Sim = Grid Monte-Carlo Simulation Using Parallel Shocks.

TABLE 5.9 Monte-Carlo Simulation VaR Report for the Sample Portfolio (Excluding Non-USD Securities, as of 1/9/97)

Security	Option-Adjusted Values for Various Parallel Interest Rate Shocks											Sim Value
Description	-200	-150	-100	-50	-25	0	25	50	100	150	200	at Risk ($)
Treasury Bonds												
TREASURY NOTE (OTR)	104,034	103,047	102,072	101,108	100,631	100,156	99,685	99,216	98,287	97,369	96,462	2,780
TREASURY NOTE (OTR)	108,310	105,964	103,677	101,448	100,354	99,274	98,208	97,156	95,090	93,076	91,112	6,180
TREASURY NOTE (OTR)	118,637	114,000	109,579	105,361	103,326	101,338	99,396	97,499	93,835	90,338	86,999	10,960
TREASURY BOND (OTR)	141,976	130,474	120,251	111,148	106,973	103,027	99,295	95,765	89,261	83,421	78,168	19,550
Agency Bonds												
FHLMC (callable)	108,929	107,788	106,541	105,137	104,362	103,546	102,676	101,768	99,831	97,777	95,643	5,750
Futures												
MAR 10YR NOTE FUTURE	14,478	10,671	6,992	3,437	1,704	0	-1,675	-3,322	-6,534	-9,640	-12,643	9,610
MAR 30YR BOND FUTURE	27,359	19,827	12,779	6,181	3,040	0	-2,970	-5,904	-11,582	-16,964	-22,096	16,910
Options												
MAR 10 YR NOTE Put	0	2	26	186	410	469	1,421	2,281	4,640	7,480	10,419	470
10 YR NOTE FUTURE Call	14,533	10,762	7,189	4,047	2,769	1,328	1,017	534	106	13	1	1,310
Interest Rate Swaps												
US Swap	27,191	22,527	18,165	14,087	12,149	10,275	8,463	6,712	3,384	276	-2,627	9,970
Caps & Floors												
6.00 3M LIBOR CAP	21	63	155	325	449	604	795	1,027	1,634	2,432	3,376	560
10YR CMT, 5-YR TENOR 6.4%	11,445	9,776	8,170	6,654	5,938	5,255	4,610	4,006	2,937	2,079	1,458	3,170
OTC Derivatives												
Swaption 1	0	5	31	130	234	393	622	934	1,843	3,151	4,823	390
Swaption 2	19,314	14,799	10,531	6,644	4,957	3,519	2,367	1,505	515	142	33	3,370

(continues)

219

EXHIBIT 5.9 Continued

Security	Option-Adjusted Values for Various Parallel Interest Rate Shocks											Sim Value
Description	-200	-150	-100	-50	-25	0	25	50	100	150	200	at Risk ($)
Generic Pass-Throughs												
FGOLD 30YR	104,599	104,116	103,732	103,333	102,999	102,521	101,876	101,045	98,994	96,639	94,167	5,860
FGOLD 30YR	106,788	106,179	105,593	104,958	104,594	104,167	103,660	103,031	101,420	99,412	97,243	4,730
GNMA Construction Loans												
FHA CREEKWOOD GN/GN	138,631	129,652	121,591	114,334	110,975	107,782	104,744	101,851	96,467	91,566	87,095	16,170
Non-Agency CMBS												
DLJMA_96-CF1 B1 144A	118,750	115,441	112,248	109,167	107,667	106,193	104,745	103,323	100,552	97,877	95,293	8,290
Inverse Floating Rate Mortgages												
CMOT13 Q	113,873	112,317	110,759	109,199	108,421	107,651	106,892	106,135	104,604	103,021	101,426	4,610
POs-Agency												
FNSTR_267 (FN 8.50)	97,248	95,941	94,221	91,898	90,499	88,813	86,947	84,834	80,539	76,462	72,818	12,310
IOs-Agency												
FHLMC_2043 (FG 7.00)	8,407	8,984	11,145	15,759	18,444	21,083	23,371	25,149	27,291	28,309	28,875	12,380
CMO Sequentials-Agency												
FNMA_93-178 (FN 7.00)	100,325	100,222	100,119	100,011	99,956	99,902	99,847	99,792	99,682	99,553	99,411	350
Corporates - Finance												
BANKAMERICA CAPITAL II	130,525	126,085	121,522	116,832	114,453	112,060	109,665	107,278	102,553	97,955	93,532	14,060
Corporates - Industrial												
PROCTER & GAMBLE COMPANY (THE)	166,712	154,889	144,304	134,806	130,423	126,264	122,316	118,566	111,612	105,315	99,601	20,880
Asset Backed - Prepay Sensitive												
CONHE 97-5 (Home Equity)	107,304	105,864	104,449	103,057	102,369	101,688	101,012	100,342	99,019	97,718	96,439	3,960
Asset Backed - Non-Prepay Sensitive												
CHVAT_98-2 (Auto)	103,735	102,957	102,189	101,432	101,057	100,685	100,315	99,947	99,220	98,501	97,793	2,180
Total Assets	1,993,125	1,912,353	1,838,030	1,770,677	1,739,152	1,707,992	1,679,300	1,650,471	1,595,198	1,543,280	1,494,820	164,171

curve risk include key rate durations, yield curve reshaping durations (Chapter 2), and bullet versus barbell (yield versus convexity) trade-offs arguments.[16] This section presents a richer approach to gaining insights into yield curve exposures of portfolios and securities – Grid Monte-Carlo Simulation VaR that uses two principal components.

Given that the explanatory power of the first principal component of the U.S. Treasury spot curve fluctuates between 86% and 95%, the vast majority of the interest rate risk in fixed income securities comes from their exposure to *directional* movements in interest rates. Therefore, it is not surprising that Grid Monte-Carlo Simulation VaR that uses the first principal component, versus the one that uses the first two principal components, often produce virtually identical results. Exhibits 5.5 and 5.6 compare such VaR estimates for a generic MBS. The addition of the

EXHIBIT 5.5   A Generic 30-yearr 7% MBS: Grid Monte-Carlo Simulation Using the First Principal Component

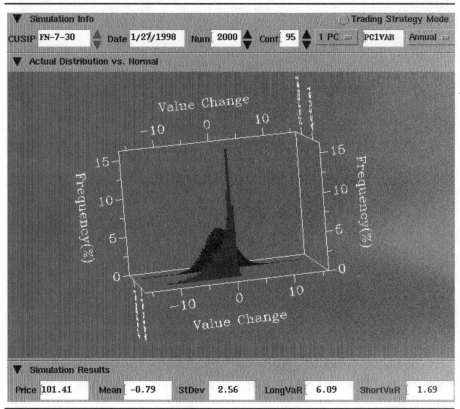

EXHIBIT 5.6   A Generic 30-year 7% MBS: Grid Monte-Carlo Simulation Using First Two Principal Components

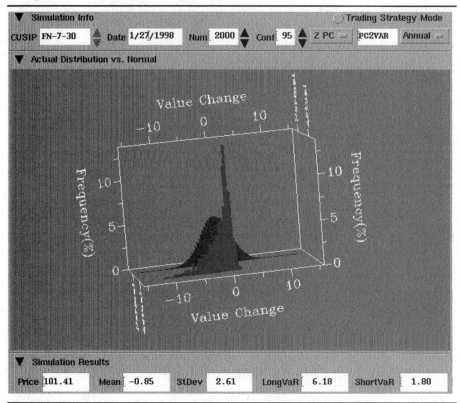

second dimension in Monte-Carlo simulation results in only a 1% improvement in accuracy (VaR of $6.09 versus $6.18 for a $100 face value) at a cost of a 400% increase in computational time because of numerous additional direct valuations. Therefore, in our experience, modeling interest rate risk using the first principal component alone is usually sufficient for most fixed income securities and portfolios.

However, this conclusion does not apply to duration-neutral yield curve trades or gaps between portfolios and their benchmarks whose durations can be close to zero. Let us elaborate on this point using the dynamics of U.S. key spot rates presented in Table 3.3. Thus, on 9/30/96, the first principal component explained 93% of the variability of interest rates, the second principal component explained 5%, and the parallel shock explained 88%. This implies that the portion of the first principal component related to nonparallel yield curve movements explained 93% – 88% = 5% of the yield curve variability, exactly as much as the second principal component did. By definition, duration-neutral yield curve trades have no sensitivity to parallel yield curve movements, and therefore the explanatory power of the first principal component with respect to such trades is comparable to that of the second principal component. From the viewpoint of duration-neutral strategies, the first two principal components are equally powerful systematic risk factors, and therefore two-dimensional Grid Monte-Carlo VaR should be employed.

Let us illustrate this numerically. Exhibit 5.7 presents the value surface of a duration-neutral "short 10-year OTR and long 30-year OTR" yield curve trade constructed via Grid Monte-Carlo Simulation with one

EXHIBIT 5.7 Duration-Neutral 10–30-year Yield Curve Trade: Value Surface Modeled Using the First Principal Component

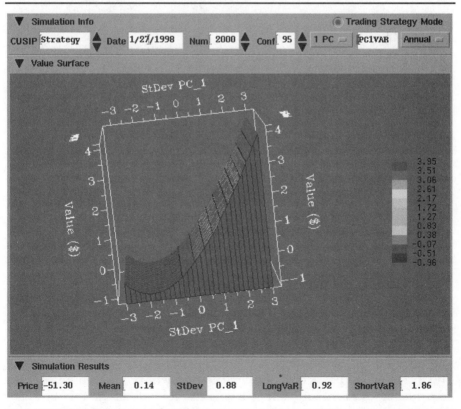

EXHIBIT 5.8   Duration-Neutral 10–30-year Yield Curve Trade: Distribution of Value Changes Modeled Using the First Principal Component

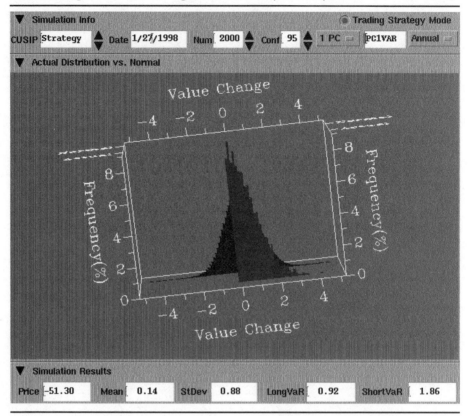

principal component. Due to positive convexity and neutrality with respect to directional interest rate movements, this strategy appears to make money irrespective of the direction of interest rate movements. Exhibit 5.8, which shows its empirical PDF, also suggests that there is virtually no downside and a lot of upside in this trade. This certainly seems too high a compensation for moderate negative carry associated with this position, suggesting an almost arbitrage-like opportunity. This clearly erroneous conclusion arises because the second principal component (a very potent systematic risk factor for duration-neutral trades) is not accounted for. Exhibit 5.9 makes the analysis complete by evaluating the value surface of this strategy as a function of two principal components. The inclusion of the second principal component provides a much more accurate assessment of yield curve risk embedded in this strategy, dramatically changing our perception of its risk/return characteristics.

EXHIBIT 5.9   Duration-Neutral 10–30-year Yield Curve Trade: Value Surface Modeled Using Two Principal Components

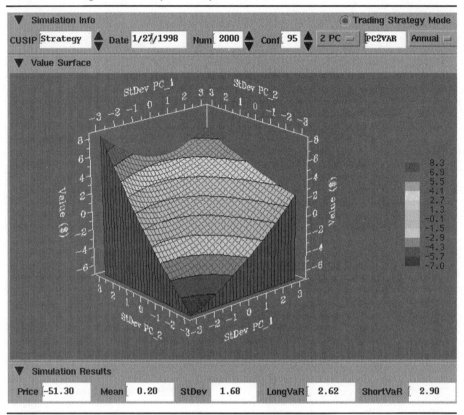

Notice that the maximal loss corresponds to a simultaneous large negative realization of the first principal component and a large negative realization of the second principal component (Exhibit 5.9). This result is not at all surprising given that a "short 10-year OTR" and long 30-year OTR trade bets on a yield curve flattening. Recall that the shape of the first principal component implies that a fall in interest rates (a negative realization in the first principal component) is accompanied by a yield curve steepening (Section 3.2.3). A negative realization of the second principal component corresponds to an additional yield curve steepening (Exhibit 3.1), exacerbating the magnitude of losses. The added second principal component dimension substantially modifies the empirical probability density function as well, making it much more symmetric and only slightly skewed to the right because of positive convexity (Exhibit 5.10). Thus, the absence of a pure arbitrage opportunity becomes clear.

EXHIBIT 5.10   Duration-Neutral 10–30-year Yield Curve Trade: Distribution of Value Changes Modeled Using Two Principal Components

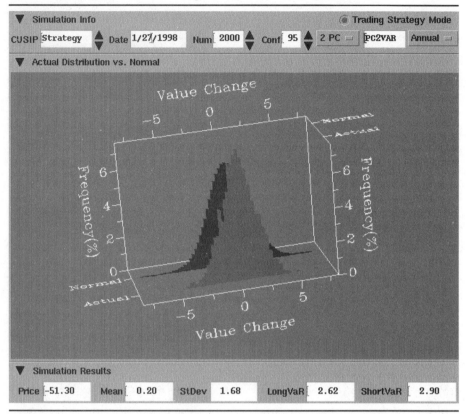

5.3.4 Incorporating Evolution of Securities through Time into VaR

For a given *confidence level,* VaR measures the magnitude of potential losses associated with holding a portfolio over a specified *horizon.* In practice, the majority of VaR methodologies estimate risk by integrating *current* market exposures of securities in a portfolio with historical correlations and volatilities of systematic risk factors. This implies that while the estimation of probability distributions of systematic risk factors is usually consistent with the selected horizon, the fact that risk characteristics of fixed income securities change over time even if the economic environment remains unchanged is rarely taken into account. Clearly, this implicit assumption is unrealistic due to the fact that fixed income securities "roll down" the curve. As a result, their durations shorten as they approach maturity, embedded options decay, and market risks associated with other types of cash flow uncertainties also change due to the passage of time. When the VaR horizon is short (one day or one week), ignoring evolution of risk characteristics over time generally does not cause any significant inaccuracies. However, failure to account for the dynamic nature of risk parameters over longer horizons (one month or one year) may significantly influence VaR and other risk measures.

The expected rate of return (EROR) framework was presented in Chapter 2. This methodology explicitly measures the following two components of expected return associated with holding a fixed income security or portfolio:

- Gain or loss due to OAV at the horizon being different from the current price
- Return associated with principal and coupon payments and their reinvestment

EROR enables the incorporation of the evolution of fixed income securities through time into Monte-Carlo Simulation VaR. As opposed to using OAVs computed via traditional scenario analysis, OAVs corresponding to various interest rate movements *at the horizon* can be employed. Exhibit 5.11 schematically demonstrates the conceptual dif-

EXHIBIT 5.11 Computing VaR: Instantaneous Interest Rate Shocks versus Shocks at the Horizon

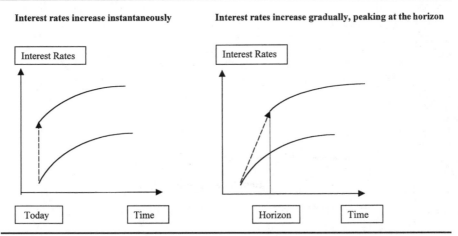

ference between these two approaches. Instead of estimating fair values corresponding to interest rates increasing *instantaneously* by a given number of basis points, interest rates are assumed to increase gradually between the valuation date and the horizon date, peaking at the horizon. The fair value of a security associated with such market scenario is then computed. In other words, EROR enables construction of more accurate empirical PDFs by sampling value surfaces corresponding to the horizon date.

Depending on the nature of cash flow uncertainties embedded in a fixed income security, scenario OAVs computed on the valuation date may be drastically different from those computed at the horizon. Exhibit 5.12 illustrates this numerically using a LIBOR interest rate cap. Because of the decay of this instrument over one year, there is almost a 100% difference between the two OAVs corresponding to a 200 basis point increase in interest rates. Clearly, VaR estimates that do not account for evolution through time would vastly overestimate the risk of a short position in this derivative.

The ability to incorporate the evolution of securities through time into VaR presents risk managers with a very interesting analytical

EXHIBIT 5.12   Scenario Analysis of a LIBOR CAP: Instantaneous OAV vs. OAV at Horizon (as of 4/30/98)

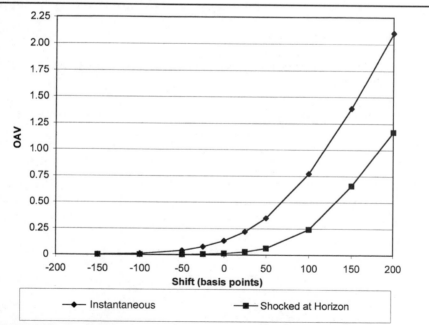

dilemma. As already mentioned, the dynamic nature of portfolio characteristics manifests itself in the following two aspects of expected return: change in the portfolio valuation over time and return due to generated cash flows and their reinvestment. While it seems logical that the former component of EROR should be always accounted for by VaR, it is unclear whether or when the (relatively) deterministic expected return considerations should be incorporated into VaR. Consider the following asset/liability management example. Suppose that the projected cash flows of a portfolio of assets are closely matched to those of the liabilities. Suppose VaR is employed to measure the capital needed as insurance against potential losses. If the (usually positive) expected return is incorporated into VaR, *the entire distribution of value changes is effectively being shifted to the right,* reducing VaR. However, this practice presents dangers of its own: Since future cash flows are used to offset potential market losses, an adverse event in the market would cause cash flows of assets and liabilities to become mismatched. Similar to the case of ALM, in hedge optimization techniques that use VaR (Chapter 6) to mitigate *unexpected* losses, the deterministic return due to the cash flow component should arguably be excluded from consideration. In portfolio management, VaR is often criticized for overestimating losses by not accounting for positive carry of fixed income portfolios. Whether cash flows should be included in VaR in this case is not as apparent and depends on the nature of the portfolio and other matters. Finally, when empirical PDFs are used to make relative value decisions or judgments about the upside versus downside of holding a security, all aspects of evolution through time should be captured, including return from cash flows and their reinvestment. Table 5.10 presents risk and return measures for a selected group of fixed income securities. When a security (e.g., U.S. Treasury) does not have any embedded cash flow uncertainties, inclusion of cash flows into the future distribution of returns simply increases the mean of this distribution by the future value of reinvested cash flows. However, when cash flows depend on the future evolution of interest rates and other basis risks, incorporation of the future value of cash flows into VaR changes both the mean and the shape of PDF, affecting the assessments of both the risk (relative to the higher mean) and the potential upside.

5.3.5 Dimensionality Reduction Tool: Principal Components in Return Space

Computational feasibility of Grid Monte-Carlo Simulation VaR relies on the ability to explain the joint dynamics of systematic market risks with a

TABLE 5.10 Incorporating Evolution of Fixed Income Securities through Time into VaR (as of 4/30/98)

	Instantaneous Scenarios			Shocks at Horizon w/o Cash Flows			Shocks at Horizon with Cash Flows		
	Current Price	Long VaR (5th Pct)	Short VaR (95th Pct)	Price at Horizon	Long VaR (5th Pct)	Short VaR (95th Pct)	Price at Horizon	Long VaR (5th Pct)	Short VaR (95th Pct)
OTR TREASURY	102.65	4.30	4.95	102.72	3.48	3.96	108.66	3.38	3.96
GENERIC MBS	99.55	5.48	3.14	99.71	5.06	2.96	111.09	5.35	19.70
GENERIC PO	70.06	8.67	17.02	70.38	8.26	17.22	81.04	8.72	27.62
PAC IO	27.53	16.14	3.48	24.29	18.77	1.93	31.47	18.77	1.93
LIBOR CAP	0.14	0.13	0.80	0.02	0.02	0.31	0.02	0.02	0.31
CALL SWAPTION	2.35	2.25	6.12	0.96	0.96	8.38	0.96	0.96	8.38

5th Pct = 5th Percentile (VaR on Long Position); 95th Pct = 95th Percentile (VaR on Short Position).

small number of random variables. Given that the vast majority of yield curve variability can typically be attributed to one or two principal components, the previous sections have illustrated that Grid Monte-Carlo Simulation VaR is one of the most comprehensive and yet computationally feasible measures of interest rate risk. Unfortunately, as illustrated in Chapter 4, the inclusion of nondollar interest rates, credit and mortgage spreads, foreign currency exchange rates, and other relatively uncorrelated risk factors into covariance matrices may dramatically reduce the explanatory power of principal components, making it challenging to parsimoniously describe the joint behavior of systematic risks. Table 5.11 presents principal components analysis (PCA) of selected U.S. interest rates, mortgage/treasury basis, MBS OASs, PO OASs, implied volatility, swap spreads, and nominal agency bullet spreads. It can be seen that the first principal component explains only 49.7% of the variability of this system, while the first two principal components explain 83.9%. The explanatory powers of principal components in this example are substantially lower than those in the U.S. Treasury market, where the first principal component typically explains between 85% and 95% of the total variability, while the first two explain between 93% and 99%.

Recall that PCA is used to study the dynamics of complex, multivariate real-life systems by describing comovements of explanatory variables as parsimoniously as possible. As mentioned earlier, PCA has two major applications in finance. First, it provides valuable insights into historical and hypothetical market movements and enables the development of the notion of historical plausibility (Chapter 3). This application of PCA deals with describing the market behavior in general, and therefore its conclusions about the observed dynamics of risk factors are independent from price sensitivities of a particular portfolio to different systematic risk factors. The second use of PCA is for reducing the dimensionality of the value surface of a particular portfolio for the purpose of Monte-Carlo Simulation VaR. This section elaborates on the latter usage of PCA by incorporating information about market exposures into the computation of principal components.

Consider a hypothetical example. Suppose a U.S. financial institution manages the following two portfolios: a portfolio invested in U.S. dollar securities and a portfolio invested in Japanese securities. To gain insight into the joint dynamics of all relevant systematic risk factors, the covariance matrix containing U.S. key spot rates, Japanese key spot rates, and the JPY/USD foreign currency exchange rate is estimated, and principal components are derived. Since U.S. and Japanese yield curves are not typically highly correlated and the JPY/USD exchange rate is usually loosely correlated with both spot curves, the cumulative explanatory

TABLE 5.11 Principal Components of Selected Interest Rates and Basis Risks

	3-mo	10-year	30-year	MTB	MBS -100	MBS -50	MBS 0	MBS 50	MBS 100	PO -50	PO 0	PO 50	Impl. Vol	Swap 2-year	Swap 5-year	Swap 10-year	Agency 2-year	Agency 5-year	Agency 10-year	PC Vol	Var Expl	CVar Expl
Implicit Exposure (years)	1.0	1.0	1.0	1.0	1.0	1.0	1.0	1.0	1.0	1.0	1.0	1.0	1.0	1.0	1.0	1.0	1.0	1.0	1.0			
Ann Vol of Changes (bp)	68	125	85	47	57	57	57	64	80	208	208	236	415	38	32	29	45	44	42			
Ann Vol of Returns (bp)	68	125	85	47	57	57	57	64	80	208	208	236	415	38	32	29	45	44	42			
Principal Components 1:	-0.8	1.9	1.0	0.1	4.4	4.4	4.5	5.3	7.1	-22.5	-22.6	-29.8	-89.1	-0.4	-1.8	-1.4	-3.2	-1.9	-1.5	4.31	49.7	49.7
2:	1.4	8.6	-1.0	-3.6	-3.6	-3.6	-3.7	-4.5	-6.8	50.4	50.5	52.4	-44.3	-2.0	-1.0	-0.7	0.2	1.8	-0.6	3.57	34.2	83.9
3:	11.9	71.1	43.5	-14.3	-21.8	-21.8	-20.8	-17.5	-21.8	-0.4	-0.4	-18.2	2.8	-6.5	-7.7	-7.2	-2.6	-3.2	-5.8	1.47	5.8	89.7
4:	12.2	-42.2	-23.1	-21.4	-31.4	-31.4	-32.0	-40.3	-44.4	-12.1	-12.1	5.8	-7.8	2.6	5.4	3.9	-0.5	0.7	-7.0	1.23	4.1	93.8
5:	38.9	-12.2	-21.9	-0.9	-7.6	-7.6	-8.6	-4.3	25.5	36.0	36.0	-64.7	3.6	-5.7	-6.2	-2.3	2.5	-10.4	-4.0	0.85	1.9	95.7
6:	59.6	10.6	-22.3	-5.1	11.7	11.7	12.7	13.4	-10.5	-13.9	-13.9	26.6	2.3	-27.0	-19.8	-12.0	-36.2	-36.3	-10.3	0.65	1.1	96.9
7:	61.4	1.2	16.7	25.0	-1.1	-1.1	0.9	7.8	-2.9	-5.4	-5.4	9.2	-3.4	25.9	32.5	31.2	9.7	35.2	32.7	0.59	0.9	97.8
8:	12.1	-48.1	74.1	1.6	-0.4	-0.4	0.0	3.4	10.2	3.3	3.6	2.6	-0.5	-16.8	-11.3	0.1	-16.5	-1.6	-36.5	0.54	0.8	98.6
9:	15.1	-5.0	10.9	1.5	-3.9	-3.9	-3.7	-0.3	13.6	-8.0	-7.9	16.0	-2.5	1.6	11.6	-6.8	80.7	-48.1	3.3	0.39	0.4	99.0
10:	0.0	15.0	-14.4	43.8	1.5	1.5	-0.5	-6.7	-7.5	0.3	0.3	0.2	0.0	44.6	-16.8	16.1	-1.3	-16.2	-70.0	0.35	0.3	99.3
11:	5.3	2.5	-11.8	43.8	3.2	3.2	5.1	-5.5	-22.1	-1.0	-1.5	-3.2	-0.8	-54.4	16.8	-19.5	31.2	48.2	-20.4	0.30	0.2	99.6
12:	12.7	12.5	-17.0	-49.9	-9.3	-9.3	-7.9	11.0	49.2	-10.2	-10.3	18.4	1.3	-3.6	4.8	7.5	13.5	40.3	-41.1	0.26	0.2	99.7
13:	15.5	-8.5	6.8	-15.7	12.5	12.5	9.8	-0.4	-15.4	1.4	2.0	-2.6	0.9	56.2	-40.8	-56.0	5.8	27.1	-1.1	0.22	0.1	99.9
14:	2.2	-0.2	2.6	-45.1	24.3	24.3	29.4	19.4	-52.7	9.7	9.7	-20.1	1.3	-6.4	24.1	24.1	24.5	-0.8	-18.9	0.19	0.1	100.0
15:	6.9	5.8	4.5	-8.3	36.3	36.3	5.6	-81.7	18.8	-1.1	-2.3	2.7	0.3	-4.8	4.0	9.5	0.5	1.8	1.8	0.09	0.0	100.0
16:	3.2	1.4	-0.6	0.7	2.2	2.2	-4.7	-0.9	4.4	-1.1	0.8	0.8	-0.2	-6.2	74.6	-65.2	-0.8	-7.7	-4.2	0.08	0.0	100.0
17:	0.1	-0.1	0.2	-0.1	0.7	0.7	-2.5	1.3	-0.2	70.7	-70.6	0.0	0.0	0.3	0.7	-1.1	0.0	-0.2	-0.1	0.05	0.0	100.0
18:	0.7	0.6	0.3	-0.2	-33.6	-33.6	84.6	-22.6	6.9	1.8	-2.2	0.7	0.1	1.5	3.5	-3.6	-1.4	-1.1	0.3	0.03	0.0	100.0
19:	0.0	0.0	0.0	0.0	0.0	0.0	0.0	0.0	0.0	0.0	0.0	0.0	0.1	0.0	0.0	0.0	0.0	0.0	0.0	0.00	0.0	100.0

	3-mo	10-year	30-year	MTB	MBS -100	MBS -50	MBS 0	MBS 50	MBS 100	PO -50	PO 0	PO 50	Impl. Vol	Swap 2-year	Swap 5-year	Swap 10-year	Agency 2-year	Agency 5-year	Agency 10-year
One StDev PC_1 (bp)	-3	8	4	0	19	19	19	23	31	-97	-97	-129	-384	-2	-8	-6	-14	-8	-7
One StDev PC_2 (bp)	5	31	-4	-13	-13	-13	-13	-16	-24	180	180	187	-158	-7	-4	-3	1	6	-2
One StDev PC_3 (bp)	18	105	64	-21	-32	-32	-31	-26	-32	-1	-27	-27	4	-10	-11	-11	-4	-5	-9

PC Vol = one standard deviation of principal components times 100; Var Expl = percentage of the variance explained; CVar Expl = cumulative percentage of the variance explained.

power of the first two or three principal components is expected to be rather low. Clearly, these principal components (that describe the joint dynamics of all factors) will be inadequate for simulating the risk of the U.S. *domestic* portfolio because of their low explanatory power. However, it seems unreasonable that principal components describing the *entire system* are used in analyzing the risk of the U.S. *domestic* portfolio despite the fact that this portfolio is not exposed to Japanese interest rates or the foreign currency rate. Principal components of U.S. interest rates should be used instead, making Grid Monte-Carlo Simulation VaR a superior and computationally feasible alternative.

Although deliberately unrealistic, this argument leads to a very important observation: when principal components are used as a pure dimensionality reduction tool, their explanatory power can be improved, sometimes dramatically, by incorporating information about the portfolio's composition into the construction of principal components. Chapter 3 described into detail how principal components are analytically derived from the covariance matrix of changes in systematic risk factors. The covariance matrix (Σ) is, in turn, a function of historical volatilities (σ_i) of changes in risk factors and the correlation matrix (ρ):

$$\Sigma = \begin{bmatrix} \sigma_1 & 0 & 0 \\ 0 & \sigma_i & 0 \\ 0 & 0 & \sigma_n \end{bmatrix} \cdot \rho \cdot \begin{bmatrix} \sigma_1 & 0 & 0 \\ 0 & \sigma_i & 0 \\ 0 & 0 & \sigma_n \end{bmatrix} \tag{5.2}$$

Imagine that historical volatility of changes in a given systematic risk factor is multiplied by the portfolio's partial dollar duration ($pdur_i$) with respect to this risk factor before computing the covariance matrix:

$$\Sigma_{\text{return}} = \begin{bmatrix} \sigma_1 \cdot \$pdur_1 & 0 & 0 \\ 0 & \sigma_i \cdot \$pdur_i & 0 \\ 0 & 0 & \sigma_n \cdot \$pdur_n \end{bmatrix} \cdot \rho \cdot \begin{bmatrix} \sigma_1 \cdot \$pdur_1 & 0 & 0 \\ 0 & \sigma_i \cdot \$pdur_i & 0 \\ 0 & 0 & \sigma_n \cdot \$pdur_n \end{bmatrix} \tag{5.3}$$

As opposed to the covariance matrix of changes in risk factors in Equation 5.2, Equation 5.3 defines the covariance matrix of one standard deviation dollar exposures of the portfolio to systematic risk factors. Principal components based on Σ_{return} are said to be constructed in the return space. They can be interpreted as the most dominant drivers of a particular portfolio's returns, given the recent dynamics of systematic risk factors. For instance, if two systematic risk factors are positively correlated but a portfolio's price sensitivities to them have opposite signs, return-based principal components will properly account for this information. In practice, it can be difficult to gain intuition behind principal components constructed in the return space. Because of that, after these principal components are derived, they can be divided (element-wise) by the portfolio's sensitivities to the corresponding systematic risk factors, converting them back into the units of changes in systematic risk factors.

By construction, principal components attempt to explain the majority of the variability of given system. Thus, principal components constructed in the return space explain *price variability*, providing risk decomposition of Global VaR (Chapter 4). The first principal component in return space is a generalization of *effective risk profile* defined in Section 4.2.3. Not surprisingly, by incorporating knowledge about market exposures into computation of principal components, their explanatory power can be improved. Thus, loosely correlated systematic risk factors reduce the explanatory power of principal components only if the portfolio's exposure to all of them is significant. Table 5.12 presents return-based principal components of a hypothetical portfolio whose partial durations with respect to each risk factor are shown in Exposure line. As compared to the traditional principal components of the same system (Exhibit 5.11), the incorporation of partial durations increased the explanatory power of the first principal component to 77%, up from approximately 50%, and the explanatory power of the first two principal components to 88%, up from 84%.

5.4 INCORPORATING NONLINEARITY INTO GLOBAL VALUE-AT-RISK

Complex real-life fixed income portfolios invested in a variety of U.S. and nondollar spread-sensitive instruments, interest rate derivatives, mortgage-backed securities and their derivatives, emerging market and high yield debt, and the like, can be exposed to a very large number of loosely correlated systematic risk factors. In these cases, a few principal components constructed via traditional methods or in return space may not be able to capture the majority of this system's variability, making Grid Monte-Carlo Simulation VaR computationally infeasible. Risk managers are therefore faced with yet another trade-off: they can either assume that the value surface is linear in all variables and employ Global VaR in estimating risk or they can exclude some of the systematic risks from the consideration, increasing the explanatory power of principal components

TABLE 5.12 Return-Based Principal Components of Selected Interest Rates and Basis Risks

	3-mo	10-year	30-year	MTB	MBS -100	MBS -50	MBS 0	MBS 50	MBS 100	PO -50	PO 0	PO 50	Impl. Vol	Swap 2-year	Swap 5-year	Swap 10-year	Agency 2-year	Agency 5-year	Agency 10-year	PC Vol	Var Expl	CVar Expl
Actual Exposure (years)	5.0	-5.0	0.2	1.0	-3.0	-0.5	4.0	5.0	1.0	-1.0	-2.5	2.2	5.0	3.3	-2.0	-1.0	0.0	1.3	4.0			
Ann Vol of Changes (bp)	68	125	85	47	57	57	57	64	80	208	208	236	415	38	32	29	45	44	42			
Ann Vol of Returns (bp)	339	-623	18	47	-170	-28	227	321	80	-208	-520	520	2077	127	-64	-29	1	57	168			

Principal Components	3-mo	10-year	30-year	MTB	MBS -100	MBS -50	MBS 0	MBS 50	MBS 100	PO -50	PO 0	PO 50	Impl. Vol	Swap 2-year	Swap 5-year	Swap 10-year	Agency 2-year	Agency 5-year	Agency 10-year	PC Vol	Var Expl	CVar Expl
1:	0.3	4.3	0.0	0.2	1.8	0.3	-2.5	-3.6	-0.9	-1.3	-3.1	5.5	99.6	0.6	-0.8	-0.3	0.0	0.3	1.3	20.9	77.0	77.0
2:	-6.6	36.9	-0.3	2.1	-9.8	-1.6	13.0	17.7	5.1	25.0	62.6	-58.3	5.1	3.4	-1.0	-0.4	0.0	-1.2	0.5	7.8	10.7	87.7
3:	7.6	-91.1	2.1	-0.7	3.3	0.6	-3.3	3.3	0.2	8.8	22.1	-31.1	6.5	-3.8	4.0	1.8	0.0	-1.6	-1.1	6.0	6.3	94.0
4:	47.3	13.8	-0.1	-6.5	32.8	5.5	-44.0	-61.0	-11.9	4.7	11.7	-17.7	-3.2	-1.5	-0.4	-0.3	0.0	-1.3	-11.6	4.1	3.0	97.0
5:	85.9	4.9	-0.6	4.5	-15.5	-2.6	21.8	38.0	7.9	-5.3	-13.2	-3.2	1.4	-6.7	1.0	-1.0	-0.1	-3.1	8.4	3.1	1.7	98.7
6:	6.6	-4.8	-0.8	1.5	4.4	0.7	-4.6	-6.9	-7.9	9.3	23.5	23.6	-2.3	37.0	-19.6	-7.4	0.2	13.1	81.2	1.7	0.5	99.2
7:	11.9	-5.0	0.9	-2.3	-5.4	-0.9	9.6	1.4	-16.6	22.6	56.7	66.6	-0.6	-17.1	4.1	1.4	-0.2	-6.2	-30.4	1.6	0.4	99.6
8:	7.3	-4.8	1.1	9.9	-2.4	-0.4	1.6	6.1	3.0	-0.4	-1.1	2.8	0.1	84.0	-20.9	-9.7	0.0	8.3	-45.9	1.1	0.2	99.9
9:	0.9	0.1	-8.0	-12.6	-18.2	-3.0	13.9	-19.8	-2.4	-0.4	-1.3	0.3	0.3	30.5	50.8	21.6	-0.2	-68.8	11.8	0.6	0.1	99.9
10:	3.9	-3.8	-6.0	29.4	-43.3	-7.2	48.3	-52.7	-29.0	-2.3	-5.5	-9.9	0.2	-4.5	-0.1	3.6	-0.1	32.0	-1.3	0.5	0.0	100.0
11:	2.8	2.7	3.1	-21.5	6.8	1.1	-7.0	10.2	4.9	1.3	3.1	3.7	0.3	15.5	63.2	34.8	-0.9	61.8	0.2	0.3	0.0	100.0
12:	0.6	-0.4	-5.0	-84.9	-6.1	-1.0	18.8	2.3	-40.5	-2.2	-7.0	-8.9	0.5	2.1	-23.2	-5.9	0.2	3.8	-3.7	0.3	0.0	100.0
13:	3.2	-3.5	-6.5	-33.2	-31.1	-5.2	2.9	-30.5	80.4	2.0	7.5	8.9	0.2	-3.7	-12.4	-7.9	0.0	8.3	-1.2	0.2	0.0	100.0
14:	1.0	1.3	81.3	-2.3	-19.2	-3.2	-21.4	-2.9	-0.7	2.0	-1.8	-0.4	-0.1	0.1	-23.3	48.2	-0.1	-6.6	1.3	0.1	0.0	100.0
15:	0.3	-0.8	-56.6	5.6	-14.5	-2.4	7.8	7.8	-2.8	-0.5	0.8	0.5	0.5	-1.8	-33.9	69.7	1.7	-1.3	-2.0	0.1	0.0	100.0
16:	0.6	-0.3	1.1	-0.2	66.4	11.1	61.7	-11.6	20.8	4.4	-1.0	1.3	0.0	1.0	-13.6	29.5	0.1	-3.5	-0.3	0.1	0.0	100.0
17:	0.0	0.1	2.6	-0.3	2.9	0.5	2.8	-0.3	0.0	-92.8	36.9	-0.1	0.0	0.2	-0.9	2.1	0.1	-0.5	0.0	0.1	0.0	100.0
18:	0.1	0.0	-0.1	-0.7	-1.2	-0.2	-0.8	0.2	-1.0	0.1	-0.1	-0.1	0.0	-0.1	0.1	-0.4	100.0	0.2	-0.1	0.0	0.0	100.0
19:	0.0	0.0	-0.1	0.0	0.0	0.0	0.0	0.0	0.0	0.0	0.0	0.0	0.0	0.0	0.0	0.0	-0.2	0.0	0.0	0.0	0.0	100.0

	3-mo	10-year	30-year	MTB	MBS -100	MBS -50	MBS 0	MBS 50	MBS 100	PO -50	PO 0	PO 50	Impl. Vol	Swap 2-year	Swap 5-year	Swap 10-year	Agency 2-year	Agency 5-year	Agency 10-year
One StDev PC_1 (bp)	1	-18	-2	4	-13	-13	-13	-15	-19	26	26	52	415	4	8	6	12	5	7
One StDev PC_2 (bp)	-10	-57	-12	16	25	25	25	27	40	-194	-194	-206	8	8	4	3	-4	-7	1
One StDev PC_3 (bp)	9	109	58	-4	-7	-7	-5	4	1	-53	-53	-84	8	-7	-12	-11	-5	-7	-2

PC Vol = one standard deviation of principal components times 100; Var Expl = percentage of the variance explained; CVar Expl = cumulative percentage of the variance explained.

and making Grid Monte-Carlo Simulation VaR computationally feasible. Exhibit 5.13 assists in classifying the universe of VaR measures.

In Exhibit 5.13, box 1 represents U.S. Variance/Covariance VaR (VaR_{IntRR}). As studied in Chapter 4, VaR_{IntRR} measures U.S. interest rate risk by assuming that value surface is linear in all key spot rates. While fully modeling the probabilistic dynamics of the U.S. spot curve, VaR_{IntRR} does not account for basis, nondollar interest rate, and foreign currency risks. Box 2 contains Grid Monte-Carlo Simulation VaR (VaR_{Sim}) computed using principal components of the U.S. spot curve. VaR_{Sim} is a measure of the U.S. interest rate risk as well; it accounts for the vast majority of the variability of the yield curve and captures the nonlinearity of the value surface at the same time. Similar to Variance/Covariance VaR, VaR_{Sim} ignores the market exposures associated with basis, nondollar interest rate, and foreign currency risks. An extension of Variance/Covariance VaR methodology, Global VaR (VaR_{Global}, box 3) fully accounts for the first-order market risk associated with all relevant interest rate, basis, nondollar, and foreign currency risk factors but assumes that the value surface is linear in all variables. Unfortunately, the construction of Comprehensive VaR (VaR_{Comp}, box 4) that simultaneously captures the nonlinearity of the value surface and exposure to all systematic risk factors is not always computationally feasible. The authors are not aware of any definitive research on the general case solution of this problem. However, given the composition of some fixed income portfolios, it is sometimes reasonable to assume that their value surfaces are nonlinear in the interest rate dimension and

EXHIBIT 5.13   Trade-offs in Value-at-Risk Modeling: Number of Risk Factors versus Nonlinearity

		Number of Risk Factors	
		U.S. Interest Rate Risks Only	**All Systematic Risk Factors**
Value Surface Modeling	**Linear Value Surface**	1. **U.S. Variance/Covariance VaR** - Fully captures U.S. yield curve dynamics - Assumes linear value surface via KRD approximation - Ignores basis risks VaR = 10% of market value per year	3. **Global Variance/Covariance VaR** - Fully captures dynamics of all systematic risk factors - Assumes linear value surface via partial durations VaR = 30% of market value per year
	Nonlinear Value Surface	2. **Grid Monte-Carlo Simulation VaR** - Approximates U.S. yield curve dynamics via PCA - Captures nonlinearity via scenario analysis - Ignores basis risks VaR = 20% of market value per year	4. **Comprehensive VaR (All Risks and Non-Linearity)** - Exact solution is too computationally expensive even with principal components constructed in return space **?**

linear in all other variables. In these special cases, the following approach to VaR_{Comp} can be used as a reasonable approximation. It builds on the previously introduced probabilistic measures of risk – U.S. Variance/Covariance VaR, Grid Monte-Carlo Simulation VaR, and Global VaR – computed for the same horizon (e.g., one year) and with the same confidence level (e.g., 95%).

Suppose that, the following risk estimates were obtained for a hypothetical fixed income portfolio (Exhibit 5.13):

- Variance/Covariance VaR: $VaR_{IntRR} = 10\%$ per year
- Grid Monte-Carlo Simulation VaR: $VaR_{Sim} = 20\%$ per year
- Global VaR: $VaR_{Global} = 30\%$ per year

Let us reason as follows. Both Variance/Covariance VaR (VaR_{IntRR}) and Grid Monte-Carlo Simulation VaR (VaR_{Sim}) estimate market risk of fixed income portfolios along the U.S. interest rate dimension alone and accurately measure the dynamics of the U.S. yield curve. Therefore, the difference between the two estimates of risk ($VaR_{IntRR} = 10\%$ versus $VaR_{Sim} = 20\%$) is solely due to the nonlinearity of the value surface. Our idea behind approximating Comprehensive VaR involves explicit modeling of this difference and its integration into Global VaR.

Consider the following familiar second-order approximation of percentage changes in price:

$$\frac{\Delta P}{P} \approx -OAD \cdot \Delta r + \frac{OAC}{2} \cdot (\Delta r)^2 \tag{5.4}$$

where OAD and OAC are option-adjusted duration and convexity, respectively, and Δr is a parallel spot curve movement that is assumed to follow a normal distribution with zero mean (Chapter 3). The term Δr^2 therefore corresponds to a χ_1^2 distribution, implying that percentage changes in price are distributed as a sum of a normal and a χ_1^2 distributions:

$$\frac{\Delta P}{P} \sim N(0, \sigma_{IntRR}) + C \cdot \sigma_{NL} \cdot \chi_1^2 \tag{5.5}$$

where $N(0, \sigma_{IntRR})$ denotes normal distribution with zero mean and standard deviation σ_{IntRR}, and C and σ_{NL} are parameters of the nonlinearity term whose meaning will be apparent momentarily.[17] Since parallel interest rate shocks are assumed to be normally distributed with zero mean, the normally distributed interest rate risk term $N(0, \sigma_{IntRR})$ and the χ_1^2-distributed nonlinearity term $C \cdot \sigma_{NL} \cdot \chi_1^2$ in Equation 5.5 can be assumed uncorrelated.[18] We now proceed to estimating the parameters of the nonlinearity term from VaR_{IntRR} and VaR_{Sim}.

Derivation of C. Because of the implicit assumption that changes in prices are normally distributed, Variance/Covariance VaR underestimates losses for portfolios with negative convexities and overestimates losses for portfolios with positive convexities. This typically manifests itself in Grid Monte-Carlo Simulation VaR being greater than Variance/Covaraince VaR of portfolios with negative convexities ($VaR_{Sim} > VaR_{IntRR}$) and in Grid Monte-Carlo Simulation VaR being smaller than Variance/Covaraince VaR of portfolios with positive convexities ($VaR_{Sim} < VaR_{IntRR}$). The constant C is introduced to explicitly account for this phenomenon:

$$C = \begin{cases} -1, & if \quad VaR_{Sim} > VaR_{IntRR} \\ 1, & if \quad VaR_{Sim} < VaR_{IntRR} \end{cases} \qquad (5.6)$$

Derivation of σ_{NL}. The purpose behind introducing the nonlinearity term is to capture the information that is contained in VaR_{Sim} but is not accounted for by VaR_{IntRR}. We define σ_{NL} as the number that makes the 5th percentile of the distribution of percentage price changes in Equation 5.5 exactly equal to Grid Monte-Carlo Simulation VaR:

$$VaR_{Sim} = 5\text{th percentile of } \left\{ N(0, \frac{VaR_{IntRR}}{1.65}) + C \cdot \sigma_{NL} \cdot \chi_1^2 \right\} \qquad (5.7)$$

where $N\left(0, \dfrac{VaR_{IntRR}}{1.65}\right)$ is the normally distributed component of the

distribution of price changes linked to Variance/Covariance VaR. Because Equation 5.7 involves a mixture of a normal and a χ_1^2 distributions, its solution σ_{NL} cannot be obtained analytically and requires application of simulation methods shown in Table 5.13.

Table 5.13 illustrates that a large number of realizations are drawn from a normal and χ_1^2 distribution.[19] Due to negative convexity of this portfolio confirmed by $VaR_{Sim} > VaR_{IntRR}$, the constant C is set to –1. A simple optimization is then used to solve for the value of $\sigma_{NL} = 4.44$ that makes the 5th percentile of the distribution of price changes exactly equal to VaR_{Sim}.[20] This enables rewriting Equation 5.5 as follows:

TABLE 5.13   Constructing Comprehensive Value-at-Risk that Captures All Risks and Nonlinearity (Computation Details)

Realizations		Derivation of σ_{NL}	Computation of VaR_{Comp}
$N(0,1)$	χ_1^2	$N(0,\sigma_{IntRR}) + C \cdot \sigma_{NL} \cdot \chi_1^2$	$N(0,\sigma_{Global}) + C \cdot \sigma_{NL} \cdot \chi_1^2$
−0.88	0.77	−7.94	−5.68
−0.11	0.01	−1.20	−0.92
0.38	0.14	−8.01	−8.98
0.00	0.00	−0.13	−0.13
−0.94	0.88	−8.92	−6.50
1.90	3.62	−3.55	−8.45
0.22	0.05	−7.69	−8.24
−1.00	1.01	−15.30	−12.72
0.68	0.46	1.02	−0.72
−0.58	0.34	−3.54	−2.05
−0.02	0.00	−6.22	−6.17
...	...	...	...
		Fifth percentile = 20	Fifth percentile = 37

$$\frac{\Delta P}{P} \sim N(0, \frac{VaR_{IntRR}}{1.65}) - 1 \cdot 4.44 \cdot \chi_1^2 \qquad (5.8)$$

Up to this point, only the interest rate dimension of market risk was considered. Our intention now is to combine information about nonlinearity with Global VaR, arriving at an approximation of Comprehensive VaR that captures first-order exposures to all relevant systematic risk factors as well as the nonlinearity of the value surface along the interest rate dimension. We achieve this by noticing that the normally distributed component of returns in Equation 5.8 only addresses the interest rate risk. If the normally distributed component of changes in prices uses Global VaR instead, a more comprehensive assessment of market risk can be obtained:

$$\frac{\Delta P}{P} \sim N(0, \frac{VaR_{Global}}{1.65}) - 1 \cdot 4.44 \cdot \chi_1^2 \qquad (5.9)$$

We define Comprehensive VaR as the 5th percentile of the distribution of the percentage price changes given by Equation 5.9:

$$VaR_{Comp} = 5\text{th percentile of } \left\{ N(0, \frac{VaR_{Global}}{1.65}) - 1 \cdot 4.44 \cdot \chi_1^2 \right\} \quad (5.10)$$

Table 5.13 illustrates the computation, showing Comprehensive VaR that incorporates interest rate nonlinearity and first-order exposures to all risk factors being 37% per year.[21] Exhibit 5.14 graphically illustrates the presented approach to incorporating nonlinearity into Global VaR.

5.5 HISTORICAL SIMULATION VALUE-AT-RISK

Monte-Carlo Simulation VaR is commonly criticized for not accounting for fat tails that are typically present in the time series of changes in systematic risk factors. Instead of postulating the functional form of the joint probability distribution of risk factors and then statistically estimating its parameters, Historical Simulation VaR[22] uses actual historical market events when constructing empirical PDFs of random returns. Because properties of fixed income portfolios and securities change over time, both Historical and Monte-Carlo Simulation methods use value surfaces that reflect *current* risk characteristics and market exposures. The most direct VaR method based on Historical Simulation is the exact analog of Full Monte-Carlo Simulation VaR discussed earlier in this chapter. Full Historical Simulation VaR uses valuation models to directly recompute the fair value of every security in a portfolio for each historical realization of systematic risk factors. Just like Full Monte-Carlo Simulation, Full Historical Simulation is therefore computationally infeasible if a portfolio contains numerous path-dependent derivatives and the number of systematic risk factors is large. If a small number of principal components can explain the majority of the variability of systematic risk factors relevant for a given portfolio, Grid Historical Simulation VaR can be a plausible alternative. Thus, multidimensional principal component scenario analysis can be used to construct the value surface. Potential gains and losses can then be sampled by expressing each historical market move as a realization of principal components (Chapter 3) and identifying appropriate points on the value surface. Alternatively, when the cumulative explanatory power of principal components is insufficient, various partial durations and convexities can be used to approximate price changes, given historical changes in systematic risk factors (e.g. Delta-Gamma Historical Simulation VaR).

Like any other risk management methodology, Historical Simulation VaR has its pros and cons. By using actual historical market events, this

EXHIBIT 5.14 Constructing Comprehensive Value-at-Risk That Captures All Systematic Risks and Nonlinearity

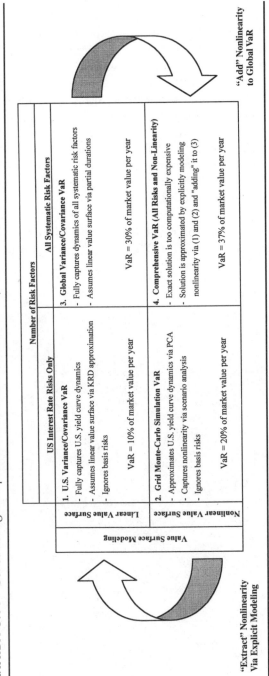

		Number of Risk Factors	
Value Surface Modeling		US Interest Rate Risks Only	All Systematic Risk Factors
	Linear Value Surface	**1. U.S. Variance/Covariance VaR** - Fully captures U.S. yield curve dynamics - Assumes linear value surface via KRD approximation - Ignores basis risks VaR = 10% of market value per year	**3. Global Variance/Covariance VaR** - Fully captures dynamics of all systematic risk factors - Assumes linear value surface via partial durations VaR = 30% of market value per year
	Nonlinear Value Surface	**2. Grid Monte-Carlo Simulation VaR** - Approximates U.S. yield curve dynamics via PCA - Captures nonlinearity via scenario analysis - Ignores basis risks VaR = 20% of market value per year	**4. Comprehensive VaR (All Risks and Non-Linearity)** - Exact solution is too computationally expensive - Solution is approximated by explicitly modeling nonlinearity via (1) and (2) and "adding" it to (3) VaR = 37% of market value per year

"Add" Nonlinearity
to Global VaR

"Extract" Nonlinearity
Via Explicit Modeling

241

methodology makes no assumptions about the joint probabilistic dynamics of risk factors, capturing various distribution asymmetries, fat tails, and so forth. It also establishes connections among actual market events and percentiles of empirical probability density functions, providing intuition behind risk measures. However, Historical Simulation VaR is by construction very susceptible to recent market trends, biasing assessments of risk. Since the number of systematic risk factors is typically large, the majority of practical implementations of Historical Simulation VaR employ local measures of risk (partial durations and convexities), resulting in potentially inaccurate results when changes in risk factors are large. Finally, this methodology does not typically allow for exponential weighting of data, placing equal importance on recent and distant history.

Exhibit 5.15 presents the results of Delta-Gamma Historical Simulation of a generic 30-year 7% MBS. This analysis employed 300 *daily*

EXHIBIT 5.15   Delta-Gamma Historical Simulation VaR

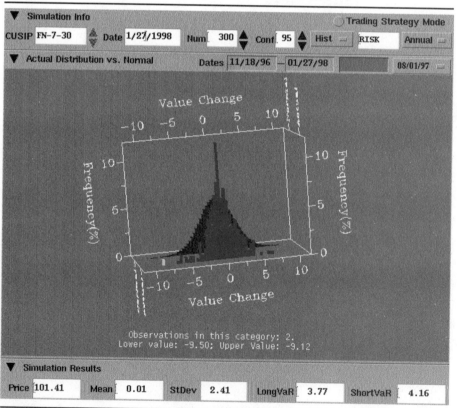

market movements, which were subsequently annualized using the *square root of time* rule.[23] It may seem counterintuitive that while distribution of annualized percentage returns obtained via Grid Monte-Carlo Simulation VaR is highly skewed to the left because of negative convexity (Exhibit 5.1), the distribution of returns obtained via Historical Simulation VaR is rather symmetric (Exhibit 5.15). This occurred because Historical Simulation approximated *daily* returns using durations and convexities and subsequently annualized them, while Grid Monte-Carlo Simulation employed annualized interest rate shocks, arriving at annualized returns directly. When the magnitude of changes in systematic risk factors is small, the impact of convexity is negligible, resulting in a symmetric PDF as in the case of Historical Simulation VaR. This highlights the importance of selecting the appropriate VaR horizon, which will be discussed in detail in the following section. Finally, Historical Simulation enables associating various parameters of empirical PDFs with the actual market events. For instance, it can be shown that the worst loss over the considered period (highlighted bar on the histogram in Exhibit 5.15) corresponds to the large market selloff on 8/1/97, which can be analyzed via approaches presented in Chapter 3 (Exhibit 5.16). It can be seen that almost the entire yield curve movement on that day was due to the first principal component. The shape plausibility and explanatory power of this yield curve shock were high, while its magnitude plausibility was virtually zero, indicating that it was an uncharacteristically large market move (a 3.6 standard deviation realization of the first principal component).

5.6 VALUE-AT-RISK HORIZON

For both risk management and portfolio management purposes, the importance of selecting the appropriate VaR horizon cannot be overestimated. Since VaR assesses large potential losses associated with a position or portfolio, the VaR horizon should be consistent with the composition of the portfolio as well as with the style of money management. Thus, daily VaR for leveraged positions that are subject to margin calls should be measured. VaR horizons are typically one month or one year for institutional portfolios managed from a longer-term perspective. However, if a financial institution decides to use VaR horizons shorter than one month, the portfolio's liquidity must be carefully examined since VaR horizon should reflect the actual time needed to liquidate positions in the event of an adverse market move without dramatically changing bid/ask spreads.

EXHIBIT 5.16   Actual Market Event Corresponding to Historical Simulation VaR

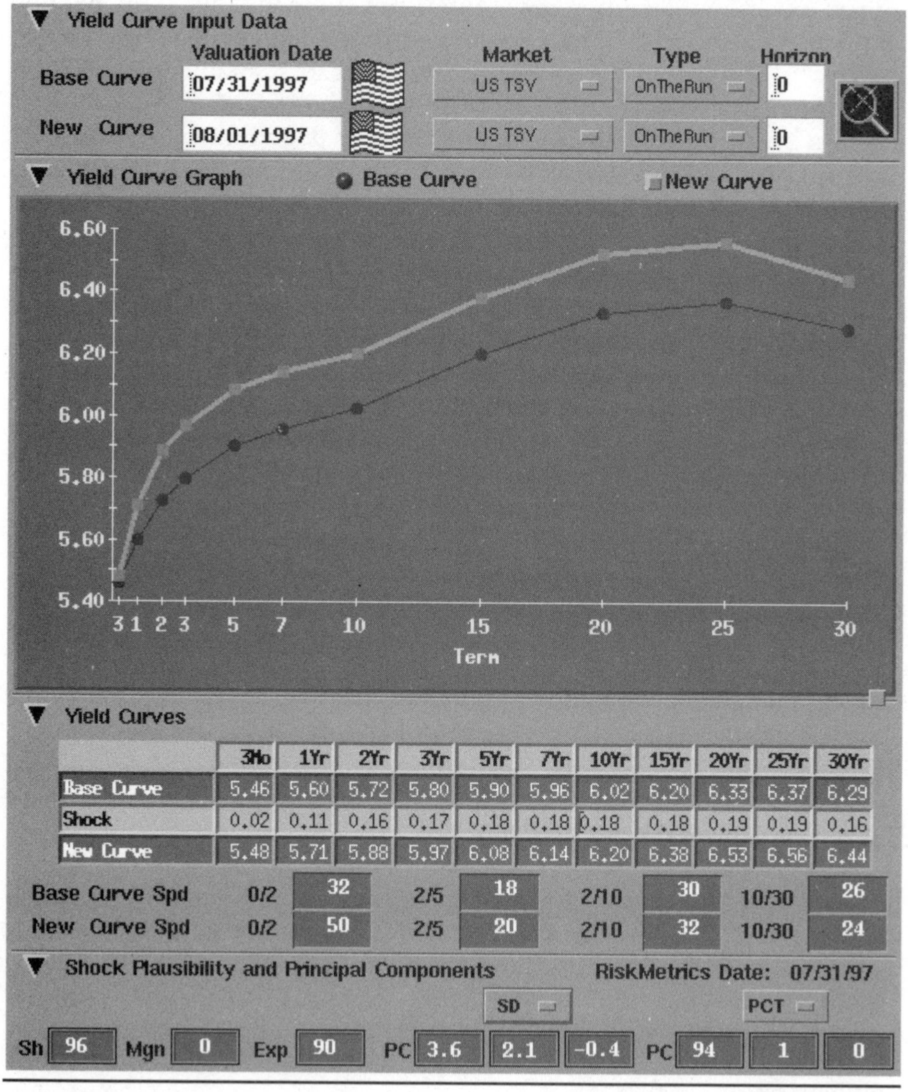

▼ Yield Curve Input Data

	Valuation Date		Market	Type	Horizon
Base Curve	07/31/1997		US TSY	OnTheRun	0
New Curve	08/01/1997		US TSY	OnTheRun	0

▼ Yield Curve Graph   ● Base Curve   ▢ New Curve

▼ Yield Curves

	3Mo	1Yr	2Yr	3Yr	5Yr	7Yr	10Yr	15Yr	20Yr	25Yr	30Yr
Base Curve	5.46	5.60	5.72	5.80	5.90	5.96	6.02	6.20	6.33	6.37	6.29
Shock	0.02	0.11	0.16	0.17	0.18	0.18	0.18	0.18	0.19	0.19	0.16
New Curve	5.48	5.71	5.88	5.97	6.08	6.14	6.20	6.38	6.53	6.56	6.44

Base Curve Spd	0/2	32	2/5	18	2/10	30	10/30	26
New Curve Spd	0/2	50	2/5	20	2/10	32	10/30	24

▼ Shock Plausibility and Principal Components   RiskMetrics Date: 07/31/97

SD ▭   PCT ▭

Sh 96   Mgn 0   Exp 90   PC 3.6   2.1   −0.4   PC 94   1   0

Different VaR horizons may lead to drastically different conclusions about risk/return characteristics of fixed income securities and portfolios. While the transformation of Variance/Covariance VaR to different horizons is governed by the square root of time rule, changing the horizon of Grid Monte-Carlo Simulation VaR cannot be done analytically and requires a separate resimulation. Let us provide the following simple illustration of this phenomenon. Suppose a monthly VaR is to be estimated for a security whose value surface is a dependency on parallel U.S. spot curve shocks. According to the square root of time rule, monthly spot curve shocks needed for Monte-Carlo simulation can be obtained from the corresponding annualized realizations via division by $\sqrt{12}$. Clearly, the only case when the change in value resulting from an annualized shock equals to the product of $\sqrt{12}$ and the change in value corresponding to a monthly shock is when the value surface is linear. However, the value surface cannot be assumed linear in this case since its nonlinearity is the reason behind using simulation methods in the first place.

Exhibits 5.17 and 5.18 present the value surface and the empirical probability density function, respectively, of the following trading strategy:

EXHIBIT 5.17   Value Surface of a Swaption Trading Strategy (Annualized Horizon)

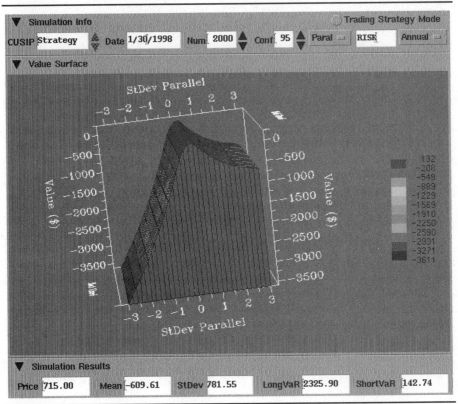

EXHIBIT 5.18   Distribution of Value Changes of a Swaption Trading Strategy (Annualized Horizon)

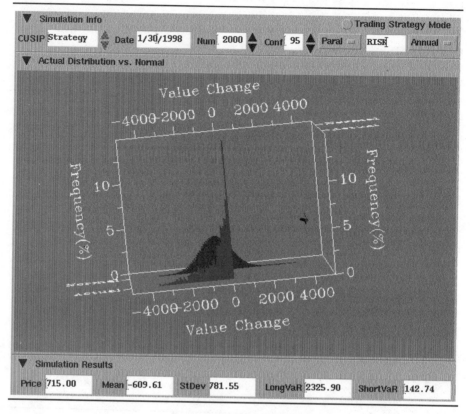

Long: $36 million (notional) of 1.5-year options on 10-year swaps

Short: $48 million (notional) of 6-month options on 10-year swaps

Monte-Carlo simulation using parallel spot curve shocks shows that holding this swaption strategy over one year has almost no upside: Both the probability and the magnitude of losses are incomparably greater than those of potential gains. However, changing the VaR horizon from annualized to daily leads to a quite different risk/return profile (Exhibits 5.19 and 5.20): Over short horizons, this strategy is a fair game with a slightly higher probability of the downside than the upside.

The example here illustrates how crucially important it is to select the most appropriate VaR horizon based on the portfolio's composi-

EXHIBIT 5.19   Value Surface of a Swaption Trading Strategy (Daily Horizon)

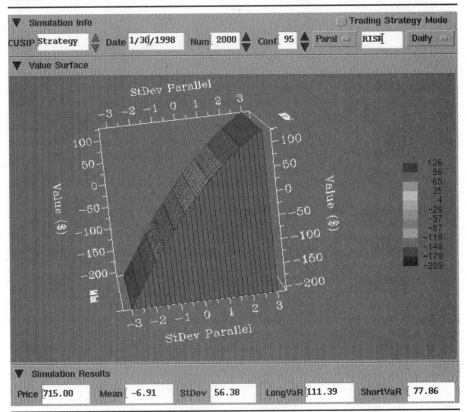

tion, rebalancing assumptions, style of money management, and the expected actions of the financial institution in times of market turmoil. The issue of establishing the VaR horizon should not be confused with the issue of selecting the time period over which historical correlations, volatilities, and other parameters of statistical distributions must be estimated.

5.7 VALUE-AT-RISK, CATASTROPHIC EVENTS, AND STRESS TESTING

Both the strength and weakness of VaR lie in its reliance on historical data of relatively short horizon.[24] Consider the following example. Suppose that the composition of a fixed income portfolio has not changed over a period of time that was characterized by a number of

EXHIBIT 5.20   Distribution of Value Changes of a Swaption Trading Strategy (Daily Horizon)

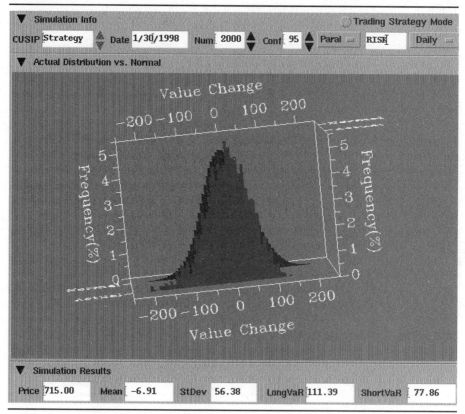

large market movements. If exponentially weighted and relatively short time series are used to estimate parameters of probability distributions of systematic risk factors, they will quickly capture the increased volatility in the market, resulting in higher VaR numbers. Despite the fact that the portfolio's composition as well as its deterministic risk characteristics have not changed, VaR will indicate that holding the same portfolio in the new market environment is more risky than before. The question is whether such behavior is desirable in a measure of risk.

There exist two philosophically opposing schools of thought on this subject. The first school argues for the relevance of long-term history for purposes of estimating VaR. From this viewpoint, VaR should not quickly capture temporary market fluctuations and should adjust risk estimates only if a particular change in the market's dynamics persists over a prolonged period of time. This argues for estimating historical correlations and volatilities over long time horizons (e.g., 5 or 10 years) and equally weighting empirical observations. The opposing view is inspired by the well-known statistical models arguing that recent history is the best predictor of future events. Following this premise, the parameters of probability distributions should be estimated by placing exponentially greater weight on more recent observations as opposed to more distant history, resulting in VaR quickly adapting to changes in the dynamics of financial markets. Depending upon the purpose of the analysis, either approach may be preferable. However, VaR measures that place heavy emphasis of the most recent data as the best predictor of future market movements can fluctuate rather dramatically, and their use as explicit firmwide risk exposure limits can create conceptual and operational problems. While a very useful trading, portfolio management, and risk management tool because it reacts rapidly to market changes, VaR must be treated with caution as a corporate risk control policy. Naïve fixed VaR limits do not necessarily work. For corporate policies constraining VaR of real portfolios to be effective, the magnitude of VaR instability needs to be fully understood, and the consequences of forcing positions to be adjusted in distressed market environments need to be realized.

VaR methodologies that use exponentially weighted empirical data can be criticized for their inability to forecast *catastrophic market events*, including extreme temporary shocks to the market as well as *regime shifts* or *structural breaks*. For instance, as mentioned earlier, using exponentially weighted observations to compute historical volatility of changes in swap spreads on 7/31/98 implied that the fall 1998 swap spread widening constituted anywhere between a 7 and 10 standard deviation event. At the same time, volatility estimates based on the longer-term history (10 years) implied approximately a 3 standard deviation event. Considering how improbable a 7 standard deviation event is, this seems to suggest that approaches based on longer-term estimates are superior to those based on exponentially weighted shorter time series. However, this conclusion is not entirely correct. For exactly the same reason that the longer-term empirical estimates provided more meaningful interpretation of the 1998 crisis, they were inferior during the long period of the benign risk behavior prior to 1998. Given their reliance on long-term history, these methods vastly overestimated risk during long periods of nonvolatile credit spread behavior, leading to excessive capital-at-risk allocations. Therefore, VaR that uses exponentially weighted data is an effective measure for forecasting unlikely but, on average, regularly occurring large losses during the *business-as-usual* market regimes. Existing VaR methodologies are neither capable of, nor should they be used for, predicting losses resulting from catastrophic market events.[25]

In the absence of probabilistic measures capable of capturing catastrophic risks, VaR must be supplemented by rigorous deterministic stress testing. By definition, stress testing estimates potential losses associated with extreme and highly unlikely adverse market movements. Some institutions use stress tests solely for informational purposes; others use them to formulate portfolio guidelines, risk limits, and other corporate risk management policies and mechanisms. Let us now discuss a variety of issues involving identification of historical and hypothetical market dislocations that can be used as stress testing scenarios.

1. *Exogenous risk factors versus the nature of business factors.* For many financial institutions, there is clear distinction between systematic risk factors that constitute the nature of their business versus a variety of other systematic risk factors that do not constitute the nature of their business but affect valuation of their portfolios. By being in the business of taking certain types of market risks, these institutions may choose to exclude risk factors that belong to the former category from VaR calculations and stress tests. As a result, market risk associated only with exogenous systematic risks will be measured and explicitly managed.

2. *Value-at-Risk horizon.* Formulation of stress tests should be consistent with the chosen VaR horizon. Thus, if the horizon is one day, catastrophic daily market movements should be considered. On the other hand, stress tests involving extreme monthly, quarterly, or even annual market movements should accompany longer VaR horizons.

3. *Actual versus hypothetical catastrophes.* When a portfolio is exposed to a very large number of systematic risk factors, identification of stress tests that possess intuitive appeal as well as economic meaning is nontrivial. Thus, historical market catastrophes can be used to test portfolios against the events that actually happened in the past. However, since it is also important to understand potential losses resulting from market events that have never happened before, historical stress tests have to be combined with hypothetical ones. Also, instead of relying on the history of a particular market, historical catastrophic events from a *proxy* market can be used.[26] Prior to 1999, for example, because there were no significant devaluations of the Brazilian real in the recent history, estimating potential losses of portfolios exposed to this currency was difficult. In formulating

stress tests at that time, one could have imagined that because it was an emerging market currency, the real could have experienced the devaluation similar in magnitude to that of the Mexican peso in 1994, the Southeast Asian currencies in 1997, or the Russian ruble in fall 1998. Interestingly enough, the magnitude of the actual losses associated with the devaluation of the Brazilian real in January 1999 was similar to the stress test involving the Russian ruble.

4. *Relevance of long-term history.* When using historical events as stress test scenarios, a determination needs to be made whether each of these catastrophes is still a plausible market event. Thus, some of the earlier historical market movements may no longer be relevant if market dynamics are believed to have *fundamentally* and *permanently* changed since then.

5. *Anticipated actions of financial institutions in times of turmoil.* Construction of meaningful stress tests should account for the way each institution is expected to react in times of crisis. Consider, for instance, a fixed income portfolio that is exposed only to U.S. interest rates and U.S. swap spreads. Then, interest rates going up by 200 basis points and swap spreads widening by 100 basis points is an example of a relevant hypothetical stress test. Suppose also that in the event that interest rates increase by more than 100 basis points, this portfolio's investment guidelines instruct portfolio managers to reduce its duration to zero by shorting U.S. Treasury futures. Clearly, given this expected action in times of turmoil, a stress test that presumes a 200 basis point increase in interest rates would vastly overestimate the actual losses.

Stress tests can be formulated in a variety of ways. The simplest and the most intuitive method specifies the exact change in each applicable systematic risk factor, for example, "interest rates sell off by 200 basis points, implied volatilities rise by 3%, all credit spreads widen by 100 basis points, and all emerging market currencies devalue by 10%." Next we present several historical events that can be used in stress testing:

- Nonfarm payrolls 3/7/96–3/8/96: the 10-year spot rate increased by more than 35 basis points (approximately a 3.7 standard deviation event)
- Beginning of the credit and liquidity crisis of 1998 (8/19/98–8/20/98): rally in the U.S. Treasury curve accompanied by the swap spreads widening by 7 basis points or 5.5 standard deviations
- The culmination of the credit and liquidity crisis of 1998 (10/1/98–10/9/98): the large selloff in the U.S. Treasury market

the (10-year spot rate increased by 57 basis points or 3 standard deviations) and swap spreads widened by 9.5 basis points or 3 standard deviations.[27]

Catastrophic market events can also be formulated in terms of standard deviations of risk factors estimated at the time of the analysis, for example, "interest rates sell off by 3 standard deviations of the first principal component, implied volatilities rise by 2 standard deviations, all credit spreads widen by 5 standard deviations, and all emerging market currencies devalue by 2 standard deviations." As already mentioned, these could be daily, monthly, or annualized standard deviations, depending on the selected VaR horizon.

Stress tests can be formulated in terms of probability distributions as well. Thus, VaR can be measured using probability distributions whose parameters were estimated *during catastrophic events*. For stress tests dealing with a variety of different markets, this approach may address the common concern of misestimating risk, given that relationships among risk factors may dramatically change during crises. Joint probability distributions computed during market dislocations by construction capture uncharacteristic changes in existing relationships.

Stress tests can be defined in terms of losses of equity rather than in terms of changes in the underlying risk factors. Thus, a financial institution may consider a 20% loss of equity over one month a catastrophic event. In this case, one can derive a set of market scenarios that would lead to such a loss given the portfolio's composition.

Table 5.14 presents a variety of historical and hypothetical stress tests for a fixed income portfolio whose sensitivities to a selected number of

TABLE 5.14   Stress Testing of a Hypothetical Portfolio (as of 7/5/99)

| | | Catastrohic Stress Tests (Horizon: One Month; Unit: Basis Points) | | | | | |
| | | Historical Events | | Hypothetical Events | | | |
Risk Factor Description	Duration	3/4/94-4/4/94	9/8/98-10/8/98	1 Monthly SD	3 SD Event	Mortgage Spreads	Simultaneous
10-year TSY Spot Rate	6.0	79	-11	37	110	0	100
ATM MBS OAS	15.0	12	45	11	32	50	75
Mtg/Tsy Basis	-2.0	12	45	11	32	50	75
10-year AAA Corp Spread	7.0	7	27	9	28	0	75
Implied Volatility	3.0	75	80	69	208	0	300
Loss (% of Market Value)		-8.98%	-9.54%	-6.31%	-18.94%	-6.50%	-30.00%

systematic risk factors (interest rates, mortgage spreads, corporate spreads, and implied volatilities) are expressed in terms of partial durations.

ENDNOTES

1. Clearly, price/yield functions are special cases of value surfaces.
2. See Mahoney, 1997.
3. See Hendricks, 1997.
4. In practice, joint sampling of a large number of interdependent variables is non-trivial since the majority of random number generators produce realizations of independent variables. In such cases, realizations of (independent) principal components can be obtained and then analytically transformed into realizations of the original systematic risk factors via Equation 3.5.
5. For the purposes of this exhibit, the Grid Monte-Carlo Simulation VaR method presented later in this chapter was used instead of the Full Monte-Carlo Simulation VaR.
6. The discussion of various properties of Variance/Covariance VaR are directly applicable to Global VaR as well.
7. See Pritsker, 1996.
8. See Jorion, 1996.
9. See Pritsker, 1996.
10. See Barber and Copper, 1996.
11. See Pritsker, 1996.
12. This IOette has a coupon of 494.14%, which explains why this bond is priced at many multiples of par.
13. After the set of grid points is determined, the scattered three-dimensional interpolation is used to create the smooth value surface.
14. In this example, interpolation is performed between −3 and +3 standard deviations and between −200 and +200 basis points for the first principal component and a parallel shock, respectively. Values outside these intervals are extrapolated.
15. For a very interesting work on estimating security-specific risk, the reader is referred to Dynkin et al., 1999.
16. See Fabozzi, 1996.
17. The presented approach makes no assumptions about the shape of the value surface and should not be confused with Delta-Gamma Simulation VaR, which uses local risk measures, duration and convexity (see Jorion, 1996).
18. Probability density function $p(x)$ of a normally distributed variable x with zero mean is a symmetric function, whereas the function x^3 is asymmetric. Therefore,

$$cov(x, x^2) = E(x^3) = \int\limits_{-\infty}^{+\infty} x^3 p(x)\, dx = 0$$

implying zero correlation as well.

19. In a single-factor setting, when prices are modeled as functions of parallel yield curve movements (Equation 5.5), the χ_1^2 random variable should be simulated as the square of the normal random varible used to model the normal by distributed component of return. In Equation 5.7, however, the χ_1^2 term represents the combined effect of nonlinearity in several dimensions (key rates). We therefore chose to model it with a separate independent χ_1^2 variable.

20. Note that $C \cdot \sigma_{NL}$ may provide an alternative way to estimate option-adjusted convexity.

21. It was previously shown that normal and χ_1^2 variables in Equation 5.5 are uncorrelated. By the same rationale, it is assumed that all systematic risks are uncorrelated with the χ_1^2 variable that represents nonlinearity.

22. See Jorion, 1996.

23. The *square root of time* rule assumes that there is no autocorrelation among changes in a risk factor corresponding to the nonoverlapping time intervals and that its volatility is constant over time. Thus, if $x_1,...,x_n$ are independent and identically distributed random variables, then the n-period volatility can be obtained by multiplying the one-period volatility σ by $\sqrt{n}$:

$$\sigma(\sum_{i=1}^{n} x_i) = \sqrt{\sum_{i=1}^{n} \sigma^2(x_i)} = \sqrt{\sigma^2(x_i) \cdot n} = \sigma \cdot \sqrt{n}$$

24. See Makarov, 1997.

25. In order to arrive at a formulation of VaR capable of capturing catastrophic risks, one can envision incorporating jump processes (see Doffou and Hilliard, 1999) and historical catastrophic events into coherent VaR measures (see Eber, 1997). Research is also being conducted on measuring risk via mixed normal distributions and using econometric models to forecast transitions from business-as-usual market regimes to catastrophic regimes (see Ghosh et al., 1999). However, these approaches are still very much a work in progress.

26. This insight belongs to Ron Dembo of Algorithmics, Inc.

27. The number of standard deviations quoted in these examples does not contradict the 7–10 standard deviation swap spread widening quoted earlier. The latter was computed by estimating volatility of changes in swap spreads on 7/31/98 and then analyzing the spread widening that occurred over the entire crisis.

6

Using Portfolio Optimization Techniques to Manage Risk

6.1 RISK MEASUREMENT VERSUS RISK MANAGEMENT

According to The Merriam-Webster Dictionary, to "hedge" means to "protect oneself financially by a counterbalancing transaction" or "evade risk of commitment." In finance, *hedging* is the process of reducing the market risk of a portfolio by buying or selling *hedge instruments* from a given set of securities (*hedge universe*). In general, many possible combinations of hedge instruments (*hedging strategies*) can reduce the systematic risk of a portfolio to a specified level. Therefore, the goal is not to merely identify a hedging strategy that decreases risk in a portfolio to a given risk tolerance, but to do this in some sort of *optimal* fashion. For a hedging strategy to be optimal, it must be cost-effective, intuitive, stable in different market environments as well as over time, and *executable*, that is, feasible to implement in practice. The complexity of identifying the optimal hedging strategy lies in balancing the hedger's risk/return preferences and market constraints. Recent financial disasters have illustrated the crucial importance of hedging. Yet hedging, while reducing potential losses, limits potential gains and may also create substantial model risk.[1] Thus, if parametric measures are inaccurate because of biased interest rate, prepayment, and other models or if historical correlations and volatilities are unsuccessful in forecasting, hedging may fail. In extreme cases, hedging may even make positions and portfolios more susceptible to certain types of risks and cause returns to become even more volatile.

In order to think about hedging, consider the following assumptions:

- *Rational economic behavior.* For a given level of expected return, investors are assumed to prefer less risk to more risk. Conversely, for a fixed level of risk, they prefer more return to less return. Given the portfolio holder's preferences, an optimal portfolio can be determined.

- *Availability of quantitative measures of risk and return.* Investors can estimate both risk and return of any security, portfolio, or portfolio vis-à-vis its benchmark.

- *Hedge universe.* The hedge universe is assumed to be sufficiently broad to cover most of the systematic risk in the original portfolio or position.

Conceptually, the task of finding the most appropriate hedge is a portfolio optimization problem. Thus, reduction of risk and enhancement of return can typically be formulated in terms of objective functions, whereas numerous portfolio and market limitations can usually be represented as optimization constraints:

- *Investment guidelines.* As discussed in Section 4.2.4, asset management mandates are typically governed by investment guidelines that determine return objectives of the assignment and ensure that the portfolio is managed according the client's risk preferences. Given that some portfolios are explicitly prohibited from owning particular security types or shorting certain asset classes, or have various cash, position size, and asset allocation limits, investment guidelines have to be translated into the language of optimization constraints. For instance, if implementing a hedge on a portfolio with no allowed leverage implies purchasing a cash instrument, the market value of the hedge must be constrained to be less than the total amount of cash currently available in the portfolio. On the other hand, if a portfolio is not allowed to short instruments, hedge optimization should be allowed to only sell securities that are currently held in the portfolio.

- *Market constraints.* When solving for the optimal hedge, numerous market considerations must be accounted for, including liquidity, relative value, and other factors. Thus, the portfolio managers' expectations that certain securities are likely to out- or underperform the market in the future should be taken into account along with knowledge that large transactions in certain securities are likely to move the market,[2] widening bid/ask spreads and increasing hedging costs. Therefore, the active involvement of traders and portfolio managers in hedge instrument selection is especially critical. Hedging is not a purely scientific process!

As is the case with most investment activities, effective hedging must rely on the synthesis of financial modeling and subjective judgement. Success in finding the optimal hedging solution is therefore contingent on the hedger's ability to translate the risk/return preferences and relative value assessments into the parameters of the optimization problem. Thus, hedge optimizations should be formulated in a flexible enough way to allow for extensive interactions with the hedger. The optimal hedge is the one that best matches the goals of the hedger. Computer programs and the underlying analytical methodologies that construct optimal hedges are merely tools that allow hedgers to explore the alternatives and more effectively search for trade-offs between their objectives and market constraints.

Finding the optimal hedge is a complex iterative decision-making and optimization process that combines mathematical modeling and market judgment. This chapter will use the previously introduced partial durations, stress tests, scenario analyses, and Value-at-Risk (VaR) approaches to minimize systematic market risk in fixed income portfolios. At the same time, various measures of return – expected rate of return, return on equity, and return resulting from instantaneous hypothetical interest rate scenarios – will be subject to maximization.

Previous chapters have discussed (1) various dimensions of market risk, (2) probability distributions of systematic risk factors, (3) different risk measures, and (4) the strengths and weaknesses of alternative risk methodologies. However, risk measurement is not risk management: The mere ability to quantify risk embedded in fixed income securities and portfolios does not protect one from financial catastrophes. Practical yet theoretically sound approaches to explicitly reducing market risk to a predefined level in a timely manner are required. The task of hedging exposures to potentially hundreds of interdependent systematic risk factors via back-of-the-envelope-type computations is, in many cases, virtually impossible. Hedging problems can be effectively solved via portfolio optimizations – techniques that formalize risk/return trade-offs and help in balancing objectives and market constraints.

6.2 TYPICAL FIXED INCOME HEDGES[3]

Hedging objectives as well as the type of market risk embedded in a security or portfolio determine the appropriate hedge instruments. Depending on whether the first-order exposure to a given risk factor or the full nonlinear shape of the value surface in one or several dimensions needs to be hedged, different fixed income securities should be included in the hedge universe:

- Instruments typically used to hedge first-order exposures:
  - U.S. Treasury securities
  - Futures on U.S. Treasury securities
  - Swaps
  - Eurodollar futures
- Instruments typically used to hedge nonlinear exposures:
  - Options on U.S. Treasury futures
  - Options on swaps
  - Caps and floors

Each of these asset classes is briefly discussed next.

Historically, U.S. Treasury securities have been among the most widely used fixed income hedge instruments due to their liquidity (inspired by many decades of U.S. budget deficits) and the absence of credit risk. These two very desirable features, coupled with the fact that many structured products have traditionally traded at a spread above a U.S. Treasury benchmark, have made Treasuries very appealing hedge instruments. Thus, hedging the interest rate risk of spread-sensitive securities with the appropriate Treasury instruments results in almost no hedge "slippage." By virtue of being extremely liquid, on-the-run (OTR) Treasuries have also had a tremendous appeal to dynamic hedgers and active money managers who typically require small friction costs when adjusting hedge ratios or implementing duration bets. In recent years, extensive use of on-the-run Treasuries in many areas of portfolio management and trading as well as decline in their supply due to U.S. budget surpluses have changed the dynamics of the Treasury market, progressively making behavior of on-the-run Treasuries materially different than the rest of the market. Thus, OTR Treasuries have increasingly begun trading "on special," exhibiting liquidity premiums reaching over 35 basis points in yield relative to the comparable off-the-run Treasury securities (Table 6.1).

Hedging with exchange traded futures on U.S. Treasury securities is common as well due to their high liquidity and the absence of upfront

Table 6.1   U.S. On-The-Run Treasury Liquidity Premiums (2/1/1999–2/1/2000)

	Liquidity Premium (basis points)				Correlations Among Liquidity Premiums			
	Mean	St Dev	Min	Max	2–year	5–year	10–year	30–year
2–year	3	2	1	11	1.00			
5–year	15	4	5	25	0.05	1.00		
10–year	29	6	8	38	0.21	0.78	1.00	
30–year	18	4	8	26	0.16	0.62	0.79	1.00

costs. Except for the 2-year contract, very large trades can be done without noticeably moving the market. While futures on U.S. Treasury securities exhibit risk characteristics similar to those of U.S. Treasuries, hedging with them may introduce additional basis risk related to the cheapest-to-deliver optionality. Also, in contrast to U.S. Treasuries, which are always positively convex, the sign of convexity of futures on U.S. Treasuries depends on the market environment (Table A.1). Given the recent developments in the U.S. Treasury market, performance of hedges involving futures on U.S. Treasuries has been increasingly influenced by supply-and-demand considerations.

From a size of zero in 1980, interest rate swaps have risen to become one of the most frequently used financial instruments in the world. Recent trends have increased their usage as generic hedging instruments as well. Today, with a net notional amount measured in tens of trillions of dollars, the interest rate swap market is one of the largest and most liquid over-the-counter markets. For instance, a 5-year swap in which an institution pays a fixed rate and receives LIBOR is usually quoted with a bid/offer spread of $1^1/_2$ basis points, but the actual execution can often be accomplished with significantly less friction of $^3/_4$ basis points or so. In liquid market environments, it is not uncommon to witness bid/ask spreads on swaps as narrow as $^1/_2$ basis points, approaching the liquidity of off-the-run Treasuries.

Decisions to hedge interest rate risk with swaps as opposed to U.S. Treasuries are influenced by a variety of considerations, including the desire to simultaneously hedge interest rate and credit spread risk, financing conditions in the U.S. Treasury market, *specialness* of the on-the-run issues, expected volatility of swap spreads, and cross-sector relative value. For example, on 1/19/2000, the 10-year Treasury was yielding 6.75% and could be financed at 4.95%, whereas the 10-year swap had a fixed leg of 7.50% and a floating leg of 6.22%. The differential cost of carry indicates that it was cheaper to short 10-year swaps than 10-year U.S. Treasuries at that time. Almost a 4 basis point swap spread tightening would have been required to eliminate this financing advantage. In general, hedging with swaps rather than U.S. Treasuries may introduce additional credit spread risk, which has been declining as swap spreads and other credit spreads appear to be evolving to a much higher correlation. This phenomenon, combined with the diminishing supply of U.S. Treasuries, manifested itself in the recent trend of quoting spread-sensitive securities in terms of spreads to LIBOR rather than the U.S. Treasury curve.

In the late 1980s, two special subsectors of the swaps market – CMT and CMS swaps – came into existence in order to permit investors to customize longer maturity hedges. The former category used Constant Maturity Treasury (CMT) rates whereas the latter used Constant Maturity Swap (CMS) rates. By entering into a CMT swap, for instance, an institution typically agrees to pay a specified CMT rate (usually, the 10-year rate) and in exchange receive LIBOR rate plus or minus a spread. In contrast with physical securities underlying the majority of asset swaps, CMS and CMT rates do not *roll down* the curve, allowing investors to better hedge certain types of relatively constant long term market exposures. CMT and CMS swaps have become fairly commonplace in the derivatives markets and are now trading at relatively low bid/ask spreads of approximately 3–4 basis points, which can be reduced even further by a competitively structured bidding process.

Emergence of total rate of return (TRR) swaps was a natural consequence of the increasing use of swaps in hedging. By entering into a TRR swap, an investor typically agrees to pay the total rate of return on a specified index (basket of fixed income securities) and in exchange receives LIBOR plus or minus a spread. The chief advantage of TRR swaps is that they can be used for hedging both interest rate as well as basis risks. They can also serve as vehicles for effectively shorting baskets of illiquid securities (CMBS, POs, etc.) that are virtually impossible to short via traditional mechanisms.

Eurodollars are U.S. dollar deposits in banks outside of the United States. Futures on Eurodollar deposits (or simply, Eurodollar futures) are effectively forward rate agreements that enable investors to lock into Eurodollar interest rates at prespecified points in the future. Eurodollar futures, which are a natural outgrowth of the futures market on U.S. Treasury Bills, trade with quarterly expirations out as far as 10 years, enabling creation of a variety of synthetic fixed-rate and floating-rate instruments (e.g., interest rate swaps). Over the past 25 years, the Eurodollar futures market went from being virtually nonexistent to "the world's center of attention for dollar-denominated short-term interest rate trading"[4] and hedging. Due to their relative analytical simplicity and high liquidity, Eurodollar futures can often provide a more flexible and less expensive alternative to hedging with interest rate swaps.

Options on U.S. Treasury futures and options on swaps (swaptions) are widely used to hedge nonlinear market exposures. Typically characterized by very large interest rate sensitivities and highly nonlinear value surfaces, options hedges may introduce significant exogenous market risks, including implied volatility risk and credit spread risk. Since risk and return characteristics of options change dramatically with their evolution through time (Section 2.7), effectiveness and stability of hedging strategies involving options and the cost of carry associated with their implementation should be judged via EROR-based rather than instantaneous risk measures. Moreover, due to their extreme sensitivity both to the passage of time and market movements, option hedges constructed using local parametric measures (see Section 6.3) require very elaborate and careful rebalancing practices, particularly if short-term options are employed.[5] As far as liquidity of options is concerned, their bid/ask spreads vary with market environments and reflect bid/ask spreads on the underlying instruments as well as bid/ask spread on implied volatility, financing, and risk premium.

Interest rate caps and floors can be thought of as portfolios of European options on various market rates, most commonly 3-month LIBOR, 1-year LIBOR, 10-year CMT, and 10-year CMS. Depending on the index, caps and floors may or may not entail credit spread risk, but their interest rate, implied volatility, and time exposures are typically very significant. While caps and floors tend to exhibit higher bid/ask spreads than options on U.S. Treasury futures and swaptions, hedging with them has all the advantages and disadvantages of other option hedges previously discussed.

6.3 PARAMETRIC HEDGING TECHNIQUES

Similar to many risk measurement methodologies that estimate risk of fixed income portfolios by approximating price changes using Taylor series expansions (Chapter 2), traditional approaches to hedging utilize various parametric measures in trying to reduce market exposures in one of several dimensions. For most fixed income instruments, whose returns are reasonably highly correlated, parametric approaches to hedging described here are practical and effective. However, these techniques may become inadequate in more general cases when no assumptions are made about the high correlation among returns on the original portfolio and those on its hedges (Section 6.4).

The simplest approach to risk reduction, *delta* or *duration* hedging, is widely used both in option pricing theory as well as in practice. Hedging exposure to small parallel changes in the yield curve is the most typical use of duration hedging in fixed income markets. Because it uses option-adjusted duration, this technique provides effective protection against small parallel changes in the yield curve but fails to address the risk associated with large or nonparallel interest rate movements.

Consider a fixed income portfolio with market value V_P and option-adjusted duration OAD_P. By using duration to hedge the interest rate risk of this portfolio, one *degree of freedom* is assumed, and therefore a single hedge instrument is required. Suppose that the selected hedge instrument has the price P_H and duration OAD_H. Hedging requires estimating the proper size in this security (i.e., unknown face value F_H) that would offset the interest rate risk to the first-order approximation. For both the portfolio and the hedge instrument, use Equation 2.24 to write the first-order approximation of price changes for a given parallel yield curve movement:

$$\Delta V_P = -OAD_P \cdot V_P \cdot \Delta r \qquad (6.1)$$

and

$$\Delta V_H = -OAD_H \cdot P_H \cdot F_H \cdot \Delta r \qquad (6.2)$$

where ΔV_P and ΔV_H are changes in the market values of the portfolio and the hedge instrument, respectively, and Δr is an arbitrary parallel change in the spot curve. To hedge the portfolio for any parallel interest rate movement is by definition equivalent to determining the face value F_H of the hedge instrument such that any change in the portfolio's market value is offset by the equal in magnitude but opposite in sign change in market value of the hedge instrument, i.e.,

$$\Delta V_P = -\Delta V_H \qquad (6.3)$$

Combining Equations 6.1–6.3 yields:

$$-OAD_P \cdot V_P \cdot \Delta r = OAD_H \cdot P_H \cdot F_H \cdot \Delta r \qquad (6.4)$$

or equivalently,

$$-OAD_P \cdot V_P = OAD_H \cdot P_H \cdot F_H \qquad (6.5)$$

The expression given by Equation 6.5 is typically referred to as *matching dollar durations*. Solving for F_H yields:

$$F_H = -\frac{OAD_P \cdot V_P}{OAD_H \cdot P_H} \tag{6.6}$$

Despite the fact that duration hedging does not require application of numerical methods, it possesses all the properties of a hedge optimization problem. The analytical solution is simply due to the fact that matching dollar durations has only one degree of freedom. The optimality of this solution can be judged via the properties of the hedge instrument, including its duration drift (and, hence, rebalancing costs), relative value, liquidity, expected return, and so forth. In the case of duration hedging, the numerous considerations that determine optimality of the hedge are implicit in the selection of the hedge instrument.

The multivariate analog of duration hedging involves simultaneous risk reduction along several dimensions and is typically formulated in terms of partial durations. Similar to the previous example, consider a domestic fixed income portfolio with a market value V_P. Assume that the market exposure of this portfolio to $n + 2$ systematic risk factors can be described (to the first-order approximation) by the following vector of partial durations:

$$Exposure_P = (krd_{1,P},\ldots,krd_{n,P}, Vol\ Dur_P, Spd\ Dur_P) \tag{6.7}$$

where $\{krd_{1,P},\ldots,krd_{n,P}\}$ are the portfolio's key rate durations, *Vol Dur$_P$* is volatility duration, and *Spd Dur$_P$* is spread duration. In order to exactly match all $n + 2$ systematic exposures of the original portfolio, the equal number of hedge instruments is needed. Each of these securities is characterized by a vector of market exposures as well:

$$Exposure_i = (krd_{1,i},\ldots,krd_{n,i}, Vol\ Dur_i, Spd\ Dur_i) \tag{6.8}$$

The exact hedging of all $n + 2$ individual exposures is equivalent to solving the following system of linear equations:

$$
\begin{bmatrix}
krd_{1,P} \cdot V_P \\
\ldots \\
krd_{n,P} \cdot V_P \\
Vol\ Dur_P \cdot V_P \\
Spd\ Dur_P \cdot V_P
\end{bmatrix}
=
\begin{bmatrix}
Exposure_1 \\
\\
\ldots \\
\\
Exposure_{n+2}
\end{bmatrix}
\cdot
\begin{bmatrix}
F_1 \\
\\
\ldots \\
\\
F_{n+2}
\end{bmatrix}
\tag{6.9}
$$

where $F_1,...,F_{n+2}$ are the unknown face values of the hedge instruments that are to be determined. In the vast majority of practical situations,[6] the system of linear equations in Equation 6.9 has a unique solution. While certainly superior to the one-dimensional duration hedging, hedging via a large number of partial durations is not always effective. First, hedging strategies obtained as exact solutions of systems of linear equations are notoriously unstable and may need frequent rebalancing. Second, since the empirical relationships among systematic risk factors are not taken into account, hedging via Equation 6.9 may lead to excessive transaction costs. Finally, if the credit spread risk is to be reduced via spread duration, it has to be ensured that the portfolio and all hedge instruments are characterized by comparable credit spread behavior. Otherwise, hedging may lead to the amplification rather than reduction of risk.

In hedging various market exposures, parametric risk measures other than partial durations can be employed as well, including cash flows, stress tests, scenario option-adjusted values (OAVs), option-adjusted convexities, and key rate convexities. While writing analogs of Equation 6.9 for these cases is straightforward and left to the reader, note that simplistic parametric approaches to hedging that attempt to account for the nonlinearity of value surface frequently result in unstable and nonintuitive hedges.

6.4 GENERALIZED APPROACH TO HEDGING (WITH WILLIAM DE LEON)

Hedging the market risk via parametric approaches has become a second nature to market participants. Thus, techniques described in the previous section are often automatically assumed to achieve reduction of the overall price volatility of a portfolio or position, which is not generally true. The goal of hedging has been classically represented as the following optimization problem:

Minimize: $\qquad\qquad\sigma(\Delta V_{\text{hedged portfolio}})$ $\qquad\qquad$ (6.10)

where σ is one standard deviation or volatility and $\Delta V_{\text{hedged portfolio}}$ is the change in the market value of the hedged portfolio:

$$\Delta V_{\text{hedged portfolio}} = \Delta V_P + \sum_{i=1}^{n}\beta_i \cdot \Delta V_i \qquad (6.11)$$

In Equation 6.11, ΔV_P is the change in the market value of the original (unhedged) portfolio, ΔV_i are changes in prices on hedge instruments, and β_i are the unknown notional amounts of hedge instruments to be bought or sold.

Recall that regression analysis uses several explanatory variables to model the variability of a single dependent variable.[7] It can be verified analytically that if the time series of ΔV_P and ΔV_i are available, solutions of the hedge optimization in Equation 6.10 are exactly equal to the coefficients of the corresponding multiple regression:

$$\Delta V_P = -\sum_{i=1}^{n} \beta_i \cdot \Delta V_i + \varepsilon \qquad (6.12)$$

since minimizing volatility of the hedged portfolio in Equation 6.10 is equivalent to minimizing variance of the residuals (the sum of the squared hedging errors ε) in Equation 6.12.

In the general case, when no assumptions are made about the relationship among the returns on the original portfolio ΔV_P and those on the hedge instruments ΔV_i, a hedge constructed via parametric techniques (e.g., Equation 6.9) may be drastically different from that obtained by solving Equation 6.10. In fact, hedging parametric measures of risk may actually lead to risk amplification rather than reduction. The following example illustrates this phenomenon by attempting to hedge spread risk of the single-B component of the DLJ High Yield Index. Since high yield securities often trade in sympathy with equities, hedging spread risk with S&P futures might be a way to hedge this exposure.[8]

Denote by R_B the percentage returns on a portfolio of B-rated corporate bonds and by $R_{S\&P}$ the percentage returns on S&P futures. Since credit spread risk is to be hedged, parametric approaches to hedging suggest that the empirical relationships between returns ($R_{S\&P}$ and R_B) and changes in high yield spreads (Δs_B) first need to be investigated, and the corresponding partial derivatives then need to be matched (Section 6.3). In doing so, the effect of changes in interest rates (Δr) on $R_{S\&P}$ and R_B should be properly separated from the effect of changes in spreads, implying the following regression:

$$R_B = \alpha + \beta_r \cdot \Delta r + \beta_s \cdot \Delta s_B + \varepsilon_B \qquad (6.13)$$

Table 6.2 presents historical correlations and volatilities of $R_{S\&P}$, R_B, Δs_B, and Δr. Note that returns on S&P futures are relatively volatile (16.53% per year) compared to returns on single-B-rated corporate bonds (6.82% per year), and that changes in single-B spreads are negatively correlated (-0.53) with changes in interest rates over the considered time interval.[9]

Table 6.2 Historical Correlations and Volatilities on Selected Returns, Spreads, and Rates (5/96–5/99)

	Annualized Volatility	Correlations			
		$R_{S\&P}$	R_B	Δs_B	Δr
$R_{S\&P}$	16.53%	1.00			
R_B	6.82%	0.61	1.00		
Δs_B	1.85%	−0.44	−0.86	1.00	
Δr	0.90%	−0.21	0.04	−0.53	1.00

Estimating the coefficients in Equation 6.13 using historical data from 5/96–5/99 yields the following results:

$$R_B = 0.007 - 4.38 \cdot \Delta r - 4.30 \cdot \Delta s_B + \varepsilon_B \qquad (6.14)$$

where the vast majority of the variability of returns R_B is explained by Δr and Δs_B ($R^2 = 98\%$); all coefficients are highly statistically significant; and one standard deviation of residuals $\sigma(\varepsilon_{S\&P}) = 1.13\%$ is relatively small compared to the price volatility (6.82%) of the original portfolio. According to Section 2.3.3, $\beta_r = -4.38$ and $\beta_s = -4.30$ are the negatives of empirical duration and empirical spread duration, respectively.

The relationship between returns on S&P futures, changes in interest rates, and changes in single-B spreads can be revealed via the analog of Equation 6.14 as well:

$$R_{S\&P} = 0.017 - 11.33 \cdot \Delta r - 6.89 \cdot \Delta s_B + \varepsilon_{S\&P} \qquad (6.15)$$

where only a portion of the variability of S&P returns is explained by interest rates and credit spreads ($R^2 = 48\%$); all regression coefficients are highly statistically significant; and volatility of the residuals is still substantial: $\sigma(\varepsilon_{S\&P}) = 12.43\%$.

Mitigating credit spread risk of the high yield portfolio in the previous example via parametric hedging techniques requires matching partial derivatives of R_B and $R_{S\&P}$ with respect to Δs_B. According to Equations 6.14 and 6.15, the empirical hedge ratio is

$$Hedge\ ratio = -\frac{-4.30}{-6.89} = -0.62 \qquad (6.16)$$

and implies shorting approximately 185 S&P futures contracts per every 100 million in market value of the single-B component of the DLJ High Yield Index.

Matching partial derivatives does not necessarily guarantee risk reduction. In fact, volatility of the hedged portfolio constructed using the hedge ratio of –0.62 is actually greater than volatility of the original (unhedged) portfolio:

$$\sigma(R_B - 0.62 \cdot R_{S\&P}) = 8.51\% \tag{6.17}$$

In contrast to parametric hedging techniques, construction of the optimal hedge requires minimizing price volatility of the hedged portfolio directly

Minimize: $\qquad\qquad\qquad \sigma(R_B + \beta \cdot R_{S\&P}) \qquad\qquad\qquad$ (6.18)

resulting in a substantially smaller hedge ratio of –0.25 obtained via the standard regression formula:

$$Hedge\ ratio = \beta = -\frac{cov(R_B, R_{S\&P})}{\sigma^2(R_{S\&P})} = -0.25 \tag{6.19}$$

This hedge in fact reduces the overall market risk of the high yield portfolio from 6.82% to 6.01% per year:

$$\sigma(R_B - 0.25 \cdot R_{S\&P}) = 6.01\% \tag{6.20}$$

In the preceding example, hedging via parametric techniques introduces a new volatile exogenous source of market risk $\sigma(\varepsilon_{S\&P})$ into the system, amplifying rather than reducing the overall price volatility. In general, both adding and omitting relevant risk factors while constructing hedges can be dangerous. For instance, consider a 10-year swap hedged with a 10-year U.S. Treasury. Since the KRD profiles of these two securities are very similar (Chapter 2), the interest rate risk of this portfolio is almost negligible. Such a hedge would have been very effective during the 1992–1997 market environment, which was characterized by an extremely benign behavior of swap spreads (see Exhibit 4.2). However, during the financial market turmoil of fall 1998, the performance of interest rate swaps was drastically different from that of U.S. Treasuries due to extreme swap spread widening, illustrating that hedging interest rate risk as a proxy for the overall price volatility is not always sufficient. As just illustrated, fixation on hedging parametric risk measures in place of minimizing the overall price volatility may cause practitioners to utilize hedge instruments whose returns are rather loosely correlated with those on the original portfolio. Low correlation is typically an indicator that either new exogenous sources of risk are being introduced into the system or important risk factors are being consciously or unconsciously omitted.

To summarize, when constructing hedges:

- No new volatile exogenous sources of risk should be introduced into the system
- No important risk factors should be omitted
- Cost of carry on the hedge should be acceptable

6.5 VARIANCE/COVARIANCE VaR AND PARTIAL DURATION HEDGE OPTIMIZATIONS

6.5.1. Basic Optimization Variables

Successful measurement and management of risks in fixed income portfolios relies on the hedger's ability to make conscious and rational trade-offs. Hedging, as an application of risk management, requires a synthesis of rigorous modeling and subjective market-based judgment. The ultimate goal of any hedge optimization is to translate the hedger's utilities into the language of mathematics so that the resulting hedge solutions are intuitive, cost-effective, executable, and stable. This section presents a simple and effective approach to hedge optimization. It will assume that all hedge instruments are reasonably correlated with the original portfolio and are selected to reflect regulatory, market, and other considerations. Consider the distinct stages of hedging in detail.

First, the *hedging target* or objective must be clarified and then expressed mathematically. Hedging targets are typically formulated in terms of the desired risk characteristics of the hedged portfolio, e.g., its duration, convexity, VaR, various partial durations, scenario analysis OAVs, ERORs, and so forth. The goal of hedging is, therefore, to determine the *optimal* combination of hedge instruments that brings the risk parameters of the hedged portfolio as close to those of the target portfolio as possible.

Second, various risk/return preferences and utilities of the hedger need to be formalized and represented as objective functions and optimization constraints. This involves asking the hedger to identify market risks and hedge costs that are subject to minimization as well as measures of expected return that are subject to maximization. All of the corresponding measures of risk, return, and cost have to be computed for both the original portfolio and all instruments in the hedge universe. The identification of various risk, return, and cost characteristics is still not sufficient for defining an effective and meaningful objective function. This knowledge has to be supplemented with information about the *relative importance* of different optimization parameters to the hedger. For instance, a hedger may believe that in order to achieve his objectives, maximization of expected return is as important as minimization of tracking error, and that they both are more important than minimization of the upfront hedging costs. Relationships of this kind can be obtained heuristically and subsequently formalized.

The third stage of hedging is developing a rigorous yet flexible mathematical formulation of the hedge optimization problem. As emphasized earlier, construction of the most appropriate hedge is a complex, iterative decision-making process. By changing the relative importance of various optimization parameters, the hedger is able to investigate the impact of various trade-offs on the risk/return characteristics of the hedged portfolio. Essentially, this allows him or her to "walk" along the efficient frontier, arriving at the solution he or she deems optimal. Numerous examples presented later in this chapter will illustrate these points.

Besides being an effective tool dealing with explicit risk reduction, hedge optimizations help solve a variety of other portfolio management and asset allocation problems. For instance, the task of maximizing expected returns while reducing risk and keeping transaction costs under control can be represented as a hedge optimization problem. This section applies simple optimizations to the tasks of hedging market risk in fixed income securities and managing portfolios against their benchmarks. Risk reduction can also be accompanied by implementation of various market bets, turning hedge optimizations into a valuable tool for active portfolio management.

Three groups of optimization parameters are used in constructing hedges:

- Measures of systematic risk
- Measures of expected return
- Measures of cost associated with hedging

Measures of Market Risk   A variety of methodologies exist for dealing with different aspects of systematic market risk in fixed income portfolios. Thus, the exposure to movements of default-free interest rates can be measured via option-adjusted duration and convexity, key rate and key treasury rate durations, principal component durations, scenario analyses, Variance/Covariance VaR, and the like. On the other hand, prepayment durations, mortgage/treasury basis durations, coupon curve and OAS curve durations, spread durations, and volatility durations can be used to estimate the first-order price sensitivity to a variety of basis risks. Finally, Global VaR presents the overall exposure to interest rate, basis, and currency risks as one summarized measure. The approach to hedge optimization presented next characterizes the market risk of fixed income securities and portfolios in terms of the following measures:

- *Price volatility* as measured by *IntRR,* Variance/Covariance VaR, or Global VaR. This measure accounts for the first-order sensitivities of portfolios to various risk factors as well as for the probability distribution of relevant systematic risk factors. Minimization of price volatility is therefore desirable.
- *Partial durations.* In addition to hedging the VaR-type measures, exposures in all relevant risk dimensions (partial durations of the hedged portfolio) should be brought as close to those of the *hedging target* as possible. The optimization variable called *dispersion of partial durations around the target* ($\Delta PDur^2$) is designed specifically for this reason. The inclusion of this variable prevents the creation of large offsetting exposures in *similar* risk factors, eliminating the implicit reliance on them remaining highly correlated and equally volatile in the future. $\Delta PDur^2$ is defined as follows:

$$\Delta PDur^2 = \sum_{i=1}^{n} \left(pdur_{i,\text{hedged portfolio}} - pdur_{i,\text{target}}\right)^2 \qquad (6.21)$$

where $pdur_{i,\text{hedged portfolio}}$ and $pdur_{i,\text{target}}$ are partial durations of the hedged portfolio and the hedging target, respectively.

Measures of Return   In addition to minimizing risk, portfolio managers often wish to incorporate their active market views into hedge optimizations. Mathematically, this task can be represented as maximization of the portfolio's return *(TotRet)* resulting from a user-specified hypothetical instantaneous market move. It can also be thought of as an optimal positioning of the hedged portfolio for a given stress test (Chapter 5), and therefore partial durations combined with hypothetical changes in systematic risk factor allow for approximating the resulting change in price:

$$TotRet = -\sum_{i=1}^{n} pdur_i \cdot \Delta F_i \qquad (6.22)$$

where $pdur_i$ are partial durations of the hedged portfolio, and ΔF_i are the anticipated changes in risk factors. Hedge optimizations should attempt to maximize $TotRet$ while minimizing the risk.

Hedge Cost Considerations   Hedge optimizations that lack a notion of hedge cost are unstable and unrealistic since large quantities of hedge instruments are bought and sold without a penalty in order to improve the objective function. Hence, such hedges are impossible to implement in practice. To ensure that sizes of the proposed hedges are feasible, an optimization variable has to be defined that prefers hedging alternatives with small total transaction sizes to those with large transaction sizes. While more elaborate measures of hedge cost that utilize bid/ask spreads can be used, the following simple measure (*TCost*) ensures that the sum of the absolute transaction sizes as a percentage of the original market value of the portfolio is minimized:

$$TCost = \frac{\sum_{\text{hedge instruments}} |Market\ Value_i\ or\ Notional\ Value_i|}{Portfolio's\ Net\ Asset\ Value} \qquad (6.23)$$

Supplementing this rudimentary transaction cost penalty with market information about bid/ask spreads on fixed income securities can make hedge optimizations even more realistic and generalized. This can typically be achieved by specifying that hedge instruments have different prices depending on whether they are bought or sold. Obviously, the simple cost penalty described in Equation 6.23 does not measure the cost of carry associated with alternative hedging strategies. This matter will be addressed later in this chapter.

Finally, we arrive at the following expression for the objective function of our hedge optimization:

Minimize: $\alpha \cdot IntRR + \beta \cdot \Delta PDur^2 + \tau \cdot TCost - \eta \cdot TotRet$ \qquad (6.24)

where Global VaR can be used instead of IntRR, where appropriate, $\Delta PDur^2$ is a measure of how closely partial durations of the hedged portfolio match those of the target, *TCost* is a transaction cost penalty, *TotRet* is a measure of instantaneous return resulting from a user-defined hypothetical market move, and α, β, τ, and η are the weights assigned to different components of the objective function. By varying these weights and reoptimizing the hedge, the hedger can sketch out the efficient frontier and arrive at the optimal solution.

In addition to defining the hedge target and describing the objective function (Equation 6.24), it is often necessary to impose a number of *hard constraints* on the solutions of hedge optimizations. These market-related and portfolio-specific limitations include information about allowable or executable transaction sizes, cash constraints, investment guidelines, duration bands, and other considerations.

6.5.2 Example: Hedging Interest Rate Risk of a Mortgage-Backed Security

This section utilizes hedge optimization given by Equation 6.24 to create simple, intuitive, and cost-effective hedging strategies. The examples here demonstrate a variety of approaches to implementing a mortgage/treasury basis trade by purchasing a mortgage-backed security (MBS) and hedging out its interest rate risk using U.S. Treasury securities and futures contracts on U.S. Treasury securities. Given the nature of this hedging objective, the systematic market risk of both the MBS and the hedge instruments can be described through the following measures of risk: *IntRR*, option-adjusted duration *(OAD)*, option-adjusted convexity *(OAC)*, and key rate durations *(KRDs)*. In a more general setting, if basis risks need to be hedged in addition to interest rate risk, Global VaR can be used instead of *IntRR* without changing the described paradigm.

Exhibit 6.1 presents a snapshot of a computer program that uses this hedge optimization methodology. In order to fully define the optimization problem, the following information needs to be specified:

1. Portfolio information (Panel A)
   - Name or CUSIP (FN_7_30YR denotes a 30-year 7% Fannie Mae MBS)
   - Net asset value ($100,000,000)
   - Available cash
   - Valuation and RiskMetrics® dataset dates (12/31/98)
2. Benchmark information, if any (Panel B)

EXHIBIT 6.1   Hedging a Generic 30-year 7.0% FNMA MBS with U.S. TSY Futures (Variance/Covariance VaR, KRD, and Cost Optimization)

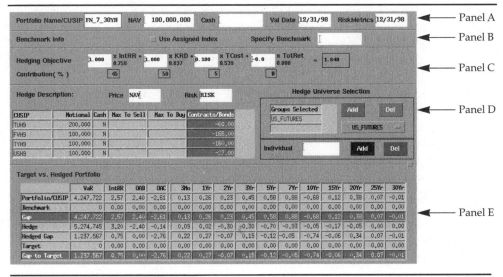

Panel A

Panel B

Panel C

Panel D

Panel E

3. Hedging objective (Panel C) denotes the objective function of the hedge optimization as given by Equation 6.24. In the considered example, $\alpha = 1$, $\beta = 1$, $\tau = 0.01$, and $\eta = 0$.

4. Hedging constraints (not shown). In this example, the following hard optimization constraint was imposed:

$$OAD_{\text{hedged portfolio}} = OAD_{\text{target}} \qquad (6.25)$$

5. Panel D describes hedge instruments, their risk characteristics, and transaction limits. Exhibit 6.1 shows that this example uses futures contracts on U.S. Treasury securities as hedge instruments. TUH9 denotes a 2-year futures contract, FVH9 a 5-year contract, TYH9 a 10-year contract, USH9 a 30-year futures contract.

6. The *optimization target* describes the desired risk characteristics of the hedged portfolio (Panel E). Targeting duration, convexity, key rate durations, and *IntRR* to be zero is indicative of the goal of hedging the interest rate risk of the mortgage-backed security as *flat* as possible.

Exhibit 6.1 presents the results of hedging interest rate risk in a generic 30-year 7.0% Fannie Mae MBS using U.S. Treasury futures. The optimal hedge implies shorting 60 contracts of the 2-year futures, shorting 165 contracts of the 5-year futures, shorting 160 contracts of the 10-year futures, and shorting 27 contracts of the 30-year futures. First, notice that the hard constraint of hedge optimization is satisfied since OAD of the hedged MBS is zero (panel E). It can be seen that U.S. futures are relatively effective in reducing *IntRR* of the MBS. Compare a 75 basis point per year *IntRR* of the hedged MBS with a 257 basis point per year *IntRR* on the unhedged MBS.

While substantially reducing *IntRR* and Variance/Covariance VaR, U.S. Treasury futures are not completely effective in hedging the individual KRDs of this MBS. KRD profiles of the MBS ("gap"),[10] the hedged MBS ("hedged gap") and the target reveal that the hedged MBS still remains exposed to yield curve risk (Exhibit 6.2).[11] Because it was impossible to completely hedge the MBS's KRD profile (large positive 7-year KRD, large negative 10-year KRD, and moderately positive 20-year KRD), the hedge optimization used correlations and volatilities of key spot rates to identify the KRD profile that implies the smallest overall interest rate risk.

EXHIBIT 6.2   KRD Profiles of a 30-year 7.0% FNMA MBS with and without the Hedge from Exhibit 6.1

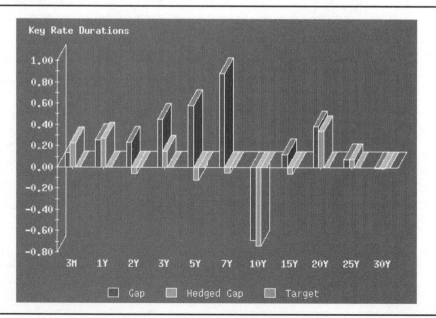

Finally, from the contribution percentages presented in panel C (Exhibit 6.1), it can be seen that *IntRR* contributed approximately 45% to the final value of the objective function, $\Delta PDur^2$ (denoted by KRD) contributed approximately 50%, and transaction penalty *(TCost)* contributed approximately 5%. In other words, the hedge optimization has found the optimal trade-off between minimizing IntRR and minimizing individual KRDs. The transaction cost factor has been deemed less influential.

Exhibits 6.3 and 6.4 show the results of the hedge optimization of the same FNMA MBS, only this time a combination of U.S. Treasury futures and U.S. OTR Treasury securities was used. Clearly, the addition of U.S. OTR TSY instruments (which are denoted by GY2Y, GY5Y, GY10Y, and GY30Y and quoted in millions of dollars) substantially improves the quality of the hedge. *IntRR* of the hedged MBS is 18 basis points per year, down from 257 basis points of IntRR of the unhedged MBS. The KRD profile of the hedged MBS is also much flatter, suggesting that this hedging strategy is superior to that presented in Exhibits 6.1 and 6.2.

EXHIBIT 6.3   Hedging a Generic 30-year 7.0% FNMA MBS with U.S. TSY Futures and U.S. OTR TSY (Variance/Covariance VaR, KRD, and Cost Optimization)

| Portfolio Name/CUSIP | FN_7_30YR | NAV | 100,000,000 | Cash | | Val Date | 12/31/98 | RiskMetrics | 12/31/98 |

Benchmark Info   ☐ Use Assigned Index   Specify Benchmark

| Hedging Objective | 1.000 | x IntRR + 0.183 | 1.000 | x KRD + 0.209 | 0.100 | x TCost + 4.425 | -0.0 | x TotRet 0.000 | = | 0.835 |
| Contribution(%) | | 21 | | 25 | | 53 | | 0 | | |

Hedge Description: Price NAV   Risk RISK   Hedge Universe Selection

CUSIP	Notional	Cash	Max To Sell	Max To Buy	Contracts/Bonds
TUH9	200,000	N			690.00
FVH9	100,000	N			-520.00
TYH9	100,000	N			-169.00
USH9	100,000	N			-26.00
GY2Y	1,000,000	Y			-173.00
GY5Y	1,000,000	Y			30.00
GY10Y	1,000,000	Y			11.00
GY30Y	1,000,000	Y			-2.00

Groups Selected: US_FUTURES, US_OTR_TSY   Add   Del   US_OTR_TSY

Individual   Add   Del

Target vs. Hedged Portfolio

	VaR	IntRR	ORD	OAC	3Mo	1Yr	2Yr	3Yr	5Yr	7Yr	10Yr	15Yr	20Yr	25Yr	30Yr
Portfolio/CUSIP	4,247,722	2.57	2.40	-2.61	0.13	0.26	0.23	0.45	0.58	0.88	-0.68	0.12	0.38	0.07	-0.01
Benchmark	0	0.00	0.00	0.00	0.00	0.00	0.00	0.00	0.00	0.00	0.00	0.00	0.00	0.00	0.00
Gap	4,247,722	2.57	2.40	-2.61	0.13	0.26	0.23	0.45	0.58	0.88	-0.68	0.12	0.38	0.07	-0.01
Hedge	4,472,271	2.71	-2.40	-0.15	-0.15	-0.09	-0.37	-0.33	-0.71	-0.90	0.61	-0.20	-0.08	-0.04	-0.14
Hedged Gap	301,738	0.18	0.00	-2.76	-0.02	0.17	-0.14	0.12	-0.13	-0.02	-0.07	-0.09	0.30	0.03	-0.15
Target	0	0.00	0.00	0.00	0.00	0.00	0.00	0.00	0.00	0.00	0.00	0.00	0.00	0.00	0.00
Gap to Target	301,738	0.18	0.00	-2.76	-0.02	0.17	-0.14	0.12	-0.13	-0.02	-0.07	-0.09	0.30	0.03	-0.15

EXHIBIT 6.4 KRD Profiles of a 30-year 7.0% FNMA MBS with and without the Hedge from Exhibit 6.3

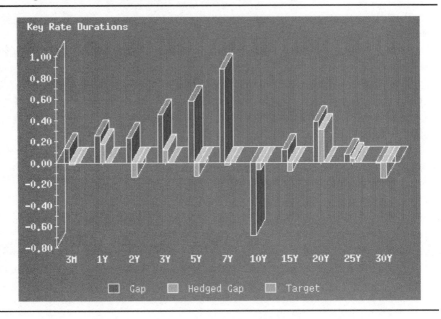

EXHIBIT 6.5 Hedging a Generic 30-year 7.0% FNMA MBS with U.S. TSY Futures and U.S. OTR TSY to Duration 1 (Variance/Covariance VaR, KRD, and Cost Optimization)

Portfolio Name/CUSIP FN_7_30YR NAV 100,000,000 Cash [ ] Val Date 12/31/98 RiskMetrics 12/31/98

Benchmark Info   ☐ Use Assigned Index   Specify Benchmark [ ]

Hedging Objective 1.000 × IntRR + 1.000 × KRD + 0.100 × TCost + -0.0 × TotRet = 0.504
                         0.126   0.152   2.266   0.000
Contribution(%)   24   30   44   0

Hedge Description: Price NAV   Risk RISK

Hedge Universe Selection

Groups Selected	Add	Del
US_FUTURES		
US_OTR_TSY	US_OTR_TSY	

Individual [ ] Add Del

CUSIP	Notional	Cash	Max To Sell	Max To Buy	Contracts/Bonds
TUH9	200,000	N			312.00
FVH9	100,000	N			-280.00
TYH9	100,000	N			-158.00
USH9	100,000	N			-14.00
GY2Y	1,000,000	Y			-82.00
GY5Y	1,000,000	Y			13.00
GY10Y	1,000,000	Y			12.00
GY30Y	1,000,000	Y			-1.00

Target vs. Hedged Portfolio

	VaR	IntRR	OAD	OAC	3Mo	1Yr	2Yr	3Yr	5Yr	7Yr	10Yr	15Yr	20Yr	25Yr	30Yr
Portfolio/CUSIP	4,247,722	2.57	2.40	-2.61	0.13	0.26	0.23	0.45	0.58	0.88	-0.68	0.12	0.38	0.07	-0.01
Benchmark	0	0.00	0.00	0.00	0.00	0.00	0.00	0.00	0.00	0.00	0.00	0.00	0.00	0.00	0.00
Gap	4,247,722	2.57	2.40	-2.61	0.13	0.26	0.23	0.45	0.58	0.88	-0.68	0.12	0.38	0.07	-0.01
Hedge	2,844,907	1.72	-1.40	-0.07	-0.05	-0.03	-0.23	-0.22	-0.54	-0.81	0.71	-0.11	-0.04	-0.02	-0.07
Hedged Gap	1,441,688	0.87	1.00	-2.68	0.09	0.22	0.00	0.23	0.04	0.07	0.03	0.01	0.34	0.05	-0.08
Target	1,505,397	0.91	1.00	0.00	0.09	0.09	0.09	0.09	0.09	0.09	0.09	0.09	0.09	0.09	0.09
Gap to Target	207,300	0.13	-0.00	-2.68	-0.00	0.13	-0.09	0.14	-0.05	-0.02	-0.06	-0.08	0.25	-0.04	-0.17

In certain cases, portfolio managers may not want to hedge out the entire interest rate risk component, combining a mortgage/treasury basis bet with a directional interest rate bet. By specifying a nontrivial optimization target, the duration of the MBS can be reduced to the specified duration target of one year while its yield curve risk is minimized (Exhibits 6.5 and 6.6).

6.5.3 Example: Managing Fixed Income Portfolios Against Their Benchmarks

In addition to hedging various components of risk embedded in individual securities, the approach to hedge optimization described in Equation 6.24 can also assist in effectively managing fixed income portfolios relative to their benchmarks. Exhibits 6.7 and 6.8 present a fixed income portfolio (named XYZ) benchmarked against the Lehman Brothers U.S. Aggregate Bond Index. The duration of this portfolio is 45 basis points longer than that of the index, which translates into ex ante tracking error of 51 basis points per year. Suppose that portfolio managers are unsure about the future direction of interest rates and decide to make this portfolio as mar-

EXHIBIT 6.6   KRD Profiles of a 30-year 7.0% FNMA MBS with and without the Hedge from Exhibit 6.5

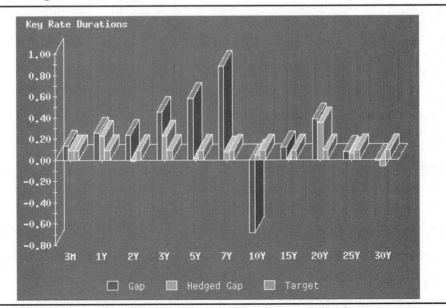

EXHIBIT 6.7　Hedging XYZ Portfolio to the Lehman Brothers U.S. Aggregate Bond Index Using U.S. TSY Futures (Variance/Covariance VaR, KRD, and Cost Optimization)

| Portfolio Name/CUSIP | XYZ_PORT | NAV | 100,000,000 | Cash | 5,000,000 | Val Date | 12/31/98 | RiskMetrics | 12/31/98 |

Benchmark Info　LEH_AGG　☑ Use Assigned Index　Specify Benchmark [

Hedging Objective　1.000 × IntRR + 1.000 × KRD + 0.100 × TCost + -0.0 × TotRet = 0.402
　　　　　　　　　　0.168　　　　0.218　　　　0.166　　　　0.000

Contribution(%)　41　　54　　4　　0

Hedge Description:　Price NAV　Risk RISK　　Hedge Universe Selection

CUSIP	Notional	Cash	Max To Sell	Max To Buy	Contracts/Bonds
TUH9	200,000	N			23.00
FVH9	100,000	N			24.00
TYH9	100,000	N			11.00
USH9	100,000	N			-60.00

Groups Selected　US_FUTURES　　Add　Del
US_FUTURES

Individual [　　Add　Del

Target vs. Hedged Portfolio

	VaR	IntRR	OAD	OAC	3Mo	1Yr	2Yr	3Yr	5Yr	7Yr	10Yr	15Yr	20Yr	25Yr	30Yr
Portfolio/CUSIP	8,710,522	5.28	4.90	-0.32	0.03	0.14	0.23	0.39	0.63	0.70	0.79	0.54	0.59	0.39	0.46
Benchmark	8,022,914	4.86	4.45	-0.12	0.05	0.18	0.29	0.50	0.65	0.75	0.45	0.45	0.57	0.36	0.21
Gap	842,119	0.51	0.45	-0.20	-0.01	-0.04	-0.06	-0.11	-0.02	-0.04	0.34	0.09	0.02	0.02	0.25
Hedge	896,335	0.54	-0.45	-0.06	-0.01	-0.00	0.09	0.02	0.05	0.00	-0.12	-0.39	-0.10	0.00	0.00
Hedged Gap	276,485	0.17	-0.00	-0.26	-0.02	-0.04	0.03	-0.09	0.03	-0.04	0.22	-0.30	-0.08	0.02	0.25
Target	0	0.00	0.00	0.00	0.00	0.00	0.00	0.00	0.00	0.00	0.00	0.00	0.00	0.00	0.00
Gap to Target	276,485	0.17	-0.00	-0.26	-0.02	-0.04	0.03	-0.09	0.03	-0.04	0.22	-0.30	-0.08	0.02	0.25

ket-neutral (relative to its benchmark) as possible, while preserving all basis, asset allocation and security selection bets. Clearly, this task can be expressed as the hedge optimization shown is Exhibit 6.7. Similar to the case of the MBS, the optimal U.S. futures hedge reduced ex ante tracking error of this portfolio to only 17 basis points per year but was unable to reduce all yield curve risks, creating a negative exposure at the 15-year key rate in order to offset those at 10- and 30-year key rates (Exhibit 6.8). By construction, the KRD profile of the gap between the portfolio and its index has the smallest ex ante tracking error given the recent historical behavior of U.S. key spot rates.

Imposing additional optimization constraints typically worsens the forecasted effectiveness of the hedge. Suppose that XYZ portfolio currently owns thirty 30-year futures contracts and its portfolio manager is reluctant to short more futures than are currently in the portfolio. This limitation can be formulated as an optimization constraint as shown in Exhibit 6.9. This additional constraint increases ex ante tracking error to 29 basis points per year, up from 17 basis points per year in the previous example and worsens the KRD profile (Exhibit 6.10).

Hedging the gap between XYZ portfolio and the Lehman Brothers U.S. Aggregate Bond Index with U.S. OTR Treasuries rather than with

EXHIBIT 6.8 KRD Profiles of the Gap between XYZ Portfolio and the Lehman Brothers U.S. Aggregate Bond Index with and without the Hedge from Exhibit 6.7

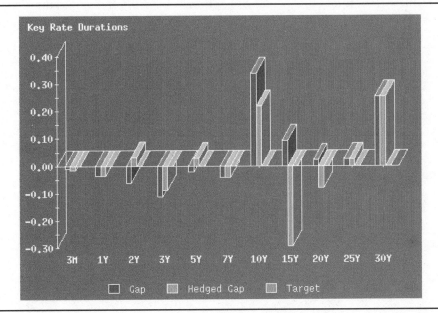

EXHIBIT 6.9 Hedging XYZ Portfolio to the Lehman Brothers U.S. Aggregate Bond Index Using U.S. TSY Futures with a Constraint (Variance/Covariance VaR, KRD, and Cost Optimization)

	VaR	IntRR	OAD	OAC	3Mo	1Yr	2Yr	3Yr	5Yr	7Yr	10Yr	15Yr	20Yr	25Yr	30Yr
Portfolio/CUSIP	8,710,522	5.28	4.90	-0.32	0.03	0.14	0.23	0.39	0.63	0.70	0.79	0.54	0.59	0.39	0.46
Benchmark	8,022,914	4.86	4.45	-0.12	0.05	0.18	0.29	0.50	0.65	0.75	0.45	0.45	0.57	0.36	0.21
Gap	842,119	0.51	0.45	-0.20	-0.01	-0.04	-0.06	-0.11	-0.02	-0.04	0.34	0.09	0.02	0.02	0.25
Hedge	901,155	0.55	-0.44	-0.04	0.01	0.00	0.03	-0.01	-0.04	-0.12	-0.06	-0.19	-0.05	0.00	0.00
Hedged Gap	478,713	0.29	0.00	-0.24	-0.01	-0.04	-0.03	-0.13	-0.06	-0.16	0.28	-0.10	-0.03	0.02	0.25
Target	0	0.00	0.00	0.00	0.00	0.00	0.00	0.00	0.00	0.00	0.00	0.00	0.00	0.00	0.00
Gap to Target	478,713	0.29	0.00	-0.24	-0.01	-0.04	-0.03	-0.13	-0.06	-0.16	0.28	-0.10	-0.03	0.02	0.25

EXHIBIT 6.10   KRD Profiles of the Gap between XYZ Portfolio and the Lehman Brothers U.S. Aggregate Bond Index with and without the Hedge from Exhibit 6.9

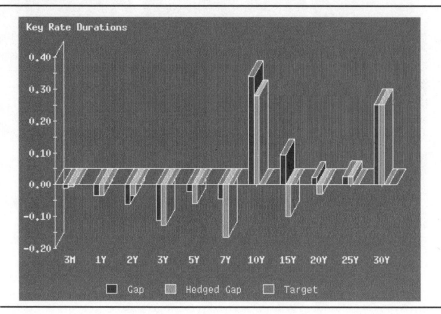

futures contracts achieves better results both in terms of the individual KRDs and ex ante tracking error. Exhibits 6.11 and 6.12 illustrate this point numerically. Notice a much flatter KRD profile and tracking error of only 6 basis points per year.

6.5.4 Example: Incorporating Yield Curve Bets into Hedge Optimizations

The examples in the previous section did not use the fourth component of the objective function *(TotRet)*, which measures returns resulting from user-specified instantaneous hypothetical market movements (Equation 6.24). This section will demonstrate an easy and computationally inexpensive way to employ this additional capability in placing active yield curve bets while reducing the overall interest rate risk. Suppose that portfolio managers had no market view on the future direction of interest rates but expected the U.S. yield curve to steepen. In this case, they may choose to eliminate the active directional interest rate bet embedded in a portfolio or restructure it for a yield curve steepener. In doing so,

EXHIBIT 6.11 Hedging XYZ Portfolio to the Lehman Brothers U.S. Aggregate Bond Index Using U.S. OTR TSY (Variance/Covariance VaR, KRD, and Cost Optimization)

| Portfolio Name/CUSIP | XYZ_PORT | NAV | 100,000,000 | Cash | 5,000,000 | Val Date | 12/31/98 | RiskMetrics | 12/31/98 |

Benchmark Info　　LEH_AGG　　☑ Use Assigned Index　　Specify Benchmark ▯

Hedging Objective　1.000 × IntRR + 1.000 × KRD + 0.100 × TCost + -0.0 × TotRet = 0.120
　　　　　　　　　　　0.055　　0.046　　0.186　　0.000

Contribution(%)　　46　　38　　15　　0

Hedge Description:　　Price NAV　　Risk RISK　　Hedge Universe Selection

Groups Selected: US_OTR_TSY　　Add　Del
US_OTR_TSY

Individual ▯　　Add　Del

CUSIP	Notional	Cash	Max To Sell	Max To Buy	Contracts/Bonds
GY2Y	1,000,000	Y			8.50
GY5Y	1,000,000	Y			3.00
GY10Y	1,000,000	Y			-4.50
GY30Y	1,000,000	Y			-2.50

Target vs. Hedged Portfolio

	VaR	IntRR	OAD	OAC	3Mo	1Yr	2Yr	3Yr	5Yr	7Yr	10Yr	15Yr	20Yr	25Yr	30Yr
Portfolio/CUSIP	8,710,522	5.28	4.90	-0.32	0.03	0.14	0.23	0.39	0.63	0.70	0.79	0.54	0.59	0.39	0.46
Benchmark	8,022,914	4.86	4.45	-0.12	0.05	0.18	0.29	0.50	0.65	0.75	0.45	0.45	0.57	0.36	0.21
Gap	842,119	0.51	0.45	-0.20	-0.01	-0.04	-0.06	-0.11	-0.02	-0.04	0.34	0.09	0.02	0.02	0.25
Hedge	792,704	0.48	-0.45	-0.11	0.00	0.00	0.15	-0.00	0.09	-0.06	-0.32	-0.04	-0.04	-0.05	-0.18
Hedged Gap	91,445	0.06	-0.00	-0.31	-0.01	-0.03	0.09	-0.12	0.06	-0.10	0.02	0.05	-0.02	-0.02	0.07
Target	0	0.00	0.00	0.00	0.00	0.00	0.00	0.00	0.00	0.00	0.00	0.00	0.00	0.00	0.00
Gap to Target	91,445	0.06	-0.00	-0.31	-0.01	-0.03	0.09	-0.12	0.06	-0.10	0.02	0.05	-0.02	-0.02	0.07

EXHIBIT 6.12 KRD Profiles of the Gap between XYZ Portfolio and the Lehman Brothers U.S. Aggregate Bond Index with and without the Hedge from Exhibit 6.11

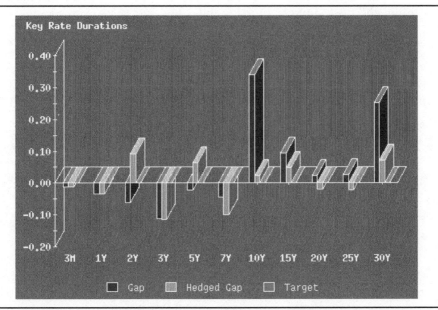

they can effectively use the approach to hedge optimization shown in Equation 6.24. Their goal is to simultaneously reduce the duration of the gap between the portfolio and its benchmark to zero, minimize interest rate risk, and maximize return in the event of a steepener (hence, the minus sign in front of the *TotRet* measure in the objective function). Exhibits 6.13 and 6.14 show the optimal hedge which not only minimizes the overall interest rate risk but also maximizes return under SEDUR interest rate shock. The KRD profile of the hedged gap between XYZ portfolio and Lehman Brothers U.S. Aggregate Bond Index reveals a clearly pronounced yield curve steepening bet.

The incorporation of yield curve bets into hedge optimizations enables searching for trade-offs among risk, return, and cost. By allowing the user to vary the weight (η) assigned to the return component of the objective function *(TotRet)*, hedge optimizations can explicitly sketch out the risk/return efficient frontier (Exhibit 6.15). An increase in the relative importance of the return component would lead to higher potential returns and, naturally enough, to higher ex ante tracking errors. Thus, for instance, the change in η from 0.0 to –0.05 results in an increase in tracking error from 6 basis points per year to 10 basis points. At the same time, the return under SEDUR hypothetical interest rate scenario increases from –2 basis

EXHIBIT 6.13   Hedging XYZ Portfolio to the Lehman Brothers U.S. Aggregate Bond Index while Incorporating SEDUR Yield Curve Bet (Variance/Covariance VaR, KRD, and Cost Minimization, Instantaneous Return Maximization)

Portfolio Name/CUSIP	XYZ_PORT	NAV	100,000,000	Cash	5,000,000	Val Date	12/31/98	RiskMetrics	12/31/98

Benchmark Info   LEH_AGG   ☑ Use Assigned Index   Specify Benchmark

Hedging Objective	1.000	x IntRR + 0.095	1.000	x KRD + 0.161	0.100	x TCost + 0.251	-0.050	x TotRet 3.252	=	0.118

Contribution(%)   [80]   [135]   [21]   [-137]

Hedge Description: Price NAV   Risk RISK   Hedge Universe Selection

CUSIP	Notional	Cash	Max To Sell	Max To Buy	Contracts/Bonds
GY2Y	1,000,000	Y			5.00
GY5Y	1,000,000	Y			10.00
GY10Y	1,000,000	Y			-7.50
GY30Y	1,000,000	Y			-2.50

Groups Selected   US_OTR_TSY   Add   Del

US_OTR_TSY

Individual   Add   Del

Target vs. Hedged Portfolio

	VaR	IntRR	OAD	OAC	3Mo	1Yr	2Yr	3Yr	5Yr	7Yr	10Yr	15Yr	20Yr	25Yr	30Yr
Portfolio/CUSIP	8,710,522	5.28	4.90	-0.32	0.03	0.14	0.23	0.39	0.63	0.70	0.79	0.54	0.59	0.39	0.46
Benchmark	8,022,914	4.86	4.45	-0.12	0.05	0.18	0.29	0.50	0.65	0.75	0.45	0.45	0.57	0.36	0.21
Gap	842.119	0.51	0.45	-0.20	-0.01	-0.04	-0.06	-0.11	-0.02	-0.04	0.34	0.09	0.02	0.02	0.25
Hedge	829.219	0.50	-0.45	-0.12	0.00	0.00	0.09	0.02	0.34	-0.08	-0.50	-0.04	-0.04	-0.05	-0.18
Hedged Gap	156.918	0.10	-0.00	-0.32	-0.01	-0.03	0.03	-0.09	0.31	-0.13	-0.16	0.05	-0.02	-0.02	0.07
Target	0	0.00	0.00	0.00	0.00	0.00	0.00	0.00	0.00	0.00	0.00	0.00	0.00	0.00	0.00
Gap to Target	156.918	0.10	-0.00	-0.32	-0.01	-0.03	0.03	-0.09	0.31	-0.13	-0.16	0.05	-0.02	-0.02	0.07

EXHIBIT 6.14 KRD Profiles of the Gap between XYZ Porfolio and the Lehman Brothers U.S. Aggregate Bond Index with and without the Hedge from Exhibit 6.13

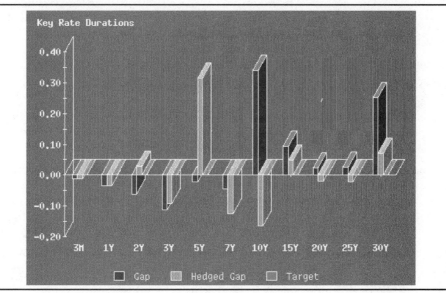

EXHIBIT 6.15 Trade-off between Ex Ante Tracking Error and Magnitude of SEDUR Yield Curve Bet

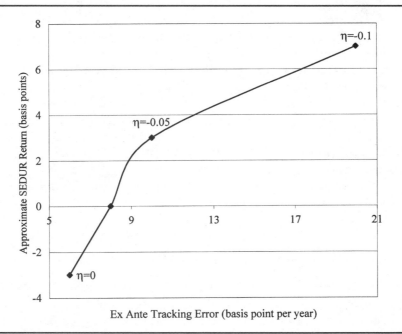

points to 3 basis points. The negative return when $\eta = 0$ (before the hedge was implemented) reveals that the gap between the portfolio and its benchmark was originally positioned for a yield curve flattener.

6.6 GENERAL PORTFOLIO OPTIMIZATIONS: RETURN VERSUS RISK AND COST

6.6.1 Additional Optimization Variables

While effective in constructing simple hedging strategies, the approach to hedge optimization presented in the preceding sections needs to be generalized to enable portfolio optimizations in more complicated settings. Next, additional measures of risk, return, and cost that help analyze various hedging alternatives from a more comprehensive perspective are introduced. This, in turn, enables hedgers to have a greater flexibility in representing their objectives, market and portfolio constraints, and other considerations in the language of hedge optimizations.

Auxiliary Measures of Risk In addition to hedging OADs, Variance/Covariance VaR, and other risk measures that presume prices to be linear functions of systematic risk factors, the nonlinearity of the value surface in the interest rate dimension can be explicitly hedged. This can be achieved by incorporating various scenario analyses (Chapter 2) into hedge optimizations or, alternatively, using Monte-Carlo Simulation VaR (which is very computationally expensive). A hedge optimization starts with the specification of the risk and return characteristics desirable in the hedged portfolio. Thus, similar to the case of various partial durations, OAVs corresponding to various interest rate scenarios can be specified as a hedging target. The new component of the objective function ($\Delta Scen^2$) is introduced in order to measure the extent to which the hedged portfolio's scenario OAVs resemble those of the target. This new optimization variable is called *weighted dispersion of interest rate scenarios* ($\Delta Scen^2$) and is defined as follows:

$$\Delta Scen^2 = \sum_{i=1}^{n} w_i \cdot (OAV_{i,\text{hedged portfolio}} - OAV_{i,\text{target}})^2 \qquad (6.26)$$

where $OAV_{i,\text{hedged portfolio}}$ and $OAV_{i,\text{target}}$ are scenario OAVs of the hedged portfolio and the target, respectively, and $w_1, \ldots, w_n$ are weights whose meaning will be discussed momentarily.

Hedging interest rate scenarios unveils a very interesting conceptual dilemma. Considering that the probability of interest rates moving by 200 basis points or more over one year is substantially smaller than that of interest rates moving by, say, 50 basis points, it is unclear whether losses corresponding to a 200 basis point interest rate move should be hedged as tightly as those corresponding to a 50 basis point move. In other words, it is up to the hedger to decide if it is reasonable to place equal emphasis on hedging different scenarios given the fact that the probabilities of the underlying events are drastically different. The answer depends on whether hedges are purchased as a protection against catastrophic events or business-as-usual market movements. For instance, in managing mortgage servicing and insurance portfolios, all interest rate scenarios are typically hedged in a similar fashion, implicitly assigning equal probabilities to the underlying interest rate moves. To summarize, the weights $w_1,...,w_n$ in Equation 6.26 can be either specified by the user or computed using the probabilities associated with various interest rate scenarios (Chapter 3). In addition to using instantaneous scenario analysis OAVs, EROR scenario analysis can be used in hedge optimizations as well.

Auxiliary Measures of Return   Return-on-equity *(ROE)* is a measure of return that can be obtained via the EROR analysis (Chapter 2). ROE accounts for both debt-to-equity (DER) ratio as well as financing assumptions:

$$ROE = \frac{(1+DER) \cdot EROR \cdot MV - DER \cdot FinR \cdot AvgMV}{AvgMV} \qquad (6.27)$$

where *EROR* is expected rate of return, *DER* is debt-to-equity ratio, *FinR* is the financing rate, *MV* is the market value of the hedged portfolio at the time when the hedge is put on, and *AvgMV* is the average market value of the hedged portfolio over the life of the hedge. Clearly, portfolio optimizations should attempt to maximize ROE.

Auxiliary Measures of Hedge Cost   In reality, financial institutions allocate limited resources to hedging programs. Therefore, the upfront costs associated with implementing hedging strategies can sometimes be an important consideration. For this reason, a hedge that consists of notional securities (e.g., futures, swaps, forward contracts) may be deemed optimal even if it provides less effective risk reduction than that consisting of cash instruments. *Upfront hedge investment (Invest)* is defined as the total market value of the hedge instruments expressed as a percentage of current market value of the portfolio. Clearly, this additional component of the objective function is subject to minimization.

Measuring the *ongoing hedge cost* or *cost of carry* associated with a hedging strategy is very important as well. Hedge cost *(HCost)* is typically defined as the total expected return (in dollars) resulting from holding hedge instruments over the life of the hedge and can be obtained via the EROR framework. While being extremely valuable in estimating hedge costs, *HCost* can be misleading if it is not used in conjunction with ROE and other measures of return. For example, one can construct a hedging strategy that reduces interest rate risk of a fixed income portfolio by shorting deep out-of-the-money interest rate caps and floors. By construction,[12] this hedge has positive EROR, seemingly implying a pure arbitrage opportunity to reduce the risk and make money at the same time. Clearly, this is not the case since the implementation of hedging strategies of this type is often associated with excessive financing costs, resulting in suboptimal ROE. A properly formulated hedge optimization is typically capable of finding the optimal trade-off between cost of carry (as measured by *HCost*), optimal use of leverage, and ROE.

By combining the newly introduced optimization variables with those discussed in Section 6.5, the general formulation of the portfolio optimization problem can be arrived at:

Risk Measures $\rightarrow$ min: $\alpha \cdot IntRR + \beta \cdot \Delta PDur^2 + \gamma \cdot \Delta Scen^2$ (6.28)

Return Measures $\rightarrow$ max: $\delta \cdot ROE + \eta \cdot TotRet$ (6.29)

Cost Measures $\rightarrow$ min: $\tau \cdot TCost + \mu \cdot Invest + v \cdot HCost$ (6.30)

As before, determination of the hedging objective should be accompanied by the appropriate optimization constraints, including asset allocation limitations, relative value, and liquidity considerations, and so forth. Depending on the nature of the portfolio, the optimization problem just described may be substantially nonlinear and have a large number of local minima. In these cases, identification of the global minimum may be problematic, and even the use of genetic algorithms may not lead to meaningful solutions. Market knowledge and subjective judgement must therefore accompany the entire hedge optimization process to ensure that optimization results are intuitive. This illustrates once again that the complexity of portfolio optimizations lies in finding trade-offs among risk, return, and cost considerations.

6.6.2 Example: Hedging Interest Rate Risk with Swaps, Caps, and Floors

Tables 6.3–6.5 present an approach to hedging the interest rate risk embedded in a portfolio of mortgage derivatives. The upper panel of Table 6.3 describes the assumptions made by the hedge optimization methodology described in Equations 6.28–6.30. The horizon of this hedging program is 1 year; 100% of the portfolio is to be hedged; the financing rate is 1-month LIBOR plus 20 basis points, and the portfolio is leveraged 10:1. The second panel of Table 6.3 shows the initial market value of both the original portfolio and its hedges; the projected average market values over the course of one year; EROR; and ROE of the original portfolio, its hedges, and the hedged portfolio. As a compensation for significant interest rate and basis risks, this portfolio has the projected ROE of 44.80%. According to Table 6.3, by hedging out the majority of interest rate risk, the ROE of this portfolio is decreased to 19.75%, illustrating again that hedging, while reducing risk, limits potential returns as well. The middle panel of Table 6.3 presents interest rate scenario analysis of the original portfolio, its hedges, and the hedged portfolio. In this example, all scenarios are equally weighted (Equation 6.26), ignoring probabilities associated with the underlying interest rate shocks. Notice that the hedge consisting of interest rate caps, floors, swaps, and PO asset swaps (Table 6.4) is very effective, dramatically reducing market exposures measured by scenario analysis, *IntRR*, OAD, and KRDs.

The composition of the optimal hedge is presented in Table 6.4. This exhibit shows that upfront costs associated with this hedge are significant (14.77% of the original portfolio's value). Because of option decay and other characteristics related to the evolution of hedge instruments over time, the ongoing hedge cost is expected to be on the order of 1.42% per year.

Table 6.5 presents the objective function and optimization constraints. As expected, the portfolio optimization has identified the optimal trade-off between the two most influential factors, ROE and weighted dispersion of interest rate scenarios, while other factors have proved to be not as influential. All constraints, including hedge instruments' size limits, interest rate scenarios, and the like, were satisfied. The results were also intuitive for portfolio managers specializing in mortgage derivatives.

6.6.3 Example: Asset/Liability Management via Monte-Carlo Simulation VaR

Similar to managing portfolios versus their benchmarks, asset/liability management (ALM) can utilize sophisticated hedging techniques as

TABLE 6.3 Portfolio Optimization: Risk, Return and Cost Summary (as of 2/19/98)

Assumptions			
Horizon: 1 year	% Hedged: 100%	Financing: 1M LIBOR + 20 bps	Debt/Equity Ratio: 10:1

	Start MktVal	Avg MktVal	EROR (%)	ROE (%)
Portfolio	582,589	610,524	9.59%	44.80%
+ Hedges	86,074	81,941	-9.60%	-166.84%
= Hedged Port	668,663	692,465	7.12%	19.75%
- Financing	607,875	629,513	5.59%	5.59%
= Equity	60,788	62,951	19.75%	19.75%

Interest Rate Scenarios (Parallel Spot Curve Shocks in Basis Points)

| Shock | -200 | -150 | -100 | -50 | -25 | 0 | 25 | 50 | 100 | 150 | 200 |
Weight	1.00	1.00	1.00	1.00	1.00	1.00	1.00	1.00	1.00	1.00	1.00
Portfolio	338,934	369,856	426,576	506,659	546,132	582,589	614,547	641,267	678,933	701,214	713,933
+ Hedges	332,266	286,099	226,679	156,035	120,049	86,074	55,356	29,392	-7,448	-25,737	-29,136
= Hedged Port	671,200	655,955	653,255	662,694	666,181	668,663	669,903	670,659	671,485	675,477	684,797
dPortfolio	-243,655	-212,733	-156,013	-75,930	-36,457	0	31,958	58,678	96,344	118,625	131,344
+ dHedges	246,192	200,025	140,605	69,961	33,975	0	-30,718	-56,682	-93,522	-111,811	-115,210
= dHedged Port	2,537	-12,708	-15,408	-5,969	-2,482	0	1,240	1,996	2,822	6,814	16,134
% Diff	0.38%	-1.90%	-2.30%	-0.89%	-0.37%	0.00%	0.19%	0.30%	0.42%	1.02%	2.41%
% Hedged	101%	94%	90%	92%	93%	100%	96%	97%	97%	94%	88%

Interest Rate Risk, Partial Durations, and Option-Adjusted Convexity

	IntRR (%)	OAD	OAC	MTB Dur	VOL Dur	Key Rate Durations									
						3mo	1yr	2yr	3yr	5yr	7yr	10yr	15yr	20yr	30yr
Portfolio	18.25	-23.09	-11.84	-29.07	1.04	0.58	0.52	0.36	0.72	-0.89	-0.93	-13.52	-8.36	-1.34	-0.23
Hedged Port	2.28	-0.58	-2.37	-25.33	0.05	0.06	0.48	0.96	1.99	1.64	0.80	-1.48	-4.75	-0.25	-0.03
%Hedged	87.51	97%	80%	13%	95%	89%	9%	-167%	-176%	284%	186%	89%	43%	81%	88%

TABLE 6.4 Portfolio Optimization: Hedge Structure (as of 2/19/98)

Instrument	Lower Limit	Upper Limit	Notional	Mid Mkt Price	Adjusted Price	Upfront Cost	Long Pos EROR	1 Year Exp $Return
4.50 Floor	-10,000,000	10,000,000	-890,000	0.48	0.44	-3,898	-36.47%	1,422
4.75 Floor	-10,000,000	10,000,000	-226,000	0.67	0.62	-1,416	-33.63%	476
5.00 Floor	-10,000,000	10,000,000	-450,000	0.93	0.87	-3,963	-31.05%	1,231
5.25 Floor	-10,000,000	10,000,000	-80,000	1.33	1.27	-1,047	-29.13%	305
5.50 Floor	-10,000,000	10,000,000	140,000	1.73	1.80	2,454	-26.22%	-643
5.75 Floor	-10,000,000	10,000,000	420,000	2.31	2.38	9,953	-13.13%	-1,306
6.00 Floor	-10,000,000	10,000,000	180,000	2.94	3.01	5,369	-4.66%	-250
6.25 Floor	-10,000,000	10,000,000	250,000	3.69	3.76	9,352	0.12%	11
6.50 Floor	-10,000,000	10,000,000	300,000	4.46	4.53	13,827	3.46%	479
6.75 Floor	-10,000,000	10,000,000	370,000	5.33	5.39	19,724	5.19%	1,024
6.75 Floor	-10,000,000	10,000,000	720,000	1.90	1.97	14,211	-32.29%	-4,589
6.00 Cap	0	10,000,000	340,000	1.56	1.63	5,496	-34.27%	-1,884
6.25 Cap	0	10,000,000	250,000	1.29	1.35	3,361	-36.24%	-1,218
6.50 Cap	0	10,000,000	77,000	1.06	1.12	866	-38.19%	-331
6.75 Cap	0	10,000,000	80,000	0.83	0.89	711	-40.43%	-288
7.00 Cap	0	10,000,000	1,400,000	0.69	0.74	10,338	-42.36%	-4,380
7.25 Cap	0	10,000,000	70,000	0.56	0.61	431	-44.27%	-191
7.50 Cap	0	10,000,000	64,000	0.46	0.50	320	-46.14%	-148
7.75 Cap	0	10,000,000					-11.94%	-10,280
Total Caps & Floors			2,951,000			86,090		
10-yr Swap	0	10,000,000	340,000	0.00	0.00	5	$0.40	1,354
5-yr Swap	0	10,000,000	130,000	0.00	0.00	2	$0.24	320
5-yr CMT Swap	0	10,000,000	150,000	-0.02	-0.02	-24	$0.43	630
Total Swaps			620,000			-16		2,304
6.5% PO FNSTR-249	0	200,000	200,000	71.63	0.00	0	-0.45%	-639
7.0% PO FHSTR-177	0	200,000	200,000	74.72	0.00	0	-0.46%	-687
7.5% PO FHSTR-188	0	200,000	200,000	79.45	0.00	0	-0.01%	-13
8.0% PO FHSTR-186	0	200,000	200,000	84.17	0.00	0	0.62%	1,048
Total PO Swaps			800,000			0		-291
Grand Total			4,371,000			86,074	-9.60%	-8,267
% Portfolio						14.77%		-1.42%

* Adjusted Price reflects the bid-ask spread and distinguishes between being long or short a hedge instrument

TABLE 6.5   Portfolio Optimization: Objective Function and Constraints (as of 2/19/98)

	Hedging Objective (to be minimized)					
	Description	**Goal**	**Weight**	**Value**	**Weight ×** **Value**	**%Contrib**
	Interest Rate Risk	MIN	1.00	2.28%	0.02	8.49%
Risk	Sum of Weighted ΔScen²	MIN	2.00	11.69%	0.23	87.06%
	Sum of ΔPDur²	MIN	0.50	3.33%	0.02	6.19%
Return	Return on Equity	MAX	−1.00	19.75%	−0.20	−73.55%
	Instantaneous Return	MAX	0.00	0.00%	0.00	0.00%
	Transaction Size Penalty	MIN	1.00	2.28%	0.02	8.48%
Cost	Upfront Hedge Investment	MIN	0.50	14.77%	0.07	27.50%
	Running Hedge Cost	MIN	1.00	9.62%	0.10	35.82%

	Constraints			
	Lower Limit	**Value**	**Upper Limit**	**Is Satisfied**
Option Adjusted Value −200	−10.00%	0.38%	10.00%	Yes
Option Adjusted Value −150	−4.00%	−1.90%	4.00%	Yes
Option Adjusted Value −100	−4.00%	−2.30%	4.00%	Yes
Option Adjusted Value −50	−2.00%	−0.89%	2.00%	Yes
Option Adjusted Value −25	−1.00%	−0.37%	1.00%	Yes
Option Adjusted Value +25	0.00%	0.19%	1.00%	Yes
Option Adjusted Value +50	0.00%	0.30%	2.00%	Yes
Option Adjusted Value +100	0.00%	0.42%	3.00%	Yes
Option Adjusted Value +150	0.00%	1.02%	4.00%	Yes
Option Adjusted Value +200	0.00%	2.41%	10.00%	Yes
Interest Rate Risk	N/A	2.28%	3.00%	Yes
Sum of Weighted ΔScen²	N/A	11.69%	N/A	Yes
Sum of ΔPDur²	N/A	3.33%	N/A	Yes
Return on Equity	16.00%	19.75%	N/A	Yes
Running Hedge Cost	N/A	9.62%	N/A	Yes
Upfront Hedge Investment	N/A	14.77%	N/A	Yes
Transaction Size Penalty	N/A	2.28%	N/A	Yes

well. While many of the previously described approaches to hedge optimization are applicable to ALM, this section illustrates the process of matching assets to liabilities using Grid Monte-Carlo Simulation VaR. As studied in Chapter 5, this approach to measuring the interest rate risk accounts for cash flow uncertainties of fixed income securities, captures the nonlinearity of the value surface, and uses information about the probability distributions of systematic risk factors.

Exhibit 6.16 presents the empirical price distribution of an income portfolio (assets). Due to large negative convexity of this portfolio, the distribution of its value changes is highly skewed to the left. The empirical price distribution of (the portfolio of) liabilities has quite different risk characteristics (Exhibit 6.17): It is rather symmetric and slightly skewed to the right due to small positive convexity. In order to partially eliminate the discrepancy between the two distributions and ensure that

EXHIBIT 6.16 Asset/Liability Management Using Monte-Carlo Simulation VaR: Distribution of Assets' Returns

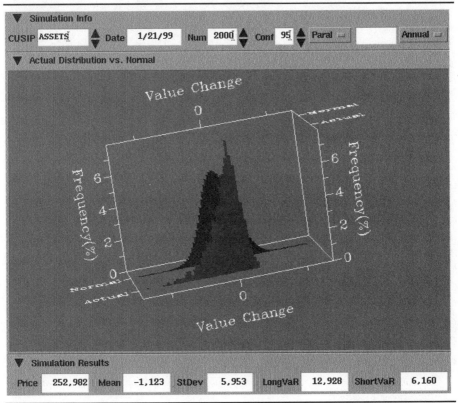

EXHIBIT 6.17   Asset/Liability Management Using Monte-Carlo Simulation VaR: Distribution of Liabilities' Returns

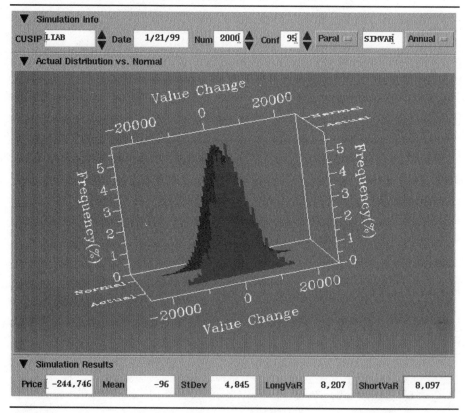

unexpected price fluctuations of liabilities are largely offset by those of the assets, a variety of options contracts whose aggregate price distribution is highly skewed to the right (Exhibit 6.18) was purchased. Finally, the hedged gap between the portfolio of assets and the portfolio of liabilities is presented in Exhibit 6.19. While assets and liabilities are still somewhat mismatched, the bulk of the differential returns is now concentrated around zero.

ENDNOTES

1. See uses of VaR by LTCM in Jorion, 1999.
2. To "move" the market means to change the existing bid/ask spreads by performing large transactions.

EXHIBIT 6.18   Asset/Liability Management Using Monte-Carlo Simulation VaR: Distribution of Hedges' Returns

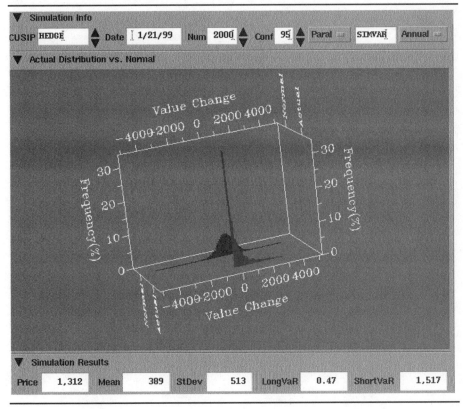

3. We would like to thank colleagues Scott Peng and Bill De Leon for their help with the discussion of hedge instruments.
4. See Burghardt et al., 1991.
5. As discussed in Section 2.7, it is very easy to misuse short-term options if parametric (instantaneous) analyses are employed because the likelihood of a given interest rate movement decreases with time (Table 2.12).
6. For this system of linear equations to have a unique solution, it is sufficient that no two hedging instruments have identical or proportional exposures to all systematic risk factors, and that for each risk factor there exists at least one hedging instrument that is exposed to it.
7. See Neter et al., 1986.
8. In practice, directly hedging high yield spreads via short positions or derivatives is not sensible.
9. The magnitude and the sign of correlation between changes in interest rates and changes in credit spreads vary dramatically with the market environment.

EXHIBIT 6.19   Asset/Liability Management Using Monte-Carlo Simulation
VaR: Distribution of Assets – Liabilities + Hedges

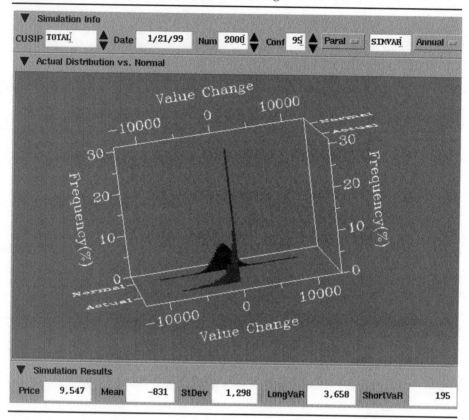

10. As shown in Section 6.5.3, this computer program can be used to hedge both the absolute risk of securities or portfolios as well as the relative risk of portfolios vis-à-vis their benchmarks. That is the reason behind using the term *gap*. When a portfolio is managed against a benchmark, *gap* denotes the active risk of the portfolio relative to its index. When no benchmark is specified, *gap* measures the absolute risk of the original portfolio or position.

11. Durations of both the hedge and the hedged protfolio are presented in terms of the market value of the original portfolio in order to enable meaningful comparison of the risk parameters.

12. Shorting options characterized by rapid decay leads to positive expected return on the hedge.

Appendix

DESCRIPTION OF THE SAMPLE PORTFOLIO

Portfolio managers, executives, practitioners, academics, and students interested in the field of risk management exhibit an extreme diversity of professional and academic backgrounds. Some of them can better understand the nature of financial risks in terms of abstract arguments and formulas, while others approach these problems from a more practical and intuition-based angle. To make this book useful and intuitive for both categories of readers, the theoretical discussions of various analytical constructs have been supplemented with numerical examples, calculation details, and screen snapshots of computer programs. A hypothetical fixed income portfolio (referred to as the Sample Portfolio throughout the book) that contains a set of fixed income securities representing a wide range of asset classes is used to illustrate the vast majority of models and approaches.[1] Table A.1 presents security details and basic risk measures of the holdings in the sample portfolio.[2] By studying various methodologies using the same set of instruments, the reader can develop intuition with respect to various risk characteristics of fixed income securities, compare and contrast alternative approaches, and understand the influence of different assumptions and intellectual trade-offs on risk estimates. The other motivation behind providing a large number of numerical examples and screen snapshots was to demonstrate that the presented concepts can be implemented in practice and used in a computationally feasible manner to make effective and timely investment decisions.

ENDNOTES

1. Occasionally, when the discussed concepts are not applicable to all asset classes, different portfolios are used. For instance, when discussing measures of mortgage risk in Chapter 2, a portfolio of 30-year generic mortgage-backed securities is used instead.
2. Please note that the standard fixed income markets' convention of dividing the actual convexity of a security by 100 before reporting it was followed. When approximating price changes using duration and convexity, the reported convexity numbers should be multiplied by 100.

295

TABLE A.1 Security Details and Basic Risk Measures Report for the Sample Portfolio

Security Description	Coupon	Maturity	Strike	Face/Contracts	Market Value	Yield	WAL	Duration	Convexity
Treasury Bonds									
TREASURY NOTE (OTR)	4.63	12/31/00		100,000	100,156	4.54%	2.00	1.89	0.05
TREASURY NOTE (OTR)	4.25	11/15/03		100,000	99,274	4.54%	4.87	4.32	0.22
TREASURY NOTE (OTR)	4.75	11/15/08		100,000	101,338	4.66%	9.87	7.76	0.73
TREASURY BOND (OTR)	5.25	11/15/28		100,000	103,027	5.09%	29.87	14.93	3.34
Agency Bonds									
FHLMC (callable)	6.33	02/13/06	100	100,000	103,546	5.75%	2.12	3.25	-0.79
Futures									
MAR 10YR NOTE FUTURE		03/31/99		1*	0			5.67	0.38
MAR 30YR BOND FUTURE		03/31/99		1*	0			9.47	0.89
Options									
MAR 10 YR NOTE Put		02/20/99	117	1*	469			-350.74	925.11
10 YR NOTE FUTURE Call		02/20/99	119	1*	1,328			266.42	452.59
Interest Rate Swaps									
US Swap	7.24	06/15/11		100,000	10,313			6.68	0.91
Caps & Floors									
6.00 3M LIBOR CAP	6.00	02/19/02		100,000	568			-114.67	95.80
10YR CMT, 5-YR TENOR 6.4%	6.40	06/17/02		100,000	5,157			50.32	11.26
OTC Derivatives									
Swaption 1	7.25	05/12/00	7.25	100,000	343			-195.71	284.47
Swaption 2	Float	06/23/99	5.85	100,000	3,880			148.11	132.62
Non USD Government Securities									
SWEDEN GOVT	10.25	05/05/00		100,000	14,220	3.51%	1.35	1.23	0.02
JGB BD 174 (10 YR)	4.60	09/20/04		100,000	1,021	1.70%	5.72	5.18	0.31
UK TREASURY	9.00	10/13/08		100,000	229,715	4.38%	9.78	6.91	0.61
CANADA GOVT	5.75	06/01/29		100,000	71,490	5.16%	30.42	14.78	3.30

Generic Pass-Throughs									
FGOLD 30YR	7.00	12/31/28		100,000	102,521	6.52%	5.37	2.52	-2.59
FGOLD 30YR	8.00	12/31/28		100,000	104,167	6.72%	3.60	1.85	-1.32
GNMA Construction Loans									
FHA CREEKWOOD GN/GN	7.30	11/30/38		100,000	107,782	6.76%	28.62	3.57	-1.13
Non-Agency CMBS									
DLJMA_96-CF1 B1 144A	8.27	01/12/08		100,000	106,193	7.40%	7.56	4.41	-0.54
Inverse Floating Rate Mortgages									
CMOT13 Q	15.55	01/20/03		100,000	107,651	9.04%	1.20	2.83	0.16
POs-Agency									
FNSTR_267 (FN 8.50)		10/01/24		100,000	88,813	4.32%	3.06	7.95	-4.02
IOs-Agency									
FHLMC_2043 (FG 7.00)	7.00	01/15/16		100,000	21,083	19.08%	4.62	-45.94	-20.82
CMO Sequentials-Agency									
FNMA_93-178 (FN 7.00)	5.25	09/25/23		100,000	99,902	6.08%	0.23	0.22	0.00
Corporates – Finance									
BANKAMERICA CAPITAL II	8.00	12/15/26	Vary	100,000	112,060	6.78%	7.96	8.72	0.05
Corporates – Industrial									
PROCTER & GAMBLE COMPANY	8.00	10/26/29	100	100,000	126,264	6.19%	30.82	12.84	2.67
Asset Backed – Prepay Sensitive									
CONHE_97-5 (Home Equity)	6.58	06/15/19		100,000	101,688	6.14%	3.02	2.27	-1.00
Asset Backed – Non-Prepay Sensitive									
CHVAT_98-2 (Auto)	5.91	12/15/04		100,000	100,685	5.69%	1.61	1.47	0.04
Total Assets	**7.02**			**2,604,000**	**2,024,653**	**5.92%**	**9.90**	**6.82**	**0.81**

* Denotes number of options and futures contracts as opposed to dollars of face value

Bibliography

Amihud, Yakov, and Haim Mendelson, "Liquidity and Asset Pricing: Financial Management Implications," *Financial Management* (1988), 5–15.

Anderson, Nicola, Fransis Breedon, Mark Deacon, Andrew Derry, and Gareth Murphy, *Estimating and Interpreting the Yield Curve*, (New York: John Wiley & Sons, Inc., 1997).

Barber, J. R., and M. R. Copper, "Immunization Using Principal Component Analysis," *Journal of Portfolio Management*, (Fall 1996).

Beder, Tanya S., Michael Minnich, Hubert Shen, and Jodi Stanton, "Vignettes on VAR," *The Journal of Financial Engineering* (September/December 1998), 289–309.

Black, Fischer, and Myron Scholes, "The Pricing of Options and Corporate Liabilities," *Journal of Political Economy*, 81, (1973), 637–654,

Boudoukh, J., M. Richardson, and R. Whitelaw, "The Best Of Both Worlds: A Hybrid Approach to Calculating Value at Risk," The Salomon Center, Stern School of Business, NYU, 1997.

Breeden, D. T. "Complexities of Hedging Mortgages," *Journal of Fixed Income*, 4, (December 1994), 6–41.

Breeden, D. T., "Risk, Return, and Hedging of Fixed Rate Mortgages," *Journal of Fixed Income* (September 1991), 85–107.

Brusilovskiy, P. M., and L. M. Tilman, "Incorporating Expert Judgement Into Multivariate Polynomial Modeling," *Decision Support Systems* (October 1996), 199–214.

Burghardt, Galen, Belton, Morton Lane, Geoffrey Luce, and Richard McVey, *Eurodollar Futures and Options*, (Chicago: Probus, 1991).

Castillo, Oscar, and Patricia Mein, "A New Method for Adaptive Model-Based Control of Economic Systems Using a Neuro-Fuzzy-Genetic

Approach: The Case of International Trade Dynamics," Proceedings from the IEEE/IAFE Computational Intelligence for Financial Engineering Conference (March 1999).

Chang, Isaac J., and Andreas S. Weigend, "Nonlinear Prediction of Conditional Percentiles for Value-at-Risk," Proceedings from the IEEE/IAFE Computational Intelligence for Financial Engineering Conference (March 1999).

Cheyette, Oren, "Interest Rate Models," Chapter 1 in *Advances in Fixed Income Valuation, Modeling, and Risk Management,* F. Fabozzi, Ed., (New Hope: Frank J. Fabozzi Associates, 1997).

CreditMetrics™ Technical Document. J. P. Morgan Publication (1997).

Dembo, Ron S., "Value-at-Risk and Return," *Algorithmics Incorporated, Canada* (December 1994).

Dembo, Ron S., and Andrew Freeman, *Seeing Tomorrow: Rewriting the Rules of Risk* (New York: John Wiley & Sons, Inc., 1998).

Doffou, Ako, and Jimmy E. Hilliard, "Testing a Jump-Diffusion Stochastic Interest Rates Model in Currency Options Market", Proceedings from the Conference Computational Intelligence for Financial Engineering Conference (March 1999).

Dunlevy, J., "Swap Spread Beta: A new Tool in Monitoring Mortgage Risk" Beacon Hill Asset Management (February 1999).

Dynkin, L., and J. Hyman, "The Lehman Brothers Return Attribution Model" (New York: Lehman Brothers, May 1996).

Dynkin, L., Hyman, J. and W. Wu, "The Lehman Brother Multi-Factor Risk Model," Lehman Brothers Fixed Income Research (March 1999).

Eber, Jean-Marc, "Coherent Measures of Risk," Proceedings of the Latest Cutting Edge Developments in Value-at-Risk Conference (November 1997).

Engle, R., and Simone Manganelli, "CAViaR: Conditional Autoregressive Value at Risk," (UCSD., June 1999)

Ericson, Joseph O., and Richard K. Singer, "Assessing the Historical Simulation to Calculate Value-at-Risk and Improving the Accuracy of Monte Carlo Simulation," Proceedings of the Latest Cutting Edge Developments in Value-at-Risk Conference (November 1997).

Fabozzi, Frank J., *Fixed Income Mathematics* (Chicago: Probus Publishing Company, 1988).

Fabozzi, Frank J., and Dessa T. Fabozzi (ed.), *The Handbook of Fixed Income Securities* (Chicago: Irwin, 1995).

Fabozzi, Frank J. (ed.), *The Handbook of Mortgage-Backed Securities* (New York: McGraw-Hill, 1995).

Fabozzi, Frank J., *Measuring and Controlling Interest Rate Risk* (New Hope, PA: Frank J. Fabozzi Associates, 1996).

Fabozzi, Frank J., (ed.), *Perspectives on Interest Rate Risk Management for Money Managers and Traders* (New Hope, PA: Frank J. Fabozzi Associates, 1998).

Fisher, Lawrence, "Determinants of Risk Premiums on Corporate Bonds," *Journal of Political Economy* (June 1959), 217–237.

Ghosh, Bunt, Milward, Ian, and Roy, Amlan, "Asset Liability and Portfolio Strategy (ALPS): An Emerging Markets Portfolio Framework," *Credit Suisse First Boston Emerging Markets Strategy* (November, 1999).

Ghoshray, Sabyasachi, "Reducing Arbitrage Risk by Fuzzy Regression Based Prediction of Exchange Rates for Composite Currencies," Proceedings from the IEEE/IAFE Conference "Computational Intelligence for Financial Engineering" (March 1999).

Golub, B. W. and L. M. Tilman, "Measuring Plausibility of Hypothetical Interest Rate Shocks," *Managing Fixed Income Portfolios,* F. Fabozzi (ed.) (New Hope: Frank J. Fabozzi Associates, 1997).

Golub, B. W., and L. M. Tilman, "Measuring Yield Curve Risk Using Principal Component Analysis, Value-at-Risk, and Key Rate Durations," *Journal of Portfolio Management* (Summer 1997).

Grundy, B. D., and Z. Wiener, "The Analysis of VaR, Deltas and State Prices: A New Approach" (working paper), Rodney L. White Center for Financial Research, The Wharton School (August 1996), 11–96.

Gulranjani, Deepak, Michael Roginsky, and Ronald Kahn, "Advanced Techniques for the Valuation of CMOs," Chapter 7 in *CMO Portfolio Management,* Frank J. Fabozzi (ed.), Summit, NJ: Frank J. Fabozzi Associates (1994), 103–120.

Gupton, Greg, "An Overview of the Credimetrics Framework for Estimating Value-at-Risk within the Context of a Credit Portfolio," Proceedings of the "Latest Cutting Edge Developments in Value-at-Risk" (November 1997).

Hendricks, D., "Evaluation of Value-at-Risk Models Using Historical Data," FRBNY Economic Policy Review (April 1996).

Hendricks, D., "Judging How Well Various VaR Models Produce Useful Risk Assessments," Proceedings of the Practical Implementation of Value-at-Risk to Quantify Risk Conference (January 1997).

Hill, Charles, and Simon Vaysman,"An Approach to Scenario Hedging," *Journal of Portfolio Management* (Winter 1998), 83–92.

Ho, T. S. Y., "Key Rate Durations: Measures of Interest Rate Risks," *Journal of Fixed Income,* (September 1992), 29–44.

Ho, T. S. Y., Chen, M. Z. H. and Eng, F. H. T. "VaR Analytics: Portfolio Structure, Key Rate Convexities, and VaR Betas," *Journal of Portfolio Management* (Fall 1996).

Ilmanen, A., *Understanding the Yield Curve* (New York: Salomon Brothers, 1995–1996).

Ilmanen, A., "When Do Bond Markets Reward Investors for Interest Rate Risk," *The Journal of Portfolio Management* (Winter 1996), 52–63.

Jensen, Michael, "The Performance of Mutual Funds in the Period 1945–1964," *Journal of Finance* (1968), 389–416.

Jensen, Michael, "Risk, The Pricing of Capital Assets, and the Evaluation of Investment Portfolios," *Journal of Business* (1969), 167–247.

Johnson, Richard, and Dean Wichern, *Applied Multivariate Statistical Analysis* (Englewood Cliffs: Prentice-Hall, Inc., 1982).

Johnston, D., "Risk Adjusted Yield Spread Model," *Lehman Brother Fixed Income Research* (November 1998).

Jones, Frank J., "Yield Curve Strategies," *Journal of Fixed Income* (September 1991), 43–51.

Jorion, P., "Risk Management Lessons from Long Term Capital Management" (UC at Irvine, 1999).

Jorion, P., *Value At Risk: The New Benchmark for Controlling Market Risk* (Chicago: Irwin, 1996).

Jorion, P., "Bayes-Stein Estimation for Portfolio Analysis," *Journal of Financial and Quantitative Analysis* 21(3): 279–292.

Kahn, Ronald N., "Fixed Income Risk Modeling," Chapter 14, in *The Handbook of Fixed Income Securities*, Fifth Edition, Frank J. Fabozzi (ed.) (Homewood, IL: Business Ones Irwin, 1995).

Kahn, Ronald N., "Fixed Income Risk Modeling in the 1990s," *Journal of Portfolio Management* (Fall 1995), 94–101.

Kahn, Ronald N., "LBO Event Risk," Chapter 17 in *Managing Institutional Assets*, Frank J. Fabozzi (ed.) (New York: Ballinger, 1990), 365–375.

Kao, Duen-Li, *Estimating and Pricing Credit Risk: An Overview* (New York: General Motors Investment Management Corporation Publication, 1999).

Klaffky, Thomas E., Y. Y. Ma, and A. Nozari, "Managing Yield Curve Exposure: Introducing Reshaping Durations," *Journal of Fixed Income* (December 1992), 5–15.

Klaffky, Thomas E., Ardavan Nozari and Michael Waldman, "Risk Management of Fixed-Income Portfolios: Applying New Duration Measures," Salomon Brothers (June 1993).

Konishi, Atsuo, Ravi Dattatreya (eds.), The Handbook of Derivative Instruments (Chicago: Irwin, 1996)

Kuberek, R. C., "Common Factors in Bond Portfolio Returns," Wilshire Associates, Inc. Publication (1990).

Ledoit, Olivier, "Improved Estimation of the Covariance Matrix of Stock Returns With an Application to Portfolio Selection" (UCLA: Anderson Graduate School of Management, 1999).

Ledoit, Olivier, "Hypothesis Testing When the Sample Covariance Matrix is Singular" (UCLA: Anderson Graduate School of Management, 1998).

Ledoit, Olivier, "A Well-Conditioned Estimator For Large Dimensional Covariance Matrices" (UCLA: Anderson Graduate School of Management, 1996).

Leibowitz, M. L., S. Kogelman, and L. N. Bader, "Statistical Duration – A Spread Model of Rate Sensitivity Across Fixed-Income Sectors," Salomon Brothers (August 1993).

Leland, H. E., "Beyond Mean-Variance: Risk And Performance Measures For Portfolios with Nonsymmetric Return Distributions" Working Paper, Haas School of Business, University of California, Berkeley (October 1998).

Lezos, Georgios, and Monte Tull, "Neural Network and Fuzzy Logic Techniques for Time Series Forecasting," Proceedings from the IEEE/IAFE Computational Intelligence for Financial Engineering Conference (March 1999).

Linsmeier, T. J., and N. D. Pearson, "Risk Management: An Introduction to Value-At-Risk," (working paper), U of Illinois at Urbania-Champaign (July 1996).

Litterman, R., and J. Scheinkman, "Common Factors Affecting Bond Returns," *Journal of Fixed Income* (June 1991), 54–61.

Litterman, R., and K. Winkelmann, "Managing Market Exposure," Goldman Sachs, Risk Management Series (January 1996).

Litterman, R., "Hot Spots and Hedges," Goldman Sachs Publication (October 1996).

Lopez, J. A., "Regulatory Evaluation of Value-at-Risk Models," (working paper), The Wharton Financial Institutions Center (September 1996) 96–51.

Mahabir, Kris, "Aggregating and Integrating Market and Credit Risk: Applying a Value-at-Risk Analysis to Both Risk Areas," Proceedings of the Latest Cutting Edge Developments in Value-at-Risk Conference (November 1997).

Mahoney, J., "Comparing Empirical-Based vs. Model-Based Approaches to VaR," Proceedings of the Practical Implementation of Value-at-Risk to Quantify Risk Conference (January 1997).

Makarov, Victor, "Comprehensive Risk Management Componenets: VAR, Stress Testing & Scenario Analysis," Proceedings from the Practical Implementation of Value-at-Risk to Quantify Risk Conference (January 1997).

Macaulay, Frederick R., "Some Theoretical Problems Suggested by the Movement of Interest Rates, Bond Yields, and Stock Prices in the

United States Since 1865" (New York: National Bureau of Economic Research, 1938)

Mausser, Helmut, and Dan Rosen, "Beyond VaR: Triangular Risk Decomposition," *Algo Research Quarterly* (March 1999).

Mausser, Helmut, and Dan Rosen, "Beyond VaR: Parametric and Simulation-Based Risk Management Tools," Proceedings from the IEEE/IAFE Computational Intelligence for Financial Engineering Conference (March 1999).

Mausser, Helmut, and Dan Rosen, "Beyond VaR: From Measuring Risk to Managing Risk," Proceedings from the IEEE/IAFE Computational Intelligence for Financial Enginnering Conference (March 1999).

Michaud, Richard, *Efficient Asset Management* (Cambridge: Harvard University Press, 1998).

Nawalkha, Sanjay K., and Donald R. Chambers (ed.), Interest Rate Risk Measurement and Management, (New York: Institutional Investor, Inc., 1999).

Neter, John, Michael Kutner, Christopher Nachtsherim, and William Wasserman, Applied Linear Regression Models, (Chicago: Irwin, 1986).

Oliver, Wyman & Company, "Modeling Liquidity Risk with Implications for Traditional Market Risk Measurement and Management" (April 1999).

Peng, Scott, and Ravi Dattatreya, *The Structured Note Market* (Chicago: Probus, 1995).

Pedrosa, Monica, and Richard Roll, "Systematic Risk in Corporate Bond Credit Spreads," *The Journal of Fixed Income*, (December 1998).

Pritsker, M., "Evaluating Value at Risk Methodologies: Accuracy versus Computational Time" (working paper), The Wharton Financial Institutions Center (1996) 96–48.

Reitano, R.R., "Multivariate Duration Analysis," *Journal of Portfolio Management* (1990).

Reitano, R.R., "Non-Parallel Yield Curve Shifts and Stochastic Immunization," *John Hancock Financial Services* (1996).

RiskMetrics™ Technical Document (New York: J.P. Morgan/Reuters, 1996).

Ronn, E.I., "The Impact of Large Changes in Asset Prices on Intra-Market Correlations in the Stock and Bond Markets," Working Paper, U of Texas in Austin (1996).

Sarig, Oded, and Arthur Warga, "Bond Price Data and Bond Market Liquidity," *Journal of Financial and Quantitative Analysis* (1989), 367–378.

Schittenkopf, Christian, George Dorffner, and Engelbert J. Dockner, "Fat Tails and Non-Linearity in Volatility Models: What is more Important?" Proceedings for the IEEE/IAFE Computational Intelligence for Financial Engineering Conference (March 1999).

Schumacher, M., "Swap Spreads Do Matter," *Journal of Fixed Income* (June 1998), 59–64.

Sharpe, W.F., "The Sharpe Ratio," *Journal of Portfolio Management* (Fall 1994).

Stoll, Hans, "Lost Barings: A Tale in Three Parts Concluding with a Lesson," *Journal of Derivatives* (Fall 1995), 109–115.

Strang, G., *Linear Algebra and Its Applications* (New York: Academic Press, 1980).

Taleb, Nassim, *Dynamic Hedging: Managing Vanilla and Exotic Options* (New York: John Wiley & Sons, Inc., 1997).

Vandaele, W., *Applied Time Series and Box-Jenkins Models* (San Diego Academic Press, Inc. 1983).

Warga, Arthur, "Bond Returns, Liquidity and Missing Data," *Journal of Financial and Quantitative Analysis* (1992), 605–617.

Weil, N., "Macaulay Duration: An Appreciation," *Journal of Business* 46 (1973), 589–592.

Weir, N. "Advances in Risk Management: Applications to Portfolio Management" (working paper), Goldman Sachs & Co. (1996).

Willner, R., "A New Tool for Portfolio Managers: Level, Slope, and Curvature Durations," *Journal of Portfolio Management* (June 1996).

Wong, Anthony, *Fixed Income Arbitrage* (John Wiley & Sons, Inc., 1993).

Index

About the Authors

Bennett W. Golub is a founding partner and Managing Director of BlackRock, Inc., a global money management and risk advisory firm based in New York. Mr. Golub is co-Head of BlackRock's Risk Management and Analytics Group and a member of its Management Committee and Investment Strategy Group. In addition to developing BlackRock's risk advisory business, he is actively involved in the creation of analytical tools used in measuring and managing market and credit risks of fixed income and equity portfolios and monitoring the risk of portfolios vis-à-vis their benchmarks. Dr. Golub also shares the responsibility for developing the firm's analytical infrastructure that supports its various lines of business. Before BlackRock, Mr. Golub was a Vice President at The First Boston Corporation where he was responsible for establishing the Financial Engineering Group. His group helped create over $25 billion of structured securities including many innovative collateralized mortgage obligations and asset-backed securities.

Dr. Golub has authored many articles, including "Measuring Yield Curve Risk Using Principal Components Analysis and Value At Risk," "Towards a New Approach to Measuring Mortgage Duration", "Measuring Plausibility of Hypothetical Interest Rate Shocks," and "Composite Portfolios Present Challenges." He is a frequent lecturer at industry conferences and meetings and is affiliated with numerous professional and academic organizations, including The American Economics Association, The American Finance Association, The Financial Management Association and The International Association of Financial Engineers. Mr. Golub earned an S.B. and an S.M. in Management and a Ph.D. in Applied Economics and Finance, all from the Massachusetts Institute of Technology.

Leo M. Tilman is Director in the Risk Management and Analytics Group at BlackRock, Inc. Mr. Tilman specializes in the creation of new risk management methodologies, marketing of risk management services, financial modeling, and risk advisory work. His primary focus is solving portfolio management, trading, and enterprise-wide risk management problems through the use of the financial modeling techniques. Earlier in his career at BlackRock, Mr. Tilman was involved in research and analytical software design and development. Prior to joining BlackRock in 1993, he was a quantitative analyst with Eastern Commercial Bank (Russia).

Mr. Tilman has published extensively on risk management, financial modeling, applied statistics, decision making, and expert systems. His recent works have appeared in *The Journal of Portfolio Management* and *Decision Support Systems* as well as chapters in several books including *Managing Fixed Income Portfolios, Interest Rate Risk Measurement and Management*, and *Perspectives on Interest Rate Risk Management for Money Managers and Traders*. Mr. Tilman's earlier research on uses of expert judgment in modeling of complex real-life systems was presented at international conferences and symposiums and published in journals and books, including those by the Russian Academy of Sciences.

Mr. Tilman is a frequent guest speaker on the topics of risk management and financial modeling. Recently, he delivered lectures at the Yale School of Management and Columbia University. He is a member of the Global Association of Risk Professionals (GARP) and the International Association of Financial Engineers (IAFE). Mr. Tilman received a B.A. in Mathematics and an M.A. in Statistics with concentration in Finance, both from Columbia University.